Islands in the City

Islands in the City

West Indian Migration to New York

EDITED BY

Nancy Foner

UNIVERSITY OF CALIFORNIA PRESS

Berkeley   Los Angeles   London

University of California Press
Berkeley and Los Angeles, California

University of California Press, Ltd.
London, England

© 2001 by
The Regents of the University of California

Islands in the city : West Indian migration to New York / edited by Nancy Foner.
    p. cm.
    Based on a conference entitled West Indian migration to New York : historical, contemporary, and transnational perspectives, which was held at the Research Institute for the Study of Man in April 1999.
    Includes bibliographical references and index.
    ISBN 0-520-22573-2 (cloth : alk. paper)—ISBN 0-520-22850-2 (pbk. : alk. paper)
    1. West Indian Americans—New York (State)—New York—Social conditions—Congresses. 2. West Indian Americans—New York (State)—New York—Race identity—Congresses. 3. Blacks—New York (State)—New York—Social conditions—Congresses. 4. Blacks—Race identity—New York (State)—New York—Congresses. 5. Immigrants—New York (State)—New York—Social conditions—Congresses. 6. New York (N.Y.)—Social conditions—Congresses. 7. New York (N.Y.)—Race relations—Congresses. 8. New York (N.Y.)—Emigration and immigration—Congresses. 9. West Indies—Emigration and immigration—Congresses. I. Foner, Nancy, 1945-
F128.9.W54 I85 2001
305.896′97290747—dc21

                                            00-046711

Printed in the United States of America
08 07 06 05 04 03 02 01
10 9 8 7 6 5 4 3 2 1

The paper used in this publication meets the minimum requirements of
ANSI/NISO Z39.48-1984 (R 1997) (*Permanence of Paper*).

CONTENTS

ACKNOWLEDGMENTS

This volume has its origins in a two-day conference, "West Indian Migration to New York: Historical, Contemporary, and Transnational Perspectives," held at the Research Institute for the Study of Man in April 1999. The conference was made possible by support from the Wenner-Gren Foundation for Anthropological Research and the Research Institute for the Study of Man.

I owe a very special debt to Lambros Comitas, director of the Research Institute for the Study of Man. The phrase "without him this book would never have been written" may be a cliché, but in this case it is really true. He suggested that I organize the conference in the first place and provided advice and assistance with great generosity and good humor. Many thanks, as well, to Lewis Burgess, also associated with the Research Institute for the Study of Man, for his help with the many details involved in arranging the conference.

At the conference, Roy S. Bryce-Laporte, Don Robotham, Roger Sanjek, and Constance Sutton made valuable contributions to the discussion and offered comments on early drafts of the papers, many of which have been incorporated in this volume. Other participants at the conference included Rachel Buff, Randal Hepner and Tricia Redeker Hepner, Winston James, and Philip Scher; their papers provided insights that I, and many of the authors, have found extremely useful. My thanks to Philip Kasinitz, not only for his formal comments at the conference—which were the basis for his concluding chapter—but also for serving as a much-valued sounding board during the preparation of the book. And, of course, my appreciation to all of the authors in the volume for their responsiveness and commitment to the project and for the quality of their contributions.

A special thanks to Naomi Schneider, executive editor at the University of California Press, for her support of the project and for shepherding the manuscript through the publication process so quickly and efficiently. Also, thanks to Ellie Hickerson and Kristina Kite for answering endless questions and helping with details along the way. Finally, I am grateful to Wallace Zane and another, anonymous reader for the University of California Press for providing useful suggestions that have, I believe, made this a better book.

INTRODUCTION

West Indian Migration to New York
An Overview

Nancy Foner

The past four decades have witnessed a massive West Indian migration to New York. The influx—the largest emigration flow in West Indian history—has had enormous consequences for the lives of individual migrants as well as for the societies they have left behind and the city they have entered. This collection of original essays explores the effects of West Indian migration, puts forward analytic frameworks to aid in understanding it, and points to areas for further research.

The focus of the book is on migrants from the nations of the former British Caribbean, who share a heritage of British colonialism, Creole culture, and linguistic background. The location is New York—the most significant destination, by far, for Caribbean immigrants in the United States. Since 1965 more than half a million West Indians have moved to New York City—about twice the size of the population of the island of Barbados and five times the size of Grenada. If one puts together all the migrants from the Anglophone Caribbean, West Indians are the largest immigrant group in New York City. More and more, New York's black population is becoming Caribbeanized. By 1998, according to *Current Population Survey* estimates, almost a third of New York City's black population was foreign born, the vast majority West Indian. Adding the second generation, census estimates suggest that roughly two-fifths of the city's black residents trace their origins to the West Indies. The dense concentrations of West Indians in certain sections of the city have created neighborhoods with a distinct Caribbean flavor. As Milton Vickerman has recently noted, West Indian New Yorkers are more likely to go to Flatbush Avenue to develop a sense of West Indian ethnicity than to Kingston or Port of Spain.[1]

In the context of the near record-breaking immigration to the United States, West Indians represent a particularly fascinating case. Because they are, in American racial terms, overwhelmingly black, West Indians bring to the fore the critical role of race in the U.S. immigrant experience. Because many West Indian migrants remain closely tied to their home societies, they highlight the role of transnational processes and practices. And because West Indian migration to New York has a long history, analysis of the city's West Indian community is able to shed light on what is new about contemporary patterns.

In providing a broad view of West Indian migration to New York, the chapters in *Islands in the City* draw on a variety of theoretical perspectives, empirical data, and methodologies. Sociologists studying West Indian migration have generally focused on immigrant incorporation and issues of identity, historians have often looked at relations between black Americans and West Indians, and anthropologists have been primarily concerned with transnational processes and cultural shifts in the United States. This volume—with authors from the fields of anthropology, history, political science, and sociology—brings together the different approaches. It includes studies of the past as well as the present, analyses of transnational connections as well as modes of immigrant incorporation, comparisons of the first and second generations, and discussions of political socialization as well as economic integration. A wide variety of methods are involved, including archival research, participant observation and in-depth interviews, and quantitative analyses of census materials.

A central question is how West Indian arrivals have been transforming New York as they settle and form communities in the city. West Indians are also changing, and being changed by, New York's system of race and ethnic relations. In the contemporary era, what kinds of racial and ethnic identities have emerged among the first generation—and are developing among the second generation? Are members of the second generation assimilating into the African American population? Is the presence of hundreds of thousands of West Indians playing a role in altering American racial conceptions? Also at issue is the question of transnational practices. What kinds of ties do West Indians maintain to their home societies? What consequences do transnational links have for West Indians at home and abroad? And how should we conceptualize the ties between New York West Indians and their compatriots in other receiving societies such as Britain and Canada?

As the chapters explore the West Indian migrant experience, they shed new light on a number of broad cultural and social processes. Among them are the nature and impact of transnational connections, the dynamics of segmented assimilation, the role of gender in migration, patterns of immigrant residential and economic incorporation, and, above all, the effects of race. Black immigrants are a significant component of America's new immigrants, but they have often been ignored in immigration debates, which typically focus on Asians and Latinos. By highlighting the distinctive experience of West Indian newcomers, the essays in this book bring out the critical role of race in immigrant incorporation. They also underscore the way "blackness" is being renegotiated in an increasingly multi-ethnic black America. Moreover, because West Indians are closely identified with African Americans, the study of West Indian migration has implications for the way West Indians fare in relation to native-born blacks—and the complex ways that West Indians utilize ethnicity to improve their image and their life chances.

In this introductory chapter I set the stage with an overview of contemporary West Indian migration to New York, setting it in the context of past migration and in terms of two issues—race and transnationalism—that are major themes in the volume. The chapters in the first section analyze some basic features of the movement to New York: where West Indians live (Crowder and Tedrow) and work (Model) and women's experiences in the migration in the early twentieth century (Watkins-Owens). The second part explores West Indian transnational practices (Basch and Olwig). Although issues of race are in the forefront throughout the book, the chapters in the third section are specifically concerned with race, ethnicity, and identity in the first and second generations (Rogers, Waters, Bashi Bobb and Clarke, and Vickerman). In the concluding chapter, Philip Kasinitz offers a review of the social science literature on West Indian Americans, explaining why they are emerging from "invisibility"—and why parts of their experience were ignored in the past and continue, even in the new body of scholarship, to be overlooked.

A few words on terminology. In this chapter, I use "West Indian" to refer to people from the Anglophone Caribbean, including the mainland nations of Guyana and Belize, and, although I have not imposed an editorial straitjacket regarding this usage, many of the contributors have followed the same convention. (A few authors use the term somewhat differently—for example, in their analysis of census data Crowder and Tedrow include people from Haiti and the Dutch and French islands under the West Indian rubric.) Several authors use "Afro-Caribbean" or "African Caribbean" to emphasize the role of race.[2] Indeed, all of the chapters focus on West Indians of at least partial African descent. Unless otherwise noted, "African Americans" or "black Americans" refer to North Americans of African ancestry, as opposed to "West Indians" or "Afro-Caribbeans"; "blacks" refers to all non-Hispanic New Yorkers of African descent, including those of Caribbean and North American origin.[3] Finally, the term "people of African ancestry," as Vickerman notes in his chapter, includes African Americans and West Indians as well as immigrants from Africa and elsewhere who can trace their heritage back to Africa.

WEST INDIAN MIGRATION
TO NEW YORK, PAST AND PRESENT

Emigration has long been a way of life in the West Indies. Its roots go deep—they are traceable to the legacy of slavery, the distorting effects of colonial rule, the centuries-long domination of the islands' economies by plantation agricul-

ture, and, in recent years, continued dependence on world powers, lending institutions, and corporations. Scarce resources, overpopulation, high unemployment and underemployment, limited opportunities for advancement—
these have long spurred West Indians to look abroad for economic security and
better job prospects, improved living standards, and ways to get ahead. "Jamaica," one man told me when I was doing research in a rural community in
the late 1960s, "is a beautiful country, but we can't see our way to make it
through" (see Foner 1973, 1978).

In the past few decades, economic crises—along with inflation and unemployment—have continued to fuel migration fever. West Indian small-island
economies simply cannot deliver the kinds of jobs, lifestyles, and consumption
patterns that people at all social levels want. And increasingly they want more,
due to such factors as improved communications, the promises of new elites,
the expansion of educational opportunities, as well as reports and visits from
migrants themselves. A national opinion survey in Jamaica in the late 1970s
found that 60 percent of the population would move to the United States if
given the chance (Stone 1982: 64).[4]

The search for a better life has taken West Indians all over the globe—to
Central America, other West Indian islands, Britain, Canada, and, of course,
the United States. Most who come to this country gravitate to New York. In
the first mass West Indian influx, which began around 1900 and peaked in the
early 1920s, New York City was the main port of entry. By 1930, more than
half of the seventy-two thousand foreign-born blacks from the non-Hispanic
Caribbean in the United States counted in the census lived in New York City.
Indeed, New York was the only city in the country where a significant proportion of the black population was of Caribbean origin. In 1920 West Indians constituted about a quarter of New York's black population, and in 1930
nearly a fifth (Kasinitz 1992: 24–25, 41–42).

Today no other U.S. city has so many West Indians, or such a high proportion of the national total. By 1998 West Indian immigrants constituted
about 8 percent of New York's population, making them the largest immigrant group in the city. Census Bureau estimates for the late 1990s put the
number of Jamaican, Guyanese, Trinidadian, and Barbadian immigrants in
New York City—the four largest West Indian groups—at about 435,000.[5] According to Immigration and Naturalization Service figures, over half of the
Jamaicans and Trinidadians and close to three-quarters of the Guyanese who
legally entered the United States between 1972 and 1992 settled in the New
York urban region, most of them moving to the city itself.[6]

New York City and its surrounding counties have been a popular destination for a number of reasons. Early in the twentieth century, steamships carrying bananas and tourists between the Caribbean and New York helped to
establish the city as a migration center. Once West Indians set up a beachhead
in New York, a process of progressive network building sustained the flow

until restrictive legislation in the 1920s and the depression of the 1930s cut it off.[7] Migrants wrote letters encouraging friends and relatives to join them, often sent back funds for the voyage, and were on hand to offer a sense of security and prospects of assistance. Like other immigrants, West Indians created what Charles Tilly (1990: 90) has called "migration machines: sending networks that articulated with particular receiving networks in which new migrants could find jobs, housing, and sociability." As Irma Watkins-Owens shows in her essay, West Indian women, as well as men, were centers of these "migration machines." At the beginning of the twentieth century as well as later, women were important figures in initiating and sustaining migration chains.

The very presence of an established (though aging) West Indian community drew immigrants to the city once mass migration resumed following changes in U.S. immigration law in 1965. Once again, New York offers employment possibilities for West Indian arrivals. Networks of friends and relatives continue to channel West Indians to the city, serving as financial safety nets for the new arrivals and sources of information about life in New York. By allocating most immigrant visas along family lines, present U.S. immigration law reinforces and formalizes the operation of migration networks. New York is appealing because it is home to vibrant West Indian neighborhoods and institutions. Moreover, New York itself has an image that draws newcomers. To many West Indians, New York is a symbol of North American influence and power and the object, as Bryce-Laporte has written, of their "dream[s], curiosity, sense of achievement, and drive for adventure" (1987: 56).

The most obvious common thread in the New York West Indian migrant experience throughout the twentieth century is the existence of racial prejudice and discrimination, a topic I take up at length later. Several chapters point to other continuities. Irma Watkins-Owens's portrait of independent West Indian women in early-twentieth-century New York—often migrating on their own, working in low-end personal service jobs, and serving as central figures in informal kinship networks—does not sound all that different from today. Contrary to stereotypes about the West Indian "genius" for business in the early 1900s, Suzanne Model's analysis of census data shows that West Indians had low self-employment rates then, just as they do now. Indeed, what self-employment existed in the earlier period, according to Philip Kasinitz (this volume), was largely in the professions, not in the types of small businesses we usually associate with immigrant entrepreneurial activity.

But despite continuities, much has also changed. Today's New York West Indian community is more than ten times the size it was seventy years ago. Whereas West Indian migration shrank to small numbers in the long hiatus between the mid 1920s and the mid 1960s, today's huge influx has already lasted longer than the earlier wave and is still going strong.[8] Barring draconian U.S. legislation, a large flow is likely to continue for years to come.

Today's immigrants come from a different Caribbean than their predecessors. West Indian societies are no longer British colonies but independent nations, with black- and brown-skinned elites and government leaders. British influence has declined, while American political, economic, and cultural influence has grown. Modern technology—especially television, telephones, and jet travel—and growing tourism allow people in the most remote West Indian villages to have an up-close view of American life before they even get here.

New York is also a very different place than it was during the first wave. The city's black population is much larger and more dispersed, as is the West Indian population. The core of the West Indian community, centered earlier on central Harlem and Bedford-Stuyvesant, has shifted to the Crown Heights, East Flatbush, and Flatbush sections of Brooklyn. Distinct West Indian neighborhoods have also developed in southeastern Queens and the northeast Bronx as well as in neighboring Mount Vernon, just across the city line in Westchester. Large numbers of post-1965 migrants flocked to neighborhoods experiencing an exodus of whites that opened up a substantial stock of decent housing (see Crowder and Tedrow, this volume; Crowder 1999).

In the post–civil rights era, West Indians (especially the better educated) have access to a much wider array of jobs in the mainstream economy; higher education, including elite colleges and universities, is more available. The political arena has enlarged for blacks. As Philip Kasinitz (1992) details in *Caribbean New York,* the first cohort of West Indian immigrants played down their ethnic distinctiveness in the public arena. Entering America at the height of racial segregation—and when they were a much smaller community— West Indian New Yorkers immersed themselves in the broader African American community. Few West Indians who rose to political prominence claimed to be Caribbean leaders; indeed, they deliberately muted their West Indianness in public life as they appealed to, and were largely supported by, a predominantly native African American electorate.[9] Today a new breed of politicians has emerged who represent distinct West Indian interests and have a political base in the city's large, densely populated West Indian neighborhoods. Dominant political interests have helped this process along; two predominantly West Indian districts in Brooklyn were created through redistricting in the 1990s, and political figures of all stripes actively court West Indian leaders and make use of West Indian symbolism in order to obtain votes. As Linda Basch (this volume) points out, mainstream New York politicians now clamor to strut down Eastern Parkway on Labor Day at the helm of the "West Indian American Day Carnival Parade," currently the city's largest ethnic celebration, which draws crowds of one to two million people.

Today's racial/ethnic hierarchy provides a radically new context in which West Indians interact with other New Yorkers. In 1920 the 152,000 black New Yorkers constituted a little under 3 percent of the city's population, and an even smaller proportion were Asian or Hispanic.[10] By 1998 the city was more than a quarter black, nearly a third Hispanic, and 8 percent Asian. In the early 1900s, newly arrived Jewish and Italian immigrants were considered as belonging to separate, and inferior, races; today their descendants make up the bulk of New York's (declining) white population, dominate leadership positions in both the public and the private sector, and are often West Indians' employers and on-the-job superiors.

A fuller understanding of what is new about the recent West Indian migrant experience requires consideration of a wide range of other factors.[11] These include not only the context—economic, political, social, and cultural—in the Caribbean and New York that shape why (and which) West Indians leave their homelands and what happens after they move, but also the different economic and power relations in the contemporary, postcolonial world order that are deeply implicated in the processes and trajectory of West Indian migration.

TRANSNATIONAL TIES

Insight into many of these dynamics arises through the analysis of transnational practices, which, like much else, turn out to be a mix of old and new. As defined by Basch in her chapter, transnational practices refer to the way migrants sustain multistranded social relations, along family, economic, and political lines, that link their societies of origin and settlement. In this way, Basch argues, migrants build "transnational social fields" that cross geographic, cultural, and political borders.[12]

As Watkins-Owens makes clear, transnational practices were alive and well in the first wave of migration (cf. Foner 1997). Then, as now, letters went back and forth between New York and the Caribbean, and migrants sent substantial amounts of money home.[13] In her chapter, Watkins-Owens mentions that handmade clothing and shoes traveled the Brooklyn–Barbados network in the early part of the twentieth century; today, migrants ship barrels filled with clothing, food, and household goods that are unavailable or exorbitantly priced back home. (One barrel sent by a Trinidadian domestic worker in the 1980s contained almost eight hundred dollars worth of goods, including three gallons of cooking oil, forty pounds of rice, twenty pounds of detergent, flour, tea, cocoa, toothpaste, and other items [Colen 1986: 62].)[14] Watkins-Owens also shows that the practice of leaving young children behind with relatives or sending them back home has a long history. And first-wave women, as well as men, were involved in New York–based voluntary associations that raised money for scholarships, school supplies, and other projects in the home societies. By the 1930s, some West Indians in New York were active in nationalist political organizations that agitated for their home country's independence (Kasinitz 1992: 113–115).

What's new? For one thing, new technologies of transportation and communication have increased the density, multiplicity, and importance of transnational connections and made it possible for migrants to operate more or less simultaneously in New York and the West Indies. In the jet plane age, it is faster, easier, and cheaper to travel back and forth. Round-trip fares to Jamaica and Barbados in the fall of 2000 ran from about $380 to $430. Admittedly, as Philip Kasinitz (this volume) points out, regular trips home are still no easy matter for the poor and undocumented. Only six of the thirty-four food service workers in Mary Waters's study (this volume) had been back for a visit; only nine of the twenty-five teachers had traveled home in the last ten years. Other researchers find more frequent contact. Four out of five of Reuel Rogers's (this volume) respondents made regular trips back. Among the forty Jamaican New Yorkers in my 1980s study, the vast majority had been to Jamaica in the previous three years. Several flew home on short notice to see sick relatives or attend funerals. Many returned for weddings or to attend to business affairs in Jamaica. Friends and relatives also often came up from Jamaica to visit in New York (Foner 1983). Caribbean-based research finds much the same thing. According to anthropologists George and Sharon Gmelch, many people in the rural Barbadian parish they studied in the 1990s visited relatives in the United States, especially Brooklyn, each year (1997: 178).

Telephone contact, impossible eighty years ago, allows migrants to hear about news and people from home right away and to participate immediately in family discussions on major decisions. Telephones have now spread to virtually everywhere on the islands. Rates have become cheap—in 2000, a three-minute call to Jamaica cost as little as $1.80 with AT&T's one-rate international plan; phone parlors and prepaid phone calls are even cheaper. Among the Jamaican New Yorkers I interviewed in the late 1980s, the vast majority had phoned someone on the island in the previous six months. They readily phoned home in case of serious problems or crises, to deal with business matters, or, in some cases, simply to chat (Foner 1983). Today, some West Indians are able to send faxes and videotapes to relatives back home—a few, whose relatives in the Caribbean have access to the Internet, can even use e-mail.

Political developments have also spawned new kinds of transnational links. West Indian New Yorkers now come from independent countries with established nationalist ideologies and institutions, and they are a potential base of support for government projects, policies, and leaders in the homeland. Political leaders at home encourage emigrants to participate politically and economically in their home country, leading Linda Basch (this volume) to write of "deterritorialized nation-state building." Government representatives of St. Vincent and Grenada, according to Basch, treat New York immigrant organizations as a basis for Vincentian and Grenadian national interests in New York and the United States. The Vincentian government not only funds an umbrella organization to link smaller Vincentian groups in New York, but also holds meetings at the consulate so that the prime minister can speak directly, by telephone, to the migrants.

Today, candidates for office in places like St. Vincent can hop on a plane to attend fund-raisers and garner support in New York. On one weekend, Basch notes, the opposition leader from St. Vincent, the mayor of Georgetown, Guyana, and the chiefs of state from Barbados and Antigua were all in New York visiting constituents. Dual nationality, granted by all the new nations of the Anglophone Caribbean, means that West Indian New Yorkers who become U.S. citizens do not lose their rights in the Caribbean.[15] Indeed, island governments see nationals who become U.S. citizens as potential lobbies that can influence American representatives on behalf of the home country.

If many West Indian New Yorkers maintain close, ongoing ties with their home societies, they do not belong to transnational villages or localities of the kind found among Mexican New Yorkers by Robert Smith (1998).[16] Migrants from Ticuani, a small *municipio* of less than twenty-five hundred people in southern Mexico, organized a New York committee that helped build two schools and rebuild parts of the municipal palace and church after an earthquake, and raised over $100,000 to install water pipes in the *municipio*. The Ticuani Youth Group, formed by young Ticuanis in New York, sponsored sports tournaments to raise funds for public works projects in the *municipio*. In Mexico, communities such as Ticuani have been historically important units for the organization of politics and society; they have a set of indigenous corporate institutions, including communal landholding and religious cargo systems with offices linked to communal rituals. The social organization of rural West Indian life is very different, as my own study of a Jamaican rural community demonstrates (Foner 1973). There are few parallel structures of the Mexican type found in West Indian communities. And, as far as I know, there are no village-based West Indian associations in New York.

By and large, West Indian migrants' connections to the home society are mediated by informal personal networks. The formal associations that link New York and the West Indies crosscut local community ties. Most are island-based, like the St. Vincent Education and Cultural Club that Basch describes in her chapter. There are voluntary associations based on shared professions (Barbadian nurses, for example, or Vincentian teachers), alumni groups based on school ties back home, church-based groups, and political associations that draw on islandwide constituencies. While the New York Ticuani Committee claimed to have a list of all Ticuani households in New York—1600 people attended the wedding of one member, representing the majority of Ticuanenses in the city—people from the rural Jamaican community that I studied in the late 1960s generally did not maintain contact in New York unless they were relatives, close associates, or happened to work or worship in the same place. When I interviewed a number of people from the community in New York in the 1980s, they knew little about their co-villagers in the city. In several cases, I was a source of gossip and information—and in one or two instances, addresses—of villagers in New York.

West Indians' transnational connections extend beyond the New York–West Indies axis. Through a detailed account of one Jamaican family's movements, Karen Olwig shows how West Indians are involved in family networks that knit members together across global space. Some family members who moved to New York later returned to Jamaica or moved elsewhere. While living in New York, they maintained ties with relatives in England, Canada, and the West Indies, as well as other parts of the United States (cf. Ho 1993). Although the family Olwig highlights was unusual in many ways, their members' global family networks were not. Many West Indian New Yorkers have kin in England as well as in Canada. According to 1991 census counts, Britain was home to some 263,000 West Indians of foreign birth, Canada to about 270,000 (Henry 1994; Peach 1995). For example, a Guyanese homecare worker I know well, who had lived in New York for about ten years, not only maintained close ties to family back in Georgetown but also kept up contact, through letters and phone calls, with her mother, who lived in London.

A number of West Indian New Yorkers are "twice migrants," who went to Britain in the 1950s or early 1960s during the mass West Indian migration there and then moved to New York in search of better incomes and/or to join relatives. Thus, one of the people Karen Olwig interviewed had lived in London for a number of years before moving to New York in the mid 1960s. Even when living in London, she made lengthy visits to her family in New York. Once in New York she kept up close contact by phone with relatives in England, Canada, and Dominica, as well as other parts of the United States. Indeed, in 1997 she was contemplating yet another move—this time to Nova Scotia, where her daughter had settled.

The case of a Trinidadian steel drum master from Port of Spain, Trinidad, whose living arrangements span two countries and several cities may be extreme, but it highlights the way some West Indians move between different locations. The steel drum master's home is in Miami, where he leads a band for the carnival on Columbus Day weekend. Around the end of November, he goes to stay with his mother in Trinidad until the spring, when he heads to California to work at Disneyland for two months. He spends July and August in Brooklyn, preparing his arrangements for the local West Indian Carnival (Pareles 1999). Most migrants' work schedules do not allow this kind of pattern, yet, during retirement, commuting becomes a possibility. Many Jamaicans I met in the late 1980s planned to spend winters in Jamaica and the warmer months of the year in New York when they retired; several had older relatives who had already adopted this strategy (Foner 1983).

RACE AND ETHNICITY

For West Indian New Yorkers of African descent, being black is the "master status" that pervades and penetrates their lives. This was true in the past and continues to be true today.

West Indians are increasingly visible now that they are an ever growing proportion of black New York, yet they still often find themselves lumped with African Americans. Even when other New Yorkers recognize them as West Indian, as foreign, or, as many whites say, "from the islands," West Indians are seen as an ethnic group within the larger black population. Their racial status, in other words, is always salient.

Today's West Indian migrants, to be sure, face much less overt prejudice and discrimination than their predecessors in the first wave. In the aftermath of the civil rights revolution, American whites are more racially tolerant and less likely to voice racial sentiments in public. A series of laws and court decisions have banned discrimination, and new agencies and systems are in place to enforce them. Still, racial stereotypes, prejudice, and discrimination against blacks have had a tenacious hold—and persist in a variety of forms. At one extreme, blatant interpersonal racism—physical attacks or threats, denials of housing or employment specifically for racial reasons, and harassment by the police—is unfortunately still with us (Waters 1999b: 80, and this volume). Indeed, a number of well-known racial incidents in New York City in the past few decades have involved West Indians. In the Howard Beach incident in 1986, the victim, Michael Griffith, a Trinidadian immigrant, was struck by a car and killed after being chased on the highway by a group of white teenagers. The victim who sparked the Crown Heights riots in 1991 was a seven-year-old Guyanese boy named Gavin Cato, killed when a car driven by a Hasidic Jew jumped a curb. Less dramatic, but still painful, West Indians tell of an accumulation of racial slurs, insults, and slights, and of their sense that whites do not want to socialize or associate with them. Young black men, whom many whites see as potentially dangerous, have an especially hard time. It is not unusual for whites to cross the street or clutch their handbags when they see a young black man approach—and they do not stop to wonder whether the man is West Indian or African American. Mary Waters notes that the teenage boys in her study reported far more racial harassment from whites and the police than did the girls, and they also felt less at ease when they left their all-black neighborhoods.

Race, as Crowder and Tedrow's chapter makes clear, is a primary factor determining where West Indians live. Choice plays a role: like other newcomers, West Indians gravitate to areas with kinfolk and friends, where they find comfort and security in an environment of familiar institutions. Yet racial discrimination and prejudice put severe constraints in their way. West Indians, as Crowder and Tedrow's analysis shows, are as segregated from whites as American blacks. Real estate agents often steer West Indians to black neighborhoods or withhold information on housing availability elsewhere, and West Indians themselves often prefer communities where they can avoid racism and rejection. "Some neighborhoods," one West Indian New Yorker said, "are not yet ready for black people. And I don't want to be a hero" (quoted in Waldman

1998). Those who have braved open hostility and branched out from West Indian areas in Brooklyn and Queens to adjacent white communities find that their new neighborhoods become increasingly black. Antiblack prejudice tends to fuel a process of racial turnover as whites begin to leave and no new whites move in; at the same time, the growing number of black families makes the neighborhood seem more welcoming to West Indians looking for homes. The result is a pattern of segregation in which West Indian residential enclaves are located in largely black areas of the city and its suburbs. Indeed, Crowder and Tedrow show that West Indians are not very segregated from African Americans.

West Indians' lack of access to white neighborhoods—and the inevitable racial turnover that takes place when middle-class "pioneers" move into white communities—confines most to areas with inferior schools, relatively high crime rates, and poor government services, and limits their informal contacts with whites. Outside of work (and sometimes at work as well), most West Indians find themselves moving in all-black, or largely black, social worlds. This is fortified by patterns of marriage, which are another indication of the continuing racial prejudice and distinctive social distance separating whites and blacks in America. Census figures show that white Americans who intermarry are far more likely to wed an Asian or Hispanic than a black person—whether West Indian or African American.

The sting of racial prejudice is especially painful because West Indians come from societies with different racial hierarchies and conceptions of race. To be sure, the legacy of West Indian plantation slavery and colonial social arrangements has left in its wake the assumption that African ancestry is inferior; dark skin, moreover, continues to be correlated with poverty. But blackness does not have the same stigma that it does in the United States, and blackness is not in itself a barrier to social acceptance or upward mobility. In most West Indian societies, people of African ancestry are the overwhelming majority (the exceptions are Trinidad and Guyana, with their large East Indian populations) and there are hardly any whites or Europeans. That people with dark skin occupy high status roles is a fact of life—and unremarkable. "Blackness," as Milton Vickerman puts it in his chapter, is normal in the West Indies the way "whiteness" is normal in the United States.

The very notion of who is considered black also differs in the West Indies. Whereas in the United States the category "black" includes those who range from very dark- to very light-skinned, in the West Indies blackness is a matter of ancestry, skin color, hair type, facial features, and socioeconomic status. People defined as "black" in the United States belong to different groups in the West Indies, where there is a keen consciousness of shade—the lighter, the better. Thus, in Jamaica, "blacks" are generally thought of as impoverished individuals with African ancestry, dark skin, and certain facial features and hair type. People who combine features from several types (African and European, Asian, or Middle Eastern) are traditionally considered "brown" or "coloured." Moreover, money "whitens"; as individuals improve their income, education, lifestyle, and wealth, they seem progressively "whiter." What matters, above all, is having education, wealth, manners, and well-placed associates, not race.

Whatever their achievements or shade, West Indians of African ancestry are considered "black" in New York. On arrival, as many migrants have told researchers (including myself), they became aware, for the first time, that they were black—and were often astonished at being discriminated against because of their skin color (Bashi Bobb and Clarke, this volume; Vickerman, this volume, 1999; see also Foner 1987). Although they knew about the structure of American racial inequalities before they came, they were unprepared for the degree of interpersonal racism they encountered in their day-to-day experiences.[17]

Given these realities, no wonder that issues of race loom so large in the literature on West Indians. Although West Indians learn to "become black" in America, several chapters in this volume demonstrate that their sense of racial consciousness is not the same as African Americans'. Rogers makes the point that West Indians do not have the same highly cultivated sense of racial group consciousness as African Americans. In Waters's study, the immigrant parents had a negative view of becoming too "racial"—that is, being overly concerned with race and using race as an explanation for lack of success at school or on the job. In general, West Indians tend to subordinate racial considerations to the overriding goal of achieving material success in America, and they believe that individual effort can overcome racial barriers (Bashi Bobb and Clarke, this volume; Vickerman, this volume; Waters 1999b: 78).

A further complication is that West Indians have a strong sense of ethnic, as well as racial, identity. It is not an either/or situation. West Indian immigrants may embrace both their racial and ethnic identities without contradiction, although one identity may be more salient than another depending on the particular contexts and circumstances (Rogers, this volume). The immigrants' ethnic identity is nurtured by their immersion in West Indian neighborhoods and social networks in New York, and their continued contact with relatives and friends in the home society. They also attempt to distinguish themselves from, and avoid the stigma associated with, poor black Americans. Many West Indians assert an ethnic identity in order to make a case that they are culturally different from black Americans, emphasizing their strong work ethic, their valuing of education, and their lack of antisocial behaviors. Although this strategy may help individual West Indians, Waters argues that it ends up reinforcing stereotypes of blacks as inferior.

West Indian identities have implications in the political arena. On the one hand, the shared experience of being black in America and West Indians' identification with African Americans around this "linked racial fate outlook" provide a basis for coalition building between the two groups (Vickerman 1999). On the other hand, because West Indians also often distance themselves from African Americans, such coalitions cannot be taken for granted. As Rogers puts it, a politically unified black community does not exist on all issues and in all political contexts, and West Indians may have very different frames of reference than African Americans for making sense of the political world.

The American racial situation has also shaped scholarship on West Indians so that they are constantly compared with African Americans rather than with other groups. Academic debates about whether West Indians are an economic success story typically focus on whether they do better than African Americans and, if so, why (for a summary of this research see Waters 1999c). In New York, West Indians' median household income is higher and the percentage of households in poverty is lower than for African Americans. A consistent finding is that West Indian immigrants have higher labor force participation rates than native-born blacks. West Indians' dense social networks connect them to jobs, and they have what Waters calls a "different metric" for judging the worthiness of jobs than African Americans; even low wages in New York look good compared to what is available back home, and West Indians' sense of self is still tied to their status in the home country. Waters also argues that white employers generally prefer foreign over native blacks; they view the latter as less reliable, less productive, and less tractable than immigrants (cf. Model, this volume; Bashi Bobb and Clarke, this volume).[18]

Important as the comparisons with African Americans are, Kasinitz points out that they have led to a situation where scholarship on West Indians has ignored or minimized the significance of other critical features of their economic incorporation. Although researchers have paid much attention to the fact that West Indians are slightly more entrepreneurial than African Americans, they have largely missed the significance of the lack of an autonomous West Indian economic enclave, and of West Indians' low self-employment rates compared with those of other immigrant groups. Without an economic enclave—characterized by multilevel structures of co-ethnic workers, bosses, service providers, and customers—less-educated West Indians in both the first and second generations may be at a disadvantage compared with other immigrants. Also, because African Americans in New York are well represented in public-sector employment, it is not considered particularly noteworthy that West Indians' rates in this sector are also relatively high (see Model, this volume, on West Indian employment patterns). Often overlooked is that they have extremely high rates of public-sector employment compared with other immigrant New Yorkers, and Kasinitz suggests that this may partly explain why so many West Indians are involved in electoral politics.

For members of the second generation, born and bred in the United States, the key question is whether they will become black American. How they identify themselves therefore takes on special significance. Waters lays out three possibilities: the assertion of an ethnic identity, an immigrant identity stressing national origins and one's own or one's parents' experiences in the home country, and an American—that is, an African American—identity, in which one chooses to be viewed as a black American. The identities may overlap, as Vickerman's study (this volume) indicates. The second-generation individuals he interviewed nearly all saw themselves as partially West Indian—but also as American. Indeed, they were more conscious of race as a life-shaping issue than their parents because they had grown up in the American, rather than Caribbean, racial system and because they were not buffered by dense West Indian immigrant social networks (see Bashi Bobb and Clarke, this volume). At the same time as they assimilated into the African American community, they saw their West Indian identity and cultural values as setting them apart from generalized negative views of blacks.

How members of the second generation identify themselves is rooted in structural circumstances; those from middle-class backgrounds and from families involved in ethnic organizations and churches are most likely to be ethnic-identified (Waters 1994a, this volume). In turn, identities can also influence economic outcomes. Being ethnic-identified and involved in the ethnic community can reinforce attitudes and behavior that contribute to success in school and protect the second generation from the negative features of American—and black American—youth culture (cf. Zhou and Bankston 1998). By the same token, the American-identified teens in Waters's study came from poorer families and attended dangerous, substandard, and virtually all-black schools. Their experiences with racial discrimination and their perceptions of blocked social mobility led many to reject their parents' immigrant dream—and to be receptive to the black American peer culture of their neighborhoods and schools that emphasizes racial solidarity and opposition to school rules and authorities, and sees doing well academically as "acting white." Such an adversarial stance is often a recipe for academic failure.

Identification with African Americans, it is critical to stress, need not lead to downward assimilation for the second generation, as notions of segmented assimilation (Portes and Zhou 1993) would suggest. Kathryn Neckerman and her colleagues (1999) argue that incorporation into the growing African American middle-class "minority culture of mobility" provides strategies for economic mobility, including black professional and fraternal associations and organizations of black students at racially integrated high schools and universities. And, as Kasinitz (this volume) notes, New York African American communities can provide West Indians, of both the first and second generations, with a market for goods and services, a base for political support, and programs promoting black educational achievement.

Looking ahead, it is unclear whether second-generation West Indians who identify ethnically in their teens and young adulthood will continue to do so as adults. Even if some members of the second generation retain a strong West Indian identity over their lifetimes, how will others view them? Will they be recognized as West Indian? As black ethnics? Or simply as black Americans? Much depends on the future of the color line in America. If, as pessimistic prognoses have it, we are moving toward a black/nonblack racial order, there could be dire consequences for the children and grandchildren of West Indian immigrants. Without an accent or other clues to immediately telegraph their ethnic status to others, they will be seen—and subjected to the same kind of racial exclusion—as black Americans (Waters 1994a).

Yet there are signs that monolithic conceptions of blackness are being "tweaked," to use Vickerman's phrase, and one factor is the growing number of black immigrants (and their children) who emphasize their ethnic distinctiveness. Since racial hierarchies within the United States vary by region, this "tweaking" is especially likely to occur in places such as New York, where foreign-born blacks and their children now represent almost half of the city's black population (and where there is also a sizable and successful black middle class).[19] Continued mass immigration from the West Indies will sustain, and probably increase, this proportion, further chipping away at notions of a monolithic blackness and enhancing West Indians' "visibility." Ongoing replenishment of the immigrant community will keep alive an ethnic awareness among the second and third generations in a way that didn't happen in the past. From the 1930s to the 1960s, migration dwindled to a trickle; in contrast, many of today's second and third generations will grow up alongside immigrants of the same age and in communities where sizable numbers retain ties to the home country (see Kasinitz, this volume).

If these forces are leading New Yorkers to have a greater awareness of ethnic diversity within the "black" population, it is also the case that West Indian influences are increasingly felt within the wider black community, leading some scholars to speak of the "West Indianization" or "Caribbeanization" of black New York (cf. Sutton 1987). Kasinitz writes of assimilation in reverse, as Brooklyn's African American teenagers incorporate Jamaican dance hall music into their repertoire and imitate Jamaican patois. "What this means for African Americans and for black identity in general," he notes, "is among the least researched, but potentially most important, aspects of contemporary black immigration to New York."

FUTURE RESEARCH

This brings us to future research needs. The studies in this volume shed new light on the West Indian migrant experience in New York, yet we still have a lot to learn.

If continued large-scale immigration makes it imperative to study the impact of West Indians on the broader New York black community, it is also important to explore the experiences of new immigrant cohorts. More than thirty-five years have passed since the Hart-Celler immigration reforms opened the door to the contemporary mass influx. How are the newer immigrants, arriving at the dawn of a new millennium, faring compared with their counterparts who came to the city several decades ago? And what kinds of relations do the newcomers maintain with their predecessors? A growing number of studies are examining the trajectories of the new West Indian second generation, yet soon a sizable third generation will emerge, and we will need research that explores their lives as well.

In *Caribbean New York* (1992), Kasinitz charted the development of West Indian politics in Brooklyn in the 1970s and 1980s, but additional studies are clearly needed to update the story. Some research has been done on West Indian organizations in New York (e.g., Basch 1987a), yet this area also deserves more attention. So does religion. Given religion's importance in the lives of West Indian New Yorkers, it is surprising that the church is barely mentioned in most scholarly accounts. Randal Hepner's (1998) study of a Brooklyn Rastafarian church is a fascinating case of cultural reinvention in the immigrant setting; future researchers should also focus on the various Protestant churches that attract large numbers of West Indians in New York.[20] We also need more studies of the dynamics of West Indian migrant family life, a topic that has both theoretical and policy implications. How do family structures and values change in New York? In what ways are family and kin ties a source of support? What kind of conflicts and strains develop in West Indian families—and what are the consequences? How widespread are the "transnational families" discussed in the literature, and how do the separations, reunions, and continued contacts between close family members "here" and "there" affect their lives?[21] The whole study of transnational practices calls for systematic research to document just how extensive these practices are and their significance—positive as well as negative—for West Indian New Yorkers.

The essays in this volume focus on West Indians of African ancestry, but a growing number of New York West Indians are East Indian—descendants of Indian indentured laborers brought to the Caribbean (particularly Guyana and Trinidad) in the nineteenth century to replace African slaves on the sugar plantations after emancipation. East Indian West Indians are a fascinating case since they typically attempt to establish an Asian identity as a way to avoid being labeled black and have developed distinctly Indo-Caribbean neighborhoods, the Richmond Hill section of Queens being an especially popular area.[22] Ethnographic studies are required to document the experiences of this "minority within a minority," to use Kasinitz's term, as well as to explore relations they have with their compatriots of African ancestry.

Also important are relations among West Indians from different national backgrounds. In New York, ties develop among West Indians from different islands and a common West Indian identity takes on new significance (see Foner 1987; Sutton and Makiesky-Barrow 1987). At the same time, home country identities remain important, as Linda Basch's chapter on Vincentians makes clear. Indeed, Crowder and Tedrow show that West Indians often cluster among their compatriots when they settle in New York. Future research should probe just how meaningful home country allegiances are—and in what contexts—as well as the particular types of bridges and bonds uniting West Indians in New York. Also relevant are West Indians' relations with other immigrant communities in the city, not just in terms of potential political coalitions but also as they affect identities and the development of popular cultural forms.

West Indians, like other immigrants, generally move to the United States as children, teenagers, or young adults. What happens as they age and reach the end of their working lives? Karen Olwig's essay demonstrates that New York is not necessarily a permanent place of residence for West Indian migrants. What proportion will remain in New York after retirement? Return "home" to the islands? Commute back and forth? Or move to join their children elsewhere in the United States? Many West Indian retirees (as well as younger immigrants and their children) are already flocking to south Florida, where the weather is warm, the Caribbean is close, and sizable West Indian communities exist. A study of transplanted West Indian New Yorkers in Florida would make a fascinating addition to the literature.[23]

Careful comparisons across cities and nations and with other immigrant groups will also deepen our understanding of the New York West Indian experience. My own comparisons of West Indians in New York and London have brought out the importance of context—particularly the racial context and the presence of a large African American community in New York—in shaping West Indian identities, achievements, and intermarriage patterns (Foner 1979, 1983, 1985, 1998a, 1998b; see also Model and Ladipo 1996; Model 1997a; Model and Fisher 1999). Additional cross-national comparisons would benefit from the inclusion of Canada since the large West Indian community in Toronto faces yet another set of opportunities and constraints.

An intriguing question concerns West Indians who have lived in Britain for many years before moving to New York. Undoubtedly, the racial and ethnic identities and understandings that develop among these "twice migrants" in New York are influenced and complicated by their earlier experiences in Britain. Such movements can also intensify and alter the shape of transnational connections. Indeed, studies of transnational practices should be sensitive to the type, frequency, and impact of ties with relatives in Britain and Canada—not just with the home societies.

Also on the agenda for the future are comparisons between New York's West Indians and and those of other U.S. cities. Most research on West Indians in the United States has been done in New York, and there is a tendency to assume that the findings and analyses of New York–based studies hold true for West Indians throughout the country. Such assumptions often are not warranted. The size of New York's West Indian community, its long history, and the presence of large numbers from so many different nations have provided a base for a much broader range of West Indian neighborhoods and organizations and a launching pad for a greater number of successful political candidates. New York's economic context shapes occupational opportunities; West Indians elsewhere, for example, do not always cluster, as they do in New York, in health care or private household work. New York's West Indians also bring with them a particular range of human capital that affects how they fare in the economy—with a smaller proportion of professionals, for example, than in the Washington, DC, area (Palmer 1995: 28–29).

The extraordinary heterogeneity of New York's immigrant population also provides a very different context than, say, Miami, the second most popular city for U.S. West Indians. In Miami, West Indians live in a city with a "Cuban ambiance" and where Cubans greatly outnumber other immigrants (Perez 1992: 83). No one immigrant group dominates New York the same way. Whereas Miami's Cubans are touted as an economic success story, New York's West Indians do better (in terms of employment rates and household income) than the city's two largest Hispanic groups: Puerto Ricans and Dominicans (cf. Grasmuck and Grosfoguel 1997). New York City's black population also has much more political clout than Miami's, and in the early 1990s an African American, David Dinkins, was mayor. Moreover, unlike New York, Miami does not have a dominant West Indian residential neighborhood (Kasinitz, Battle, and Miyares, forthcoming). An important task for further analysis is to untangle the way particular structural features in each receiving city—including the size, composition, and historic pattern of settlement of the West Indian population—interact to create distinctive West Indian experiences.[24]

Within New York itself, comparisons with other immigrant groups are useful in highlighting and explaining what is distinctive about West Indians and what gives them an edge in relation to other groups. The role of West Indians' human capital, their fluency in English upon arrival, and their race are obviously critical in such comparisons, though it is important not to slight the cultural orientations that West Indians bring with them. While much has been made of West Indian culture in the contrasts with black Americans, there is a risk it may be overlooked in comparisons with other immigrants precisely because West Indians are native English speakers, come from nearby societies that are heavily influenced by American culture, and do not have "exotic" customs such as arranged marriages or patrilineal kinship. Scholars should bear this in mind.

The essays that follow then, are, a challenge for further study. They offer a rich, detailed, and complex portrait of a major immigrant group in America's quintessential immigrant city. In doing so, they illuminate fundamental issues concerning immigration, race, and ethnicity in American society and global interconnections in the modern world. And they raise new questions that take on added significance as growing numbers of West Indians continue to migrate to New York and transform the city, and are inevitably changed by their own journeys.

NOTES

1. Comments at conference on "Transnationalism and the Second Generation," Harvard University, 4 April 1998.

2. Strictly speaking, the category *Afro-Caribbean* encompasses people of African ancestry from Haiti, the Dominican Republic, and other non-English-speaking islands, but the authors who use the term in this volume have in mind people from the former British colonies. Hispanic and Anglophone Caribbean immigrants form separate communities in New York. Language as well as differences in historical and political background distinguish Haitians from their English-speaking Caribbean counterparts.

3. This follows the convention adopted by Kasinitz, who has a useful discussion of terminology in *Caribbean New York* (1992: 14–15).

4. On the causes of West Indian migration see, for example, Deere et al. (1990), Foner (1978), James (1998), Marshall (1982), Palmer (1995), Richardson (1983, 1992), and Thomas-Hope (1992).

5. The breakdown: foreign-born from Jamaica (137,725), Guyana (130,252), Trinidad and Tobago (127,764), and Barbados (39,903) (March 1997 and March 1998 Current Population Survey, Annual Demographic Supplements, calculated by John Mollenkopf, Center for Urban Research, City University of New York (CUNY) Graduate Center).

6. Flores and Salvo (1997); Salvo and Ortiz (1992); Department of City Planning (1999).

7. Between the late 1930s and 1965, net migration from the Commonwealth Caribbean to the United States probably never exceeded three thousand a year. "Immigration virtually came to a halt at the height of the Depression, climbed slightly after World War II, but was cut back again in 1952 when the McCarran-Walter Act restricted the use of 'home country' quotas by colonial subjects" (Kasinitz 1992: 25–26). This act imposed a quota of one hundred visas on the colonial dependencies of Europe (Palmer 1995: 10).

8. Immigration and Naturalization Service figures show some decline in Jamaican, Guyanese, and Trinidadian immigration to New York City in the mid 1990s, yet the numbers are still very large: about 100,000 legal immigrants entered New York City from these countries in the period 1990–96 (Department of City Planning 1999: 6–7).

9. See Winston James, *Holding Aloft the Banner of Ethiopia* (1998), for a detailed and richly textured account of Caribbean radicals in early-twentieth-century America.

10. The city's black population mushroomed between World War I and the 1960s, largely the result of a huge internal migration from the South. A huge migration of Puerto Ricans after World War II brought large numbers of Hispanic migrants to the city; since the 1960s, immigration, particularly of Dominicans, Mexicans, Colombians, and Ecuadorians, has fueled the growth of the city's Hispanic population. Large-scale Asian immigra-

tion is a post-1965 phenomenon, with Chinese by far the largest Asian group in the city (see Foner 2000).

11. Many of these changes are discussed in Foner (2000), which offers a broad comparison of today's immigrant New Yorkers and their predecessors at the turn of the twentieth century.

12. In her earlier influential work, with Nina Glick Schiller and Cristina Szanton Blanc, Basch (1994) used the term *transnationalism,* which has gained widespread currency in scholarly circles. In a recent publication, Alejandro Portes, Luis Guarnizo, and Patricia Landolt restrict the concept of transnationalism to "occupations and activities that require regular and sustained contact over time across national borders for their implementation" (1999: 219).

13. Migrant remittances have long been critical in West Indian societies at both the national and household levels, leading some academic analysts to speak of them as "remittance societies." On the role of remittances (from Central America, Britain, and the United States) in these societies see, for example, Manners (1965), Philpott (1973), B. Richardson (1983, 1985), and Stinner, Albuquerque, and Bryce-Laporte (1982).

14. The most commonly shipped barrels are "super jumbos," which stand nearly four feet tall, are two feet around, and can hold up to five hundred pounds. In 1999, the barrels cost sixteen to twenty-five dollars, depending on size. The shipping cost of a five-hundred-pound barrel through a small storefront company was around sixty dollars (Beshkin 1999).

15. See Kasinitz (1992: 32). On the importance of dual nationality provisions among New York immigrants today, see Foner (2000), chapter 6.

16. See Levitt (2000) on transnational villages among Dominican migrants in Boston.

17. Waters (1999a: 153) makes a distinction between West Indians' expectations of structural racism—blocked mobility for blacks in society and a hierarchy in which whites have economic and political power—and the realities of interpersonal racism they encounter in daily life upon arrival. See also Foner (1987).

18. Waters (1999b) contends that West Indians' preparation for and militancy toward structural racism, in combination with their lack of expectation of interpersonal racism, have helped them make progress in the service economy. They push for promotions and perks, yet have easygoing relations with whites on the job.

19. This estimate is based on the March 1998 Current Population Survey, tables provided by John Mollenkopf, Center for Urban Research, CUNY Graduate Center. The majority of foreign-born blacks in New York City are West Indian.

20. See Zane (1999). In this regard, it is interesting that the literature on West Indians in Britain has paid more attention to the role of religion, from the very beginning of the influx (e.g., Calley 1965) to the present (e.g., Toulis 1997).

21. In my work, I have explored changes in West Indian women's family roles in New York (Foner 1986, 1997). See Waters (1997, 1999a) on the strains that result when children left in or sent back to the West Indies are reunited with parents in New York. In an unpublished paper, Thompson and Bauer (n.d.) note that, in their exploratory study of members of ten Jamaican families in Jamaica, Canada, Britain, and the United States, one family held biennial family reunions with their extended family successively in Jamaica, Canada, and New York.

22. Indo-Caribbeans are becoming involved in ethnic politics in Richmond Hill. In the 2000 primary contests, for example, an Indo-Caribbean lawyer from Guyana was running for City Council and another Indo-Caribbean candidate from the area, a community-college professor, was a State Assembly hopeful (Thottam 2000).

23. By 1990, Dade County, Florida, was home to 53,676 Anglophone West Indian immigrants, and Broward County to 32,208 (Kasinitz, Battle, and Miyares, forthcoming). Also see Ho's (1993) interesting study of thirty Afro-Trinidadians living in Los Angeles, the majority having moved there from the New York metropolitan area. Los Angeles appealed to them because of the mild climate and because they believed they would get ahead more easily there.

24. As a beginning step in this direction, see Ransford Palmer's (1995: 27–30) brief profile of the West Indian communities in Hartford and Washington, DC, and my own comparison of Haitians in New York and Miami (Foner 1998b). Also see Johnson (1995) on Boston's West Indian community and Kasinitz, Battle, and Miyares (forthcoming) on the children of West Indian immigrants in south Florida.

PART ONE

Gender, Work, and Residence

ONE

Early-Twentieth-Century Caribbean Women

Migration and Social Networks in New York City

Irma Watkins-Owens

Around 1900, African Caribbean women began migrating in increasing numbers to the United States, settling mainly in clusters of compatriots in African American communities of New York City.[1] The migration of women—which increased steadily for the next two and one-half decades— was a key factor in making possible the formation of culturally distinct Caribbean communities for the first time in New York City. The history of African Caribbean women migrants, however, remains absent from the growing body of literature on women and U.S. immigration during the late nineteenth and early twentieth centuries (Cordasco 1985; Gabaccia 1989). Recent historical work on Caribbean immigrants of this period notwithstanding, a fuller discussion of early women's experience is warranted (Hathaway 1999; James 1998; Holder 1998; Watkins-Owens 1996; Johnson 1995).[2]

In this chapter I focus on the participation of African Caribbean women within migration and social networks in New York City between 1900 and the beginning of the Second World War. Early-twentieth-century women's migration experience and the informal and organizational networks they participated in reflect significant aspects of migration yet to be incorporated into the larger story of Caribbean migration. A goal of this essay is both to identify issues specific to women's migration experiences and to reengage the often gender-neutral narrative of early Caribbean upward mobility. The period under discussion encompasses roughly the last fifty years of the formal colonial era in the British-held Caribbean and a time of significant movements toward independence and nationhood. To reconstruct migrant women's stories and to bring their issues into public focus, their writing, letters, and oral interviews are important resources. While this evidence reveals both men's and women's involvement in social networks, sisters, daughters, mothers, and wives often sustained relations with people back home through a continuous stream of correspondence, parcels of clothing and food, remittances, gossip, match-making, child fostering, and rotating credit. Women's involvement in what social scientists would now call a transnational field or arena was linked to conditions and cultural practices that defined their roles as independent economic providers.

While women's social networks are important to understanding Caribbean community formation in New York as well as transnational connections, migrant women's networks were not forged without conflict (Pessar 1999; Hondagneu-Sotelo 1994). African Caribbean women migrated within colonial and patriarchal structures that subordinated them on the basis of sex, class, and color; in New York they entered another arena of race and sex discrimination. They both adapted to and challenged the gender order, and their activities and experiences reflect multiple strategies. Investigating migrant's networks—and the specific conditions affecting women—not only begins the recovery of hidden histories and concerns previously ignored but also allows for a scholarly reengagement with the larger record of black immigrants in the first half of the twentieth century (Pessar 1999).

MIGRATION, GENDER, AND SETTLEMENT IN NEW YORK CITY

Nearly every immigrant to New York arrived or participated in a network in which female family members played important roles. In some cases, self-supporting women were the first in a family to migrate. A few examples involving well-known public figures illustrate this point. In 1900 Hubert Harrison, later a radical intellectual and leader among Caribbean anticolonialists and known to Harlem audiences as the black Socrates, joined his wage-earning older sister in New York after the death of his father. Nevis native Cyril Briggs, editor of the radical journal *Crusader,* joined his mother in New York in 1905 after completing his secondary education. W.A. Domingo, a Harlem importer and the well-known radical activist founder of the nationalist Jamaica Progressive League, arrived in Boston in 1910, where he joined a sister who ran a boardinghouse for Jamaicans. Richard B. Moore, the Harlem radical intellectual from Barbados, came with his widowed stepmother, Elizabeth Moore, who joined a wage-earning sister on the upper West Side of Manhattan in 1909 (Hill 1983: 528; Turner and Turner 1988: 23).

If working women were central to the formation and support of networks involving male and female kin, migrating women especially relied upon other women. Sisters, mothers, or grandmothers helped care for children while female friends most often assisted with finding jobs and making social contacts in New York. When the widowed Elizabeth Moore found herself with three stepchildren and almost no income, "she consulted her sisters, who advised going to America where opportunities for the children would be better." She and her young stepson, Richard B. Moore, lodged with another sister already settled in Manhattan

(Turner and Turner 1988: 22). Other women lodged with friends and compatriots. Ties to home were reinforced by these informal connections.

Organizing migration often encompassed a consciousness about and a practical approach to life circumstances imposed by the Caribbean colonial social economy. In spite of racial barriers the United States represented an opportunity to realize a future of otherwise impossible dreams. Many immigrants could be detached from and defiant about America—viewing it as someone else's country—while at the same time recognizing it as a place that offered a chance to overcome the severe economic constraints at home. In Paule Marshall's novel *Brown Girl, Brownstones* about first-generation Barbadian migrants in Brooklyn, one character critically assesses the circumstances that compelled her to move to New York: "One Crop. People having to work for next skin to nothing. The white people treating we like slaves and we taking it. The rum shop and the Church join together to keep we pacify and in ignorance. That's Barbados" (Marshall 1959: 70). And, she adds, "I wouldn't let my mother know peace 'til she found the money and send me to this man country."[3] As in so many other Barbadian families, the mother-daughter network in Marshall's family was responsible for financial organization of the passage.

Migration within the Caribbean was historically rooted in slavery and colonial and imperialist exploitation, as well as the structural, geographic, and population pressures of the region. Migration was necessary for family survival and was structured in favor of males, though women were always participants in the various movements. Many migrating women, even among the "the better laboring" and middle classes, came from backgrounds where women were socialized to support themselves and their children, often within a network of kin. Particularly in seafaring families, women became accustomed to running household economic affairs and relying on each other for social life. In her "biomythography"/autobiography, *Zami*, Audre Lorde describes a culture of women in the early-twentieth-century village of her maternal great-aunt on the island of Carriacou:

> Aunt Anni lived among the other women who saw their men off the sailing vessels, then tended the goats and groundnuts, planted grain and poured rum upon the earth to strengthen the corn's growing, built their own women's houses and the rain water catchments, harvested the limes, wove their lives and the lives of their children together. Women who survived the absence of their seafaring men easily, because they came to love each other, past the men's returning (Lorde 1981: 14).

The year 1898 and the onset, formally speaking, of American empire in the Caribbean with intervention in Cuba and elsewhere, had a direct effect on migration streams to the United States. In the nineteenth century and earlier, the United States attracted small communities of Caribbean intellectuals, churchmen, and students and continued to do so after the turn of the twentieth century. These individuals were mainly men who came with exceptional educational and other skills and found opportunities within the African American community.

The expansion of U.S. investments in commercial agriculture in the Caribbean, the construction of the Panama Canal between 1904 and 1914, the introduction of regular shipping lines between the region and the eastern seaboard, and the growing number of American tourists helped facilitate the travel of larger numbers of men and women. Demographer George Roberts dates 1904 as the beginning of large-scale emigration from Barbados, when work on the Panama Canal resumed under American sponsorship. "Also developing at the time," he writes, "was an extensive movement to the United States of America." In the first two decades of the century, working women were increasingly part of the movement of people within and outside the Caribbean. According to Roberts, between 1911 and 1921 an estimated 44 percent of the population decline in Barbados was due to the emigration of women (1955: 270).

Colonial administrations tried to regulate, encourage, or select emigrants based on the perceived interests of the colonies. Between 1891 and 1900 the Barbados government sponsored the emigration of 1569 women "in reduced circumstances who cannot earn a living in this country" (Roberts 1955: 269). In the last three years of the nineteenth century the government-sponsored Victoria Emigration Society helped 179 white women and 50 colored or mixed-race women emigrate to the United States. Although "many people such as widows and children approached the government for assistance," money was generally not made available to fund such requests (264). In keeping with color stratification practices, the Barbados government selected a few poor white and biracial women for emigration assistance.

In the ensuing decades a growing number of women of all colors seeking better opportunities arranged their own travel. Unemployment was behind the movement of many skilled and semiskilled female workers from some countries. The aging Harriet Dowridge wrote her daughter from Barbados in 1907, "It will give me great pleasure to come to nue york next sumer as I feels stronger now and could work but can get nothing to dow for things are very dull hear."[4] Rhoda Reddock cites the effect of post–World War I unemployment in Trinidad and Tobago that "led to a high rate of emigration of women, mainly to the United States, in the early 1920s. The *Labour Leader,* the newspaper of the Trinidad Workingmen's Association, noted in 1923 that a 'review of the passenger list for the last six months showed that 90 percent were women'" (1993: 252).

In an essay with Norma Steel, Margaret Prescod-Roberts, whose mother and grandmother preceded her to New York in the 1930s and 1940s, describes the women's motivation: "Looking around us, we knew that our lives in the Village were about work . . . centuries of hard work. And it was clear that the wealth that we were creating was not there—we had to go and get it" (1980: 26). Migration for these women was strategic, goal-oriented, and practical.

According to census reports, over forty-eight thousand foreign-born black women as compared to fifty-seven thousand foreign-born black men lived in the United States in 1930. As Table 1.1 indicates, in terms of numbers women

TABLE 1.1   Year of Arrival of Immigrants of African Descent, by Sex

Years of Immigration	Female		Male		Total	
	Number	%	Number	%	Number	%
1900–1930	48,135	100.0	57,887	100.0	106,202	100.0
1900 or earlier	3,050	6.3	4,551	7.9	7,601	7.2
Unknown	4,129	8.6	7,448	12.9	11,577	10.9
1901–10	6,178	12.8	9,178	15.8	15,356	14.5
1911–14	4,943	10.2	6,008	10.4	10,951	10.3
1915–19	8,482	17.6	9,699	16.8	18,181	17.1
1920–24	13,981	29.0	13,391	23.1	27,372	25.7
1925–26	1,667	3.4	1,822	3.1	3,489	3.3
1927	609	1.2	652	1.1	1,261	1.2
1928	615	1.3	558	1.0	1,173	1.1
1929	725	1.5	632	1.1	1,357	1.3
1930 (to April 1)	160	0.3	142	0.2	302	0.3
1925–30	3,776	7.8	3,806	6.6	7,582	7.1

SOURCE: Adapted from Reid (1969 [1939]: 236), based on U.S. Census of Population, 1930.

were a "tremendous human resource" within Caribbean migrant communities (Marshall 1982: 91). Well over half of all black immigrants settled in New York City—over 90 percent of them had been born in the Caribbean (Kasinitz 1992: 25). Not surprisingly, the highest number of women arrived when the migration peaked between 1915 and 1924. The permanent emigration of so many young men and women alarmed the colonial ruling class, who described the movement as an "exodus." "From one small island 500 negroes have gone to America," observed one upset member of the Jamaican ruling elite in 1920.[5]

Although they were a minority of those immigrating in most years of the mass movement, Caribbean women may have been more permanent members of the African Caribbean immigrant community by virtue of their legal entry. Ira Reid suggests one reason for this: "The ease with which males can cross the borders, leave their occupations as seamen, and arrive surreptitiously by various devices, is much greater than among females. While statistical verification is not possible, there is every reason to believe that this factor accounts, in part at least, for the relatively unequal sex proportions indicated by the statistics of arrivals" (1969 [1939]: 81).

In general, a woman's departure for New York required more careful orchestration than a man's, and the support of kin and friends in the city was crucial. Almost all oral narratives identify the friend or relative a woman "came to" in New York. Single black men (76.9%) and women (68.39%) predominated among black immigrants arriving in the United States between 1923 and 1932 (Reid 1969 [1939]: 243). Still, it is important to note the participation of married Caribbean women. In fact, just before the 1924 Immigration Act nearly shut down entry from the region, the rush to reunite families may have accounted for the heavier flow of women.

In *Zami*, Audre Lorde writes about her parents, who had been married just one year before their arrival in New York in 1924. Her father was a native of Barbados and her mother was born in Carriacou, a small island near Grenada. Her mother, Linda, who was reunited in New York with two of her sisters, "lied about her age in immigration because her sisters who were here already had written her that americans wanted strong young women to work for them, and Linda was afraid she was too old [at 27] to get work." She did find work however, and together the sisters were better able to confront "being black female and foreign born in New York City. . . . My mother and her two sisters were large and graceful women whose ample bodies seemed to underline the air of determination with which they moved through their lives in the strange world of Harlem and america" (Lorde 1981: 9, 16–17).

Work may have been a primary motivation for migrating, but African Caribbean women also had a sense of adventure and high expectations about life in the city. Their letters home describe jazz music, visits with friends, and other socializing. A letter from a female friend in New York captures one young woman's feelings about the excitement of the times. "Well girl how are things in the old home? From all I can hear [Barbados] is getting quite gay. Some of the New York Spirit seems to have been diffused over there. I don't know perhaps it gets there in the people's trunks as they leave here." And she continues, "Did you see anything of the Halley's comet? Girl, the people here made a time of it."[6] Caribbean and southern migrant women in Alice Brown Fairclough's 1929 study listed recreational and social life as one, though not the primary, attraction of New York City. Topping the list were their occupational and educational aspirations and the desire to join relatives already in the city.[7]

What were the profiles of the African Caribbean women who migrated to New York? Scholars generally agree that the early Caribbean immigrants were a select, even highly select group (see Holder 1987; James 1998; Model, this volume). Prospective migrants needed resources to be able to afford the journey. The cost of the trip could be prohibitive for the average wage-earning family in the Caribbean: a Caribbean emigrant needed forty-five dollars in 1900, sixty-five in 1915, and ninety-five in 1924 (Holder 1987: 14). Women and men who left for the United States were mainly from the stable-wage-earning to middle stratum of Caribbean society; colonial elites, mainly males, also continued a pattern of immigration begun in the nineteenth century and before. "Panama Money" was one of the most dependable sources of passage money to the states, but sometimes a "bit of family ground" had to be sold (Marshall 1982: 88). "My mother sold her property [one quarter-acre]; she got very little for it," recalled Vera Clarke Ifill, a native of Christ Church, Barbados (Ifill 1986).

A majority of female immigrants, especially those entering legally after passage of the 1917 Literacy Act, possessed at least a grammar school education and knowledge of a skilled trade, such as needlework. In addition, social-class skills and manners were highly valued by immigrants in their home communities as well as in New York. "She was thoroughly British in her ideas, her manners and her plans for her daughters," writes Shirley Chisholm about her Barbadian mother (1970: 13). Novelist Rosa Guy, a native of Trinidad, writes, "I started school in that British colony, dedicated to upholding British traditions. My family was the proud product of that colonial system, churchgoing lower middleclass. We looked down upon our more unfortunate brothers and sisters. . . . They were poor, and never allowed stepping into our charmed circle. Indeed we guardians of British culture had been well chosen" (Guy 1990: 128).

In terms of education, African Caribbean migrant women were generally at a disadvantage as compared to men. In all of the British-held colonies, race and class restricted access to secondary education (especially for the dark-skinned masses), but gender was an added dimension for girls (Mayers 1995: 261). Migration in pursuit of education was a long tradition among the sons of the colonial elite but seems to have been less common for daughters. For example, between 1869 and 1932 only 29 of 1047 Caribbean students attending Howard University were women (Smith 1933: 238). Equal access to educational opportunities for women was a key concern of early-twentieth-century Caribbean women's rights activists. In 1901, Cathryn McKenzie, a Jamaican feminist activist in the People's Convention and the Jamaica-based Pan African Association, called for "The Rights of Women" to be incorporated into a nationalist agenda (Ford-Smith 1988: 73). In addition to education, she wanted the franchise and women's equal participation in politics.

Although they faced discrimination, in New York immigrant men had more opportunities than women did to take advantage of higher education that led to professional status (Mayers 1995: 272; Henry 1977: 462–471). First-generation Caribbean men held visible roles in the African American community as lawyers, physicians, and political leaders. The public roles of key first-generation Caribbean women have yet to be fully assessed in the historical literature (Bolles 1996; Richards 1994). But adult immigrant women, including those from middle-class backgrounds, were more likely than men to continue as wage earners. While many Caribbean immigrants experienced downward mobility, such a downslide was probably more permanent for first-generation adult women than for men. Women may have been reconciled to such status loss when they gained independence as wage earners in New York and more opportunities for their children.

The story of Emily Matilda Wilkin and Charles Steber illustrates the status loss that was initially experienced by many Caribbean immigrants. Their story is based on a narrative written by the eldest son of the Wilkin-Steber family, who arrived in Manhattan's Tenderloin district in 1900. Twenty-five-year-old

Emily Matilda Wilkin of Montserrat, fearing her widowed tyrannical father would require her to keep house for him indefinitely, secretly left for the United States after "borrowing" her passage from his strongbox. Wilkin was apparently from the fair-complexioned colored class, for according to the narrative, her father was "related" to the white owner of the large estate that he managed. With the help of two cousins, she made good her escape, leaving behind a note for the old man, known to everyone as Mas Johnny. Her plan was to join a former sweetheart, a medical student at Meharry in Tennessee, and pursue her own education. But these plans changed when she met and courted a young seaman aboard ship, Charles Joseph Steber, a native of Dominica. She changed her destination from Nashville to New York, and after a brief courtship the two were married. The family's narrative reports an eventual reconciliation with Wilkin's father but does not recount the networks she may have utilized to find lodging or a job in the garment industry where she worked to help support the family in the early years of her marriage. Between 1902 and 1908 she gave birth to three children. After moving from tenement to tenement in the Tenderloin district, the family made a permanent removal uptown to Harlem in 1906, where Charles, a printer by trade, established his own business.

Previous chain migrations and Charles's prior lodging arrangements probably pulled the couple to the Tenderloin, a crowded and deteriorating section of African American and Irish tenements in the West 20's and 30's where Gimbel's Department Store and Pennsylvania Station would later be built. The section extended to Ninth and Tenth Avenues and was identified with vice and other underworld activities. Emily Wilkin's move from a big house on a Montserrat estate "over which she presided in a tropical climate to come to New York and live in a cold-water railroad flat in America was a devastating experience," according to the family narrative. "There were no leases for these sub-standard, low-cost living quarters in those days. If you agreed to stay for a year, you got a bonus of one month rent-free. At the end of the year, families shopped around for better quarters and a better bonus" (Steber 1987: 2). In a 1906 speech before YMCA clubs, the Rev. Charles Morris, a well-known African American Baptist minister, described the blocks filled with dives and taverns as "little less than a corner of hell." Like other African American reformers of the era, Morris was worried about the neighborhood's threat to the uplift ideology values of nuclear family, righteous living, and self-help.[8] "Fathers and mothers away down south or far off in the West Indies, little know of the shame and degradation that have overtaken many of their sons and daughters who have come to this city to improve their condition and perhaps aid their parents, but have been lost to them and the world."[9]

The Wilkin-Stebers, like many other young black people from the south and the Caribbean, had few choices for housing in New York. Had they not settled in the Tenderloin, the couple might have resided in San Juan Hill, a section of Manhattan in the West 50's and 60's that remained heavily represented by new

Caribbean immigrants as late as 1920. More prosperous and experienced African Americans and Caribbean migrants moved uptown to Harlem by 1915. According to one contemporary study, 58 percent of San Juan Hill's residents were foreign born in 1924. They came "for the most part from the BWI where English is spoken, though with a few, Spanish is the native tongue."[10]

San Juan Hill was an area well known as a site of Caribbean entrepreneurship. Several male members of the prosperous Bermuda Benevolent Association established shops there in the 1890s.[11] Because of the denser concentration of Caribbean migrants in the area, it may have been more important than other centers of black population as an immigrant business district. Two churches in the San Juan Hill area—St. Cyprian Episcopal and St. Benedict the Moor—catered to immigrants, providing services, programs, and recreation. St. Cyprian had been founded in 1905 as part of the Protestant Episcopal Mission City Society's effort to avert integration when black immigrants began frequenting the previously all-white Episcopalian churches in the area (Woofter 1969: 254–255; Watkins-Owens 1996: 56). Its parish house was the "outstanding social center" of the district. (St. Martin, St. Cyprian's sister church in Harlem, later became a stronghold of Caribbean professionals.) Also, other institutions in the area, such as Sloane Maternity Hospital and New York Nursing and Child Hospital, served immigrant and southern migrant women and children. Although they lived in the West 30's, the Wilkin-Steber family attended church and used the services in the San Juan Hill district. Wilkin gave birth to her first child at Sloane in 1902, and the child was baptized at the Roman Catholic Church of St. Benedict the Moor on Fifty-third Street. While San Juan Hill was "one of the most congested colored districts in New York City,"[12] the area continued to draw new immigrants long after the Wilkin-Stebers moved uptown (Steber 1987: 15).

The family moved to 134th Street in Harlem only after Charles Steber, who worked as a seaman until 1902, established a steady income as a printer. He had been trained in this occupation in his native Dominica. In Harlem the couple solidified their ties to the community by joining twenty-seven different fraternal, civic, religious, benevolent, and homeland associations. Steber also organized the British Colonial Society, with the "blessing of the British Consul," to aid new immigrants and, according to the family narrative, to "combat prejudice of southern blacks" directed against Caribbean newcomers.[13] Emily Wilkin worked in her husband's print shop and volunteered her time in the women's auxiliaries of many associations, rising to leadership positions and organizing fund-raising activities. In 1914, the Wilkin-Stebers bought a brownstone house at 159 West 136th Street, becoming the fourth black family to move into the block (Steber 1987: 20).[14]

Because the family history was written by the Wilkin-Stebers' eldest child and constructs an upward mobility narrative of immigrant success, we cannot be certain of Emily Wilkin's real feelings or motivations. She apparently was a willing and active partner in the creation of formal social networks designed to enhance her own and her husband's social standing. "Besides being a loving and devoted wife," according to the narrative, "[she] did everything she could to enhance the stature of her husband and the well-being of her family." According to the narrative, she took "night classes in a variety of subjects" while a working mother. Participation in so many Caribbean and African American (including southern migrants') associations was a careful and not uncommon strategy, intended to gain clients for the family printing business. Steber's close ties to the British Consul may have been a strategic manipulation of his own immigration status as much as a way to ensure protection for the immigrant community. Though he was well known in Harlem business and political circles, according to the family narrative, he never became a citizen of the United States. Perhaps as a seaman he had entered the country without obtaining legal status. His community involvement effectively neutralized this detail. As for Wilkin, she escaped the constraints of her father's household in Montserrat and, in Harlem, reinvented her status as a middle-class wife, mother, and community leader.

Middle-class status in the New York African Caribbean community carried with it certain norms and expectations. In spite of the "dens of iniquity" near which respectable immigrants settled, most were careful to avoid becoming objects of gossip among compatriots. Reproductive norms, which reinforced patriarchal family structure, could especially shape the migration experiences of single women. In her essay about Barbadian women immigrants, Paule Marshall writes: "Most of these women were unmarried although a number already had children. In some cases this was the reason for them being sent to the States. An aunt of mine was banished to New York for having disgraced the family with a child fathered by a pan-boiler from British Guiana, who came to Barbados every year during the grinding season to work in the sugar factory" (P. Marshall 1987: 88). In most cases, children were left behind with female kin to enable a young mother to emigrate and provide support.

However, reproductive and sexual politics affected women's migration experience in distinctive ways. African Caribbean women's increasing visibility as migrants on the move threatened patriarchal conventions about the place of women and families in a stable colonial society. One official Jamaican publication warned that women and children could expect to find it more difficult than men to obtain visas for the United States.[15] In addition, migrating black women, like other immigrant women, were constantly under suspicion for prostitution (Sheperd 1995: 239; Friedman-Kasaba 1996: 206–207). As a result, women's movements were subject to surveillance by British and American authorities. Claims that Caribbean women were being imported to Panama in 1906 for purposes of prostitution—"the United States authorities had imported at considerable expense several hundreds of colored ladies"—prompted U.S. government officials to require migrating women to sign affidavits swearing to the "voluntary nature of their immigration" (Bigelow 1906: 20; see also McCullough 1977: 577).

Because of prevailing sexual stereotypes about women of color, all migrating black women's movements were subject to policing by reformers. Operating under the assumption that "the race can rise no higher than its women," female progressives often placed undue responsibility on women (White 1999: 55). African American feminist Victoria Earle Matthews, who founded the White Rose Home in 1898, cautioned women about traveling alone to the city. "Unless a girl has friends whom she and her family know are to be trusted, unless she has money enough to pay her way until she can get work, she cannot expect to be independent or free from question among careful people" (Matthews 1898: 68). At Ellis Island, committees of African American club-women and social workers, concerned about unscrupulous employment agents, met women without family in the city and escorted them to their lodgings or to the White Rose Home, a boarding facility for black working women. In 1923, clubwomen organized the Welcome Stranger Committee to meet single black women migrants at Ellis Island and Pennsylvania Station.[16]

Despite reformers' concern with public representation, most migrating women were anxious to settle and find a job. Like southern migrant women, Caribbean women were mainly employed as household workers or in other personal service jobs—in 1925, this description fit over 75 percent of African Caribbean migrant women in Manhattan's labor force (see Table 2.3 in Model, this volume). During the First World War, European immigrant women—cooks, house servants, and laundry workers—found jobs in munitions factories and as clerks, but southern and Caribbean black migrant women were excluded from these occupations in New York. As Model's data show, some Caribbean women (just over 10 percent in 1925) worked in manufacturing, mainly in the garment industry, but most were at the lower end of the wage scale. Maida Springer Kemp, a garment union organizer and African Panamanian of Caribbean descent, recalled: "When I came in [the garment industry] in 1932, I came in as a finisher, a hand worker, sitting at the table doing the hems, and the buttons and the trimming and the necks." According to Kemp, black women worked mainly as pinkers, examiners, cleaners, and finishers (Richards 1994: 292–294).

Personal service and garment workers used coethnic networks to find work, but Model's figures suggest that this was easier for household workers. Fred Challenor's query to his wife Aletha about her interest in a possible job was typical. "I saw Adamson and Fay last Sunday, they are working together in a private family and the same party wants me in a job similar to it but I would have to get you along. . . . What do you think about it?"[17] In New York in 1928, the average weekly wage was $9 for a female household servant, $13 for a female elevator operator, and $11 for a female laundry worker. Garment factory work was better paid. A 1934 Urban League article reported that unionized black women finishers started at $22.75 for a thirty-five-hour week. "Negro women workers in the dress industry are among the best paid of their race in Harlem," the article noted (Kine 1934: 108–109; Fairclough 1929: 63). In 1940, domestic service and laundry work were still the top two occupations employing Caribbean immigrants (Waldinger 1996: 119).

Because of race, the working lives of Caribbean women closely resembled those of their African American sisters. Unlike European immigrant women, a majority of black women from both groups continued as wage earners after marriage, primarily as household servants. Some New York employers appear to have preferred black immigrant women over southern migrants, but they still restricted black immigrant women to jobs as servants or sweatshop workers (Marshall 1959: 287). These restrictions were maintained in spite of Caribbean women's skills and high literacy levels. All black wage earners were restricted to low-wage jobs, as Carole Marks points out, because of the advantages that accrued to both employers and white workers (Marks 1989: 136). What appeared on the surface as preferential treatment was actually manipulation of a disadvantaged workforce, which strained ethnic relations between some African American and African Caribbean women (Erickson 1996: 26; Alexander and Mohanty 1997: xv). Individual southern and Caribbean women devised various ways to negotiate New York City's racialized landscape.

Women quickly noticed that skin complexion often influenced hiring practices. This made finding alternatives to household work difficult or impossible for many. Employers sometimes listed "fair complexion" in their ads for doctor's attendants, elevator operators, or restaurant workers, though conditions of employment in those jobs were not necessarily better than in the most demanding housework positions (Fairclough 1929: 46–47). "Passing" could be one temporary, though unreliable, method of finding work, as Audre Lorde's mother discovered. Light enough in complexion to pass for white (or Spanish), she found a job as a scullery maid in a teashop on Columbus Avenue and Ninety-ninth Street during the 1920s. "She went to work before dawn, and worked twelve hours a day, seven days a week, with no time off. The owner told my mother that she ought to be glad to have the job, since ordinarily the establishment didn't hire 'spanish' girls. Had the owner known Linda was Black, she would never have been hired at all." In the winter of 1928, Linda became ill and sent her husband to the teahouse to collect her uniforms so they could be washed. "When the owner saw him, he realized my mother was Black and fired her on the spot" (Lorde 1981: 9).

During the depression, some African Caribbean women, like their southern black migrant counterparts, were unable to find steady work and resorted to the so-called slave markets. These were street corners where black women went daily to sell their labor to white housewives. Some estimates put the number of slave markets as high as two hundred. Wages were as low as thirty cents an hour (Baker and Cooke 1935: 331).

Finding alternatives to domestic service for themselves and their daughters was a major goal of immigrant women. Self-supporting occupations such as hairdressing, real estate, and boarding and lodging operations attracted enterprising women. "The very first attempt to introduce Virgin Island produce in New York was made by a Miss Isabel George, who started with little finance and proved conclusively that fruits and vegetables shipped to her at the time were without the least sign of decay."[18] In fact, small transnational enterprises featuring homemade specialties afforded a small income for some immigrants. Around 1907, Harriet Dowridge wrote her daughter in Brooklyn, "You must collect all the jelley pots and send [them to me] by [Miss Innis] as I am still boiling and also let me know if Aunt Lue can sell some for me."[19] Women with financial backing could engage in more ambitious enterprises. Louise Burnham, a native of Barbados, helped finance her own home and two boardinghouses in Harlem from her hairdressing business and her rotating credit association.[20]

Many Caribbean women enrolled in vocational or occupational schools, which, like the professional workplace, remained segregated both in the city and nationally. African Caribbean women were well represented in the Lincoln School of Nurses, founded in 1898 as a training program for black women. New York black nurses, led by Mabel Keaton Staupers, a native of Barbados, initiated the fight to desegregate nursing training and the workplace during the depression and the 1940s (Hine 1989). In the same period, trade unionists Maida Springer Kemp of the International Ladies Garment Workers Union and Charlotte Adelman, a Trinidadian, of the Laundry Workers Union emerged as activists for women's labor. By this time, workplace advancement and unionization had become an important goal for Caribbean women's organizational activity in New York.

MIGRATION AND SOCIAL NETWORKS

Clearly race, class, color, and gender had an enormous impact on African Caribbean women's migration, settlement, and work experiences. I now turn to their stories as reflections of family networks and lodging, reproductive issues, child fostering, and voluntary associations, all of which shaped women's lives in the city.

Family Networks and Lodging

Most African Caribbean, as well as southern migrant, women "came to" a relative or respectable compatriot in New York City as the first step in the settlement process. Constance Payne established one migration network in 1900 from Barbados to 246 Adams Street in Brooklyn. Payne, a family leader, arrived in Brooklyn from St. Michael at the age of thirty-three. Of fair complexion, she was one of the fifty "coloured" women assisted by the Victoria Emigration Society between 1897 and 1900. She came from a family of experienced, hardworking women, and had previously earned a living by working for and traveling with privileged colonial families. Her aunt Annette, famous in the family for her world travels, once worked in the household of a ship's captain.

In 1900, jobs with respectable wages were hard to find in Barbados, even in the bustling port of Bridgetown. According to census reports, between 1891 and 1921 approximately ten thousand Barbadian women listed occupations in needlework, dressmaking, or millinery. A majority of these workers were found in the urban parish of St. Michael, in Bridgetown, "where competition [was] exceedingly keen."[21] Qualifying as a woman in "reduced circumstances," Payne received help from the Emigration Society. When she arrived in Brooklyn, she worked for several years as a household worker. After saving enough money, she left the job and rented a three-story frame house on Adams Street, near Brooklyn Heights, which she set up as a boardinghouse for Barbadians.

In contrast to the Wilkin-Stebers, who settled in a predominantly African American and Caribbean immigrant neighborhood, Payne's house was located on a block of predominantly working-class first- and second-generation Europeans. Several other Barbadian and southern migrant families also lived on this block. The boarding house, within walking distance of Brooklyn's then-important ports, provided her with a good income. Indeed, she was able to help with the emigration of two nieces and a nephew, the children of different siblings. "I am glad you are with Constance," Annette wrote her recently married and pregnant niece in Brooklyn. "I know she will take care of you."[22] In 1915, seventeen people lived in her house. All except the infants had been born in Barbados, and they ranged in time spent in the city from two weeks to fifteen years. There were three families with infants, as well as other kin-related networks in the household, which contained eight men and six women. Only two people in the household were over forty years of age.[23]

Constance Payne's lodgers were all employed. Mainly they worked in personal service jobs, including several male elevator-operating and female domestic work positions. The prevalence of male elevator operators and domestic workers in Payne's house and in the house next door at 248 Adams suggests that residents cooperated in finding work. The family correspondence between St. Michael and Brooklyn indicates that Payne ran a rotating credit association, or informal savings club, from her boardinghouse. At least one member lived in Barbados while participating in the Brooklyn rotating credit association. The correspondence also indicates that Payne and others sent parcels back and forth to St. Michael, probably via seamen who lived on her Adams Street block.

The letters also reveal that discussion and negotiation of a family member's travel to New York could continue for years before the actual event took place. Aletha, Constance Payne's niece, received this letter in 1913 from a cousin living in New York: "I got a letter from Ethel and Lettie last week, but I am quite undecided what to do, send and tell me when you are thinking about coming back, and what you think about bringing Lettie. I don't think I will be able to send any more than her passage money." Although Aletha left for New York soon after receiving the letter, Lettie, a young woman of twenty, did not travel to New York until two years later in 1915.

Some relatives went back and forth between Barbados and New York. Ethel initially immigrated in 1906. Following a common practice of immigrant mothers, she returned to St. Michael some seven or eight years later to give birth to her first child. By 1915 she had rejoined her husband at Constance

Payne's Brooklyn boardinghouse and given birth to a second child.[24] Wilhemina was not so fortunate. She experienced great discomfort and homesickness during a first pregnancy, as she explains in a 1907 letter to Aletha: "It seems as if I am multiplying. I can hardly eat anything, continually throwing up, which weakens me a deal. I want golden apples, green mangoes, eddoes & yams, things I cannot get here. Not able to attend to the house, so that everything is neglected & you know what sort of place this is, everybody has to work for themselves and especially beginners, as I smell food I am in a state, if it is a baby, apart from the Lords will not offending him I would never like another."[25] Wilhemina did not survive the birth of this child.[26] While no details survive about the circumstances, migrating women from the south and the Caribbean often returned home to be attended by family during childbirth because of inadequate prenatal and obstetric care for mothers in the city.

When Constance Payne died in the flu epidemic of 1918, the chain migration to Adams Street was broken. Lettie, who remained single, continued to assist in the emigration and settlement of other, mostly female, kin. She eventually found a job in the garment industry as a presser, bought a Brooklyn brownstone on Pacific Street, and sent for her nieces, whom she supported while they attended school.[27]

Constance Payne's story illustrates how a central female figure in a migration network could facilitate the settlement of a small community of people. She also exercised considerable influence over them. The family correspondence reveals that family members were reluctant to offend her. She provided housing, a mini-transport business through her seamen contacts and interest-free loans as head of a rotating credit association; as the longest-term resident in her household, she also served as an invaluable source of information.

In addition, Payne's network provided a support system for women, female kin, and close friends. Hers was a "very tight community."[28] In novelist Paule Marshall's recollections of her mother's generation, she writes that "the women looked to each other for their social life. . . . This consisted mainly in sitting around the kitchen table and talking. . . . Much of the talk had to do with home—meaning Barbados; the places people and events there as they remembered them" (Marshall 1987: 89). Women often imparted their traditions and outlook to children in these spaces. "Home was . . . a place I had never been to / but I knew well out of my mother's mouth," writes Audre Lorde (1981: 13). But if the family and female networks were a source of support and other rewards for migrant women, there were complications for them, particularly in their role in bearing and raising children.

Child Fostering and Remittances

Child fostering of female and male children by grandmothers and other female kin was an important function of women's primary social networks, and such arrangements usually meant that a family member would return to the

Caribbean, at least for visits. Child fostering also facilitated the emigration of single mothers who, once in New York, could be a reliable source of remittances to aging parents and other dependents back home. In her study of St. Vincentian immigrants, Joyce Toney observes that grandmother-centered families in the working class were important in facilitating the migration of young mothers and that children sent back to St. Vincent or left behind "sometimes accepted the grandmother as the real parent" (1986: 46). In the absence of a grandmother, an aunt or another relative might take care of children.

Child fostering was a mixed blessing for some families. "The story is told that my grandmother tried very hard not to get my parents to bring me here," reports Maida Springer Kemp, who arrived in New York from Panama with her Caribbean father and African Panamanian mother in 1917 at age seven.

> She wanted them to leave me in Panama until they found their way. But my *wonderful*, young mother with not a clue as to what she would entail here told my grandmother that if she had to suck salt in the United States, I would be right beside her. She wasn't trained for anything in the United States. She had never worked anywhere. When she first came here, she worked as a domestic. But she told her mother she would give me a little salt, and we would drink salt water together. She would *never* leave me with anyone.

Separations from parents could indeed be painful for children and adults, and relatives were not always good caregivers. According to Springer Kemp, she appreciated her mother's decision "because many of the women that my mother knew and who came here after her had stories. They left their children behind at first and brought them when they were ten, twelve, thirteen years old. So I saw some of what could happen first hand" (Richards 1994: 115).

But for many mothers a supportive child fostering network was critical to establishing a livelihood in New York and maintaining cultural links to home. Vera Clarke Ifill, whose parents came to Brooklyn from Barbados in 1904, was sent back to Christ Church parish until after her grandmother's death in 1914. "It was easier for the parents to send the children back to their grandparents, and it would give them a better chance . . . to make a way for themselves and maybe help with the children later" (Ifill 1986). In 1928, Shirley Chisholm's mother, Ruby St. Hill, sailed back to Barbados "with her three little girls, three, two and eight months, and ten trunks full of food and clothing. . . . She planned to board us there until she and Father had saved enough to assure our future in the States" (Chisholm 1970: 5). The children remained with their grandmother until 1934, when they returned to Brooklyn.

This common pattern of child fostering reinforced migrant women's relationships with relatives in the home society. As a study of contemporary fostering argues: "As adults circulate between home and host societies, channeling their resources from one to the other, children provide the link in the exchange systems between the mobile adult and the more stationary ones left at home.

For all the individuals involved, this exchange is an investment. For the participating adults, fostering opens up a wide spectrum of active social ties across which goods flow and commitments are sustained" (Soto 1987: 133). Consider the case of Aletha Challenor, who lived at her aunt Constance Payne's boardinghouse on Adams Street. Around 1910 she brought her first child, Elise, to the child's grandmother, Harriet, in Barbados, so that she could return to work in Brooklyn. The family correspondence reveals the deeply rooted nature of the exchange. Harriet's fostering of Elise not only allowed Aletha to go back to work, but the child's presence filled an emotional void for Harriet, who was alone after the death of her husband. "She is so loving . . . you must take care of yourself for her sake. . . . Lea you would be surprised to see how happy she is with me."[29] Fostering also reinforced bonds of trust and blurred boundaries between Brooklyn and St. Michael. Remittances, as well as handmade clothing, shoes, and other items, traveled this network. Elise remained with her grandmother until Harriet's death around 1917. Aletha meanwhile gave birth to two other children in Brooklyn, whom Harriet never met.[30]

In general, remittances were an important aspect of women's roles within social networks. Community sanctions among immigrants in the city and people back home functioned as a form of social control, ensuring regular support for dependents (see Philpott 1968: 473). Although both men and women sent money home, absent mothers may have experienced especially harsh community sanctions if they failed to do so, as well as higher expectations to keep up regular support. According to Prescod-Roberts, people in her Barbados village believed that families who sent women abroad were the "lucky ones" because if the migrants "left . . . children or they had a mother or grandmother back home, they will send money. . . . Quite often the men would come over, maybe leave a family in Barbados, but pick up with another woman . . . in New York and start a new family. So when the men went by themselves, you were taking a chance because you didn't know what you were going to get. . . . Sometimes in the village there would be occasions when Mr. So and So would come back . . . and he would bring his new wife and child. But meanwhile Mr. So and So had a woman and two children up the road" (Prescod-Roberts and Steel 1980: 26). As Soto reminds us, consanguinal rather than conjugal bonds were culturally important and transferable to the international arena (Soto 1987: 141). The belief that daughters were more likely than sons to send money home was realistic given patterns of social relations, which located women at the focus of the parent-child relationship (Philpott 1968: 469).

Remittances also helped to solidify and bolster contact with the homeland, thus ensuring the immigrant a place should she return permanently. Just before her death, Harriet Dowridge wrote her daughter in Brooklyn: "My [dear] girl, when I am gone home, you may have to come home with your girls and you will have some[where] to live."[31] A sense of responsibility or of obligation to kin was not the only meaning attached to remittances. They also reflected a migrant's commitment to the idea of "home," and concern for reputation in the home community.

Migration and Women's Reproduction

Child fostering facilitated the immigration of single mothers, but in some families a woman's reproductive life came under stringent family sanctions and surveillance. Certain social class and respectability requirements, as well as parental domination, probably led many women to seek greater control over their reproductive decisions through migration.

A 1926 study of five hundred black single women in New York City, conducted by Ruth Reed for the Welfare Council, provides a rare look at women's interior lives. Based on the records of women who applied and received aid from several private and public agencies and hospitals, the study qualifies as women's narrative because each woman constructed her own personal history in order to receive assistance.[32] The women's appeal for assistance did not necessarily mean that they received no support from their families or the fathers of their children. Because of the well-known ineffectiveness of city-run and private agencies (including employment agencies), African American and Caribbean migrant women generally rejected them, instead relying largely on friends and relatives for mutual assistance. They also shared information about the institutions that most effectively provided services to the community. These included the New York Colored Mission (founded in 1870), the White Rose Working Girls Home (1898), the Lincoln Settlement in Brooklyn (1908), Hope Day Nursery (1911), the 137th Street YWCA (1918), Utopia House (1928), and Club Caroline (1928). These community-based institutions provided housing, childcare, and job training and placement.

A majority of the women in Reed's study were not native to New York City. Thirty-five percent had been born in the Caribbean and an equal number in the southern states. The percentage of Caribbean women making appeals to the agencies was higher than their proportion of the city's total black population. This frequent appeal of Caribbean women to agencies reflected their recent arrival. Fifty-two percent of the Caribbean women had been in the city less than three years, 25 percent three to five years, and 23 percent longer than five years. The Caribbean women had a higher average age than new mothers born in the state of New York or the South; they also emigrated at a later age than other migrants, probably because of the distance and expenses involved in making the journey.

A brief summary of one woman's case history is useful in demonstrating the special conditions that recent female migrants encountered in the city.

> Roseanna H. was sent to [an] agency for guidance by the social service department of the hospital where her child had been born. The young woman age 23 was born in Jamaica and had been in New York City three years. She was a mem-

ber of the Protestant Episcopal Church and a regular attendant. She had three years of high-school work and had been a teacher in Jamaica. She had come to New York hoping to [earn money to pay for singing lessons]. Unable to secure employment until her savings were used up, she finally secured a position at general housework. The work was physically taxing and she became ill and lost her job. She lived in an inexpensive but not very respectable lodging house because she was unable to afford better quarters. She stated that the man whose room adjoined hers offered to loan her money during the time she was out of employment. On one occasion she asserted that he forced himself into her room and that after that occasion she had continued on terms of intimacy with him for several months and that he had given her money and presents. When the man learned that she was pregnant he wished to marry her but she refused. She said the man was of "unsuitable ideals and low standards of life" and that she did not wish to be associated with him. When she refused to marry him he called on her several times and was abusive. She wished the agency to assist her to secure another situation, away from the man where she would never see him again (Reed 1926: 67–68).

Reed reported that this woman was ashamed to take her child to be christened at her church or to write her mother about the situation. When the agency dispatched a letter, the mother wrote back, refusing to have anything to do with the daughter because of her "disgrace." She recounted the sacrifices that she had made to give Roseanna "cultural advantages" and declared that Roseanna had "thrown herself away." A second appeal failed to soften the mother, who responded that Roseanna had "forgotten her God, her bringing up, and herself." Rejection by a mother on the basis of class or moral sanctions was usually temporary. As Insley-Casper noted, the "Negro unmarried mother appears almost always with her new baby in her arms, both of them in the home of the mother's family" (1934: 172).

The agency found a live-in household job for Roseanna outside of New York City where she could keep her child with her. Soon, both mother and child appeared to be doing well. With this job, Roseanna could be independent of the child's father and did not have to turn to a fault-finding parent or face the condemnation of a church. Roseanna's experience was unusual. Most women would not have been able to bring a child to a live-in job, and many single mothers, as discussed earlier, ended up sending a child to relatives back home so they could work in New York.

We will never know how Roseanna's life turned out. But her story and the stories of others in Reed's study highlight the significance of reproductive issues and strategies in the lives of migrating women.

Voluntary Associations and Women's Social Networks

African Caribbean women's participation in various voluntary associations, especially homeland and fraternal, was widespread in New York. In addition, their involvement in and leadership of labor and political groups was more significant than has been recognized. Much of women's work in associations reflected the kind of relations they had already constructed in networks with family, friends, and acquaintances back home and in New York. As in many activities, joining homeland associations reflected dual perspectives. Such affiliations promoted social class standing and status, served as sites of socialization for children, and provided places to meet appropriate marriage partners from one's home community. On the other hand, women's work in these associations also reflected collective consciousness and opposition to colonial and racial oppression.

Women were involved in the earliest associations as organizers and fundraisers. Records of the Bermuda Benevolent Association, organized in 1898, identify several women as founding members.[33] Women also formed their own female self-help and benevolent associations and formed networks with African American and other Caribbean women in labor and political organizations. Typically, women worked directly on projects for their communities back home. For example, a main goal of the Dorcas Committee of the Virgin Islands Congressional Council was to "raise a large sum of money" to purchase clothing for those in need in the islands during Christmastime.[34] Projects of other associations included support for education, money for scholarships and school supplies, and attention to other material needs of home communities. Women raised money by various means: excursions, dances, picnics, dinners, and other social activities.

The key officeholders and spokespeople of most of the early African Caribbean associations (those whose names survive in the public record) were males. Male benevolent association leaders were often long-time New York residents with professional or entrepreneurial status in both the African Caribbean *and* African American communities. Women's activities were often directed toward social welfare concerns in their homelands, while for many men the associations served as stepping-stones to political influence in New York and the Caribbean. The limited number of leadership roles for women, as well as the absence of a more assertive political anticolonial outlook, concerned Helena Benta, the secretary of the Montserrat Progressive Society. Benta's own leadership, along with that of key males in the Montserrat Progressive Society, was derived primarily through status already achieved as a member of a prominent Harlem business family (Benta 1933).

One group of women from the then-Danish Virgin Islands felt that the interests of women were specific enough to justify forming a society expressly for women. In 1915, they organized the Danish West Indian Ladies Aid Society for mutual aid and social welfare. After 1917, when the United States purchased the Virgin Islands from Denmark, the women changed the name to the american Virgin Islands Ladies Aid Society. The organization remained active into the mid 1950s despite the presence of numerous other Virgin Islands associations, led by powerful males such as the numbers banker and fraternal leader Casper Holstein. Leaders of the organization engaged in working-class political activity in Harlem, such as the protests of the Harlem Tenants League and the Jobs Campaign of the 1930s. In addition, leaders supported the work of the Brotherhood of Sleeping Car Porters and Maids. The Ladies Aid Society paid sick and burial benefits to members and their families, and the association sustained and gained new members and secondary migrants from Florida over the years.

Women were actively involved in another type of association in New York—rotating credit associations brought from home. These associations, which still thrive in the New York Caribbean community, are basically informal savings systems. They provide a simple method of accumulating capital by pooling an agreed-upon sum among a small group and rotating the total amount to each member, usually on a weekly basis. As Violet Johnson found among her Boston informants in a recent study, men might participate in rotating credit associations but women often controlled them (1995: 66). According to Aubrey Bonnett, all strata of early African Caribbean migrant society participated in rotating credit associations. "From the daily domestic worker, the sleep-in maids, the elevator operator to the government servant, the migrants got together to form their 'susus' as they called their RCAs" (1981: 55). While we need to know more about the actual impact of rotating credit associations on women's networks, Roger Waldinger's (1996: 119) observation points to their important role in the Caribbean community: "Raising capital through rotating credit associations they had imported with them from the islands, Caribbean immigrants engaged in considerable property speculation, with the result that real estate had emerged as a small, but still significant, Caribbean niche by the eve of World War II." Several of Bonnett's female informants also saw the associations as social networks "providing mutuality, group cohesion and intense bonds of friendship" (1981: 66).

High levels of female participation and leadership in voluntary associations were most noticeable when these organizations combined the social welfare concerns of the transnational community with politics. In addition, women were most effective when they created their own organizational space. Such participation reflected home country patterns in which, as Rhoda Reddock notes, working people organized themselves, despite anticombination legislation, in "friendly societies, workingmen's associations, political associations, and women's organizations—often called unions." (1994: 149). Women's involvement in strikes and labor disturbances (in Jamaica, Trinidad and Tobago, and British Guiana) was a key component of anticolonial activism, which reached its peak in the regionwide disturbances of the late 1930s. Heavy unemployment and low wages were key grievances of women involved in the public protests and often violent demonstrations.

The precise link between working women's activism in the Caribbean and the activities of mostly middle-class immigrant women in New York is unclear. However, by the late 1930s the growing mass discontent reflected in labor strikes in British-held countries was the focus of special homeland association meetings in New York. For example, the British Virgin Islands Benevolent Association appointed a special committee to address the demand for representative government in the British Virgin Islands; the committee called a mass meeting to discuss the issue in November 1938.[35] British complicity in the Italian invasion of Ethiopia also led to indignation meetings within the homeland associations. In general, as one contemporary noted, "[There is] a great spread in anti-British feeling precisely among her former loyal subjects" (Robinson 1939: 10).

The organization most closely resembling the omnibus anticolonial associations in the Caribbean was Marcus Garvey's Universal Negro Improvement Association (UNIA), which attracted Caribbean migrant women in New York from all walks of life. As Barbara Bair explains, the UNIA promoted culturally constructed gender roles to project an image of women as mothers, virtuous wives, and daughters, and men as leaders and decision makers (1992: 156–157). In fact, the organization's structure provided for public (although separate) roles for women. In 1914 the organization's cofounder, Amy Ashwood (Garvey), organized a ladies' division (not auxiliary), which held its own meetings and provided space for women's leadership development. Honor Ford-Smith (1988) reminds us that the movement attracted large numbers of migrant women precisely because the organization was an outlet for the kind of work these women were already doing. For instance, the initial mutual aid and fraternal nature of the organization formalized social networks that migrant women had already formed through personal ties. In addition, the UNIA's emphasis on entrepreneurship attracted many immigrant women who were members of provider networks and already engaged in enterprises such as boardinghouses, real estate, and rotating credit associations.[36] The UNIA's importance to first-generation immigrant women lay primarily in providing space for those women who remained isolated from African American women's clubs and associations. The organization gave these women an opportunity to engage in public sphere leadership outside their immediate communities. As Springer Kemp recollected a UNIA meeting, "You listened to great oratory. At nine years old. I was listening to great stuff. . . . The woman that made a great impression on me—because I had never heard a woman speaker before—was Henrietta Vinton Davis. . . . When I saw all of these men posturing and talking and reshaping the world, this woman could just hold you. I would sit there in attention and with awe. She commanded an audience" (Richards 1994: 132–133). Her mother's involvement in the UNIA and her own exposure influenced Springer Kemp's decision to become politically involved. The UNIA also inspired other future political activists. In New York as in the Caribbean, Garveyite women became trade unionists and other public figures (Bolles 1996; Reddock 1994). Springer Kemp began working in the garment industry in 1933 and later became Educational Director of Local 33 of the International Ladies Garment Workers Union. A Pan-Africanist, she continued a long public career as a union organizer both in New York and internationally, particularly in East and West Africa. Springer Kemp maintained a close female social network of trade unionists, especially with black women from the South and the Caribbean. These contacts were established through the Women's Trade Union League (WTUL) as well as through local unions. In 1936 one associate, Trinidadian Charlotte Adelman, began organizing laundry workers who were mostly African American and Caribbean women. These workers were among the most exploited groups in New York City. A Garveyite, Adelman was described as the "moving force" behind the Laundry Workers' Joint Board of the Amalgamated Clothing Workers Association (Richards 1994: 347).

Garveyism did not spawn all political activity among New York's Caribbean women activists. On the opposite side of the spectrum was the Communist party, which attracted men and women interested in social change with respect to both class and race. Trade unionist and Communist women worked from different fronts, and little has been written about their activities. Both groups advocated economic justice for wage-earning women. The African Caribbean activist Bonita Williams, who headed the Communist Workers' Alliance, led a mass movement of housewives against price increases in Harlem butcher shops and other markets during the depression. She also helped women lobby for increased relief benefits.[37] Both trade unionist and Communist women endorsed the economic rights of women as independent wage earners, despite experiencing sexism and racism within their own movements. Trinidadian Claudia Jones, who became the Negro Affairs editor of the Young Communist League during the 1930s, pointed out to her colleagues—in a 1949 essay entitled "An End to the Neglect of the Problems of Negro Women"—that black women's particular problems and labor issues ought to be at the center, not the margins, of political organizing (Jones 1949).

Any analysis of Caribbean immigrant women's collective behavior must recognize the centrality of their transnational networks in fermenting their identities in the city. Although most women were not visible in New York public sphere activities, many were the informal organizers and central figures of widespread family networks. Prescod-Roberts's description of her grandmother's activities during World War II no doubt mirrors the orientation of many migrating women:

> My grandmother was one of those 'upwardly mobile' West Indians. She used to work cleaning people's houses, and during the war she worked in a factory. She saved her money. She learned how to sew so she could make every piece of clothes, so she didn't have to go into the store and buy anything, because she knew she had a daughter with children back home. It was her that was sending those parcels and she had to have the money to do that. And also there was her dream that some day her daughter and her grandchildren would be able to come, and she had to provide for them (Prescod-Roberts and Steel 1980: 27).

In Prescod-Roberts's representation, the grandmother's political orientation was strategic and practical. "Cleaning people's houses" was a means to realizing her goal and did not define who she was.

CONCLUSION

Women were numerically significant in the first wave of immigration from the Caribbean. Barely visible in the historical literature on U.S. immigration of this period, African Caribbean women's experiences and perspectives are critical to understanding the larger story of Caribbean migration and the black diaspora in the twentieth century. As wage earners in New York, women were often the first members of a family to migrate and set up households in the city. The earliest female immigrants, who arrived in 1900 or before, established networks that incorporated both males and females and proved especially crucial in sustaining a community of migrant women. Some Caribbean women in New York subscribed to gender and class conventions associated with middle-class status in the colonial societies they left behind. At the same time, their activities reflect collective consciousness and a strategic orientation to the migration experience.

Migrating women and men settled mainly in clusters in African American and black immigrant areas, but they also sometimes settled in predominantly white areas near households where they worked as servants. Many African Caribbean women, like southern migrant women, helped shift the pattern of household service from live-in to day work and were critical to the formation of the permanent Caribbean communities to which women returned at night.

A closer look at women's particular experiences and problems reveals a more complete narrative of migration and immigrant community. Although Caribbean women, like Caribbean men, were a highly select population in terms of literacy levels and other class advantages, gender influenced their mobility in New York. Men with educational and other advantages became involved in professional careers, business, and electoral politics in the African American community. Women relied more directly on transnational social networks in their public as well as private lives. They were affected by a sexual and reproductive politics rooted in colonial patriarchy and had to negotiate the attendant restrictive categories in the public spaces of New York City. Recent arrivals were often more vulnerable to poor lodging situations and the multiple obstacles of an unfamiliar city. Women used coethnic contacts to find work, but here again migrants had to negotiate the color line to get the "best" job in the few categories set aside for black women. The limited opportunities for good work were the source of conflict between African American and Caribbean women, but complexion may have been a stronger force shaping women's opportunities—at least for the very light-skinned. Some colored or biracial women, members of a relatively privileged class in the Caribbean, were able to "pass" as white in order to find work in New York. Dark-skinned women faced greater challenges related to race, color, gender, and foreign status. Caribbean women sought and created alternatives to household work and developed their own income-earning enterprises. They probably played a larger role than previously acknowledged in shaping the small real estate niche that Caribbean immigrants had established by the beginning of the Second World War. Their role in organizing rotating credit, as well as their management of boardinghouses and other lodgings, influenced the development of women's involvement in real estate.

Women were central in the family-based social networks that linked relatives in New York and the home community. Utilizing cultural skills acquired at home, women established child fostering networks, formed female mutual aid societies, and engaged in collective social welfare efforts for their home communities. The Garvey movement, with its all-female divisions, attracted immigrant women isolated from African American women's organizations and served as a training ground for future labor and political activists. It is clear that women were actively engaged in what has long been thought to be a male sphere, the African Caribbean voluntary associations and political and labor organizations of New York. The full extent of women's contributions and political thought has yet to be uncovered. But involvement in social networks, generally relegated to the private domain, did not preclude women's vocal, even radical participation in public affairs. Indeed, transnational networks were key to their political consciousness and orientation.

This chapter is a beginning attempt to uncover and chart the dynamics of Caribbean migrant women's lives at the beginning of the twentieth century, in the first large wave of Caribbean migrants to New York. The initial task of investigation points to a transnational migration system that incorporated both sexes in equal proportions. Previous interpretations of the period based on a male-led migration model are in need of careful revision. The migration experiences of first-generation Caribbean women are not merely hidden chapters waiting to be inserted into a larger framework. When more fully accounted for, they will reshape our understanding of the entire early Caribbean immigrant experience.

NOTES

Research for this chapter was supported, as part of a larger study, by the Schomburg Center for Research in Black Culture, Scholar-in-Residence Program and the National Endowment for the Humanities.

1. In this chapter *African Caribbean* (or *West Indian*) refers to people of African descent who migrated from the region including Bermuda and the Bahamas as well as British Honduras (Belize) and British Guiana (Guyana). My focus is primarily on women from the English-

speaking areas. However, migrating women came from other European-held colonies of the Caribbean, including Suriname.

2. A number of studies of post-1965 African Caribbean diasporic and transnational communities do focus on and provide detailed discussions of women's experiences (see Foner 1986; Mortimer and Bryce-Laporte 1981; Davis 1994).

3. See also Marshall's 1987 essay about the novel.

4. Harriet Dowridge to Aletha, August 1907, Challenor-Dowridge Family Letters, 1904–1917, Manuscripts, Archives, and Rare Books Division, Schomburg Center for Research in Black Culture (SCRBC).

5. Quoted in the *Daily Gleaner* (Jamaica), 20 July 1920.

6. Addie to Aletha, 6 September 1910, Challenor-Dowridge Family Letters. The correspondence belonging to Aletha Dowridge Challenor contains letters to her posted St. Michael to Brooklyn from her mother, Harriet, and posted New York to St. Michael from her husband, friends, and relatives.

7. Alice Brown Fairclough conducted a study of 334 mostly migrant women, a third of whom had come from the Caribbean.

8. For a discussion of uplift ideology see Gaines (1996).

9. *New York Age,* 29 March 1906.

10. Association for Improving the Conditions of the Poor (1924: 5).

11. See Moore (1913) and Records of the Bermuda Benevolent Association 1898–1969, SCRBC.

12. Association for Improving the Conditions of the Poor, p. 5.

13. For a discussion of Caribbean immigrant and native-born African American relations, see Watkins-Owens (1996).

14. Due to a downturn in fortune, the Wilkin-Stebers were later required to sell this house and move back into an apartment. But their status as members of Harlem's middle class was well established. Eventually the family moved to East Elmhurst, Queens.

15. *Gazette* (Jamaica), 10 October 1918.

16. *Negro World,* 3 March, 7 April 1923; *Amsterdam News* (New York), 7 March 1923. Earlier in the century the social purity movement affected most single women. In 1904, for instance, the Council of Jewish Women placed a full-time Yiddish-speaking worker at Ellis to record the names of all unaccompanied Jewish females ages twelve to thirty and to intercede on their behalf (Schneider and Schneider 1994: 138).

17. Fred to Aletha, 22 January 1913, Challenor-Dowridge Family Letters.

18. Ashley Totten, "The Truth Neglected in the Virgin Islands," *Messenger,* August 1926.

19. Harriet Dowridge to Aletha, c. 1907, Challenor-Dowridge Family Letters.

20. Dorothy Burnham, interview with author, New York, 12 November 1993.

21. Massiah (1993: 17).

22. At least one of these nieces worked in a white household on Pineapple Street in Brooklyn Heights. Dorothy Burnham interview; Aunt Nett to Lee (c. 1907 or 1908), Challenor-Dowridge Family Letters.

23. New York State Manuscript Census, Kings County 1915, Assembly District 2, Election District 8.

24. New York State Manuscript Census, ibid.; Challenor-Dowridge Family Letters.

25. Wilhemina to Aletha, 14 September 1907, Challenor-Dowridge Family Letters.

26. Harriet Dowridge to Aletha, c. spring 1908, ibid.

27. Dorothy Burnham interview; Violet Murrell, interview with author, St. Michael, Barbados, 2, 3 September 1994.

28. Dorothy Burnham interview.

29. Harriet Dowridge to Aletha, 4 November 1910, Challenor-Dowridge Family Letters.

30. Dorothy Burnham interview; Burnham also indicated that a sense of isolation from the Brooklyn family was one result of the separation from parents and younger siblings.

31. Harriet Dowridge to Aletha, 20 July 1917, Challenor-Dowridge Family Letters.

32. For a discussion of early social welfare and mother's aid programs, see Gordon (1995). Reed's 1926 study was in the tradition of the mother's aid reformers, who applied morals testing and background investigations before granting eligibility. The agencies in Reed's study included the Katy Ferguson Home for unwed mothers, Sloane Maternity Hospital, the Department of Public Welfare, and the Association for Improving the Condition of the Poor.

33. Records of the Bermuda Benevolent Association.

34. Margaret Samuel to the Officers and Members of the American West Indian Ladies Aid Society, Inc., 11 November 1930, AWILAS Records, SCRBC.

35. Report of Special Committee to Officers and Members, 26 November 1938, Records of the British Virgin Islands Benevolent Association of New York, Inc., 1926–1989, Box 2, Legislative Committee Folder, SCRBC.

36. Dorothy Burnham interview.

37. *Daily Worker*, 3 June 1935.

TWO

Where New York's West Indians Work

Suzanne Model

Where do New York's West Indians work? This question can be answered in many ways: geographically, occupationally, even organizationally. The present chapter offers an industry-centered answer and pays particular attention to a phenomenon known as the *ethnic niche*. Simply put, an ethnic niche is an industry in which members of an immigrant or minority group are overrepresented (Model 1993, 1997b; Waldinger 1996; Wilson 1998). The tendency to concentrate in some industries—and to eschew others—is typical of ethnic minorities. Equally important, industrial location affects minority earnings. Two effects have been identified. First, there are often systematic pay differentials across industries, even for workers with the same qualifications and the same occupation (Krueger and Summers 1988). Second, ethnic niches occasionally offer pay differentials, differentials that advantage workers belonging to backgrounds that are overrepresented in the industry (*insiders*) and disadvantage workers from other backgrounds (*outsiders*).[1] Like interindustry differentials, these intraindustry differentials hold irrespective of qualifications or occupation. In Waldinger's words, for insiders, a niche is "an arena in which they are treated more favorably than in jobs of lower ethnic density" (Waldinger 1996: 95).

Scholars have offered several explanations for the tendency of immigrants and minorities to congregate in particular industries. Immigration laws are a factor because they target occupations that certain nations produce in abundance, such as nurses. Another cause is the tendency for immigrants' social networks to be ethnically homogeneous. Job seekers often rely on relatives and friends for information about vacancies, and the more one's employment contacts are like oneself, the more inbred the work experience becomes. Discrimination is yet another way that niches develop. Exclusion from one form of employment crowds applicants into others or into entrepreneurship. Similarly, any group whose members encounter favoritism in hiring or promotion acquires the potential for clustering. And since most individuals rank members of their own group highly, when minority group members hold positions as employers, managers, or hiring agents, nepotism results.

Until relatively recently, scholars assumed that niching, like speaking broken English or living in ethnic neighborhoods, was associated with poverty. One reason later generations outperformed their parents was that they assimilated, a pattern that included moving into mainstream jobs. However, recent scholarship reveals that immigrants and minorities do not always concentrate in the worst industries; indeed, for some groups, niching is an advantage and assimilation a disadvantage. For instance, at mid-century, New York's Jews were disproportionately employed in the apparel industry, where they earned more than similarly qualified compatriots in other industries (Model 1997b). African Americans are another case in point. Since the 1970s, they have been disproportionately employed in government, where they have received benefits (Durr and Logan 1997). Conversely, Chinese immigrant earnings plummeted in the 1980s, a situation probably related to their clustering in low-paying industries (Farley 1996). In short, sometimes niching carries an economic benefit, sometimes not.

The purpose of this chapter is to identify the industries in which New York's West Indians concentrate and to measure the effect on earnings associated with those industries. Some research on this topic has already appeared (Waldinger 1996; Wright and Ellis 1996; Kasinitz and Vickerman, forthcoming). The present effort supplements these studies by adding a historical dimension as well as by attending to generational and gender distinctions. In addition, African Americans are incorporated into all phases of the present analysis. Including African Americans is useful because the two groups of blacks are both each other's closest companions and each other's closest competitors. Their companionship is based first and foremost on the experience of racism. In Vickerman's words, "West Indians, like African Americans, must constantly negotiate racial obstacles in the job market, and they do not overcome these easily" (1999: 76). Racism likewise restricts their housing possibilities, with the result that, in New York at least, the two groups of blacks share neighborhoods (Crowder and Tedrow, this volume). This fact is not irrelevant to employment, because neighbors often serve as conduits to jobs. Another way that housing segregation affects employment patterns is that it creates a pool of customers with similar tastes. It has long been believed, for instance, that in the first half of this century West Indian blacks were the shopkeepers of the African American community (Haynes 1968 [1912]; Domingo 1925; Foner 1985; Kasinitz 1992; Waldinger 1996). Such small businesses represent the prototypical ethnic niche.

But there is evidence of competition as well as cooperation. African Americans have complained that Caribbean immigrants take jobs from native blacks (Foner 1985). Ethnographic studies offer some support for this charge. For instance, Mary Waters conducted interviews with black and white personnel in a large New York City catering firm that relies heavily on foreign-born black labor. White managers stated without hesitation that West Indians were the more desirable workers. "If I had one position open and if it was a West Indian versus an American black, I'd go with the West Indian," reported one white manager. When asked why, he replied, "Their reliability, their willingness to do the job . . . they have a different drive than American blacks" (Waters 1999a: 116). A number of hypotheses have been advanced to explain this preference. Waters proposes that whites find immigrants' demeanors less disconcerting than African Americans'. Faye Arnold (1996) speculates that whites associate British West Indian accents with England and hence with high-status origins. Yet another possibility is that employers' preference for West Indians is a special case of a general preference for immigrants over natives. In a recent study, 81 percent of Detroit employers and 88 percent of those in Los Angeles told interviewers that they believe foreign-born workers have a stronger work ethic than natives (Moss and Tilly 1996). Frequently this perception translates into a preference for Hispanics over African Americans, but a preference for West Indians over African Americans is an equally plausible result.

A quantitatively informed, niche-oriented perspective is well suited for examining African American–African Caribbean competition because it can compare outcomes of similarly qualified individuals across an entire labor market. Initial insights about the relationship between West Indians and African Americans can be obtained by comparing their industries of overrepresentation across time. Within these industries, the pay of overrepresented groups, be they West Indian or African American, deserves scrutiny. Recall that in some instances, niches pay insiders more than outsiders. In addition, West Indians and African Americans are sometimes overrepresented in the same industries. When this situation obtains, a comparison of the two groups' earnings relative to each other—and to that of outsiders—proves helpful. Achieving such a comparative perspective on niches is the task undertaken in the present chapter.

DATA

The data come primarily from four censuses: the New York State Census of 1925, the Public Use Sample of the 1970 U.S. Census, and the 1980 and 1990 Public Use Microdata Samples. The labor market focus of the research necessitated excluding persons under eighteen or over sixty-five. The 1925 data were extracted from the Manhattan census manuscripts using a strategy designed to obtain a disproportionately large number of minority households. However, a representative sample was taken within each minority. The key variables for implementing the sampling strategy were the birthplace and race of the household head and the household's Assembly District. Because no information exists for 1925 on the distribution of West Indians by Assembly District, the strategy proceeded under the assumption that West Indians were distributed across these districts in the same way as African Americans. If this assumption is correct, it is permissible to generalize from the sample to Manhattan's West Indian households.

The U.S. Census samples were obtained from the Inter-university Consortium for Political and Social Research and the Integrated Public Use Microdata Series. To maximize the number of cases in the 1970 Public Use Sample, the analysis includes foreign-born West Indians from both the 5 percent and 15 percent samples. Native-born West Indians are only identifiable in the 15 percent sample. The 1980 and 1990 data include foreign- and native-born West Indians extracted from the 5 percent Public Use Microdata Samples of those years.[2]

Because the focus is on labor market outcomes, beginning in 1970 all individuals living in the area that the U.S. Census Bureau defines as the Greater New York labor market are candidates for inclusion. Not surprisingly, the area in question grows over time. A second, definitional issue concerns identifying the ethnic and racial groups of interest. In 1970, 1980, and 1990, a foreign-born West Indian is considered to be an individual described as black, non-Hispanic, and born in the British West Indies. The definition of a native-born West Indian changes from year to year because of a revision in the census questionnaire.[3] African Americans are identified in 1970 as all native-born non-Hispanic blacks with two parents born in the United States. In 1980 and 1990, following Kalmijn (1996), all native-born non-Hispanic blacks whose response to the ancestry question was either black, African American, American, or unreported are categorized as African American. Finally, for comparative purposes, the analysis includes a random sample of "all New Yorkers."

Before leaving this topic, some of the shortcomings associated with census data deserve acknowledgement. First and foremost is the tendency of censuses to exclude some segments of the population, particularly the less affluent and the undocumented (Warren and Passel 1987). A second problem concerns the unreliability of the ancestry question as a mechanism for identifying native-born West Indians. Research by Waters (1994a) suggests that less-educated second-generation West Indians may identify more strongly as African Americans than their more-educated counterparts. Finally, the census fails to inquire about such things as number of jobs held, residency status of immigrants, biracial identities, and so on. In short, though census data are the preeminent source of information about immigrants and minorities, they suffer from problems of external and internal validity.

EMPIRICAL RESULTS
Self-Employment

Scholars interested in ethnic niches are curious about self-employment because high rates of entrepreneurial activity usually imply a skewed industrial distribution. One of the best-known stereotypes about early-twentieth-century West Indian New Yorkers is that they were heavily entrepreneurial. This description probably appeared first in George Haynes's classic study, *The Negro at Work in New York City*. Examining the characteristics of persons listed in the city's Negro Business Directory of 1909, Haynes concluded that about two-thirds of the proprietors were born in the southern United States and one-fifth were born in the West Indies. The West Indian figure is about twice that expected on the basis of the West Indian proportion in the black population (1968 [1912]). Herbert Gutman (1976) was the first to subject this claim to a test. Drawing a sample of West Indian–born and American-born blacks from the Manhattan portion of the 1925 New York State Census, he found that 1.2 percent of West Indian men (N = 5123) were entrepreneurs, compared to 1.8 percent of African American men (N = 14,623). Unfortunately, this finding received little scholarly attention, and most West Indian specialists remain unaware of it. More recently, Holder (1998) reported the proportion of West Indian immigrants who were entrepreneurs or proprietors in the 1905, 1915, and 1925 New York State Censuses as 1.5 (N = 1152), 1.4 (N = 4600), and 1.4 percent (N = 16,926), respectively.[4] To be sure, after the appearance of publications based on the 1970 census, awareness that contemporary West Indians have a low rate of self-employment began to spread. Nevertheless, most scholars interpret the new figures as evidence of a decline in West Indian entrepreneurship rather than as evidence of a long-standing error (Waldinger 1996).

In an effort to yet again examine the evidence, this study scrutinizes two data sources. The earliest data come from the *Reports* of the U.S. Immigration Commission (1911). The unstated goal of the *Reports* was to paint immigrants in a disagreeable light so that immigration restrictions would follow upon publication, a consequence that indeed occurred. The volume *Immigrants in Cities* contains a list of occupations subdivided by nativity/ethnicity/race for a sample of household heads dwelling in seven major cities in 1908. Not surprisingly, only the tables for New York City contain foreign- as well as native-born blacks. Chosen for study were "the blocks inhabited by the largest number of households per lot and consisting of the poorest representative dwellings" (1911: 7). Most of the black families selected lived on West Sixty-second Street between Tenth and Eleventh Avenues. The occupations of household heads are reported in considerable detail, and distinctions between proprietors and employees are noted. The occupations of 166 African Amer-

TABLE 2.1   Class Distribution (in %) of Manhattan Male Labor Force
Participants by Race/Ethnicity, 1925

	FB West Indians	African Americans	All New York Men
Employers	0.24	1.03	4.67
Own account	1.45	3.21	12.00
Workers	78.41	76.77	74.58
Uncodable	19.91	18.99	8.75
Number of unweighted cases	340	419	3001
Number of weighted cases[a]	8294	26,473	637,788

[a]In order for a stratified sample to reflect the population, it must be weighted; therefore, the percentages reported here are based on the total number of weighted cases rather than the total number of actual cases.

ican males are identified; six of these are proprietors. The occupations of 110 foreign-born black men are identified; none of these are proprietors.

Of course, these figures are not representative of black New Yorkers. The second data source is the previously described representative sample of Manhattan's blacks, drawn from the New York State Census. This census contains a "class" question with three possible responses: "EMP" (employer), "OA" (own account or self-employed without employees), or "W" (worker). Table 2.1 summarizes these responses by race/ethnicity. Typically, the "EMP" and "OA" responses are considered to indicate entrepreneurs. These figures reveal a higher proportion of entrepreneurial African Americans (4.24%) than Gutman's data, while all three census samples concur that the rate for West Indians is a very low figure.

Using samples from the three most recent federal censuses, Table 2.2 provides self-employment rates for foreign-born West Indians, native-born West Indians, African Americans, foreign-born New Yorkers, and all New Yorkers, subdivided by sex.[5] In general, men's rates are much higher than women's, the West Indian rate is slightly higher than the African American rate, and the black rates are far below those for all New Yorkers. One unexpected number is the high rate (8.93%) for native-born West Indian males in 1970. In considering this figure, it is wise to keep in mind that it is based on only 112 cases, a very small sample. This anomaly aside, it is obvious that self-employment has played an inconsequential role in the socioeconomic attainment of West Indian New Yorkers. Similarly, it must play an inconsequential role in the degree to which West Indians have clustered in particular industries, an issue to which the discussion now turns.

TABLE 2.2 Percent of New York SMSA Labor Force Participants Self-Employed, by Race/Ethnicity, Nativity, Gender, and Year

	Men			Women		
	1970	1980	1990	1970	1980	1990
FB West Indians	3.88	4.11	6.12	2.32	1.17	3.36
	(541)	(3625)	(4221)	(777)	(4616)	(5583)
NB West Indians	8.93	4.39	4.23	0	1.34	2.52
	(112)	(433)	(537)	(126)	(521)	(664)
African Americans	3.84	3.90	4.22	1.75	0.84	1.99
	(4271)	(4075)	(4949)	(4409)	(4738)	(6504)
FB New Yorkers	12.62	11.28	11.75	3.73	3.31	5.80
	(618)	(8068)	(12,230)	(510)	(6897)	(10,693)
All New Yorkers	10.22	10.72	11.02	2.20	3.12	5.07
	(4597)	(41,890)	(49,517)	(3911)	(36,634)	(47,116)

Industrial Concentrations

The distinctive job patterns of immigrants and minorities often persist for decades. Thus, it is appropriate to begin an analysis of the industrial locations of New York's blacks in 1925, a time when record numbers of newcomers—both from the Islands and from the South—were flocking to the city. Unfortunately, the New York Census asked only about "occupation" and "class," not about "industry." As a result, industrial affiliations had to be inferred from the available data. Table 2.3 contains the eight major industrial categories that this approach yielded. The "uncodable" row conveys the proportion of persons whose employment information could not be assigned an industry; for instance, "shop," "cleaning," "cutlery," or "working."

Looking first at men, observe that, compared to all Manhattan men, West Indian males are underrepresented in manufacturing and trade and overrepresented in transport. African American men exhibit the same pattern even more strongly. Both groups of men are also slightly more likely to work in personal service than all men, but the industry total is low. Historical studies of urban black men discover large concentrations of employment in transport and personal service, in both the North and the South (Lieberson 1980). Thus, in 1925, African American New York men were pursuing the few urban jobs open to them. West Indians found themselves taking the same road. Of course, it is possible that a disproportionate number of West Indian immigrants were stevedores or teamsters in the Islands, and that they too were continuing a premigration trend. But a more likely scenario is that discrimination kept most black men out of manufacturing and trade. Still, the percent of

TABLE 2.3 Industrial Distribution (in %) of Manhattan Labor Force Participants by Race/Ethnicity and Gender, 1925

	Men				Women		
	FB West Indians	African Americans	All New Yorkers		FB West Indians	African Americans	All New Yorkers
Construction	5.68	8.38	7.68				0.06
Manufacturing	7.90	2.32	15.42		11.50	3.21	11.62
Transport, communications, utilities	8.22	11.25	3.76			0.13	0.68
Trade	10.95	12.54	24.03			12.87	8.68
Finance, insurance, real estate	1.57	1.81	2.69				1.06
Business services	1.21	3.10	1.65				
Personal services	5.29	6.61	3.61		76.76	66.52	23.59
Professional services	1.21	1.26	2.08		0.38	2.24	2.46
Other	2.90	6.85	4.30		0.38	1.79	1.93
Uncodable	55.06	45.88	34.78		6.86	13.23	49.90
Number of unweighted cases	339	417	2993		199	269	944

missing cases is so large that generalizations on the basis of these data must be viewed as tentative.

Unexpectedly, among women, half the cases in the "All New Yorkers" category could not be assigned an industry. Among blacks, it is not uncodable job titles but the presence of several blank or small cells in the table that is noteworthy. On the one hand, this result is a consequence of small sample size. The larger the sample, the greater the chance that a few women will fill each cell. On the other hand, sample size is not the reason that women are more industrially clustered than men or that black women are more clustered than white women. These patterns reflect powerful norms regarding the effects of race and gender on work. Three-quarters of West Indian women worked in one industry: personal service. Another 11.5 percent held manufacturing jobs, mostly in apparel. African American women were more often found in trade than in manufacturing, but two-thirds of them likewise toiled in personal service. These patterns reflect premigration traditions that extended not only to the South but also to the Islands. Indeed, a New York job more often meant downward mobility for a Caribbean-born man than for a Caribbean-born woman because job opportunities for women in the Islands were not much different from job opportunities for African American women in the United States (Eisner 1961).

Few hard data are available on West Indian employment patterns in the New York metropolitan area between 1925 and 1970 because public use samples were too small until the post-1965 migrant influx augmented population counts. However, using the state rather than the metropolitan area as the unit of analysis, Ladipo (1998) reports some fascinating figures on government employment among men. His earliest data, for 1940, show 18.3 percent of foreign-born West Indians in government jobs, 21.6 percent of African Americans, and 12.0 percent of all men in New York State. For 1960, the numbers are 15.9 percent, 15.0 percent, and 12.2 percent, respectively. That year is also the first to generate data for enough native-born West Indians to justify a tabulation. A striking 40.9 percent worked in government. In other words, blacks were concentrated in public employment well before affirmative action; indeed, in the case of native-born West Indians, they were very highly concentrated. Most likely, this tendency reflects both the public sector's greater tolerance for diversity and the prestige that Caribbean culture traditionally accorded civil service (Lowenthal 1972).

Table 2.4 reports concentrations by major industrial category for 1970, 1980, and 1990. Government employees are here assigned their own industry. The bottom of the table presents the index of dissimilarity, a summary measure for distributions. The index conveys the percentage of each subgroup that would have to change industries in order to have the same industrial distribution as "All New Yorkers." The higher the number, the more skewed the minority distribution. In

TABLE 2.4 Industrial Distributions (in %) of New York SMSA Labor Force Participants by Race/Ethnicity, Gender, and Year

	Men			Women		
	1970	1980	1990	1970	1980	1990
Construction						
FB West Indians	5.55	7.50	11.09	0.13	0.28	0.61
NB West Indians	3.60	3.23	5.70	0.00	0.38	0.46
African Americans	6.06	4.81	7.30	0.29	0.37	0.52
FB New Yorkers	8.43	7.34	9.65	0.59	0.47	0.85
All New Yorkers	6.29	6.08	8.73	0.69	0.71	1.13
Manufacturing						
FB West Indians	21.44	20.50	12.51	13.16	9.79	6.28
NB West Indians	11.71	15.24	11.10	14.52	9.02	5.76
African Americans	22.34	19.27	13.97	19.37	15.20	10.24
FB New Yorkers	28.50	25.56	17.58	32.74	32.85	20.44
All New Yorkers	24.09	21.75	15.42	22.20	19.18	13.25
Transport, communication, utilities						
FB West Indians	10.54	8.61	10.68	2.19	3.03	3.57
NB West Indians	8.11	7.39	10.31	4.84	4.80	5.75
African Americans	11.07	8.38	10.67	5.42	4.56	5.71
FB New Yorkers	6.97	7.41	8.16	3.55	2.69	3.59
All New Yorkers	9.76	8.36	8.82	4.39	4.04	4.45

(continued)

TABLE 2.4 (continued)

	Men			Women		
	1970	1980	1990	1970	1980	1990
Wholesale trade						
FB West Indians	3.14	4.33	3.89	1.81	1.71	2.15
NB West Indians	4.50	3.00	2.50	1.61	1.54	2.08
African Americans	4.26	4.10	5.09	1.54	1.97	2.21
FB New Yorkers	6.65	5.40	5.64	3.75	3.63	4.05
All New Yorkers	5.36	5.78	5.64	3.39	3.93	3.88
Retail trade						
FB West Indians	7.76	10.54	11.22	6.97	7.99	9.00
NB West Indians	6.31	8.08	13.84	8.87	12.28	9.63
African Americans	13.16	11.53	11.20	10.39	10.31	9.09
FB New Yorkers	17.83	17.54	19.50	14.00	11.68	14.32
All New Yorkers	14.99	14.76	14.85	16.47	15.69	14.31
Finance, insurance, real estate						
FB West Indians	10.72	9.74	9.85	8.77	11.81	13.25
NB West Indians	10.81	7.85	7.98	6.45	8.25	13.77
African Americans	5.01	4.81	5.28	5.74	8.07	8.88
FB New Yorkers	5.51	7.01	7.85	7.89	7.89	9.70
All New Yorkers	7.10	7.25	8.82	8.84	9.89	11.42
Business services						
FB West Indians	7.76	8.50	9.09	2.58	5.05	4.84
NB West Indians	2.70	7.16	9.03	4.84	4.80	4.21
African Americans	5.78	7.62	8.11	3.27	4.79	4.03
FB New Yorkers	5.02	6.50	7.26	3.16	4.55	4.99
All New Yorkers	5.25	6.54	6.71	4.32	5.37	4.97

Personal service						
FB West Indians	5.18	2.79	2.03	23.10	12.56	8.83
NB West Indians	3.60	0.69	1.96	1.61	2.69	3.83
African Americans	3.42	2.65	2.40	17.03	6.74	4.24
FB New Yorkers	4.38	3.05	2.98	9.27	6.98	7.61
All New Yorkers	2.33	2.02	1.95	6.68	4.15	4.04
Professional service						
FB West Indians	12.01	11.89	11.76	25.94	28.86	33.43
NB West Indians	4.50	8.31	11.47	14.52	16.89	25.99
African Americans	5.15	7.08	9.47	12.79	15.06	23.24
FB New Yorkers	6.16	9.19	9.83	15.58	16.06	22.05
All New Yorkers	6.75	8.76	11.43	14.18	17.50	24.14
Government						
FB West Indians	13.12	14.54	16.30	14.58	18.44	17.90
NB West Indians	41.44	36.49	25.13	41.13	38.39	26.95
African Americans	19.64	28.36	25.00	21.48	32.22	31.13
FB New Yorkers	7.78	9.37	9.36	6.90	12.37	11.52
All New Yorkers	14.81	16.29	14.76	16.01	17.95	16.69
Other						
FB West Indians	2.77	1.08	1.56	0.77	0.48	0.35
NB West Indians	2.70	2.54	0.98	1.61	0.96	1.58
African Americans	4.10	1.40	1.51	2.68	0.70	0.71
FB New Yorkers	2.76	1.64	2.19	2.56	0.83	0.88
All New Yorkers	3.27	2.40	2.86	2.83	1.58	1.72

(continued)

TABLE 2.4 *(continued)*

	Men			Women		
	1970	1980	1990	1970	1980	1990
Index of Dissimilarity						
FB West Indians	15.02	10.00	9.58	28.18	22.18	17.02
NB West Indians	31.62	21.56	14.22	26.43	21.20	15.76
African Americans	8.59	13.79	13.94	16.85	17.38	15.90

the interests of space, the following discussion emphasizes the years 1970 and 1990, with little discussion of the intervening census.

To begin with foreign-born West Indian males in 1970, this group held far fewer jobs in retailing and somewhat more jobs in finance, business services, and personal service than the entire male workforce. But the most obvious disparity involves professional service, where 12.01 percent of male West Indian immigrants worked, compared to 6.75 percent of all men. Moving to native-born West Indians, observe that, with an index of dissimilarity (ID) of 31.62, their 1970 distribution was more skewed than that of the foreign born (ID = 15.02). Native-born West Indians were underrepresented in all industries except government and finance, the last an industrial concentration they shared with their foreign-born compatriots. The public sector was a native-born West Indian niche; 41.44 percent worked there, about the same rate that Ladipo (1998) observed among New York State native-born West Indians a decade earlier. Interestingly, African American men had a relatively unremarkable industrial distribution (ID = 8.6), yet they too concentrated in government. Their percentage (19.64%) was well above average but less than half the native-born West Indian rate. Indeed, the public sector turns out to be the only industry where African Americans and a West Indian group both clustered, but the West Indians clustered there were not immigrants. Additional analysis (not shown) reveals that, in most years, foreign-born West Indians worked in the public sector at rates roughly 6 percent higher than all foreign-born New Yorkers but at unremarkable rates compared with "All New Yorkers." In other words, considering that they were foreign-born, West Indian immigrants worked in government at high rates.[6]

The industrial distribution of foreign-born West Indian men moved much closer to that of all men between 1970 (ID = 15.02) and 1990 (ID = 9.58). Structural changes were partly responsible for the convergence. Three industries where West Indian immigrants clustered in 1970 employed proportionately more New Yorkers in 1990: finance, business services, and professional service. Retail trade employment stayed about the same, but immigrants nevertheless improved their representation there. The most distinctive feature of foreign-born West Indian men's 1990 industrial pattern was a modest increase in government employment and a new visibility in construction. Wright and Ellis (1996) likewise note a public-sector gain of foreign-born blacks in 1990. They associate this growth with a decline in government employment among native-born blacks in the same year, an interpretation taken up below. Waldinger (1995) likewise notes a construction gain and attributes it to the arrival of Caribbean immigrants with experience in the building trades and the commitment of government agencies to favoring minority business enterprise.

The industries of native-born West Indian men also became less distinctive, but for a different reason: only a quarter of their numbers worked

for government in 1990. To be sure, this was still a high figure, but many
had to find new jobs. These jobs were predominantly in retail trade, where
native-born West Indian concentrations doubled to 13.84 percent, and in
business services (9.03%). While native-born West Indian industrial distinctiveness fell, African American distinctiveness rose. Nor were these
phenomena independent. Rather, the data suggest that, between 1970 and
1980, African American men may have gained public service jobs at native-
born West Indians' expense. Even in 1990, public-sector employment remained the most remarkable feature of the African American industrial
distribution, but by that date the group had begun to lose ground in this
niche.

Moving to black women, note that their IDs are higher than their black
male counterparts', indicating that they were more industrially concentrated. Since the benchmark for each ID is all New Yorkers of the same gender and year, the reason that black women have higher IDs than black men
is not that women have long been more concentrated industrially than men.
Rather, black women are more concentrated relative to all New York
women than black men are concentrated relative to all New York men.
Black women's domestic service concentration plays a role, as well as their
stronger concentration in government. Another gender difference is that the
ID values for native-born West Indian women are slightly lower than those
for foreign-born West Indian women. Recall that the industrial distribution
of native-born West Indian males was *more* skewed than that of the foreign
born.

In 1970, just two industries employed nearly half of foreign-born West Indian females: personal service and professional service. Simultaneously, these
women were strongly underrepresented in manufacturing and retail, two industries quite popular among New York's women as a whole. The contrast
with native-born West Indian women is strong—the native born eschew personal service (1.61%), are half as likely to work in professional service
(14.52%), and flock instead—like their male counterparts—to government
(41.13%). As for African American women, they are overrepresented in some
of the same industries as foreign- and/or native-born West Indian women,
but generally at less impressive levels. For instance, 17.03 percent of African
American women had personal service jobs and 21.48 percent worked in government.

In 1990, foreign-born West Indian women were still overrepresented in
personal service, but that percentage had dropped by a third to 8.83 percent.
Concurrently, they had increased their representation in professional service
from a quarter to a third of all workers. Other, less impressive gains for West
Indian immigrant women were made in finance and government. Like native-
born West Indian men, native-born West Indian women lost considerable
ground in government between 1970 and 1990. Their compensatory strategies

were different, however. The most obvious were increases in finance and professional jobs; less obvious was a small rise in personal service (1.61% in 1970, 3.83% in 1990). Finally, African American women paralleled West Indian immigrants in abandoning personal service for professional service. Their other area of growth was government, in which their representation, though down slightly between 1980 and 1990, was still a healthy 31.13 percent.

As mentioned earlier, Wright and Ellis (1996) interpret the shifts in government jobs among blacks as the substitution of foreign workers for natives. Reliance on different levels of analysis—city versus metropolitan area—renders the two studies not strictly comparable. Partly for this reason, the numbers in Table 2.4 suggest a different interpretation. Taking into account fluctuations in the size of government, women's gains were smaller than men's and came in the '70s; men's larger gains came in the '80s. As for declines, the big losers were native-born West Indian men and women, who lost jobs in both decades. African American men gained many government posts in the '70s, then lost a few in the '80s; African American women gained many government posts in the '70s, then gained a few more in the '80s. In sum, public services were replacing native blacks with foreign-born blacks, but the native blacks being replaced were West Indian, not African American. One potential explanation for this shift is that it was voluntary rather than discriminatory. After all, few employers can distinguish a native-born West Indian from an African American. However, census data are not very helpful in the attribution of motives; additional qualitative research is needed instead.

Niche Distributions

Having shown that neither West Indians nor African Americans have been randomly distributed across industries, the discussion now turns to an examination of these groups' niche industries. First, as recommended by Logan, Alba, and McNulty (1994), the more than two hundred detailed industries defined by the Census Bureau are reduced to forty-seven, then further divided into private, federal, state, and local "subindustries." Because, more often than not, men and women work in different subindustries, the two genders are analyzed separately. In order to qualify as a niche, a subindustry must employ at least one thousand people of the same sex. And because this restriction does not adequately screen out small subindustries, about which generalizations are error prone, a subindustry must also employ at least 2.5 percent of an ethnic group to qualify as a niche. The final defining characteristic of a niche is that minority men or women must be represented in the subindustry at a rate at least 1.5 times greater than the proportion of the New York labor force of the same sex employed in the subindustry (Waldinger 1996; Waldinger and Bozorgmehr 1996; Model 1997).

The first column of Table 2.5 presents a listing of all subindustries that served as niches for West Indians or African Americans in at least one of the following years: 1970, 1980, 1990. The remaining columns contain the percentage of the gender/generation subgroup employed in the niche. If that figure is at least 1.5 times greater than expected, the degree of overrepresentation (the location quotient) appears in parentheses. Several cells do not include location quotients; for instance, banking for native-born West Indian men in 1980 and 1990. The absence of a location quotient means that the group was not overrepresented in the subindustry at a rate 1.5 times greater than expected in that year. In this situation, rather than present a blank cell, it seemed appropriate to include the percentage of the group employed in the subindustry, because the niche definition is somewhat arbitrary. Thus, any subindustry that met the niche definition in one year is assumed to have provided important employment opportunities for the relevant gender/generation subgroup in all three years.

One generalization that can be made is that several subindustries are related. Among men, transportation is a major arena, here including both trucking, private transport (primarily taxi services), and public transport (mostly bus and subway services). Interestingly, a glance at the occupations associated with the repair category (not shown) reveals that most are jobs in automotive repair. Hospitals are a significant cluster for both sexes, with private institutions the largest employer but local and state-run hospitals attaining significance in at least some years. A third arena is public administration, at all three levels of government. Welfare services, both local and private, compose the final shared category.

There are, in addition, six independent subindustries: banking, apparel, communications (telephone), department stores, private households, and local schools. Two of these, apparel and local schools, have no linkages to other subindustries, attain niche status only in 1970, and consist only of native-born West Indian men or women. Recall that the number of native-born West Indian men and women available for study in 1970 was small (see Table 2.2). This fact, coupled with the stand-alone nature of these two subindustries, suggests that their appearance in Table 2.6 may be a matter of chance. The legitimacy of the other stand-alone niches—banking, department stores, communications, and private households—is indisputable, however.

As has already been suggested, these niches represent a mix of old and new opportunities. As shown above, transport and personal service (private households) are traditionally associated with black men and women, respectively. Still, the fact that America's post-1965 immigration law favored the entry of household workers certainly exacerbated the long-standing association between black skin and household labor. Even so, this niche has undergone extensive erosion. Note that private household service never attains the status of a niche for native-born West Indian women. Of course, part of the reason for

TABLE 2.5 Niche Distributions (in %) and Location Quotients of New York SMSA Labor Force Participants by Race/Ethnicity, Gender, and Year[a]

	Men			Women		
	1970	1980	1990	1970	1980	1990
Banking						
FB West Indians	4.07 (2.24)	4.33 (1.91)	3.86 (1.68)	6.33 (1.99)	7.00 (1.63)	6.74 (1.60)
NB West Indians	4.07 (2.23)	2.31	2.57	3.42	4.03	6.66 (1.58)
Apparel						
NB West Indians	4.07 (1.96)	1.85	1.21			
Trucking, warehousing						
African Americans	3.11	3.03 (1.63)	3.74 (1.66)			
Private transport						
FB West Indians	5.00 (1.50)	4.30	2.11			
NB West Indians	4.87	3.93	2.61 (1.85)			
Local transport						
NB West Indians	4.07	4.16 (4.76)	3.44 (5.29)			
African Americans	2.05	3.03 (3.47)	2.06			
Repair						
FB West Indians	4.07 (2.42)	4.13 (2.06)	2.92 (2.00)			
Communications						
NB West Indians				3.42 (1.59)	3.26 (1.92)	3.51 (1.82)
African Americans				3.41 (1.58)	2.91 (1.71)	3.07 (1.60)

(continued)

TABLE 2.5 *(continued)*

	Men			Women		
	1970	1980	1990	1970	1980	1990
Department stores						
NB West Indians				5.48	7.68 (1.93)	2.83
Private households						
FB West Indians				17.7 (5.83)	9.82 (5.59)	5.79 (3.86)
African Americans				9.39 (3.09)	4.58 (2.61)	2.22
Local schools						
NB West Indians				11.0 (1.66)	8.83	6.26
Private welfare						
NB West Indians				3.42 (2.19)	2.87	2.05
Local welfare						
NB West Indians				0	4.22 (3.73)	3.39 (4.21)
African Americans				2.66	3.54 (3.13)	2.68 (3.33)
Private hospitals						
FB West Indians	6.00	6.88 (3.36)	5.62 (2.77)	20.8 (4.76)	21.7 (3.24)	19.4 (2.62)
NB West Indians	0	3.70 (1.81)	4.75 (2.34)	8.22 (1.88)	8.25	12.8 (1.73)
African Americans	1.75	2.78	3.26 (1.60)	7.30 (1.67)	7.62	9.32
Local hospitals						
FB West Indians				3.46	4.86 (3.41)	3.84 (3.09)
NB West Indians				3.42	4.41 (3.10)	4.64 (3.74)
African Americans				2.29	3.74 (2.62)	2.76 (2.22)

State hospitals						
African Americans			1.60	2.50 (2.80)	1.93	
Post office						
NB West Indians	7.32 (2.57)	6.00 (3.80)	2.90 (2.11)			
African Americans	3.69 (2.14)	2.94 (1.86)	2.64 (1.92)			
Federal administration						
NB West Indians	2.44	3.93 (3.36)	0.69	4.11	3.83 (3.43)	1.28
State administration						
NB West Indians	1.62	2.54 (2.87)	0.76			
Local administration						
NB West Indians	8.94 (3.20)	9.01 (2.60)	2.45	1.37	4.80 (2.51)	2.63
African Americans				1.00	3.35 (1.75)	3.53 (1.91)
Total % of group in niches						
FB West Indians	19.1	19.6	14.5	48.3	43.4	35.8
NB West Indians	35.8	37.4	21.4	43.9	52.2	46.0
African Americans	10.6	11.8	11.7	27.6	28.2	25.5

[a]Location quotients are provided in parentheses if the niche industry absorbs more than 2.49 percent of minority workers and the location quotient is greater than 1.49. See text for further details.

the declining percentages in private household service (but not for the declining location quotients) is that such opportunities diminished over the course of the twentieth century. Hospital jobs, conversely, expanded over time, a fact that facilitated black entry into this subindustry. Again, immigration regulations contributed—nurses can more easily enter the United States because their occupation is officially in short supply. As Palmer (1974) has noted, this policy has resulted in a disproportionate number of Jamaican nurses moving to the United States. Yet less than half of the West Indian women in hospital jobs hold professional posts. Hence, appropriate qualifications are only part of the explanation for the evolution of this West Indian niche. Ethnically homogeneous social networks are a likelier cause, with employed West Indians of all skill levels passing on vital job information to the unemployed. Moreover, African Americans also populate this niche, and not only in New York, but in Los Angeles as well (Wright and Ellis 1997). This discovery suggests that other factors common among the three groups, perhaps English-speaking ability, are responsible for the disproportionate number of black women employed in American hospitals.

Public administration is another arena that attracts blacks, for a combination of reasons. To be sure, since the public sector has taken the lead as the exemplary affirmative action employer, the most obvious reason for black preponderance is social policy. Yet, as mentioned above, as early as 1940 New York State's African Americans were overrepresented in government; by 1960 native-born West Indians were as well. Thus, affirmative action policies only enhanced an earlier black concentration, or perhaps improved access to an arena that by mid-century was already practicing "fair employment." In any event, Table 2.5 shows that public administration is even more a native-born West Indian niche than an African American niche. Yet the absence of any location quotients for native-born West Indians in public administration in 1990 means that, by this date, the group was no longer overrepresented there. The location quotients also show that African American women increased their visibility in local administration in the eighties, at the very time native-born West Indian representation was falling. Thus, results of the fine-grained analysis mesh with those of the earlier, coarse-grained analysis: the group losing ground in the public sector is not African Americans but native-born West Indians.

The last niche to note is welfare services, once a growing field, if only because the impoverishment of urban blacks created new opportunities for the black middle class to serve as intermediaries between the state and the truly disadvantaged (Collins 1983). Since politicians massively cut public welfare programs in the late 1990s, jobs in local welfare may have declined.

Another way of categorizing the information in Table 2.5 is to distinguish African American niches from West Indian. Of the nineteen niche subindustries in the table, two are unique to African Americans (trucking and state hospitals), nine are unique to West Indians, and eight are shared by the two groups. These findings fit with a pattern noted earlier, the greater propensity of West Indians to hold niche jobs. Not only are West Indians represented in more niches than African Americans (seventeen versus ten), but generally, when the two groups share a niche in the same year, a higher percentage of West Indians than African Americans are employed therein. (These patterns are also evident from the indexes of industrial dissimilarity in Table 2.4.)

Similarly, native-born West Indians are more attracted to niche employment than are foreign-born West Indians. This generalization holds in terms of the number of niches, four each for foreign-born West Indian men and women, nine for native-born West Indian men, and ten for native-born West Indian women. It also holds in terms of the total percentage of each subgroup in niche jobs. This conclusion is suggested by the last three rows of Table 2.6, which sum the percentage of each ethnic/racial gender category across niches by year. For instance, in 1970, 19.1 percent of foreign-born West Indian men worked in a niche.[7] Thus, if niche employment is broadly defined as working in any subindustry that attained niche status at least once over the surveyed period, the figures show that men are less likely to hold niche jobs than women, that, controlling for gender, African Americans are less likely to hold niche jobs than West Indians, and that native-born West Indians are more likely to hold niche jobs than foreign-born West Indians. In addition, both foreign- and native-born West Indians were more likely to work in niches in 1970 than in 1990, while time has had little effect on the tendency for African American New Yorkers to hold a wide variety of jobs.

Two factors underlie the African American pattern of industrial dispersal: first, the group's long history as Americans, which tends to dilute a propensity toward job concentrations, as assimilation theorists have long maintained. Equally important, however, has been the long-standing reluctance of white employers to hire many blacks in one firm, plant, or company (Bodnar, Simon, and Weber 1982; Model 1988). With some significant exceptions, such as the auto industry or household service, few industries have relied on a disproportionately African American workforce. Given the ethnographic material in support of the claim that white employers favor West Indians over African Americans, the discovery that West Indian immigrants register higher levels of job concentration than African Americans is not a complete surprise (Foner 1979; Arnold 1996; Waters 1999a). Additional evidence that employers might prefer immigrants to native blacks comes from the higher representation (larger location quotients) of foreign-born West Indians within the niches that immigrants share with African Americans. Three of these exist: private households (women), private hospitals (men and women), and local hospitals (women). Within these niches, West Indian immigrants are consistently more strongly represented than their African American same-sex, same-year counterparts. With one exception (local hospitals in 1990), this generalization also holds for native-born West Indians. Thus, if location quotients indicate levels of demand for labor, these figures imply that West Indians are outpacing African Americans in the competition for jobs. But location quotients summarize the effects of both supply *and* demand, leaving the observer in the dark with respect to how much the numbers convey what workers want (supply) versus what employers want (demand). For instance, West Indian immigrants probably pursue domestic service opportunities more vigorously than African Americans; hence their high representation in this field is probably more a result of worker than employer preference. Unfortunately, the two groups' attitudes toward hospital work are less clear. As before, quantitative analysis does a poor job of explaining people's motives.

Niche Earnings

Having shown that West Indians are not distributed at random across New York's industrial structure, the analysis turns to the consequence of this fact for earnings. In order to address this issue, attention focuses first on whether or not the logged hourly earnings of group members inside a niche are statistically distinguishable from the logged hourly earnings of similarly qualified group members outside the niche. If so, two potential explanations deserve consideration. The niche may be a relatively more (or less) remunerative place for everyone; that is, all its employees may earn, on average, more (or less) than workers in other industries. Or, the niche may reward group members (insiders) differently than non–group members (outsiders). One or both of these scenarios may obtain.

Three regressions were estimated, each on a different subsample. The dependent variable was always the log of hourly earnings for the year preceding the census and the control variables were always age, age squared, years of schooling, and a dummy variable coded one for married persons and zero for all others. All equations were estimated separately by sex and year and were limited to persons aged 25–64 who had minimum annual earnings of $500 in 1969, $750 in 1979, and $1000 in 1989. The first equation tested whether or not members of a particular group earned more or less in a niche industry, all else being equal. The subsample for this model was all members of the same racial/ethnic, generation, and gender group in the same year. Along with the controls, the model included a dummy coded one for those group members working in the niche industry and zero for all others. A statistically significant coefficient for the group-membership dummy indicated that group members fared better (or worse) as a result of niche jobs. Such a finding required further inquiry. In contrast, a statistically insignificant coefficient for a particular dummy terminated the analysis of earnings in that niche for the racial/ethnic, generation, and gender group in that year.

When a significant finding obtained, two more regressions were estimated. The subsample became all employed individuals of the same gender and in the same year. The dummy included with the controls was coded one for all individuals of the same gender working in the niche, irrespective of race, ethnicity, or nativity, and zero for all others. A significant coefficient for this dummy indicated that jobs in the niche paid everyone better (or worse) than jobs in the economy as a whole. Regardless of the findings revealed by this step, a second model, for which the subsample included all employed individuals of the same gender working in the niche in the year of interest, was estimated. The dummy variable was coded one for insiders and zero for all others. A significant coefficient for this dummy indicated that insiders earned more (or less) than outsiders. Because of variations in sample size and in the size of the group membership coefficients, steps two and three did not always yield significant coefficients.

Table 2.6 lists the niches that paid significantly more or less than other job opportunities, by group and by year. The absence of an entry for a group in a given year means that, in the given year, niches paid the same as other job opportunities. Eleven of the nineteen different niches identified in Table 2.5 appear at least once in Table 2.6. Perhaps the most striking feature of the table is the gender difference. There are fewer entries for men than for women, a partial reflection of the previously noted smaller propensity of men than women to work in industrially concentrated jobs. But other factors must contribute, for native-born West Indians have the largest proportion of men in niche jobs, yet they are wholly absent from Table 2.6. Note too that the earnings effects of niche jobs are far more often the result of industrywide differences (column 3) than of differential treatment by group membership (column 4). In other words, *the wage effects of niches more often accrue to all who work there than to a select group of insiders.*

To begin with men, West Indian immigrant males appear in the table only in 1990. In that year, they received a pay shortfall in two niche industries, repair and transport. The significant effects in column 3 and absence thereof in column 4 mean that repair and private transport paid all men poorly, not just the West Indian born. A larger number of niche effects accrued to African American males. In local transport, they enjoyed a premium in all three years. Yet neither column 3 nor column 4 records a statistically significant result. Additional analysis (not shown) indicates that the African American advantage is more closely tied to a group-specific premium than to an industry-specific premium. Conversely, the African American shortfall in private hospitals in 1970 and the surfeit in post office jobs in 1980 result from industrywide wage patterns, though again the first of these industrial effects falls short of statistical significance.

All told, niches contribute little to black men's financial well-being. This conclusion holds because the proportion of men employed in the few niches

TABLE 2.6 Net Effects of Employment in Niches on Logged Hourly Earnings of New York SMSA Earners by Race/Ethnicity, Gender, and Year[a]

Group, gender, year, niche industry	Group inside niche vs. group outside niche		All inside niche vs. all outside niche		Group inside niche vs. non-group inside niche	
FB West Indian men						
1990						
Private transport	-0.1848*	(0.0746)	-0.2921***	(0.0269)	0.0041	(0.0938)
Repair	-0.1383*	(0.0636)	-0.2515***	(0.0288)	0.0193	(0.0720)
NB West Indian men						
1990						
Local administration	0.3383	(0.1753)	0.1758***	(0.0182)	0.0141	(0.1250)
African American men						
1970						
Local transport	0.1364*	(0.0600)	0.0080	(0.1110)	-0.0820	(0.0793)
Private hospitals	-0.1462*	(0.0693)	-0.1844	(0.1091)	-0.1892	(0.1323)
1980						
Local transportation	0.1456*	(0.0602)	0.0180	(0.0337)	-0.0332	(0.0472)
Post office	0.2500***	(0.0644)	0.0740**	(0.0260)	0.0336	(0.0455)
1990						
Local transportation	0.2132**	(0.0681)	0.0321	(0.0387)	0.0441	(0.0498)
FB West Indian women						
1970						
Private households	-0.4726***	(0.0680)	-0.2868**	(0.0875)	-0.1492	(0.1167)
Private hospitals	0.3401***	(0.0619)	-0.1098	(0.0609)	0.2851**	(0.0903)
1980						
Private households	-0.3595***	(0.0380)	-0.3249***	(0.0350)	0.0800	(0.0638)
Private hospitals	0.1586***	(0.0256)	0.1050***	(0.0151)	0.1230***	(0.0252)
Local hospitals	0.1214*	(0.0480)	0.0677*	(0.0321)	0.1191*	(0.0543)

	(1)		(2)		(3)	
1990						
Private households	−0.4664***	(0.0348)	−0.3390***	(0.0284)	−0.0600	(0.0424)
Private hospitals	0.1482***	(0.0216)	0.1130***	(0.0119)	0.0107	(0.0214)
Local hospitals	0.1100**	(0.0434)	0.1106***	(0.0278)	−0.0164	(0.0478)
NB West Indian women						
1970						
Banking	2.2416***	(0.4095)	0.0268	(0.0841)	2.2375***	(0.2400)
Local administration	1.4856*	(0.6500)	0.1141	(0.1025)	1.2296*	(0.5416)
1980						
Department stores	−0.2709*	(0.1203)	−0.1788**	(0.0244)	0.1432	(0.1161)
1990						
Private hospitals	0.1567*	(0.0749)	0.1130***	(0.0119)	0.1046	(0.0657)
African American women						
1970						
Private households	−0.2357***	(0.0453)	−0.2868**	(0.0375)	−0.0845	(0.1273)
1980						
Communications	0.1852**	(0.0583)	0.3103***	(0.0280)	−0.1245*	(0.0616)
Private households	−0.3735***	(0.0659)	−0.3249***	(0.0350)	−0.0243	(0.0844)
1990						
Communications	0.1995***	(0.0434)	0.2302***	(0.0231)	−0.0665	(0.0421)
Private households	−0.2779***	(0.0527)	−0.3390***	(0.0284)	0.0480	(0.0672)
Local administration	0.0949*	(0.0445)	0.0650**	(0.0236)	0.0512	(0.0425)

[a]Values are regression coefficients, with standard errors in parentheses. In each model, the control variables are age, age squared, years of schooling, and a dummy coded one for married individuals and zero for all others. See text for further information.

* $p < .05$, ** $p < .01$, *** $p < .001$.

that offer pay differentials is small. Conversely, among black women, niche employment has a substantial impact, though primarily on foreign-born West Indian women's earnings. The reason for the small impact on the native born is not a lack of niches—each of the women's groups has three or four—but the small proportion that each niche absorbs. However, for West Indian immigrants, two niches absorb very large percentages: private households and public hospitals. Together these employed nearly two out of five immigrants in 1970 and one out of four in 1990. Interestingly, these two niches affected earnings in opposite ways. Private households paid below-average wages and public hospitals paid above. Fortunately for West Indian immigrant women, their representation in household service diminished over time, eventually rendering niche jobs more of an asset than a liability.

Before continuing, it is worthwhile to elaborate on the mechanisms responsible for these earnings effects. In the case of private households, the cause is low pay for all employees. For private hospitals, in the latter two years, the cause is high pay. In addition, in 1970 and 1980 foreign-born West Indian women in private hospitals received higher salaries than outsiders. This is an intriguing finding, especially considering that, in this industry, all three groups of black women were insiders. A similar but less striking pattern holds in local hospitals; in 1980, foreign-born West Indian women received higher wages in this niche than outsiders. These results raise the possibility that foreign-born West Indian women obtained higher remuneration in both types of hospitals than did other black women.

Additional analyses (not shown) pursued this possibility, finding that West Indian immigrant women earned *more* than equally qualified African American women in one niche: private hospitals.[8] And this earnings advantage obtained in all three census years. At the same time, no intrablack wage difference surfaced in the other two niches that West Indian and African American women shared: local hospitals and private households. In sum, the evidence on intrablack competition is mixed. In most niches that the three black groups in this study shared, their earnings are statistically indistinguishable. Private hospitals, however, are an exception to this rule. Again, only further study can ferret out the reasons why.

CONCLUSION

This chapter has focused on the industrial distribution of New York's blacks and the difference it makes for earnings. The descriptive part of the research uncovered several intriguing trends. First, contrary to popular opinion, West Indian immigrants have never been heavily entrepreneurial, at least in New York City. Second, some of the industries to which West Indians gravitated as early as 1925, such as transportation and domestic service, continue to absorb a disproportionate number today. Third, West Indian women's industrial distributions are more skewed than West Indian men's. More surprising, within both genders the distribution of the native born is more skewed than that of the foreign born. Finally, controlling for gender and nativity, West Indian job distributions became more like those of all New Yorkers during the 1980s. These trends are hard to interpret, since they reflect the preferences of both employers and workers. But they do set West Indians apart from other immigrant groups.

As for earnings consequences, among men there are surprisingly few, and those that are measurable turn out to be negative. For women the consequences are greater, and those that are measurable are both positive and negative. The arena that absorbs the most West Indian women, private hospitals, imparts a premium, while one of the arenas that absorbs relatively few, private households, imparts a penalty. On the one hand, U.S. censuses count household workers far less reliably than hospital workers. Thus, the figures in this chapter underestimate the earnings disadvantage of niche employment for West Indian–born women. On the other hand, far more West Indian women work in hospitals than households. Thus, on balance, niche jobs help these women more than hurt them.

Also noteworthy is the discovery that, prior to 1990, very high proportions of native-born West Indians worked in government. The reason for their decline surely merits investigation. Fortunately, the analysis offers little evidence that native-born West Indian earnings suffered as a result of their declining representation in government. Yet this conclusion may be unduly optimistic, because studies of earnings are restricted to those with jobs. If a large number of native-born West Indian ex–government employees remained unemployed in 1990, their "zero earnings" also merit consideration in any assessment of the consequences of the drop in government employment on native-born West Indians. Moreover, government employment is widely assumed to bring advantages other than earnings, such as job security and opportunities for advancement.

This point suggests a useful closing reminder: this research has paid scant attention to the nonpecuniary side of employment. Perhaps New York's West Indian niches are more consequential in terms of on-the-job training, internal labor markets, and generosity of benefits than in terms of earnings. Unfortunately, census questionnaires do not inquire about nonpecuniary outcomes of employment. Moreover, as this chapter has repeatedly stressed, census analysis cannot uncover human motives. Hence, the ideal strategy would be for scholars to conduct qualitative research to supplement the findings reported here, with greater detail from both West Indians and the New Yorkers who employ them.

NOTES

1. Some scholars use occupations rather than industries as the unit of analysis in niche research. See, for example, the work of Reitz (1990). However, industries are preferable because they more closely approximate firms, and most scholars conceptualize niche effects as operating in firms. Unfortunately, good information at the level of firms is rarely

available. Hence, most studies that utilize large-scale surveys and censuses for niche research focus on industries.

2. The support of the Russell Sage Foundation and the assistance of Dan Kryder and Andy Schlewitz are acknowledged in association with the New York State data. Eleanor Weber assisted in extracting the 1970 files from data obtained by the University of Massachusetts from the Inter-university Consortium of Political and Social Research at the University of Michigan. The 1980 and 1990 files were obtained from the Integrated Public Use Microdata Series (Ruggles and Sobek 1997).

3. The British West Indies are here defined, following Sowell (1978), as Belize, Guyana, Bermuda, all past and present British colonies in the Caribbean, and those areas that the U.S. Census has coded "West Indies, not elsewhere classified." As for identifying U.S.-born West Indians, the relevant census question changed in 1980. In 1970 the U.S. Census inquired about parents' nativities, and, if both parents were born abroad, the father's birthplace was recorded. If only the mother was born abroad, her birthplace was recorded. Thus, for 1970 any non-Hispanic, U.S.-born black with one or more parents born in the British West Indies is here defined as a native-born West Indian. Beginning in 1980, the U.S. Census substituted an ancestry question for parents' birthplaces. Respondents could choose up to two ancestries. Thus, for 1980 and 1990 any non-Hispanic, U.S.-born black with one or more British West Indian ancestries is here defined as a native-born West Indian.

4. Unfortunately, Holder says nothing about the geographic limits of his sample. Neither Gutman nor Holder gives details about his sampling strategy or about his definition of "entrepreneur."

5. Table 2.2 also provides totals by gender, ethnicity, and year. Most of the analyses in this chapter are based on the number of cases described here.

6. The author wishes to thank Philip Kasinitz for alerting her to this unusual pattern.

7. The relevant calculation is: $4.07 + 5.00 + 4.07 + 6.00 = 19.14$. See Table 2.5 for the source of these figures.

8. The results of all additional analyses described in this section are available from the author. She may be contacted at model@sadri.umass.edu.

THREE

West Indians and the Residential Landscape of New York

Kyle D. Crowder
and
Lucky M. Tedrow

It is nearly impossible to sensibly compare the plight of West Indians in New York City to that of any other racial or ethnic minority group. West Indians face a unique constellation of barriers, challenges, and advantages in their efforts to cultivate a sustainable niche in the complex mosaic of the city. They share with the massive numbers of Asian and Latino immigrants the challenge of acquiring equal access to the opportunities available in the United States. But unlike most other immigrant groups, West Indians bring with them a phenotype that results in their classification as black under the country's inflexible system of racial categorization, a factor carrying a social weight much different from that in their countries of origin. But, complicating matters, West Indian blacks also possess an ethnic status that distinguishes them from African Americans. Finally, like most migration flows, West Indian immigration has been fairly selective: many immigrants entering the United States from the Caribbean enjoy the benefits of education and occupational experience attained in their country of origin (Butcher 1994; Model 1995; Model and Ladipo 1996).

Despite the complexity of their position, the plight of West Indian blacks has a somewhat universalistic quality. Precisely because their situation embodies such a wide range of barriers and advantages, West Indians provide a rare opportunity to examine the nexus of race, ethnicity, class, and immigrant status as these categories play out in processes of social, economic, and spatial assimilation. This chapter explores the ways in which these factors have interacted in reshaping the residential landscape of New York City. Our purpose is to trace the development of West Indian neighborhoods in the five central boroughs of New York City during the last two decades. We utilize 1980 and 1990 census data from several sources to examine the emergence, solidification, and metamorphosis of these neighborhoods over a ten-year period. In addition to focusing on the shape and ethnic composition of these neighborhoods, the chapter provides information on their general socioeconomic quality, contrasting them with comparable African American neighborhoods. Finally, to the extent that it is possible with a singularly quantitative approach, we attempt to identify some of the ecological and socioeconomic forces that have facilitated the development of these residential enclaves.

The results of our analysis suggest that, like African Americans, West Indians tend to be confined to areas with large black concentrations, residentially isolated from non-Hispanic whites and most other racial and ethnic groups. Contrary to theoretical expectations, this racial isolation has become somewhat more pronounced over time. However, rather than being evenly dispersed throughout predominantly black neighborhoods, by 1980 West Indians had carved out a set of distinct enclaves within the larger black sections of the city, and these enclaves have only solidified over time. Perhaps most importantly, these residential niches appear to be not only spatially distinct but also somewhat more socioeconomically advantageous than other predominantly black neighborhoods. The result is that West Indians, despite comparable levels of residential segregation, face somewhat more favorable neighborhood characteristics, on average, than their African American counterparts. We view the formation of these distinct neighborhoods as an important means through which West Indians maintain and cultivate their ethnic distinctiveness. Through such enclaves, West Indians in New York have sought to avoid the social and spatial stigma attached to being black in America.

WEST INDIANS IN NEW YORK

The first significant flow of West Indian immigration to the United States began near the turn of the twentieth century. This wave, which peaked in the early 1920s before declining by the 1930s (in response to worldwide economic depression and restrictive U.S. immigration laws), was modest in comparison to the massive European immigration of the time. At its peak, this first wave of West Indian immigration represented only about 2 percent of the total immigration to the States (U.S. Immigration and Naturalization Service 1997). By 1930, West Indian immigrants constituted only about 1 percent of the country's black population. Following the 1965 implementation of the Hart-Celler Immigration Reform Act, immigration from the Caribbean resumed in massive numbers. By 1980 over fifty thousand West Indians were entering the United States annually. Since 1970 over one million West Indians have been granted legal immigrant status, with over six hundred thousand of these arriving between 1981 and 1996 alone (U.S. Immigration and Naturalization Service, 1997). The immigrants have come mainly from former or current British colonies, especially Jamaica, Guyana, Trinidad and Tobago, and Barbados, but also from the French-speaking countries of Haiti and Martinique, and in relatively small numbers from the Dutch-speaking islands of Aruba and Curacao. The majority has been English-speaking, and almost all are black, at least by American standards (Kasinitz 1992).

As for other black immigrant groups, New York City has served, and continues to serve, as a primary destination for each wave of West Indian immigration (Bryce-Laporte 1987; Kasinitz 1992). The city served as port of entry for well over half of all Caribbean immigrants entering the United States in 1996, with the vast majority of these reporting their intended state of residence as New York (U.S. Immigration and Naturalization Service 1997). Census data for 1990 indicate that over half of all those reporting a West Indian first ancestry reside in the greater New York metropolitan area.

The experience of West Indians in New York City has fueled a good deal of debate among scholars about the relative importance of race and ethnicity in the determination of socioeconomic advancement in the United States. By emigrating, West Indians gain improved economic prospects but also take on the burden of a pronounced racial stigma. In the United States these immigrants find themselves subject to an institutionalized racial dichotomy in which they are likely to be stigmatized solely because of their skin color and largely regardless of their class origins (Vickerman 1994). This predicament contrasts sharply with the malleable spectrum of racial identification characterizing many Caribbean societies (Bryce-Laporte 1987; Dodoo 1991), where access to education, employment, and occupational opportunities are less circumscribed by racial phenotype (Foner 1979, 1985; Vickerman 1994). The divergence of social positions between origin and destination is often especially pronounced for those hailing from the British Caribbean, where blacks are the majority and make up a large part of the upper class (Foner 1985; Kalmijn 1996).

Yet by most accounts, the West Indian experience (to the extent that it is possible to identify a single, collective experience) has differed dramatically from the recent experience of African Americans. The earliest depictions of West Indian immigrants touted their business acumen and ability to carve out an important niche among New York's black elite (Reid 1969 [1939]). Similarly, more recent research points to a persistent advantage of West Indians over African Americans in terms of income, occupation, and educational attainment (Foner 1979, 1985; Harrison 1992; Kalmijn 1996; Kasinitz and Vickerman, forthcoming; Sowell 1978; Steinberg 1989). Data from the New York metropolitan area show that, as of 1990, West Indian black adults had higher average levels of income and education than did adult African Americans and were more likely to be employed and to own their own homes (Crowder 1999). Several authors have advanced the idea that this relative economic success is rooted in the ability of recent cohorts of West Indian immigrants to carve out profitable niches in New York's growing service industries (Kasinitz 1992; Garcia 1986; Petras 1986; Light 1972).

Other scholars have countered that the data on the economic plight of early West Indian immigrants are quite scant and what is available indicates that, like their African American contemporaries, early West Indian immigrants had low rates of self-employment and were concentrated in low-wage jobs (Gutman 1976). Moreover, recent research has demonstrated that the magnitude of the current West Indian socioeconomic advantage over African Americans is by no means large and varies sharply by gender (Model 1991, 1995), ancestry (Kalmijn 1996; Butcher 1994; Model 1991), nativity (Model 1995; Model and Ladipo 1996), and length of residence in the United States (Chiswick 1979; Kalmijn 1996; Model 1995).

Sparking even more controversy than the existence of a West Indian socioeconomic advantage is the source of this advantage. Early explanations identified a superior cultural ethos among West Indian blacks, one that emphasizes economic progress through hard work and education (Glazer and Moynihan 1970; Sowell 1978). Several writers have dubbed the case of West Indians *the* black success story (Glazer and Moynihan 1970; Reid 1969 [1939]; Sowell 1978), and, as Kasinitz (1992) points out, some have used the relative socioeconomic success of West Indians to question the role of race as a primary determinant of the economic plight of African Americans. On the other side of this debate are those who point out that much of the economic difference between African American and West Indian families can be attributed to the educational and occupational selectivity of West Indian immigration (Butcher 1994; Kalmijn 1996; Model 1995; Model and Ladipo 1996) and to West Indians' greater likelihood of having multiple earners in the household (Farley and Allen 1987; Kasinitz 1992) rather than to the alleged superiority of West Indian culture.

According to existing theories of residential attainment, the relative socioeconomic advantage of West Indian New Yorkers over their African American counterparts, regardless of its source, should translate into an advantage in terms of residential integration. The spatial assimilation theory assumes that residential segregation of racial and ethnic groups is a natural phenomenon reflecting group differences in acculturation and human capital (Alba and Logan 1993; Massey 1985). Upon entry into the country, immigrant groups presumably become segregated from the white and native-born majorities simply because they lack the education, income, and, to a lesser extent, the language ability and knowledge of the U.S. social system necessary for access to nonimmigrant residential areas. As a result, immigrant groups, including early European groups, have historically formed somewhat homogeneous ethnic residential enclaves in American cities (Lieberson 1963, 1980; Philpott 1979; Zhou 1992). The resulting separation from members of the ethnic majority, however, is assumed to be a temporary phenomenon. Over time, successful group members gain the economic resources and acculturation necessary for access to majority-dominated areas, thereby dispersing the original minority population (Alba and Logan 1991, 1993). This residential assimilation, it is assumed, is an important step toward more complete, structural assimilation (Massey and Mullan 1984).

For the most part, the spatial assimilation model has been supported by the residential assimilation of European immigrant groups (Alba, Logan, and Crowder 1997) and many racial and ethnic minority groups entering the country more recently (Alba and Logan 1991, 1993; Denton and Massey 1988; Massey and Denton 1987). But the residential experiences of black Americans necessitate an important caveat to this general assessment. Research on the process of residential attainment has indicated that black race represents a substantial disadvantage in the assimilation process (Goldstein and White 1985; Denton and Massey 1989; Massey and Denton 1993). For example, Massey and Denton have demonstrated that, unlike the prevailing situation with regard to Asian and Hispanic groups, metropolitan-area levels of, and trends in, segregation of blacks from whites are fairly unrelated to the aggregate socioeconomic status and acculturation characteristics of group members in the area (Denton and Massey 1988; Massey and Denton 1987). At the individual level, moreover, blacks are less able than members of other groups to translate their human capital characteristics into access to better-quality neighborhoods and residence near whites (Alba and Logan 1993; Logan and Alba 1993; Alba and Logan 1991; South and Crowder 1997, 1998). As a result, levels of black/white segregation remain high, with even relatively well-off blacks often confined to racially isolated neighborhoods (Massey and Denton 1993; Massey, Gross, and Shibuya 1994).

This racial disadvantage is quite relevant to the assimilation of West Indians in New York. Unlike European and most other immigrants, West Indian immigrants face the prospect of assimilating spatially and socially into the country's most stigmatized racial group. As Mary Waters notes, "if these immigrants assimilate they assimilate to being not just Americans but black Americans" (1994a: 799). This racially circumscribed assimilation process may provide the motivation for West Indians to avoid assimilation altogether. Given the strong negative stereotypes attached to black Americans, maintaining ethnic distinctiveness may be particularly important for West Indian blacks. There is little doubt that West Indian immigrants are aware of the stigma attached to being black in America and that, especially among first-generation West Indians, there is a strong motivation to maintain their distinction as West Indian ethnics (Waters 1994a). Thus, many West Indian immigrants go to great lengths to differentiate themselves from American blacks, despite the pressure of the country's racial system to classify them only as black (Foner 1987; Kasinitz 1992; Waters 1994a; Vickerman 1994; Woldemikael 1989). Given that relegation to predominantly black residential areas often means relegation to areas of concentrated poverty, physical decay, and social degradation (Massey and Denton 1993; Massey and Eggers 1990;

Wacquant and Wilson 1989), such differentiation may be advantageous. Much like the intentional maintenance of ethnic dress and speech patterns (Kasinitz 1992; Waters 1994a), the establishment and maintenance of enclaves may be an important way for West Indians to maintain the distinction between themselves and American blacks and to avoid relegation to poor black neighborhoods.

To say that the plight of West Indian blacks is complex is a monumental understatement. On the one hand, West Indian immigrants face the dual repercussions of their immigrant status and black skin. On the other hand, they are a selective and ethnically distinct group that has experienced a measure of socioeconomic success that stands in contrast with that of most African Americans. In the pages that follow, we focus on the ways in which this unique combination of ethnic, racial, economic, and social barriers and advantages has played out as the West Indian population has helped to reshape the spatial structure of New York City.

In this analysis we examine the residential patterns of those individuals reporting a West Indian first ancestry in the 1980 and 1990 Censuses of Housing and Population. One disadvantage of this census-based ancestry definition is that it tends to undercount the number of some West Indian subgroups. For example, West Indians of Guyanese or Trinidadian descent might report an Indian or Asian ancestry, while members of other groups might report an African ancestry (see Crowder 1999).[1] However, for the purpose of the present analysis, this disadvantage is outweighed by the advantages of an ancestry-based definition over the alternative delineation based on "place of birth" reports. By potentially capturing first, second, and later generations of West Indians, ancestry generally provides for a more inclusive definition of the West Indian population than does place of birth. More importantly, census ancestry items provide a more accurate estimate of the number of individuals, regardless of their place of birth, who maintain a West Indian ethnic identity. This is an important advantage, given that the main purpose of the present analysis is to examine the extent to which a West Indian ethnic identity and the utilization of group resources attached to this identity help to shape residential patterns.[2]

Using ancestry items from the 1980 and 1990 censuses, it is possible to consistently identify eight main West Indian national-origin groups. The numbers of these groups in New York City's five boroughs are provided in Table 3.1. According to the data, in 1980 there were just under 275,000 West Indians living in the five boroughs. This number had grown to over 420,000 by 1990. In both years Jamaicans dominated the West Indian population, alone making up over 38 percent of the total West Indian population in 1980 and almost a third in 1990. The next largest group in 1980 was the somewhat amorphous "other West Indian" group, which included those reporting origins in the Dutch West Indies, Belize, or one of several other

TABLE 3.1   Distribution of West Indian Population in
New York City Boroughs, 1980 and 1990

	1980		1990	
	Population	Percent	Population	Percent
Haitian	43,468	15.8	84,011	19.9
Jamaican	106,073	38.7	140,024	33.2
U.S. Virgin Islander	1,653	0.6	2,162	0.5
Trinidadian & Tobagonian	24,072	8.8	37,052	8.8
Guyanese	18,216	6.6	49,243	11.7
British West Indian[a]	20,215	7.4	41,310	9.8
French West Indian[b]	819	0.3	837	0.2
Other West Indian[c]	59,850	21.8	67,535	16.0
Total West Indian	274,366	100.0	422,174	100.0

NOTES: [a]For 1980 "British West Indian" includes: Bahamian, Cayman, British Virgin Islander, Dominica Islander, St. Lucia, other British West Indian; for 1990: Bahamian, Barbadian, Bermudan, British West Indian. [b]For 1990 "French West Indian" includes Cayman Islander. [c]For 1980 "Other West Indian" includes: other Caribbean/Central & South American (except the Spanish category), Dutch WI/Aruba/Curacoa/Saba, Caribbean, WI/Arawak/Belizean (British), San Andrés, Providencia, Suriname; for 1990: Dutch West Indian, West Indian, Belizean, but not Suriname, Providencia, or San Andrés.

small islands, as well as those reporting "West Indian" as their primary ancestry. However, by 1990 this group was surpassed in size by the Haitian population and nearly equaled by the rapidly growing Guyanese population. The Haitian population nearly doubled and, with a count of 84,011, made up almost one-fifth of the West Indian population by 1990. Even more striking, the population of individuals reporting a Guyanese ancestry grew by over 250 percent to almost fifty thousand in 1990. Also experiencing rapid growth during the decade was the population reporting under the "other British West Indian" category, which included those from the Bahamas, Barbados, Bermuda, St. Lucia, Dominica, and, in 1980, the Cayman Islands. The Trinidadian and Tobagonian population also showed strong growth during the decade but slipped from being the fourth largest West Indian group in 1980 to the fifth largest in 1990. The numbers of French West Indians (excluding Haitians) and those from the U.S. Virgin Islands remained fairly small during the decade.

Given the diversity of groups included in the West Indian ancestry category, we attempt to differentiate the residential patterns of these national-origin groups to provide a more fine-grained depiction of the area's neighborhoods. We focus on the emergence and metamorphosis of West Indian neighborhoods in New York City's five boroughs: Bronx, Brooklyn, Queens,

Manhattan, and Staten Island. These five counties alone contained about 80 percent of the first-ancestry West Indians living in the New York–New Jersey–Long Island Consolidated Metropolitan Statistical Area and almost half of the nation's West Indian population as of 1990.

THE RESIDENTIAL ASSIMILATION
OF WEST INDIAN NEW YORKERS?

How well does the spatial assimilation model fit the case of West Indian New Yorkers? An initial answer to this question is found in the examination of the level of residential segregation experienced by West Indians at two different points in time. We examine two measures of residential segregation: the index of dissimilarity and the exposure index. The index of dissimilarity indicates how evenly a population is distributed across the census tracts[3] of an area (White 1986; Massey and Denton 1988). It compares the residential distribution of two groups and is commonly interpreted as the proportion of either group's population that would have to change tracts of residence in order to be evenly distributed across tracts in the city.[4] It is a symmetrical measure and ranges in value from zero (indicating a perfectly even distribution of the populations and thus no segregation) to one (indicating complete segregation). Massey and Denton (1988, 1993) suggest a general rule of thumb for interpreting these indexes, arguing that values above .60, between .30 and .60, and below .30 respectively indicate high, moderate, and low levels of segregation.

Exposure indexes capture a slightly different dimension of residential segregation. Rather than measuring prevailing residential patterns against some abstract population distribution, exposure indexes are meant to gauge the "experience" of segregation (Massey and Denton 1988) by calculating the actual likelihood of sharing the same neighborhood—the level of residential contact—with members of the comparison group (Lieberson and Carter 1982; White 1986; Massey and Denton 1988). The measure of exposure calculated here is the commonly used interaction index,[5] or $_xP_y^*$-index. It measures the extent to which members of group X are exposed to members of group Y by virtue of sharing a common census tract. Related to this index is the isolation index, or $_xP_x^*$-index, which measures the extent to which members of group X are exposed only to other X-group members rather than to members of other groups. Both the interaction index and the isolation index vary from zero to one and are interpreted as the proportion the comparison group (group Y for the interaction index and group X for the isolation index) forms of the total population in the tract of the average member of group X. Unlike the index of dissimilarity, the exposure index is asymmetrical, since the probability of a member of one group interacting with a member of another group is a function of the relative size of the two groups in addition to their residential distributions. Specifically, the smaller a group's proportion of the total population, the less likely that a member of another group will come into contact with a member of the first group on the basis of sharing a residence tract. This fact is important to keep in mind in interpreting the interaction indexes for relatively small population groups such as West Indians.

Table 3.2 presents indexes of dissimilarity comparing West Indians to several other racial and ethnic groups of significant size in both 1980 and 1990. For further insight, we also present indexes comparing African Americans[6] to these other groups. There are several important results to note. Beginning with the figures for 1980 (first column), the level of segregation of West Indians from almost all other groups were well within the high range defined by Massey and Denton. For example, the index comparing West Indians and non-Hispanic whites indicates that, in order to attain an even distribution of these populations, over 81 percent of the West Indians or Anglos in the region would have had to relocate to a different tract. The West Indian population was also highly segregated from each of the large Asian groups in 1980. Among these, only the index comparing West Indians and Asian Indians fell below .80.[7] Similar high levels of segregation are revealed in the comparisons of West Indians and most Hispanic subgroups. Indeed, it is interesting to note that, as of 1980, the segregation of West Indians rivaled that of African Americans, the nation's most segregated racial group. West Indians were only slightly less segregated than were African Americans from the Anglo population (.811 versus .832) and had comparable levels of segregation from other groups.

Despite this similarity, West Indians and African Americans were also somewhat segregated from each other in 1980. This residential unevenness should not be overstated, since the dissimilarity index comparing West Indians and African Americans (.438) is in the mid-moderate range. Indeed, West Indians appear to have been substantially less segregated from African Americans than from any other group. On the other hand, the moderate level of segregation between West Indians and African Americans appears to indicate that, as of 1980, West Indians were not evenly distributed within black communities either. Such an indication of somewhat separate pockets of West Indian populations within larger black residential areas is consistent with the patterns of segregation revealed by Waldinger's (1987) examination of 1980 community-board-level data for New York City.

The high level of residential separation of West Indians from Anglos and most other racial and ethnic groups is consistent with the spatial assimilation model's assumption about the initial segregation of new groups in the city. Although West Indians had established a strong presence in the city by 1980, it was only fifteen years after the population's rapid growth was made possible by more liberal immigration laws. It was not until the early 1970s that West Indians began entering the city by the tens of thousands each year. The segregation of West Indians in 1980 may have simply reflected the initial accommodation of these new immigrants. According to the assimilation model, this initially high segregation should have eroded over time.

TABLE 3.2   Indexes of Dissimilarity between Selected Groups
in New York City Boroughs, 1980 and 1990

	West Indians			*African American*		
	1980	1990	Difference	1980	1990	Difference
West Indian	—	—	—	0.438	0.420	−0.018
African American[a]	0.438	0.420	−0.018	—	—	—
Non-Hispanic white	0.811	0.829	0.018	0.832	0.843	0.012
Japanese	0.899	0.918	0.019	0.896	0.906	0.010
Chinese	0.830	0.850	0.020	0.855	0.865	0.010
Filipino	0.839	0.838	−0.001	0.852	0.869	0.017
Korean	0.902	0.907	0.005	0.914	0.914	−0.001
Asian Indian	0.754	0.737	−0.017	0.787	0.807	0.020
Vietnamese	0.949	0.902	−0.047	0.965	0.919	−0.045
Other Asian	0.831	0.780	−0.051	0.828	0.807	−0.021
Mexican	0.700	0.767	0.067	0.629	0.750	0.121
Puerto Rican	0.675	0.667	−0.007	0.571	0.553	−0.018
Cuban	0.731	0.721	−0.011	0.728	0.703	−0.025
Other Hispanic	0.671	0.657	−0.014	0.650	0.638	−0.012
All others	0.609	0.604	−0.006	0.690	0.659	−0.031

[a]Refers to non-Hispanic, non–West Indian blacks.

The index of dissimilarity scores for 1990 (Table 3.2), however, tell a different story. By 1990 the West Indian population had become slightly *more* residentially segregated from non-Hispanic whites (.811 to .829) and from many other groups as well. In general, other ten-year changes in the segregation of West Indians (third column) and African Americans (sixth column) followed similar patterns: both groups became slightly less segregated from Vietnamese, "other Asians," and three of the four Hispanic subgroups. West Indians also experienced a small measure of integration with Asian Indians during the decade. However, both West Indians and African Americans became more segregated from all other groups.

Thus, it does not appear that West Indian New Yorkers experienced any noticeable level of spatial assimilation during the decade, at least in terms of gaining access to majority-dominated areas. Instead the segregation levels of West Indians and the changes therein are quite similar to those of the rest of the non-Hispanic black population—both groups remain highly segregated from the Anglo majority and most other groups. On the other hand, while a slightly lower index of dissimilarity between West Indians and African Americans (.420 versus .438) hints at the possibility of a kind of racially circumscribed assimilation process, these latest data point to a persistently moderate level of segregation between the groups and suggest that West Indians were still not evenly distributed across the black areas of the boroughs.

The exposure and isolation indexes presented in Table 3.3 describe the level of potential residential interaction between the various racial and ethnic groups in the region. These indexes provide further detail to the story conveyed by the indexes of dissimilarity—that the residential patterns of West Indians are similar to those of African Americans, but that important differences exist. The West Indian/non-Hispanic white exposure index of .182 in panel A (third column) indicates that, with the residential distributions prevailing in 1980, a randomly drawn West Indian had about an 18 percent chance of interacting, on the basis of sharing a neighborhood, with a member of the white majority. Similarly, the index of exposure of African Americans to non-Hispanic whites indicates that a randomly drawn African American had about a 13 percent chance of interacting with a white neighbor. Thus, both West Indians and African Americans were subject to residential contexts that were substantially separate from those occupied by non-Hispanic whites.

By 1990 the level of residential contact between these groups and Anglos had declined even more (see panels B and C). In 1990, Anglos made up only 13 percent of the population of the average neighborhood occupied by West Indian New Yorkers and only 10 percent of the average neighborhood occupied by African Americans. These numbers are particularly striking given the fact that non-Hispanic whites alone constituted nearly half of the region's population in 1990.

The isolation indexes presented along the diagonals (in italics) of the panels in Table 3.3 bolster the contention that West Indians occupied somewhat separate residential spaces within the larger black areas of the city. The isolation indexes for African Americans (.563) and non-Hispanic whites (.784) in panel A indicate that, as of 1980, the average member of each of these groups lived in tracts in which their own group represented a strong majority of the population. The high level of isolation experienced by each of these groups represents, in part, the ability to dominate entire census tracts simply by virtue of their large shares of the city's total population. Anglos and African Americans respectively made up 52 and 20 percent of the total population in 1980.

In contrast, West Indians constituted less than 4 percent of the total population in 1980, meaning that it would be far more difficult for the group to make up a majority in any one census tract, even given the highly uneven distribution of the population revealed in the dissimilarity scores in Table 3.2. Nevertheless, in 1980 the isolation index for West Indians was .180. Thus, the average West Indian New Yorker lived in a census tract in which 18 percent of her or his neighbors were also West Indian—a figure well above the 3.9 percent predicted on the basis of population size alone. Moreover, the figures in panel B of Table 3.3 indicate that the level of isolation experienced by West Indians in the city actually *increased* by 1990 ($_xP_x^* = .222$). Again, this figure represents, at least in part, the growing size of the

TABLE 3.3   Indexes of Exposure ($_xP_y{*}$) and Isolation ($_xP_x{*}$)
for New York City Boroughs, 1980 and 1990

A. 1980 Exposure and Isolation Indexes[a]

X-group	Y-group		
	West Indian	*African American*	*Non-Hispanic white*
West Indian	*0.180*	0.440	0.182
African American[b]	0.085	*0.563*	0.129
Non-Hispanic white	0.014	0.049	*0.784*

B. 1990 Exposure and Isolation Indexes

X-group	Y-group		
	West Indian	*African American*	*Non-Hispanic white*
West Indian	*0.222*	0.415	0.132
African American	0.120	*0.521*	0.102
Non-Hispanic white	0.018	0.047	*0.730*

C. 1990–1980 Differences in Exposure and Isolation Indexes

X-group	Y-group		
	West Indian	*African American*	*Non-Hispanic white*
West Indian	*0.042*	−0.026	−0.051
African American	0.035	*−0.043*	−0.027
Non-Hispanic white	0.004	−0.003	*−0.054*

[a]Isolation indexes and their differences are in italics.
[b]Refers to non-Hispanic, non–West Indian blacks.

West Indian population. However, it does directly contradict the expectations of the assimilation model by implying that the level of isolation experienced by the growing West Indian population was maintained and even heightened over time. In contrast, the level of isolation experienced by both African Americans and non-Hispanic whites decreased during the decade (see panel C).

On the one hand, the exposure and isolation indexes in Table 3.3 indicate that, by 1980, West Indian New Yorkers occupied areas in relatively close proximity to their African American counterparts. West Indians were almost two and one-half times more likely to interact with another black on the basis of sharing the same tract than with a member of the white majority (exposure indexes of .440 versus .182), despite the fact that there were nearly three times as many non-

Hispanic whites as African Americans in the five-borough area as of 1980. These numbers reveal the role of race in determining the location of West Indians in New York.

On the other hand, the difference between the score for the interaction of West Indians with African Americans (.440) and the African American isolation index (.563) supports the idea that West Indians remained concentrated in distinct residential areas, somewhat separated from African Americans as well. If West Indians were residentially distributed in the same manner as African Americans, the average West Indian's chances of interacting residentially with an African American would have been more similar to the chance of the average African American interacting with another African American. In essence, the average African American lived in a tract that was just over 56 percent African American, while the average West Indian lived in a tract that was 44 percent African American. Moreover, the residential distinction of West Indians from African Americans became more pronounced over the following decade. By 1990 the representation of African Americans in the tract of the average West Indian had declined (exposure = .415), while the representation of other West Indians in their neighborhoods had increased (isolation = .222).

Overall the patterns of residential segregation experienced by West Indians and the changes therein are fairly inconsistent with expectations based on the spatial assimilation model. West Indians were highly segregated from the Anglo majority by 1980 and actually became somewhat *more* segregated in the following decade, despite the passage of time and the apparent accumulation of socioeconomic resources. Indicating the possibility of assimilation into the larger black community, the segregation of West Indians from African Americans remained less pronounced than their segregation from other groups. But the persistence, and even slight increase, in the segregation of West Indians from African Americans also indicates that the residential incorporation of the West Indian population was far from complete. Instead, the available evidence suggests that a substantial proportion of the city's West Indian population was concentrated in distinct residential enclaves within larger black areas.

THE LOCATION OF WEST INDIAN NEIGHBORHOODS

The maps presented in Figures 3.1–3.3 provide the means to more directly identify and locate the West Indian enclaves hinted at by patterns of segregation in the city. The two separate maps in Figure 3.1 display the residential distribution of all non-Hispanic blacks in 1980 and 1990. Both maps clearly illustrate the persistently high level of segregation experienced by the group as a whole. In both years, the non-Hispanic black population was confined to a few well-defined residential areas, each composed of tightly clustered, mostly black census tracts, largely separate from those areas occupied by whites and other groups. Specifically, three main black areas can be identified from the map: one in the eastern part of Queens, one in central Brooklyn, and one somewhat

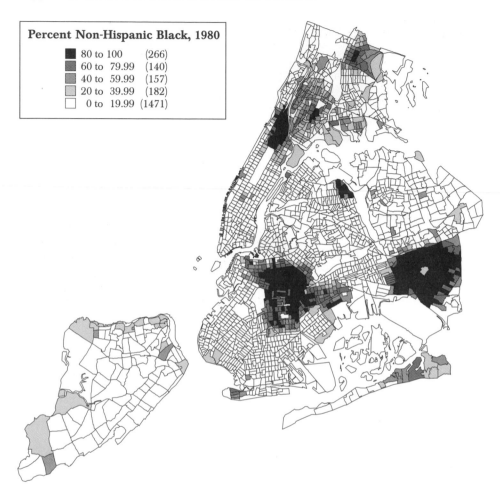

Percent Non-Hispanic Black, 1980

■	80 to 100	(266)
■	60 to 79.99	(140)
■	40 to 59.99	(157)
■	20 to 39.99	(182)
□	0 to 19.99	(1471)

Figure 3.1. Distribution of Non-Hispanic Blacks in New York City, 1980 and 1990

more diffuse area spreading from northern Manhattan through much of the Bronx. Over time, all three of these areas have become somewhat better defined and more solidly black. In 1980 each of these areas were defined by a solid core of census tracts in which the non-Hispanic black population made up between 80 and 100 percent of the total population, surrounded by a contiguous group of tracts that were between 20 and 80 percent black. By 1990 the number of core areas—those between 80 and 100 percent black—had increased in each of these areas, and more peripheral tracts had been added to each agglomeration. But, consistent with segregation scores presented in Tables 3.2 and 3.3, the overarching story conveyed in these maps is that non-Hispanic blacks in New York City's five boroughs remained highly concentrated in well-defined, predominantly black residential areas.

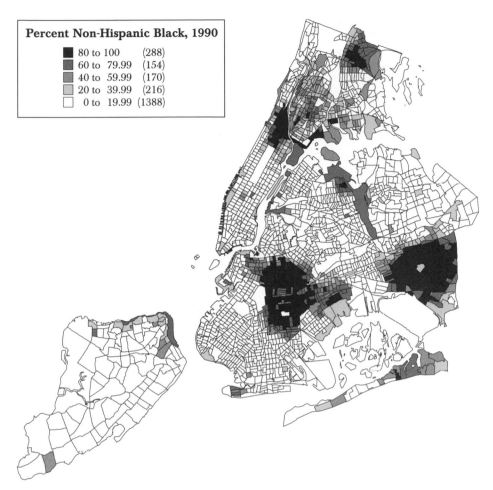

Percent Non-Hispanic Black, 1990

■ 80 to 100   (288)
■ 60 to 79.99   (154)
■ 40 to 59.99   (170)
□ 20 to 39.99   (216)
□ 0 to 19.99   (1388)

Figure 3.1. *(continued)*

More important for the purpose of this chapter are the distributions of West Indians presented in Figures 3.2 and 3.3. Figure 3.2 presents a map with all census tracts in the five boroughs shaded according to the percentage of their total population in 1980 that was made up by first-ancestry West Indians. Figure 3.3 follows the same format in showing the distribution of West Indians in 1990. The clearest conclusion to be drawn from these maps is that the West Indian residents were not distributed evenly across the areas of the city. Instead, by 1980 they were highly concentrated in distinct West Indian neighborhoods constituting highly discernible subsections of each of the city's three large black agglomerations, and these distinct West Indian enclaves persisted into the 1990s.[8] While these West Indian tracts are clearly within the boundaries of the largely black areas illustrated in the maps of Figure 3.1, they also tend to be highly concentrated on the fringes

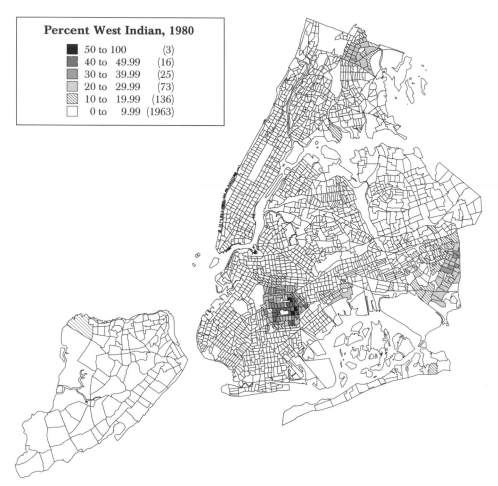

Percent West Indian, 1980

■	50 to 100	(3)
▨	40 to 49.99	(16)
▨	30 to 39.99	(25)
▨	20 to 29.99	(73)
▨	10 to 19.99	(136)
□	0 to 9.99	(1963)

Figure 3.2. Percent West Indian Ancestry in Tracts in New York City, 1980.

of the larger black agglomerations. These maps are quite consistent with the segregation indexes presented in Tables 3.3 and 3.4, which indicate that West Indian New Yorkers experienced greater residential contact with non–West Indian blacks than with members of other groups but were not evenly distributed across the city's black areas.

The maps in Figures 3.2 and 3.3 also make it clear that the distinct West Indian enclaves underwent important changes between 1980 and 1990 that are again consistent with the increase in the group's residential segregation level over the same period. Specifically, each of the enclave areas increased in geographic scale, spreading into adjacent areas. Perhaps more importantly, many of the tracts that had been included in West Indian residential enclaves had become

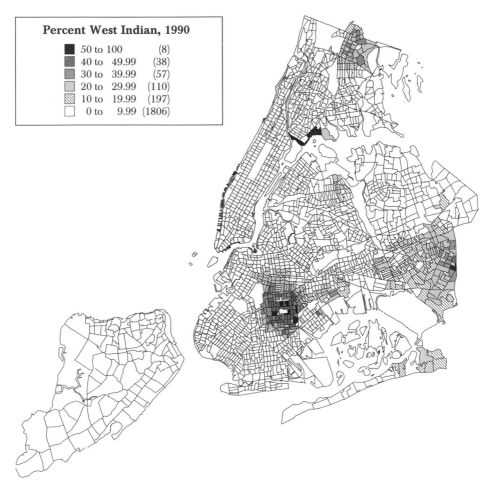

Figure 3.3. Percent West Indian Ancestry in Tracts in New York City, 1990.

more solidly West Indian, with substantially larger group concentrations. For example, in 1980 the north Bronx enclave was clearly centered around Eastchester and in a group of tracts, each 20 to 30 percent West Indian, running along East Gun Hill Road to Williams' Bridge. By 1990 this enclave had expanded south of Gun Hill Road and solidified considerably throughout the area. Eight census tracts surpassed the 30 percent West Indian threshold during the ten-year period.

In a similar fashion, the number of tracts with West Indian concentrations of at least 40 percent and those with concentrations of at least 30 percent both doubled in the East Queens enclave. The tracts defining the core of this enclave, near Laurelton and Cambria Heights in the extreme eastern section of the borough,[9] experienced substantial increases in their West Indian concentrations, and the West Indian population came to constitute over 50 percent of the population in one of these tracts. In addition, by 1990 the enclave had spread considerably, adding new tracts to the west, south, and north within Queens.

Most pronounced was the expansion and solidification of the already well-pronounced central Brooklyn enclave encompassing much of Crown Heights, East Flatbush, and Flatbush. Here the number of tracts in which West Indians constituted 50 percent or more of the total population increased from three in 1980 to five in 1990, and the number of tracts with West Indian concentrations of at least 40 percent nearly tripled. On average, the West Indian population percentage in the tracts making up these three enclaves grew from 17.3 to 25.6 percent.

In addition to the solidification of existing West Indian areas, the decade also saw the possible emergence of new West Indian residential enclaves.[10] Most notably, one small tract near 125th Street and Amsterdam, just north of Morningside Park in Harlem, was over 30 percent West Indian by 1990, with a few surrounding tracts with West Indian concentrations of 10 to 15 percent. In addition, West Indian concentrations increased in the small group of tracts around East Elmhurst in north central Queens, although only three tracts were as much as 20 percent West Indian by 1990.

THE SOURCE OF WEST INDIAN ENCLAVE GROWTH

The pronounced increase between 1980 and 1990 in the West Indian percentages of New York City's West Indian enclaves does not merely reflect the exodus of non–West Indian residents. In fact, the total population in these enclave tracts increased by an average of 7.7 percent (2829 to 3046) during the decade, well exceeding the average population growth for the tracts outside of these enclaves (−0.5%). More importantly, the total *number* of first-ancestry West Indians increased in these enclave areas by an average of over 53 percent (from 528 to 810 per tract). As a result, these enclave areas easily retained their share of the city's growing West Indian population. In 1990 the 330 tracts making up the enclaves constituted just 14.7 percent of the total number of tracts in the city but contained about 64 percent of the city's population of first-ancestry West Indians, up slightly from 63 percent in 1980.

Not surprisingly, one of the most important sources of growth in the numbers of West Indians in these tracts was new immigration from the Caribbean. The number of Caribbean immigrants entering the United States between 1980 and 1990 exceeded that of any previous decade. As Figure 3.4 shows, existing West Indian enclaves and some adjacent areas received more than their share of the new immigrants. The figure makes use of the Census Bureau's "year of entry by place of birth" item to show the percentage of Caribbean immigrants entering New York City between 1980 and 1990 that had settled in each census tract by 1990. It should be noted that these figures are based on census categories that exclude some important groups. For example, the

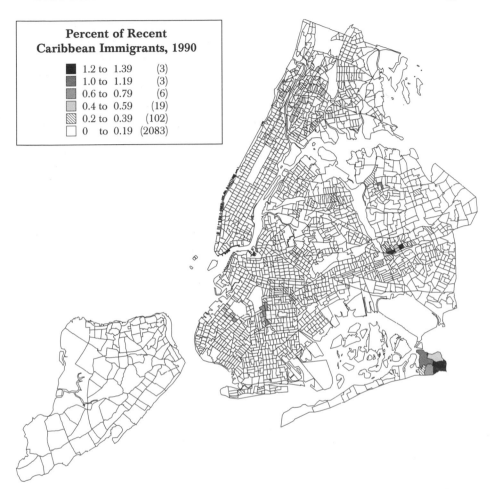

Percent of Recent Caribbean Immigrants, 1990

■	1.2 to 1.39	(3)
■	1.0 to 1.19	(3)
■	0.6 to 0.79	(6)
▨	0.4 to 0.59	(19)
▨	0.2 to 0.39	(102)
□	0 to 0.19	(2083)

Figure 3.4. Percentage of All Recent Caribbean Immigrants to Tracts in New York City, 1990

counts exclude Haitian immigrants, who were included in a less-than-ideal category along with immigrants from Brazil and some other South American countries. Thus, the map in Figure 3.4 likely understates the concentration of recent immigrants settling in enclave areas.

Nevertheless, the story conveyed is fairly clear and not particularly surprising: Caribbean immigrants entering the United States between 1980 and 1990 settled disproportionately in New York's existing West Indian enclaves. Concentrations of recent West Indian immigrants were particularly pronounced near Far Rockaway, in Flatbush, and, appropriately, near Jamaica, Queens—each within or on the fringes of already existing West Indian enclaves. Several of the tracts received a full 1 percent or more of the city's total immigrant population—well above the

0.045 percent expected on the basis of an even distribution of immigrants across all tracts of the city. Together the 326 tracts making up the main West Indian enclaves contained just over 20 percent of the city's recent immigrants. This concentration of recent immigrants is quite consistent with the theory that ethnic enclaves serve as an important resource for the incorporation of new immigrants. And the fact that new immigrants have tended to settle in areas on the fringes of existing West Indian enclaves likely marks an important mechanism through which enclaves have expanded into adjacent areas.

SOCIOECONOMIC CHARACTERISTICS OF WEST INDIAN ENCLAVES

Many of the areas constituting the main West Indian enclaves of New York are near long-established black enclaves, but not long ago they contained significant numbers of white residents. This is especially true of the central Brooklyn enclave, the city's largest and most concentrated West Indian residential area. In the 1970s many whites abandoned their Brooklyn neighborhoods for the city's outer boroughs and suburbs. This white exodus, likely spurred in part by the encroachment of black households, created significant numbers of vacancies and made possible the expansion of the growing black population into these neighborhoods. According to several reports, West Indians may have been among the pioneers in this succession process (Foner 1987; Kasinitz 1992), but other blacks soon followed, and the racial turnover of central Brooklyn was nearly complete by the 1980s. Today African Americans are the largest population group in the area, next to West Indians.

However, as Kasinitz (1992) points out, the West Indian neighborhoods of Brooklyn did not suffer the level of deterioration experienced by areas in the Bronx and Brownsville that underwent similar magnitudes of racial turnover. Thus, there is some indication that the enclaves carved out by West Indians in largely black areas were not only distinguishable by their population composition, but by their relative quality as well. Table 3.4 addresses this issue by examining the characteristics of census tracts separately by the percentages of their populations that are West Indian and those that are African American. The table makes it possible to directly compare the tracts with large West Indian concentrations to those with comparable concentrations of African Americans. Since the table figures are weighted by the total group populations in the tract, they represent, in essence, the average neighborhood characteristics experienced by African Americans and West Indians living in neighborhoods with the given racial and ethnic concentration.

Focusing first on median household income, Table 3.4 indicates that West Indians had established residential niches in relatively affluent neighborhoods. The average median household incomes in West Indian tracts were consistently higher than those in tracts with similar percentages of African Americans. In addition, median household incomes were highest in those tracts with the highest concentrations of West Indians. Income levels in African American neighborhoods at all levels of concentration fell below the city average (see the last column), and African Americans living in areas with the largest concentrations of their own group faced the worst economic conditions.[11] In contrast, West Indians tended to improve their neighborhood economic context by locating themselves in more isolated areas dominated by their own group.

Similarly, at each level of group concentration the West Indian neighborhoods, compared with their African American counterparts, had larger percentages of their population with at least some college education and higher proportions of college graduates. Among West Indian communities, the proportion of the population with at least some college education was highest in those neighborhoods with the largest concentrations of West Indians (50 to 59.99%), substantiating the conclusion that the most ethnically distinct West Indian communities were also of the highest quality. Finally, the relative quality of New York's West Indian enclaves is reflected in figures showing, for each type of neighborhood, the percentage of housing units occupied by the owner. Again, the level of aggregate home ownership experienced in the neighborhood of the average African American was below the city average (24.91%) at all levels of group concentration. Home ownership was consistently more common in West Indian neighborhoods than in comparable African American neighborhoods, and the level of home ownership exceeded the city average in neighborhoods with the most pronounced West Indian concentrations. In areas with 50 to 60 percent of the population comprising members of the given group, only about 27 percent of the housing units in the largely African American communities were occupied by the owner, compared to almost 42 percent of those in West Indian areas.

The stronger socioeconomic conditions of neighborhoods occupied by West Indian New Yorkers in comparison to those occupied by African Americans likely has two sources: the greater income, education, and prevalence of home ownership among West Indians themselves; and the greater ability of West Indians to access neighborhoods occupied by higher-status non–West Indian residents. Regardless of their source, the more favorable socioeconomic characteristics of West Indian neighborhoods relative to those of African American areas also imply a West Indian advantage in terms of access to other locational amenities. Higher median household incomes were an important quality of the neighborhoods in which West Indians settled, since an area's income distribution is crucial in determining the strength of its tax base and, in turn, the quality of its public services, parks, schools, police protection, and even political patronage (Schneider and Logan 1982). Thus, these numbers suggest that West Indians, by carving out somewhat separate residential niches within the larger black community, may have gained some measure of protection from relegation to those largely African American neighborhoods where access to quality public services is most limited.

The second panel of Table 3.4 presents figures on the racial composition and change of those areas occupied by different concentrations of West Indians and

TABLE 3.4 Characteristics of Tracts by Concentration of West Indians and African Americans,[a] Weighted by Total Group Population in the Tract, 1990

| Mean Tract Characteristics | Group Presence in Total Tract Population (in %) | | | | | | | | | | Total Five Boroughs |
| | 20 to 29.99 | | 30 to 39.99 | | 40 to 49.99 | | 50 to 59.99 | | 60 and above | | |
	West Indian	African American	West Indian	African American	West Indian	African American	West Indian	African American	West Indian[b]	African American	
Socioeconomic Characteristics											
Median household income ($1000s)	32.42	21.95	31.96	24.10	32.24	22.57	35.92	27.62	—	22.16	31.48
Percent of adults with some college education	39.34	29.68	38.72	33.17	38.65	30.38	41.09	36.21	—	30.48	38.62
Percent of adults college graduated	14.85	11.84	13.70	13.22	13.58	10.50	14.09	13.52	—	9.64	19.53
Percent of housing units owner occupied, 1990	37.48	17.70	29.24	18.94	29.44	18.00	41.68	27.39	—	24.91	34.67
Racial Composition											
Percent non-Hispanic white, 1980	24.18	27.13	15.41	24.04	14.24	12.92	15.84	12.05	—	3.07	53.31
Change in percent non-Hispanic white, 1980–90	−12.33	−10.99	−9.43	−10.31	−10.57	−6.04	−12.93	−5.82	—	−1.29	−8.53
Percent Asian, 1980	1.85	2.50	2.43	1.95	1.64	1.50	1.51	1.18	—	0.50	3.05
Change in percent Asian, 1980–90	1.41	1.88	−0.57	0.97	0.02	0.19	−0.56	0.26	—	0.06	3.52

Percent											
Hispanic, 1980	13.10	42.49	11.28	31.21	9.34	25.49	7.58	15.94	—	9.15	18.98
Change in percent											
Hispanic, 1980–90	0.93	5.05	−0.79	4.67	−2.92	2.89	−2.78	1.10	—	2.03	3.10
Number of tracts	110	143	57	116	38	114	7	107	—	283	2106

[a]Refers to non-Hispanic, non–West Indian blacks.
[b]Only one tract had a West Indian population higher than 60 percent.

African Americans. At the highest levels of group concentration, the areas occupied by West Indians had larger white populations in 1980 and experienced
greater reductions in these populations between 1980 and 1990 than did areas
occupied by African Americans. The few areas with the highest concentrations
of West Indians (50% and more) had populations that were, on average, almost
16 percent white in 1980. In the following decade, however, the white population of these same tracts declined by an average of thirteen percentage points.
In contrast, areas occupied by comparable concentrations of blacks started out
with lower white percentages and experienced less change in these populations
between 1980 and 1990. Similarly, neighborhoods with high concentrations of
West Indians experienced larger declines in the relative populations of Asians
and Hispanics as well. These racial composition trends are consistent with the
idea that West Indian New Yorkers carved out residential niches with better
socioeconomic characteristics by gaining access to areas formerly occupied by
whites and other nonblack groups.

Overall the figures in Table 3.4 provide an idea of the benefit gained by
West Indians in establishing residential enclaves. Given prevailing patterns of
residential segregation, it can be assumed that West Indians in New York City
would be distributed, on the basis of their race, fairly evenly among highly
black areas if their ethnicity made no difference. The comparison of neighborhoods occupied by West Indians and African Americans suggests that the
average neighborhood context experienced by West Indians would be substantially lower in terms of socioeconomic status without the establishment of
distinct residential enclaves.

DIVERSITY WITHIN WEST INDIAN ENCLAVES

To this point we have focused on New York's emergent West Indian enclaves
as a single entity. In reality, these enclaves have developed with distinct subareas whose diversity mirrors that of the West Indian population itself, with
one of the most important lines of differentiation being defined by specific
ancestries. Figure 3.5 provides maps of each of the three main West Indian
enclaves, shaded according to the specific ancestry composition of each tract
in 1990. These maps provide the opportunity to identify, at least roughly, concentrations of specific ancestry groups within larger West Indian enclaves.

Examining the distributions of eight different West Indian ancestry groups,
we can distinguish a huge number of potential neighborhood group combi-
nations. For this analysis we have chosen to adopt a relatively simple categorization of neighborhoods that allows for an examination of the distribution
of various groups, and their proximity to each other, without the complexity
of considering every possible combination of groups. Specifically, we categorize each tract according to which ancestry group made up the largest share
of the West Indian population in 1990. If no single ancestry group held at

least a ten-percentage-point advantage over the next largest group, the tract is categorized as "ethnically mixed." Since neither U.S. Virgin Islanders nor French West Indians represent the largest group in any one tract, this categorization scheme results in seven primary categories.

Because Jamaicans represented by far the largest West Indian group (see Table 3.1), this simplest scheme potentially hides a good deal of neighborhood diversity, simply classifying the vast majority of neighborhoods as Jamaican. Thus, for those neighborhoods in which Jamaicans constituted the largest group but did not represent at least half of the total West Indian population, we further elaborate on the tract's ancestry composition by distinguishing which group made up the second largest portion of the West Indian population. If no single group held a clear size advantage over other non-Jamaican West Indian groups, we classify the neighborhood as "Jamaican and mixed composition."

Using this system, Figure 3.5 shows some interesting patterns of concentration by ancestry. The simplest composition is found in the north Bronx enclave, where Jamaicans were the largest West Indian group and made up at least half of the total West Indian population of almost every tract. In only three tracts Jamaicans constituted the largest group but made up less than half of the population. In one of these tracts Trinidadian-Tobagonians made up the second largest group, while those classified in the amorphous "other West Indian" category constituted the second largest group in the other two tracts. The dominance of Jamaicans in the Bronx enclave represents the clearest group concentration in the five-borough area.

Jamaicans also represented the largest group in many of the tracts making up the enclave of east Queens. However, there was also a strong concentration of predominantly Haitian tracts in the northeast corner of the enclave, surrounded by a group of tracts in which Jamaicans or a mix of Jamaicans and Haitians made up the West Indian population, along with a set of tracts in which no single group dominated. Also notable is the concentration of Guyanese in a set of tracts in the Richmond Hill area on the western edge of Queens, as well as the area in which non-Jamaican British West Indians and Trinidadian-Tobagonians constituted the largest or second largest group. Each of these groups represented less than 10 percent of the total West Indian population of the city, so their representation as a primary group in this handful of tracts represents a significant level of clustering in these areas. The Queens enclave, more than the enclaves in other boroughs, demonstrates a high level of subgroup concentration even *within* the city's West Indian enclaves and points to the salience of ethnic identity in the determination of residential patterns.

Finally, the enclave in central Brooklyn, which had the highest concentration of West Indian residents in the metropolitan area, clearly contained the greatest diversity of ancestry groups as well. A majority of tracts in the area

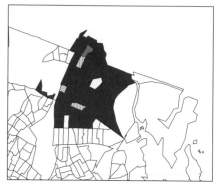

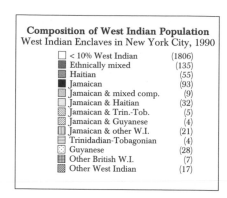

Composition of West Indian Population
West Indian Enclaves in New York City, 1990

☐	< 10% West Indian	(1806)
■	Ethnically mixed	(135)
▦	Haitian	(55)
■	Jamaican	(93)
▨	Jamaican & mixed comp.	(9)
☐	Jamaican & Haitian	(32)
▨	Jamaican & Trin.-Tob.	(5)
▨	Jamaican & Guyanese	(4)
▥	Jamaican & other W.I.	(21)
▤	Trinidadian-Tobagonian	(4)
▨	Guyanese	(28)
▦	Other British W.I.	(7)
▨	Other West Indian	(17)

Map 1: North Bronx Enclave

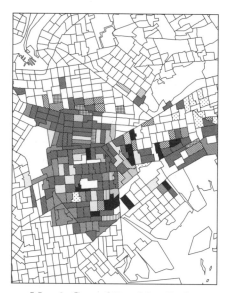

Map 2: Central Brooklyn Enclave

Map 3: East Queens Enclave

Figure 3.5. Composition of West Indian Population in New York City Enclaves, 1990

contained West Indian populations in which multiple groups were roughly equally represented. These diverse tracts included areas identified in Figure 3.3 as having some of the highest overall concentrations of West Indian populations in the city. Also present were four other kinds of areas: a cluster of predominantly Guyanese tracts on the eastern edge of the enclave leading into the Guyanese enclave of western Queens; areas dominated by Haitians, most pronounced in the southwestern corner of the enclave; areas dominated by Jamaicans dispersed throughout the enclave; and areas in which Jamaicans were the largest group but in which Haitians constituted the next largest group, again grouped near the predominantly Haitian southwest. Thus, as was true in the other two enclaves, Haitians and Jamaicans made up a large part of the West Indian population in many of the Brooklyn enclave tracts. In fact, Haitians and Jamaicans were strongly represented in a good many of those tracts categorized as "ethnically mixed." Again, the strong representation of Haitians and Jamaicans should not be surprising, given the large relative size of these groups' populations. However, the fact that Haitian and, to a lesser extent, Jamaican neighborhoods tended to cluster in separate sections of the enclave is noteworthy. Similarly, the fact that tracts defining the northern and eastern fringes of the enclave were dominated by ancestry groups with considerably smaller overall populations is also of interest. In particular, the second map in Figure 3.5 indicates that Trinidadians were the largest group in two adjacent tracts north of Prospect Park in an area with tracts in which British West Indians and "other" ancestry groups also defined the West Indian populations.

Overall, the distribution of ancestry groups leads to two primary conclusions. First, many tracts making up the West Indian enclaves of New York contained a strong diversity of West Indian ancestry groups, with two or more groups making up roughly even proportions of the total West Indian population. But, secondly, there were some pronounced concentrations of specific ancestry groups—even those with relatively small total populations—that highlight the diversity within the West Indian population and the residential cohesion of specific West Indian subgroups.

The diversity of the West Indian enclaves is further highlighted in Table 3.5, where the mean racial, ethnic, and socioeconomic characteristics of the tracts making up the three main West Indian enclaves are presented. For comparison, the table's final column also presents the average characteristics of tracts lying outside of the West Indian enclaves but in which at least 40 percent of the total population is non-Hispanic black.

The table's first panel again shows that, as of 1990, West Indian concentrations were greatest in the large central Brooklyn enclave, followed by the north Bronx, and then east Queens. The next seven lines of the table summarize the specific group composition of these three enclaves. Consistent with the first map of Figure 3.5, the north Bronx was most homogeneous in terms of ancestry composition, with Jamaicans making up, on average, about 70 percent of the total West Indian population of these tracts and the amorphous "other West Indian" category constituting most of the remainder. In contrast, Jamaicans made up just 40 percent of the West Indian population in the less concentrated enclave of east Queens, and Haitians made up over 25 percent. The figures in Table 3.5 also confirm the much stronger diversity

TABLE 3.5   Mean Tract Characteristics of West Indian Enclaves, 1990

| | West Indian Enclave Locations | | | |
	N. Bronx	C. Brooklyn	E. Queens	Nonenclave black[a] tracts
Racial and Ethnic Composition				
Percent West Indian	22.59	30.16	20.66	6.14
Haitian	0.27	6.75	5.18	0.64
Jamaican	15.93	8.60	8.27	1.95
U.S. Virgin Islander	0.17	0.05	0.03	0.07
Trinidadian & Tobagonian	0.58	3.38	1.44	0.48
Guyanese	1.16	3.23	2.05	0.69
British West Indian	1.35	3.78	1.15	0.78
French West Indian	0.01	0.01	0.06	0.02
Other West Indian	3.11	4.35	2.47	1.50
Percent African American	40.12	51.66	61.41	65.49
Percent non-Hispanic white	15.70	8.78	7.54	4.59
Percent Asian	2.10	1.85	3.13	1.17
Percent Hispanic	20.19	10.44	8.58	22.89
Socioeconomic Characteristics				
Percent of housing units owner occupied	42.00	29.40	71.64	18.96
Median household income ($1000s)	33.04	29.81	41.83	19.90
Percent of adults with some college education	36.95	37.83	42.11	28.30
Percent of adults college graduated	14.07	14.08	15.52	9.71
Number of tracts	47	162	118	263

[a]Refers to non-Hispanic, non–West Indian blacks.

of the central Brooklyn enclave, in which Jamaicans made up less than one-quarter of the total West Indian population and the average representation of every other ancestry group was larger than in the tracts making up the other two enclave areas.

The figures in Table 3.5 also cast additional light on the socioeconomic quality and racial and ethnic composition of the three enclaves. Their locations on the outskirts of the city's predominantly black areas but closer, relative to these black areas, to nonblack areas is indicated by the fact that non-Hispanic white and Asian residents were represented in greater numbers in the tracts of all three enclaves than in the city's other black tracts. Most pronounced is the fact that

Anglos made up, on average, more than 15 percent of the population in the tracts of the north Bronx enclave. Nevertheless, even within these enclaves, African Americans are the single group with which West Indian New Yorkers have their greatest residential contact. Only in the north Bronx did African Americans make up less than a majority of the average tract population. From these figures and the maps presented in Figures 3.1–3.3, West Indian enclaves appear to form a kind of physical, if not social, buffer between African American neighborhoods and those occupied by other groups.

The figures in Table 3.5 also reveal the socioeconomic differentiation of New York's three main West Indian enclaves. In general, the east Queens enclave appears to be of markedly higher status than both the Brooklyn and Bronx enclaves. The average median household income of the tracts in east Queens was almost $42,000 in 1990, substantially higher than the averages for the central Brooklyn ($29,810) and north Bronx ($33,040) enclaves. Similarly, the percentage of people owning their own home was almost two and one-half times as high in the Queens enclave as in the Brooklyn enclave and over 70 percent higher than in the Bronx. But perhaps the most important contrast to be drawn from these figures is between the enclave and nonenclave black areas. Despite their diversity, the socioeconomic characteristics of the tracts in all three of the enclaves were substantially more favorable than those of the average nonenclave black tract. On average, the tracts making up these enclaves not only had greater relative numbers of college-educated residents, but also home ownership levels that were between 55 and 278 percent higher and average income levels between 50 and 110 percent higher than in the average nonenclave black tract.

CONCLUSION

The incorporation of West Indian blacks has had a profound impact on the social, economic, and political structure of New York City. By virtue of their shear numbers alone, and especially by virtue of their rapid growth in the past three decades, Caribbean New Yorkers have helped to alter the ethnic composition of the city's population. More importantly, in the process of adapting to their unique set of social, economic, ethnic, and racial barriers and advantages, and in carving out a niche in the city, Caribbean New Yorkers have altered the city's social context. Few would disagree that the incorporation of West Indians has added to the complexity of what it means to be black in New York.

The impact of West Indians has perhaps been most pronounced in the reshaping of the city's neighborhoods. In this chapter we have attempted to trace recent developments in the creation of West Indian neighborhoods. Data from the 1980 and 1990 censuses were used to examine the emergence, solidification, and metamorphosis of these neighborhoods over a ten-year period. The residential patterns revealed reflect the complex intersection of race, ethnicity, and collective and individual resources shared by West Indian New Yorkers.

One conclusion to be drawn from this analysis is that race remains a primary determinant of the residential incorporation of West Indian blacks. Despite their somewhat more favorable socioeconomic position (Crowder 1999; Foner 1985; Harrison 1992; Kalmijn 1996), the potential social advantages associated with a distinct West Indian ancestry (Bryce-Laporte 1972; Foner 1979, 1985; Waters 1994a), and the supposed superiority of West Indian culture (Glazer and Moynihan 1970; Sowell 1978), West Indians were no more able than African Americans to gain residential access to neighborhoods occupied by the Anglo majority. Presumably on the basis of their race, West Indians in the area were concentrated in largely black areas of the city and remained highly segregated from all but the African American population. In contradiction to the expectations of the assimilation model, the segregation of West Indians from non-Hispanic whites and most other major racial and ethnic groups actually *increased* between 1980 and 1990. Thus, to the extent that they are assimilated residentially, West Indians appear to face relegation to black residential areas.

But the story is more complex than this assessment implies. Even a casual observer on the streets in Flatbush or Cambria Heights realizes that, despite their racial composition, these are not just black neighborhoods—they are West Indian neighborhoods. Consistent with earlier studies (Crowder 1999; Waldinger 1987), the present analysis shows that West Indians were not evenly distributed throughout the black residential areas of the five boroughs. Instead, by 1980 West Indians had established somewhat separate, ethnically distinct residential enclaves within black areas, and over time these enclaves became both larger, in terms of geographic area, and more consolidated. These areas and adjacent neighborhoods have served as primary destinations for a disproportionate share of West Indian immigrants entering New York City between 1980 and 1990. As a result, over 60 percent of New York's West Indian population lived in one of three main West Indian enclaves as of 1990. Further indicating the impact of ethnicity in shaping residential patterns is the fact that, within the West Indian enclaves, distinct subareas dominated by specific national-origin groups emerged. While Jamaicans dominated many areas, especially in the north Bronx, Haitians showed a strong concentration in Brooklyn and the east Bronx enclave, while the fast growing Guyanese population carved out a distinct niche in western Queens. Similarly, Trinidadians and other non-Jamaican ancestry groups dominated a few West Indian enclave tracts. Only in central Brooklyn were tracts with fairly even mixtures of West Indian ancestry groups the norm.

Perhaps most importantly, the evidence suggests that New York's West Indian residential enclaves have been established in some of the most favorable parts of larger black residential areas—that is, in formerly white neighborhoods with more affluent and highly educated occupants and higher rates of home ownership. Thus, the evidence suggests that, while largely confined to predominantly black areas, the West Indian population has avoided relegation to the most depressed black neighborhoods by establishing relatively high-quality residential niches in racially changing neighborhoods on the fringes of larger black sectors.

The establishment of these niches points to the relative advantage of West Indian ancestry in altering the impact of race on residential patterns. What is less clear is the source of this advantage. One possible explanation for the entry into better-quality neighborhoods by West Indians, and especially their more ready access to formerly white areas, is that they face less intense racial discrimination than do African Americans (Foner 1985; Garcia 1986; Kasinitz 1992). However, the fact that West Indians and African Americans experience similar overall levels of segregation from Anglos suggests that any West Indian advantage in this regard is minor at best.

An alternative explanation is that West Indians' establishment of separate, somewhat better-quality neighborhoods, even in the face of racial discrimination, is rooted in the combined effect of their higher average socioeconomic characteristics and their utilization of various ethnic resources. Insofar as securing capital is an important factor in residential self-determination, the modest socioeconomic advantage of West Indians relative to African Americans—whether rooted in a distinct West Indian culture (Glazer and Moynihan 1970; Sowell 1978), the selective nature of West Indian migration (Light 1972; Model 1995; Steinberg 1989), or their unique mode of incorporation into the broader black community (Foner 1979, 1985; Kasinitz 1992)—may be important in explaining the groups' divergent residential patterns. Moreover, the impact of even a modest West Indian advantage in this respect is likely to be magnified by the utilization of informal, ethnically based systems of credit and capital accumulation, which have likely provided many West Indians access to the resources necessary to purchase homes (Foner 1979; Bonnett 1981; Garcia 1986; Kasinitz 1992; Light 1972), thereby increasing their access to better-quality neighborhoods dominated by owner-occupied housing. In contrast, African Americans have been forced to deal with often discriminatory outside lending associations and banks (Massey and Denton 1993; Yinger 1995), further limiting their opportunities for home ownership. In addition, formal and informal realty networks that steer West Indian clientele into ethnic areas are perhaps crucial to the formation and maintenance of distinctly West Indian neighborhoods. High ownership levels and informal ethnic networks help to maintain ethnic neighborhoods, as West Indians often adhere to ethnic and familial ties when deciding where to buy a home (Kasinitz 1992). Even in tracts with limited numbers of single-family homes, West Indians often purchase apartment buildings and rent almost exclusively to other West Indians (Kasinitz 1992; Laguerre 1984; Waldinger 1987). Once established, enclaves are maintained and grow through the influx of new immigrants, being bolstered, as are many other immigrant enclaves, by ethnic networks and chain migration.

To varying extents, each of the mechanisms supporting the creation of West Indian enclaves hinges on the strength of ethnic solidarity. In particular, the maintenance of ethnic ties and the utilization of ethnic and class resources facilitate the development and maintenance of distinctly West Indian neighborhoods in fairly high-quality black areas and serve to channel ethnic resources into these areas. In a reciprocal fashion, the development of enclaves may be an important tool in the maintenance of a somewhat protective ethnic distinctiveness. The incongruence between the more complex, if not more innocuous, racial dynamics of their origin society and the problematic racial dichotomy of the United States creates a dilemma for West Indian immigrants. In the United States, West Indians often share with African Americans a racial identity forged by common experiences with racism (Vickerman 1994). But most West Indians also view themselves as distinct from African Americans (Foner 1985; Waters 1991, 1994a; Vickerman 1994), and, as Foner (1985) points out, they have a vested interest in maintaining this distinction. Insofar as West Indian blacks are viewed in a more favorable light than are African Americans, maintaining ethnic distinctiveness may lessen the sting of racism and provide a measure of protection against relegation to America's lowest social position.

In many instances, this complex interaction of race and ethnicity forces West Indian blacks to carve out an intermediate social position that allows them to maintain ethnic distinctiveness within a society that regards them as black. An important mechanism for maintaining ethnic identity may very well be the formation of ethnic neighborhoods with distinctive Caribbean institutions, businesses, and cultural flavor (Conway and Bigby 1987; Kasinitz 1992) and that are themselves supported by West Indian ethnic solidarity. In essence, the maintenance of ethnic identity and the creation of ethnic neighborhoods with relatively favorable socioeconomic characteristics are reciprocal processes that provide a measure of social protection for West Indian blacks.

The analysis presented here leaves many questions unanswered, two of which are of particularly high priority for future research. First, more work needs to be done to distinguish the specific mechanisms through which distinctively West Indian neighborhoods are supported. Specifically, research should concentrate on the relative impacts of racial barriers, socioeconomic advantages, and ethnic resources in the formation and maintenance of West Indian enclaves. Second, and perhaps more importantly, future research should focus on the repercussions of enclave life on the individual and collective levels. An analysis of secondary data like the one presented here cannot capture the nature of social relationships within these neighborhoods and falls short of distinguishing how these relationships help to shape economic, political, and social opportunities for individual West Indians. Nevertheless, the patterns described in this study do provide important insights into the impact of the interactions between race, ethnicity, and socioeconomic status on the ever changing residential landscape of New York.

NOTES

1. Our definition of West Indian first ancestry includes individuals who report their first ancestry as Jamaican, Haitian, U.S. Virgin Islander, Trinidadian or Tobagonian, Guyanese, French West Indian, British West Indian, or in the panethnic West Indian category. West Indians may also be undercounted because of incomplete census coverage (Fern 1990), a problem exacerbated by the fact that some West Indians living in the United States are undocumented residents (Foner 1987; Model 1995; Warren and Passel 1987). Undercount is likely to affect our conclusions regarding aggregate population distributions. It is also likely to affect estimates based on a census's ancestry or place-of-birth items. However, this bias may be fairly small given improvements in census coverage (Fern 1990) and generally modest differences between the characteristics of undocumented immigrants included in the census and those not enumerated (Chiswick 1988).

2. It should be noted that the substantive conclusions obtained using a place-of-birth definition of the West Indian population are virtually identical to those presented here.

3. Census tracts are an imperfect operationalization of neighborhoods because they represent only "statistical neighborhoods" defined without regard to the level of interaction between residents (Tienda 1991) and because they fail to capture the highly variable social construction of neighborhood boundaries (Guest and Lee 1984; Hunter 1974). However, the wide availability of census data for tracts makes them an attractive and popular choice for describing residential patterns and for the calculation of segregation indexes.

4. The indexes of dissimilarity are calculated as

$$D_i = \sum [t_i \, |p_i - P| \, / \, 2TP(1 - P)],$$

where t_i and p_i are the total population and minority proportion of areal unit i, and T and P are the population size and minority proportion of the city as a whole. A full description of the index's properties is found in Massey and Denton (1988).

5. Exposure indexes are calculated as

$$_xP^*_y = \sum [x_i \, / \, X][y_i \, / \, t_i],$$

where x_i, y_i, and t_i represent the number of X-group members, Y-group members, and total population of areal unit i, respectively, and X represents the number of X-group members in the entire city. Isolation indexes are calculated in the same manner but compare exposure of X-group members to other X-group members rather than to Y-group members.

6. For this analysis the African American reference group is defined as all non-Hispanic blacks not reporting a West Indian ancestry. It should be noted that the designation of this non-Hispanic, non–West Indian black population as African American undoubtedly disguises a great deal of ethnic diversity within the black population and is used here simply as a convenient basis for comparison.

7. This somewhat lower (but still high) level of segregation of West Indians from Asian Indians probably reflects the residential patterns of Trinidadian and Guyanese West Indians, many of whom are themselves of Asian Indian descent and tend to live in relatively close proximity to other Asian Indians, especially in the Richmond Hill area of Queens.

8. Using 1990 population figures, an enclave is identified as a group of *contiguous* tracts containing at least one *core tract* in which 30 percent or more of the population reports a West Indian first ancestry and whose other tracts have West Indian concentrations of

above 10 percent. Tracts were also classified as enclave tracts if they were removed from the contiguous enclave tracts by no more than a single tract. It should be noted that the 10 percent threshold used here is nearly twice the representation of first-ancestry West Indians (5.7%) in the five-borough region's total population in 1990.

9. The enclave also stretches outside of the borough into Nassau County.

10. The one long tract near Port Morris at the southern edge of the Bronx is somewhat anomalous. This tract had a population of zero in 1980 and increased to only thirty-two by 1990, with six occupied housing units. Since all of the residents in 1990 were Haitian, the area is shaded consistent with the "50 to 100 percent" category, but it would be misleading to classify this tract as a true enclave.

11. It is possible that the mean characteristics of the African American neighborhoods in Table 3.4 reflect the influence of a few poor and predominantly African American tracts dominated by public housing. To test for this influence, the data were reanalyzed excluding those predominantly black tracts in which the percentage of households receiving public assistance lay above the 90th percentile. This reanalysis produced differences between African American and West Indian neighborhoods that were only slightly diminished and supported the same conclusions as those presented here.

PART TWO

Transnational Perspectives

FOUR

Transnational Social Relations and the Politics of National Identity

An Eastern Caribbean Case Study

Linda Basch

Over the past eighteen years I have continued to attend—and be dazzled by—vibrant political meetings in Brooklyn at which political leaders from the small, eastern Caribbean nation-states of St. Vincent and Grenada, visiting New York, meet with immigrants from their countries.[1] The political leaders generally inform the migrants in detail of affairs "at home" and identify numerous ways migrants can—and need to—remain involved "at home" by participating in elections, investing in local undertakings, sponsoring projects for the good of "the nation," and informing their relatives of world affairs. The most dramatic meeting, despite its uncharacteristically somber demeanor, occurred in April 1984. As described in my field notes,

> Herbert Blaize, a former colonial chief minister of Grenada, was addressing a crowd of approximately six hundred Grenadians of varying ages and seemingly different classes. The venue was a well-appointed catering hall owned by a Grenadian immigrant. It was only a few months after the assassination of the Grenadian prime minister, Maurice Bishop. Blaize, who had declared himself a contender for the prime ministership, had come to New York to seek the financial support and influence of the immigrant community. The meeting had been organized by a support group for Blaize located in New York. The group was headed by Lamuel Stanislaus, a highly respected political leader in the Grenadian immigrant community and a long-time friend and former political ally of Blaize.
>
> The audience raised many questions and expressed apprehension about the direction in which Blaize would take Grenada if elected. Bishop's assassination had been followed by the military occupation of Grenada by U.S. forces. Bishop, in his attempts to lessen Grenada's dependence on the United States and steer a more autonomous course, had established close ties with Cuba and the Soviet Union. Although some Grenadians had applauded this seemingly

independent course, others were worried that Grenada's new alliances would enable the spread of communism in the Caribbean.

Some in the middle classes who owned property in Grenada were concerned that their property might have been confiscated by the Bishop government and redistributed to the peasantry. They asked what safeguards Blaize would create to protect property owned by immigrants abroad. Others wondered whether there would be overseas voting registration so that immigrants could vote in the upcoming election.

Blaize underscored his party's respect for personal property, at the same time drawing on a rhetoric of autonomy to assert that "anyone who gives aid must come with clean hands, with no strings attached." This included all outside interests—Soviet, Cuban, and American. He also emphasized the importance of the immigrant constituency to Grenada, pointing out that, while there were 90,000 Grenadians living in Grenada, only 32,000 of whom were adults, there were 60,000 adult Grenadians living in North America, many of whom owned property at home.

This vignette illustrates the many ways Grenadian and Vincentian immigrants remain involved with their home countries. Several of the immigrants attending this meeting owned land and houses in Grenada, and some had business interests and investments there, such as hotels, farms, and transportation companies. Others were involved in activities spanning Grenada and New York, such as small shipping companies. Still others, like Stanislaus and the other organizers of the meeting, were involved in politics at home— campaigning for candidates during elections or returning to Grenada to run for political office themselves. These involvements continue, even though many of the same immigrants also own homes and businesses in Brooklyn— the very catering hall in which the meeting was held was immigrant- owned—and are U.S. citizens. Lamuel Stanislaus, for example, left Grenada in the mid 1940s to attend dental school at Howard University, is a prominent dentist in Brooklyn, where he owns his home, is a U.S. citizen, and has been involved in various ways in New York politics, including heading the Caribbeans for Koch Committee.

These simultaneous involvements in the United States and in the countries that the immigrants still call home, constitute *transnational social practices*.[2] Transnational practices are the processes by which migrants forge and sustain simultaneous multistranded social relations that link together their societies of origin and settlement. These relations occur along the lines of family, economic, and political relations. As in the case of many of the Grenadian immigrants attending this meeting, immigrants, through their transnational practices, build *transnational social fields* that cross geographic, cultural, and political borders (Basch, Glick Schiller, and Szanton Blanc 1994: 7). Immigrants who maintain relationships that span these borders are *transmigrants*.

The behavior of the transmigrants attending this meeting also demonstrates the multiple forces shaping immigrant identity. On the one hand, the immigrants' identities are influenced by their everyday experiences in U.S. society and in Brooklyn—as residents (and some as homeowners and even citizens), parents of school children, workers, and as black immigrants in a multicultural society that both "ethnicizes" and "racializes." But immigrants' identities are also shaped by their experiences in their home societies and their continuing ties to home. The transmigrants at this meeting were responsive to the exhortations of Blaize and Stanislaus because of these ties. Blaize's statements carefully sought, in the wake of the political turbulence of the previous decade in Grenada, which had exacerbated Grenadian social divisions, to strengthen the immigrants' identifications with the Grenadian nation and make new claims on their loyalty. By underscoring his party's respect for private property and the attraction of industrial investments at home, and by invoking a rhetoric of autonomy, Blaize was attempting to reach out to Grenadian immigrants of all classes and unite them behind an encompassing national ideology.

The claims made by Blaize and Stanislaus on the immigrants' loyalties and identities demonstrate a particular strategy of nation-state building. In this paper, the *state* is defined as the policies, practices, and bureaucratic structures that organize a population within a given territory. *Nation* represents the ideology that creates a sense of peoplehood and unity among those individuals encompassed by the state. *Nation-state building* is therefore the set of practices that link the diverse populations associated with the state and forge a loyalty to the institutions, practices, and ideologies of the state (Basch, Glick Schiller, and Szanton Blanc 1994: 36–38). Confronted with situations of extreme economic impoverishment and dependency and the large-scale emigration of large sectors of the more educated and skilled among their populations, Caribbean[3] political leaders treat transmigrants residing abroad as part of the body politic and make claims on them as active and loyal members of their nation-states, even though the transmigrants may be citizens of the states in which they reside. Leaders call on symbols and representations that can unite immigrants across class, gender, and generational differences and encourage them to view themselves as a single people. This strategy, which treats the boundaries of nation-states as elastic, defining them in social rather than geographic terms, is called *deterritorialized nation-state building.*[4]

In this chapter, I explore processes of deterritorialized nation-state building occurring in the transnational social fields created by Vincentian and Grenadian migrants to New York, depicting how this construct of the nation-state and its claims builds on multistranded transnational practices. I also identify the forces that give rise to and make transmigrants responsive to deterritorialized nation-state building, forces that are grounded in the present conditions of global capitalism but are also shaped by the particulars of Caribbean history and culture and U.S. nation-state building. First, however, I turn to the ways Vincentian and Grenadian transnational social practices, and the immigrants' responsiveness to the claims of political leaders from their home countries, shed light on some thorny theoretical issues in transnational studies.

SITUATING VINCENTIAN AND GRENADIAN MIGRATION WITHIN TRANSNATIONAL STUDIES

Over the past decade, transnational processes have become a focal point of analysis in a number of fields such as anthropology, sociology, political science, and cultural studies. While the general focus of transnational studies has been on processes that transcend or cross the borders of nation-states, the units of study have been diverse, and have included capital, individuals, groups, organizations, corporations, social movements, states, identities, citizenship, cultural representations, and ideas. Because of the complexity of transnational processes and the multiple levels involved, a number of tough questions have emerged. These questions probe what actually constitutes an appropriate unit of analysis in transnational studies, whether transnational processes are in fact a new historical phenomenon and how they differ from previous cross-border movements, and what can be inferred from processes of transnationalism, in this era of globalization, regarding the continuing salience of nation-states. Vincentian and Grenadian transnational practices, and the construct of the deterritorialized nation-state, contribute in various ways to our understanding of all these questions.

Migration as a Key Unit of Study for Understanding Transnational Practices

Increasingly, theorists have expressed concern that the broad use of the concept transnationalism threatens to diminish its analytic potential (see Portes, Guarnizo, and Landolt 1999; Guarnizo and Smith 1998; Mahler 1998) and have endeavored to bring analytic clarity to transnational studies. A number of studies that have contributed to the development and refinement of transnational theory have centered on migrants moving across borders.

My own work is in this camp. My understanding of transnational processes emanates from my comparative research on the social, cultural, political, and economic relations of eastern Caribbean migrants moving regionally to Trinidad and internationally to New York. My research questions have built on the early work of Sutton (1969), who documented the number of relatives and friends of Barbadian villagers who lived off the island and the ideas that were filtering across the borders of villages, nations, and states as villagers kept in touch with their relations abroad. Later, Sutton and Makiesky-Barrow (1987) documented the bidirectional exchange of ideas occurring during the Black Power movement in a space that encompassed the migrants' home country

(Barbados) and migration destinations (New York and England). My research also owes a debt to the early studies of migrants to the African Copperbelt of Northern Rhodesia (now Zambia) (Epstein 1958; Mitchell 1956, 1969). Copperbelt migrants were entering into an urban social system while at the same time maintaining their social ties and identifications with their regions of origin. In trying to capture the experience of these migrants, Copperbelt researchers discussed a wider social field that encompassed both the rural and urban areas of Northern Rhodesia. Finally, my insights into the implications of transnational processes for understanding the role of nation-states, race, and ethnicity at the present moment in history emanate from my collaborative work with Nina Glick Schiller and Cristina Szanton Blanc (Basch, Glick Schiller, and Szanton Blanc 1994; Glick Schiller, Basch, and Blanc-Szanton 1992).

In trying to delimit the present scope of transnational studies, Portes, Guarnizo, and Landolt (1999: 219) have argued that transnational processes must include a "high intensity of exchanges, . . . new modes of transacting, and the multiplication of activities that require cross-border travel and contacts on a sustained basis." They assert that the unit of analysis must be defined (and in their own research argue that individuals and their networks are the most viable point of departure). Nonetheless, in recognizing the diversity and multilevel character of transnational processes, they and others (Appadurai 1996; Guarnizo and Smith 1998; Mahler 1998) have tried to distinguish between *transnationalism from above*—meaning transnational corporations, media, commodification, and other macrolevel structures and processes including "mediascapes," "technoscapes," and "the global cultural economy" (Appadurai 1990)—and *transnationalism from below*. The latter phrase refers to the grassroots or everyday activities of migrants and their relations, to social movements, and to coalitions. Using a broad brush, this distinction provides a heuristic device for distinguishing between structural forces and agency. As this chapter illustrates, to understand transnational processes in the context of the small island states of the former Anglo-Caribbean, it is important to look at both macro- and micro-processes, that is, transnationalism from both above and below. Transnational social fields are forged by a variety of multistranded, multilevel transnational relationships and processes.

How Unique Are Present-Day Transnational Practices?

Several analysts have emphasized the importance of identifying the conditions underlying transnational relations—that is, the particular relations of global capital and politics (Basch, Glick Schiller, and Szanton Blanc 1994; Kearney 1995; Portes 1995b; Rouse 1992; Robotham 1998) and the level of technology, communications, and transportation available (Portes, Guarnizo, and Landolt 1999). These factors are seen as especially important in distinguishing present transnational processes of migration from those of earlier periods, when migrants also went back and forth between countries of origin and destination. In fact, many of the political movements that led to the demise of colonialism in Africa, Asia, and the Caribbean were built by immigrants living in diasporas. Yet, for the most part, the transnational exchanges among diverse sectors of the population and the multiplicity of transnational activities were less intense prior to the 1980s.

In part, the migrants' heightened interactions with home societies after 1980 can be related to the ready availability of cheap, frequent, and fast communications and transportation and, by the mid 1990s, to advances in cyberspace. Even more important, however, are current relations of capital and the way these relations have enmeshed most of the world in a global mode of production. The chief features of the present system are the slipping of parts of the world economy into economic crises, the transformation of local and global labor markets, and the trend toward an increased internationalization of capital. In the 1970s, corporations owned and controlled by interests in core capitalist countries began to set up production in areas previously marginal to industrial capitalist development, where they found low-cost labor that was politically controllable. In countries like the United States and England, well-paying, unionized manufacturing employment declined, to be superceded by service-sector and clerical employment. Factories closed, wages and benefits declined, and underemployment grew, as did a contingent labor force.

The global restructuring of capital had particularly negative effects on local economies in the Third World. The recipients of large loans from the World Bank, the International Monetary Fund, and international banks, Third World countries found themselves committed to an increasing level of debt service. In 1980 these countries were the net recipients of 39.6 billion dollars of capital; by 1986, however, the amount of capital that flowed into these countries through private investment and foreign aid was exceeded by a net outflow of 24 billion dollars (Knight 1989: 32). The effect was a disruption of local economies and an increased pool of available labor as whole families migrated to urban areas, drawn by the possibility of jobs with foreign-capitalized industrial undertakings. Such opportunities were usually short-lived, however. Foreign-owned firms, ever in search of lower costs and resistant to fair labor practices that would increase production expenses, soon took off to other countries, leaving behind a displaced labor pool ready for further, often international migration. As Robotham shows for Jamaica, the structural adjustment policies of the 1980s "threw broad segments of the [Jamaican] people . . . as traders and owners of small property . . . into the transnational marketplace as migrants" (1998: 317).

But the present mode of global production also provides opportunities for migrants with certain sets of skills and educational backgrounds. International organizations and corporations have hired many West Indian professionals, thereby turning them into transmigrants. And U.S. institutions of higher education actively recruit West Indian students, whom they find well prepared for U.S. college curricula.

Regardless of the conditions underlying their migration, however, most migrants at some point confront fragile circumstances in their countries of migration, and they often find themselves socially, politically, and economically vulnerable. As Ballard points out, "[a]s long as they are identifiable, they will always be in danger. In times of adversity, outsiders make ideal scapegoats" (Ballard 1987: 18).

The Continuing Salience of Nation-States

In the social sciences and in cultural studies, transnational processes have been seen as part of the broader phenomenon of globalization linked to the restructuring of capital. This analysis has emphasized the diminishing significance of national boundaries in the production of goods and services and has been extended to trying to understand the movement of people and ideas across national borders. To many analysts, transnationalism suggests an emerging "postnational world" in which the salience of nation-states recedes as people become involved in "postnational movements, organizations, and spaces" (Appadurai 1993: 428). Some observers, such as Kearney in his work with Mixtec Indian migrants in California, have seen transnational space as liberated, counterhegemonic political space (Kearney 1991) in which the practices and identities of migrants constitute "counternarratives of the nation" (Bhabha 1990: 300).

Other observers, such as Verdery in her research on post-Soviet Eastern Europe, see transnationalism and nationalism as "mutually constitutive," even within a global context (Verdery 1998: 292). Verdery grounds her analysis in issues of citizenship and property rights and observes that, for individuals confronting state policies and practices of exclusion both at home and abroad, citizenship "ties [members of the state] to the state as the guarantor of their rights, thus incorporating them as subjects" (293). In the case of Eastern European migrants, voting rights for those residing abroad are an important component of "transnational citizenship rights" (296). Verdery also underscores the "nexus among state, property, and national identity," for "landholding is the ultimate insurance policy and pension plan" (296). Similar to the East Europeans Verdery is observing, eastern Caribbean migrants from St. Vincent and Grenada are actively caught up in the nation-building projects and values of their home countries as well as their host countries. Citizenship, property, and voting rights are key elements in their relationship to both. While transnational space or social fields provide migrants with options, rather than being hegemonically liberated, eastern Caribbean migrants experience the simultaneous pulls of their home nation-states and of their host countries, which create myriad contradictions for migrants' loyalties and identities. The "deterritorialized nationalism" Verdery has observed among East Europeans seems similar in some ways to the deterritorialized nation-state building Glick Schiller, Szanton Blanc, and I have observed among Caribbean and Philippine migrants.

SHAPING VINCENTIAN AND GRENADIAN TRANSNATIONAL SOCIAL FIELDS: KIN, ECONOMIC, AND POLITICAL NETWORKS

Transnational social fields are important sites of opportunity for individuals, families, communities, and nation-states. Through relationships that extend across this space, status and class positions can be advanced, educations gained, and political and economic positioning maximized as well as challenged. In order to understand transnational processes in the context of the tiny islands of the Anglo-Caribbean, it is necessary to look at both macro- and micro-processes—that is, transnationalism from both above and below. The contours of present-day Vincentian and Grenadian transnational practices and of Vincentian and Grenadian nation-state building are shaped in part by the historical experiences of these island states.

West Indian Migration Traditions: A Building Block of Transnational Social Relations

Transnational migration is a central part of the histories of Vincentian and Grenadian political economy and social life. As creations of global capitalist expansion, with peasant agricultural resource bases that were too scant to sustain growing populations, St. Vincent and Grenada early on became sources of migrant labor for capital development elsewhere. The first migrations, beginning in the mid 1800s, shortly after the end of slavery, remained within the nearby Caribbean—first to the late developing, more resource-endowed British colonial territories of Trinidad and Guyana, and then in the nineteenth and early twentieth centuries to Panama, Cuba, and Costa Rica, where Vincentian and Grenadian workers took on seasonal, short-term plantation and construction work and helped to build the Panama Canal. From 1888 to 1911, at least one quarter of the forty thousand inhabitants of St. Vincent were reported to have emigrated (Toney 1986: 22), and between 1911 and 1921, out-migration was so heavy that Grenada actually experienced a reduction in population (Singham 1968: 68). In the early 1900s, Vincentians and Grenadians joined other West Indians in migration streams to the United States. By the 1950s, these international migrants began fanning out to England, where Vincentians and Grenadians, along with other West Indians, provided needed skilled and semiskilled labor for the labor-scarce postwar economy. At the same time, migration continued within the Caribbean to such local economic growth poles as the oilfields and sugar plantations of Trinidad, Aruba, Curacao, and Cuba, as well as the gold fields of Guyana.

Both remittances home and plans for eventual return were important parts of Vincentian and Grenadian migration from the outset, so much so that migrants' savings were seen as important components of their islands' economies and out-migration was actively encouraged by colonial administrators. In 1951, the colonial administrator of St. Vincent publicly proclaimed, "the employment of workers outside the colony greatly assists the social and economic well-being of the people" (cited in Toney 1986: 23–26). At this time, both the Vincentian and Grenadian governments actively supported efforts to recruit their populations as contract farm labor for the United States. Whether emigrating as short-term contract workers or longer-term migrants, the vulnerability that surrounded their economic situations led the migrants to maintain bases at home, to which many returned. During the depression, from 1932 to 1937, the number of West Indians returning home exceeded those entering (Reid, cited in Kasinitz 1992: 24). To this day, West Indian immigrants, who are often at the lowest rungs of occupational hierarchies and are frequently low in seniority, are among the first to be laid off in times of economic trouble.

Labor migration patterns have contributed to what ethnographers of social life on these and other small Caribbean islands have described as *migration traditions* (Philpott 1973; B. Richardson 1983; Thomas-Hope 1978). These traditions have been characterized as "a widespread desire to leave the island, a 'definition' of migration as a temporary phase, an obligation to *have in mind* those left at home, manifested in the requirement to send remittances to and/or sponsor the migration of close relatives and good friends, and a continued involvement with the household from which migration took place" (Rubenstein 1987: 198). The house construction and land improvements that dot the landscapes of both St. Vincent and Grenada are a visible display of the strength of West Indian migration traditions. It is these traditions that frame the practices of Vincentian and Grenadian transmigrants in New York. They are traditions built on the fragility of the migrants' economic and social circumstances: born into economies too resource-poor to support them and their families, residing in societies and economies that at times could not economically sustain them, and penalized, in the case of North America and Europe, by racializing practices that scapegoated immigrants of color.

Although in outline the earlier migrations contained some of the transnational features that characterized post-1965 migration to the United States, they lacked the intensity and multistranded character of more recent transnational processes. It was not until decolonization in the early 1960s and political independence in Grenada (1974) and St.Vincent (1979) that migrants found political, economic, and social opportunities at home in which to invest their resources and themselves. Today the transnational social field provides a safety valve for migrants and is also a source of opportunity through which they can build social and political capital and advance their status and class positions. But these involvements often require a thick web of kin, organizational, and even political networks and relationships that migrants must carefully cultivate, and that span both immigrant-sending and -receiving societies. Indeed, the basis of the deterritorialized nation-state construct is grounded in the kin, economic, and organizational ties with which migrants engage in the transnational social field.

Kin Ties, Status, and Class Mobility

The West Indian family has historically served as the primary social unit and central survival strategy for its members. Never exclusively residentially based, the survival of the family and its members has often depended on individuals stretched across several sites, both on- and off-island. Today, kin are often the central pegs of migrant transnational social fields. Relatives help migrants accumulate the capital to launch their migrations, and mind the migrants' children and property while they are away. At the migration destination, kin provide immigrants with much-needed shelter, assistance in locating employment, and knowledge that makes negotiating their new settings possible, at the same time diminishing the trauma of the migration experience. But careful nurturing is needed to build the social relationships that enable such transnational assistance. Visits, telephone calls, gifts, and cash remittances are some of the forms of reciprocity developed by migrants to cultivate and strengthen transnational family ties. Of our sample of 130 Vincentian and Grenadian immigrants interviewed in the mid 1980s, 66 percent reported sending money home at least annually, while a majority (56%) remitted funds more often; 54 percent sent goods at least annually, though barrels of clothing and foodstuffs were usually shipped more often; and half owned property in St. Vincent or Grenada, which their kin either lived on or cared for.

Kin deployed in various locations in the transnational social field help migrants in other crucial ways. Education of children, for example, is frequently a transnational project. Young children may be sent home for schooling in the Caribbean, where the streets are safer, the racial situation less oppressive, and learning more structured. Leaving or sending children home for education and to be minded by close kin is an especially important interim strategy when immigrants first come to New York, their incomes are low, and they cannot afford the fees for parochial schools or the growing number of private West Indian schools or to finance the move to suburban neighborhoods, where schools are safer and academically stronger.

For many children, education takes place in an interconnected transnational social space abetted by kin, a situation that leads parents to be concerned about the continuity between the curriculum children experience at home and that encountered in New York City schools. At Expo '95, for example, a Trade and Cultural Fair sponsored by the Caribbean American Chamber of Commerce included a panel discussion that focused on this very issue.

Transnational social fields also provide migrants and their families with new opportunities for material and social gains. Central to these projects is the differential access to economic, social, and cultural capital provided by kin in various locations in the social field. The limited education and training opportunities in St. Vincent and Grenada have meant that many immigrants come to New York without having completed secondary school degrees. For middle- and working-class Vincentians and Grenadians, New York is a place where they can attend schools at night, earn a high school equivalency certificate, participate in various training programs, and even earn a college degree. Of the 130 Vincentians and Grenadians we interviewed, more than 60 percent had earned a high school degree plus a vocational certificate, and over 35 percent had gained a college degree as well. For most, the payoff of these educational advancements has been a better job with greater earnings.

Joan is a good example of a migrant who, through advancing her education, has been able to improve her own and her family's social status in St. Vincent. Like many migrants, Joan was able to move from domestic to secretarial work by obtaining a high school certificate in New York. With her savings, she was able to build a substantial "middle-class" house with modern amenities in St. Vincent, which has increased the family's symbolic and cultural capital in both St. Vincent and New York. Her brothers, who are employed in Trinidad, where they sustain themselves at a subsistence level and hence are not able to contribute to the family income, have also benefited from the family's elevated social status. Building and maintaining the house was a process initially dependent on Joan's willingness to remain in New York City for eleven years as an undocumented immigrant, unable to return home to visit her family. And caring for the family property is now dependent on Joan's mother remaining in St. Vincent rather than migrating to New York or Trinidad to join her children or to work herself.

Such returns from migration have an impact on class formation in St. Vincent and Grenada. Migrant remittances and savings enable the production and reproduction of middle social strata that would not be possible through internal forces alone, given the fragile economic conditions of these countries. Many families in St. Vincent and Grenada are sustained beyond subsistence levels by monetary transfers from abroad. In fact, these infusions of funds seem to mute the incentives of many to emigrate. Some 71 percent of the ninety-four relatives of migrants we interviewed in St. Vincent and close to 51 percent of the ninety Grenadians interviewed said they were satisfied with their own lives and did not wish to emigrate.

Transnational Economic Activities

Immigrant transnational economic activities give further shape to and reinforce the transnational social field forged by migrants. Such activities take a variety of forms and draw in different ways on people—often family members—and capital located at both ends of the migration stream.

Some transnational economic activities are small, commercial undertakings in which family members in New York provide capital, generated from their wages, that enables their relatives at home to import consumer goods, which they then sell in St. Vincent or Grenada. These items range from clothing and other dry goods, records, tapes, and videos to raw materials for dried floral arrangements or candied fruits for cakes, to larger electronic equipment, furniture, refrigerators, washing machines, automotive parts, and so on. Some immigrants send these goods home, while in other situations immigrants serve as a base for relatives when they come to New York on buying trips.

Some economic activities have developed in direct response to the transnational needs of migrants. Carl's shipping company is an apt example. Capitalized through savings from his job as a junior administrator at the United Nations, Carl ships barrels of goods for immigrants between New York and St. Vincent. The business is dependent on Carl's brother in St. Vincent, who ushers the barrels through customs and organizes the shipment of migrants' goods to New York. Carl can keep the business open only a few hours a week because of his full-time job, but this limitation is offset by the personalized service both he and his brother can provide to their customers. Importantly, Carl is active in a number of immigrant organizations in New York, which increases the visibility of his shipping company.

The immigrant press and growing West Indian entertainment industry also operate in the nexus of the transnational social field, at the same time giving further shape to this field. Both arenas are major means of facilitating flows of cultural productions and ideas that bring together the experiences of immigrants with those remaining in St. Vincent and Grenada. The entertainment industry provides the channel for calypsonians and other musical entertainers to circulate between New York and St. Vincent or Grenada throughout the year, performing much the same music in both locations. The growing record and tape industries, different stages of which are located in New York and the West Indies, further the production of commonly appreciated music. And the immigrant press, by focusing on social and political events in both the West Indies and New York, reinforces the transnational social field and suffuses it with content.

Transnational Organizational Ties

With decolonization and political independence in St. Vincent and Grenada, a more public and encompassing transnationalism, expressed through immigrant organizations, began to take hold. Previously, many immigrants had become transmigrants through remittances sent home and through investments in land and houses. By the 1960s, with decolonization, St. Vincent and Grenada became more than places to retreat to during hard times, to retire to, or to look to as sources of distinctive cultural roots. In the new political context, even meager savings invested at home in community projects, through organizations, could confer upon migrants the status of benefactors. Moreover, such involvements by transmigrants enhanced their standing and respect not only in their home communities, but in the Vincentian and Grenadian immigrant communities in New York. Velma, a practical nurse in a New York hospital, recently received an award from a key St. Vincent club in New York for her donations to a "home" for girls in St. Vincent. Her charitable work in St. Vincent enhanced her status in the island's New York immigrant community.

By the 1970s, as these islands became independent, transnational projects initiated by organizations began to penetrate deeper into island social and political life and to more actively shape the transnational social field. A network of Vincentian organizations in New York, for example, initiated the development of a hall for Carnival celebrations in St. Vincent to be built with immigrant savings. New York–based organizations spurred immigrant involvement in election campaigns on both islands by providing information and various means of support to specific candidates, from influencing relatives and friends at home to providing financial backing. At the same time that these organizations facilitated immigrant engagement in their home nation-states, they also aided immigrant incorporation into New York social, political, and economic life. Of the twenty voluntary organizations built by Vincentian migrants, thirteen have come into existence since 1970, and most have transnational agendas.

The St. Vincent Education and Cultural Club is one example. Founded in 1977, the club has about thirty active members, ranging in age from their late twenties to their late forties (Basch 1987a). Most members were of lower-middle-class or middle-class background in St. Vincent and emigrated to New York after 1965. The club's goals—to enhance the educational and cultural life of Vincentians in both New York and St. Vincent—are explicitly transnational. The club plays a role in fashioning Vincentian identity in New York by constantly bringing St. Vincent and its cultural representations into the consciousness of Vincentian immigrants. It does this through the cultural fairs it organizes, through cosponsoring calypsonians and other entertainers from home with other Vincentian immigrant organizations, and through newsletters that transmit the latest from home.

The club also fosters immigrant incorporation into the social and economic structures of New York City by addressing in its newsletters and meetings such matters as education, real estate investing, black economic upliftment, and the merits of U.S. citizenship. The club, along with other Vincentian immigrant organizations, also serves as an important location in the city's Caribbean ethnic infrastructure. While the club's active membership may be relatively small, its reach is broad and makes it a potential site of significant immigrant mobilization.

Like other immigrant transnational organizations, the club enhances its active members' status both at home and in the U.S. immigrant community. As Earl Cato, the club's current president, told me, "It doesn't hurt that we're often interviewed on television when we go home and asked what immigrants are thinking, or that politicians from home want to hear our views or want our support." These sentiments (and experiences) of immigrant organizational leaders, as well as the increasingly nationalist orientation of immigrant organizations, provide a fertile foundation for deterritorialized nation-state building.

TRANSNATIONAL IDENTITIES AND DETERRITORIALIZED NATION-STATE BUILDING

Grenadian migrants' active involvement in questioning the legitimacy of Maurice Bishop's regime and launching the candidacy of Herbert Blaize (portrayed in the opening vignette) clearly demonstrates migrants' engagement in political affairs at home. In effect, the migrants at the meeting I described were acting as political citizens of their home country, even though several had lived in the United States for many years and were U.S. citizens. Stuart Hall discusses "identity as a 'production,' which is never complete, always in process, and always constituted within, not outside representation" (Hall 1990: 222). For Hall, an important component of the identity of postcolonial peoples, in particular, is the "imaginative rediscovery" of "hidden histories," which become a way of "imposing an imaginary coherence on the experience of dispersal and fragmentation" (224).

Hall emphasizes the centering of postcolonial Caribbean identity in Africa, but, for many postcolonial Caribbean immigrants situated in the diaspora of the United States, "acts of imaginative rediscovery" increasingly focus on their home societies. Immigrants' responsiveness to the exhortations of politicians from home to identify with, support, and be supremely loyal to their countries of birth reflects a politics of identity linked to an ancestry and culture rooted in the Caribbean. This "imaginative rediscovery" of the meaning of the nation-state underlies their willingness to participate in the deterritorialized nation-state building strategies of St. Vincent and Grenada. But there is a further, pragmatic edge to this politics of identity: the assumption that migrants are identified with and can have influence in the United States as well as their countries of origin. As the meeting I described illustrates, politicians and immigrants are together complicit in forging this "imagining."

Deterritorialized nation-state building has continued with a vibrancy over the past ten years among Grenadian and Vincentian, as well as other West Indian, immigrants in New York. Politicians from Caribbean nation-states visit in even larger numbers than before. On one Saturday evening, a buffet reception for an opposition leader from St. Vincent attracted a full house at thirty-five dollars per plate and was followed on Sunday by a public meeting and rally attended by another few hundred. The purpose was to garner both political support and funding from migrants. That same weekend the chiefs of state from Barbados and Antigua were visiting constituents in New York, as was the mayor of Georgetown, Guyana. Migrants respond to these political efforts by investing in the nation-states they still call home—in beer factories, development bonds, bank certificates of deposit, and political campaigns, with many going home to campaign for candidates.

Migrants can also actively oppose political actions by leaders at home. The recent efforts of the Vincentian prime minister to sell an island in the Grenadines to Italians created a furor. As one migrant said, "The number of letters in the Saint Vincent press from New York against this—you would think the people are living and working in St. Vincent, but they're living and working in New York." One migrant, a successful salesman for a major U.S. company and a U.S. citizen politically active in the Vincentian communities in New York and St. Vincent, planned to develop a videotape to air on St. Vincent television that would put forth the negative implications of the island sale for St. Vincent. In another immigrant's words, "People in St. Vincent see this sale as a job, immigrants look at it as selling out your birthright."

Forces Underpinning Vincentian and Grenadian Deterritorialized Nation-State Building

Deterritorialized nation-state building in St. Vincent and Grenada gives a peculiar twist to European-derived understandings of the nation-state, which were built on ideologies (Gellner 1983; Hobsbawm 1990) that evolved in nineteenth-century Europe. The European notion of nation-statehood postulated a single people residing in a common bounded territory, who had undivided loyalty to a sovereign government and shared a cultural heritage. Although this definition of the nation-state never reflected the realities of European nations, let alone colonial or postcolonial states, it continued to shape political identifications and ideologies throughout the world (Anderson 1991). Autonomous nation-states were viewed as part of the natural order (Miles 1993).

By defining the boundaries of the nation-state in social rather than geographic terms, Caribbean political leaders are able to treat nationals residing abroad as part of their nations' bodies politic. They can make claims on migrants as loyal members of their nation-states even if the migrants are also citizens of other states. Such a strategy makes sense for Caribbean political leaders given their islands' static or deteriorating economic situations and the strictures imposed by international structural adjustment policies. This strategy is also increasingly being utilized by leaders of other, more populous and more resource-endowed postcolonial states. In recent years, Mexico, Greece,

Portugal, India, Pakistan, the Philippines, and El Salvador have launched similar practices to enhance their emigrants' identifications with and allegiances to their home states and to attract emigrants' savings to investments at home (Feldman-Bianco 1994; Glick Schiller and Fouron 1998; Lessinger 1992; Smith 1993). Mahler (1998: 70–71) addresses the instrumental features of this strategy for El Salvador. Remittances from migrants, estimated at seven hundred million to over one billion dollars annually, are the largest source of hard currency in El Salvador and provide hundreds of millions of dollars more than export earnings. The success of such strategies on the part of migrant "home" countries is illustrated by a fifty-thousand-dollar fund-raiser hosted by Pakistani professionals on Staten Island in March 2000 for Hillary Clinton, the U.S. Senate candidate from New York. It was timed to influence President Clinton's decision on whether to visit Pakistan on an upcoming trip. According to a front-page article in the *New York Times,* the hosts "wanted to press the case to the first lady that her husband should visit Pakistan and that his administration should become engaged in finding a solution to the war in Kashmir, a territory claimed by both Pakistan and India" (Bonner 2000: 1). President Clinton did indeed include Pakistan in his trip.

The growing number of nations that are defining emigrants as part of their bodies politic suggests that deterritorialized nation-state building is in large part a response to late-twentieth-century capitalism and the economic fragility resulting from global practices of flexible accumulation, structural adjustment, and postcolonial countries' historical positioning in the global economic order. But there are other factors at work, including the specific historical experiences and practices of postcolonial nation-states.

In the Caribbean, the meaning of sovereignty has always had a peculiar shape. The European-derived model of autonomous, territorially bounded, sovereign nation-states comprised of people with a single history developed in tandem with colonial empires and the accompanying interconnections of politics and people that spanned great distances of geography and culture. The experience of the Caribbean—with its long history of colonial domination and regional migration—is in some ways paradigmatic of a number of postcolonial nation-states. Embedded in the very definition of a Crown colony government was the geographic separation of governing institutions, located in England, from the people in the colonies. The legacy of this system was that, in St. Vincent and Grenada, "the political community . . . [was] thought of as external to the island" (Singham 1968: 71).[5] Moreover, even during the colonial period the populations of both Grenada and St. Vincent were dispersed across national and territorial boundaries as civil servants, professionals, and laborers left in search of projects that would yield a daily wage. This context gave birth to simultaneous localized, regional, and colonial identities.

With the change from colonial to decolonized status and then, in the 1970s, to political independence, another ideology began to take hold, that of the nation-state. Chatterjee (1986) has pointed out how the European vision of politically and economically autonomous nation-states has become woven into the postcolonial narratives of states such as India. Not unlike those constructing the nation-state in India, Vincentians and Grenadians began to see themselves as equal players in the world body of nations. With independence, they developed a new national identity and cultural pride—in Hall's vocabulary, an "imaginative rediscovery" of "hidden histories"—and sense of position. For Vincentians and Grenadians, the dominant images were animated by Africa, their peasant pasts, and Caribbean folklife. Migrants participated in this imagining and became actively involved with social and political projects at home, beyond the remittances they had always sent to individual family members. Concerning the impact of independence, a Vincentian social scientist friend of mine said, "We could now turn inward and embrace other nationals rather than outward to an inferior status and the stigma attached to blackness."

The historical experiences of St. Vincent and Grenada thus created a double-stranded understanding of the nation-state. The European version of a politically and economically autonomous nation-state coexists with the sense of "partialness" embedded in both states' colonial experiences. The result of these interpenetrating ideologies has been that, for both states, definitions of nation have rested on their populations, not their geographic territory.

Identity Politics and Vincentian and Grenadian State Practices

Gupta (1992: 72) has observed that whether "a master narrative of the nation succeeds in establishing itself or not depends a great deal on the *practices* of the state." The governments of both Grenada and St. Vincent have instituted a number of practices to engage their populations abroad socially, culturally, economically, and politically, as part of their hegemonic construction of the deterritorialized nation-state. These practices include allowing migrants to maintain dual citizenship in their home country even if they become U.S. citizens, allowing them to vote in elections at home if they register beforehand, and changing Carnival from the traditional time just before Lent to the summer, when migrants and their children are more likely to visit. Both governments have also given funds to initiate broad-based immigrant organizations in New York, which have provided them access to the city's immigrant communities.

Government representatives of St. Vincent and Grenada treat immigrant organizations in New York as though they were bases for Vincentian and Grenadian national interests in New York and the United States. The Vincentian government provides funding for an umbrella organization, meetings of which are often set up by the consulate in New York and are held at the consulate's office so that St. Vincent's prime minister can speak by telephone with transmigrants. Frequently, the conversation focuses on ways Vincentians with U.S. citizenship can pressure the U.S. government to provide aid to St. Vincent, allow the importation of various food products from St. Vincent, and encourage American companies to invest there.

Government representatives also treat migrants as though they were part of the home country body politic. Maurice Bishop, the prime minister of Grenada in the early 1980s, frequently stated that Brooklyn was Grenada's largest constituency. His government looked to Grenadian migrants in the United States to help influence the U.S. government, which had cut off relations with Grenada in response to its agreements with Cuba and the Soviet Union. At one point Bishop's government encouraged Grenadians in the United States to organize a meeting in Washington to advance the possibility of the United States reinstituting relations with Grenada. A number of immigrants established an alliance with the Caribbean Action Lobby (an umbrella organization of Caribbean associations) and the Congressional Black Caucus in order to organize the meeting. This broad-based coalition managed to attract the attention of a representative from the State Department, who spoke at the meeting. Several immigrants from Brooklyn—many associated with immigrant organizations—also attended. Although some of these immigrants were not in total accord with Bishop's policies, their loyalty was to their home nation-state, and they acted in this meeting as constituents of Grenada, trying to influence the United States on behalf of their homeland, much as the Pakistani Americans would later do at the fund-raiser for Hillary Clinton.

Identity Politics and U.S. Nation-State Building: The Shaping of a West Indian Caribbean Identity

Also important in shaping an immigrant identity linked to home are ideologies and practices prevalent in the United States, including those pertaining to race and ethnicity.

The U.S. response to the growing immigrant populations of color and their tendency to participate in the political processes of both the United States and their "home societies" has been an invigorated incorporation process that leads West Indians to emphasize both their racial and ethnic identities. To be sure, ongoing racial discrimination and prejudice based on the bipolar racial structuring that still dominates American social relations help account for West Indians' continuing identification with "home" and their emphasis on ethnic identity. At the same time, in the aftermath of immigration legislation in 1965, and in response to the large number of immigrants streaming in from postcolonial countries, the United States, as part of its incorporation strategy, moved toward a more culturally pluralistic definition of the nation. A revised and layered vision of the American nation began to take hold. Coexisting with the emphasis on whiteness as a cultural ideal (Omi and Winant 1994) was a view of the "American people" as a multiplicity of ethnic populations, culturally different but equal in potential (Glazer and Moynihan 1970). In this model the role of race has been muted, and populations viewed as racially different, such as African Americans or Puerto Ricans, have been equated with ethnic Europeans such as Italians, Poles, and the Irish.

These incorporative efforts have generated a heightened and politicized ethnicity among Vincentian, Grenadian, and other West Indian immigrants. Especially striking is the strong West Indian political identity that has begun to emerge in the U.S. diaspora. West Indians share many common experiences as British colonial subjects from islands originally based on plantation slavery, where economic migration has long been a survival strategy. But the development of regional political strategies that override the policies, practices, and visions of individual nation-states has been slow in coming within the West Indian Caribbean, and such strategies are only now gaining momentum. Throughout most of the twentieth century, the diaspora has been the major source of West Indian political coalitions. Moreover, these coalitions are now showing themselves capable both of united action in the United States and of influencing their home countries.

In contrast to the earlier incorporation of West Indian immigrants as part of a black racial bloc by U.S. political leaders (Basch 1992), by the late 1970s and 1980s West Indian immigrants were seen as a distinctive Caribbean ethnic group by New York politicians. For example, West Indians were invited to join the Mayor's Commission on Ethnic Affairs, and in the 1980s the Brooklyn Borough President inaugurated Caribbean Awareness Day. Although the West Indian Day Parade has dominated Brooklyn's Eastern Parkway on Labor Day for several decades, until the late 1980s it was publicly ignored. Today it is publicly acknowledged to be part of the "U.S. cultural mosaic" and is the largest ethnic festival in the nation, with mainstream New York politicians clamoring to strut down Eastern Parkway at its helm.

West Indians have also been encouraged by politicians to organize Caribbean support groups for candidates in exchange for promises of political resources and to cast votes for politicians who speak to the West Indian immigrant experience. After the twin murders in Brooklyn of Guyanese-born Gavin Cato and Australian-born Yankel Rosenbaum in the early 1990s, Governor Mario Cuomo of New York approached Lamuel Stanislaus, a political leader in the Grenadian and broader Caribbean community, to help organize meetings between the governor and the Caribbean community. As part of negotiations over creating a support committee for Cuomo, West Indians were promised that the state of New York would create and finance Caribbean House, a place in the center of the Brooklyn Caribbean community where cultural organizations and projects for young and old could be developed. In 1996, active efforts to incorporate the Caribbean community as ethnics included the creation, by the Clinton campaign, of a Caribbean desk in New York Democratic headquarters. Further, Una Clarke, a recently elected New York City councilwoman from Jamaica, was invited to join the Clinton/Gore Platform Committee. She had been elected to her political position as a result of a New York City charter revision in 1991 that created a predominantly Caribbean voting district in Brooklyn.

These incorporative strategies have contributed to the "ethnicizing" of West Indians as a larger group, creating sites for political mobilization and laying a foundation for deterritorialized regional ideologies . The strength of this generalized West Indian identity surfaced in the recent banana crisis—or, as the Caribbean press has framed it, the "Banana Blow-Out"[6]—which has had similar negative effects on most small nation-states in the English-speaking Caribbean. The issue centers on Chiquita and Dole, U.S.-based transnationals, and their suit in the World Trade Organization against the continuing preference that bananas from former Caribbean colonies receive in the European market. Chiquita and Dole argued that their bananas were being discriminated against. The issue electrified the West Indian immigrant press as well as immigrants themselves. Leaders from the various island-based immigrant communities joined together, in the name of their shared Caribbean interests, and allied with Caribbean and African American politicians, Caribbean ambassadors to the United Nations, and their local consuls to put pressure on the U.S. government to reconsider this suit. Una Clarke carried the West Indian argument into meetings of the Clinton/Gore Platform Committee in the 1996 election and continued to do so in 2000 as a candidate for the U.S. Congress.

Interestingly, some Caribbean immigrants have been critical of their home governments' resistance to developing greater regional cooperation in the banana crisis. In their view, politicians at home should have been quicker to mobilize as a block against the efforts of Chiquita and Dole. They have asserted that the present multi-island initiative was spearheaded by immigrants in the United States. According to one immigrant, West Indians in the States "see NAFTA and the EEC as the way the world is going. We have to unify as a block in the Caribbean. But the sense of unity is not as great in the islands. Since we're in a melting pot in New York, we see ourselves as Caribbeans."

Such coalitions also provide a nexus where politicians from the Caribbean and politicians in New York representing Caribbean interests can collaborate to further shared interests. For example, the African American congressman Major Owens was quoted in the Caribbean immigrant press as urging Caribbean foreign ministers to encourage their constituents in the United States to become involved in U.S. political processes in order to protect the interests of their homelands. In New York, Caribbeans seeking office campaign under a banner of Caribbean unity; both they and their fellow immigrants know that, without the entire Caribbean community's support, the candidates could not win elections. Councilwoman Una Clarke told me, in a September 1997 interview, "Like all other immigrant groups, Caribbeans have emerged because history and the numbers are right."

Although Vincentian and Grenadian immigrants see themselves as an intermediate category in the multicultural, multicolored world of the United States, they are vulnerable to the flammable racism of the United States, which identifies them as black, and to the recent anti-immigrant, antiwelfare backlash.[7] Paradoxically, this backlash may well lead to greater West Indian participation in U.S. politics. Moves in Congress in 1996 to curtail social services to immigrants as part of welfare reform legislation, combined with the passage of a California ballot initiative to cut social services to undocumented immigrants, may have contributed to the surge in U.S. citizenship applications in the late 1990s (Van Slambrouck 1999). While research has shown that Jamaicans—and by extension other West Indians—have had relatively low naturalization rates (Bouvier 1999), this pattern may be shifting. As Una Clarke told me, "Welfare reform was a blessing in disguise for me; it doubled the number of citizenship applications from West Indians. With our growing number of citizens, we stand on the edge of being a very powerful community."

This surge in naturalization has complex and contradictory implications. In part it is a defensive strategy, aimed at retaining rights in the United States. At the same time, exclusionary practices in American society stoke immigrants' identifications with the nation-states they still call home and thus provide a position of resistance to U.S. xenophobic policies and practices. Broad-based regional alliances and identifications among migrants can influence political processes in their home countries as well as in the United States. Indeed, politicians from "home" may well encourage immigrants to seek U.S. citizenship as a means of protecting and advancing the interests of their home countries and the migrants' investments in these countries.

CONCLUSIONS

Transnational kin, economic, and political practices are crucial elements in providing the framework for West Indian deterritorialized nation-state building, and I have outlined many of the forces that underpin this nation-state building strategy. In part, migrants' continuing political identification with their homelands derives from the insecurities arising during this historical moment of global capitalism. A transnational social field that encompasses two nation-states offers both economic flexibility and options to migrants and their kin. But this transnational strategy is also the result of practices and policies of exclusion in the United States that contribute as well to migrants' economic, political, and social insecurity.

Dual citizenship, the guarantor of rights for migrants in the United States and in their home countries, reinforces the strength of deterritorialized nation-state building. Dual citizenship demonstrates some of the properties of "flexible

citizenship" described by Ong (1993) with regard to Hong Kong and other overseas Chinese, who take on citizenship in various nation-states depending on
their economic interests. If home countries allow dual citizenship in part to ensure the flow of remittances and investments, they also often view their citizens
abroad as potential lobbies in the United States (Foner 2000). Moreover,
Caribbean politicians in New York clearly benefit from a wider pool of citizens.
In fact, recent anti-immigrant sentiments and legislation in the United States
stimulated well-organized campaigns by politicians in both New York and the
Caribbean to assist immigrants in becoming U.S. citizens.

If West Indians see U.S. citizenship as providing them with, among other
things, influence as voters in the New York political arena, it also has advantages linked to transnational practices.[8] Several immigrants I talked with want
to ensure that they will be able to receive social security payments when they
retire to their home states and are worried that this may someday be impossible if they are not U.S. citizens. One Vincentian told me, "If you go to a
'swearing-in' of citizens, you see people from the other nations moved to tears.
West Indians don't have that feeling. Quite the contrary." Many West Indians
think that U.S. citizenship will enable them to better represent the interests of
their home countries. Moreover, dual citizenship augments the power of
Caribbean politicians in the United States by providing them with a political
base in both New York and the Caribbean, each of which buttresses the other
in a transnational social field. For example, Jamaica-born New York City
councilwoman Una Clarke ups her political capital within the broad New
York Caribbean community by visiting several Caribbean nation-states to
learn about local conditions and concerns, which she then seeks to represent
to the U.S. government. At the same time, her influence in the Caribbean is
derived from her political position in the United States, a position built upon
the support of the broad Caribbean immigrant community.

Vincentians and Grenadians say they see no contradictions in being subject
to the hegemonic agendas of two nation-states. In part this corroborates Michel
Foucault's assertion that a heterogeneity of forms of consciousness can exist at
once among particular groups of actors (Foucault 1990). However, this dual incorporation of immigrants into the hegemonic visions of two nation-states can
cause contradictions between the nation-states and lead to contestations. For example, the broad-based regional alliances encouraged by the "ethnicizing" practices of Vincentian, Grenadian, and other West Indian immigrants in New York
constitute a potential base of resistance that can lead to political challenges organized around race and ethnicity. Examples are the "rainbow coalitions" that
took shape in the late 1980s, in which West Indians joined forces with Latinos
and African Americans to try to unseat particular elected officials, and the notions of appropriate political behavior among Vincentian immigrants that led
them to mobilize to unseat the government in St. Vincent in the late 1990s because of its proposed sale of a small Grenadine island to Italian interests. In this

latter case, what the St. Vincent government perceived as selling alienable property the immigrants viewed as "selling their birthright."

Despite the potential for contradictions, deterritorialized nation-state building seems to be an emerging force among several migrant-sending countries. States as varied as Mexico, India, the Philippines, Greece, Portugal, Haiti, the Dominican Republic, St. Vincent, and Grenada are encouraging practices of dual citizenship and granting voting rights and opportunities for property ownership and investment to nationals who have taken citizenship in other countries. At the same time, these countries are encouraging their nationals to use citizenship in their new host countries to represent the interests of their home nation-states. Moreover, host countries such as the United States, through incorporation practices that ethnicize West Indian immigrants, further reinforce immigrants' identifications with their home countries and the West Indies.

Deterritorialized nation-state building is linked to the contemporary moment of globalization and transnationalism. As Verdery (1998: 302) points out in her discussion of the nationalizing tendencies of East European states amid the growth of transnationalism, "the history of state forming, like the history of global capitalism, has not produced uniform effects everywhere." In the case of St. Vincent and Grenada, two mini-states of the eastern Caribbean, the insecurities linked to late-twentieth- and early-twenty-first-century capitalism, the states' historic economic fragility and positioning within the global economic order, and their specific experiences have combined to give special force to deterritorialized nation-state building. The question is whether this phenomenon is a harbinger of a new, more elastic definition of the nation-state, given the heightened transnational and global interactions that underpin the new century, and what the implications of this identity formation, and the state practices that fuel it, will be.

But there is another dimension to these practices that must also be considered. While broad transnational social fields offer options and opportunities to families in an insecure world, the lived experience of migrants in this expanded global space is often marked by dislocation and fragmentation. Joan, the woman I mentioned earlier who had improved her family's status in St. Vincent through educational gains in New York, had to live separately from her mother and siblings, her only support base, and was unable to see them for eleven years while waiting to obtain her green card. Many transnational families are scattered across three or more nation-states and are subject to different structures and policies in each. When transnational migrants try to return home to work, they often find themselves unwelcome, viewed as having "jumped ship." As one transnational political activist pointed out regarding the attitudes of Grenadians at home to transmigrants abroad, "They like the money, but they don't want the advice or the competition." Moreover, when transmigrants return home there are often new separations to endure, since they often leave their children in the country of migration. Transnational social fields contain myriad contradictions for both migrants and nation-states. These contradictions raise issues only now beginning to be addressed in the social science literature, issues to which greater attention needs to turn.

NOTES

An earlier version of this chapter was presented as a paper at the 1996 Annual Meeting of the American Anthropological Association in the invited session "Fight the Power!" Critical Reflections on Changing Forms of Consciousness and Protest (Papers on the Influence of Constance R. Sutton, II: Trans/Inter/Dynamics and Forms of Consciousness and Struggle). This paper is dedicated to Constance R. Sutton in appreciation of her mentorship, guidance, and friendship. This version of the paper has benefited from discussions with and clarifications provided by Earl Cato, Lamuel Stanislaus, Joyce Toney, and Joel Toney. All are greatly appreciated. Portions of this chapter appear in Basch, Glick Schiller, and Szanton Blanc (1994), especially in chapters 3 and 4.

1. Initial field research on Vincentian and Grenadian migration was undertaken from 1982 to 1985 among immigrants living in New York and Trinidad and their kin living in St. Vincent and Grenada, and was conducted under the auspices of the United Nations Institute for Training and Research. My coresearchers included Rosina Wiltshire, Winston Wiltshire, and Joyce Toney (see Basch, Wiltshire, Wiltshire, and Toney 1990; Wiltshire, Basch, Wiltshire, and Toney 1990; Toney 1987). Interviews were conducted with 130 Vincentians and Grenadians living in New York and 80 living in Trinidad; close to 200 relatives of these immigrants living in both St. Vincent and Grenada were also interviewed. Research assistance in New York was provided by Colin Robinson, Isa Soto, and Margaret Souza, of whom the first two are transmigrants themselves. The initial research was funded by the United Nations Fund for Population Activities and the International Development Research Centre of Canada.

2. My first awareness of *transnationalism* and early probing of its implications occurred while working collaboratively with Rosina Wiltshire and Winston Wiltshire. My recognition of the pervasiveness of these processes, and their implications for understanding nationalism, race, and ethnicity, were developed through collaborative work with Nina Glick Schiller and Cristina Szanton Blanc.

3. The people of this area use the terms *West Indian* and *Caribbean* interchangeably to describe themselves. In this chapter, however, I use *West Indian* to describe the peoples of the former Anglo-Caribbean and reserve *Caribbean* to describe peoples from all the islands in the Caribbean Sea, as well as the countries of Suriname, French Guiana, and Guyana, which lie along the northern rim of South America.

4. The concept of the *deterritorialized nation-state* was developed in collaboration with Nina Glick Schiller and Cristina Szanton Blanc.

5. The situations on the small islands of St. Vincent and Grenada contrast with those on larger islands such as Jamaica, where members of the planter class remained on the islands and where island councils had administrative authority.

6. There have been a spate of articles in the *Carib News*, "the weekly voice of the Caribbean-American community," underscoring the "greed" of the United States in its at-

tempts to "peel away at the benefits for Caribbean bananas" in the European Union (see Best 1998, 1999).

7. For example, the front page of the 8 October 1996 *Carib News* carried the following banner headline: "Immigrants' Nightmare. Attack on Legal Aliens—Restricts Benefits—Roadblock to Sponsor Relatives—Deportation Easier—Harsh Penalties for Fraud Papers—Restriction on Foreign Students."

8. West Indian immigrants see citizenship as providing other benefits as well, for example, access to various government jobs and, perhaps most important, the ability to sponsor relatives.

FIVE

New York as a Locality
in a Global Family Network

Karen Fog Olwig

Throughout the history of the United States, New York has served as the most important migrant destination and port of entry into the country. One result of New York's central role in the making of the United States is that migration research has viewed the city as a place of incorporation into American society, where newcomers are turned into new citizens. This, in turn, is compatible with the stereotype of migration as a process by which poor, honest folk, fleeing poverty and oppression in the home country, become free and upwardly mobile Americans. In recent years, however, a number of migration scholars have noted that the process of incorporation is more complex than hitherto realized and may involve segmented, or partial, forms of integration into American society. In the case of Caribbean migration, scholars point to an increasing Caribbeanization or transnationalization of New York.

I argue here that the focus on processes of incorporation in migration research is informed by knowledge gained by hindsight. I am not questioning that, in the long run, migrants who move to the United States undergo some degree of integration into American society. The incorporation perspective, however, says little about the migrants' understanding of their move: how they experience migration to and initial settlement in New York, and what significance they attach to their lives in New York. In this chapter I examine New York from the vantage point of the members of one large family network of Caribbean middle-class background who have lived in the city for various periods of time. Their narratives shed light on the importance of New York both as a destination and place of residence for migrants and as an economic, cultural, and social site of significance in the wider spectrum of movement characteristic of the Caribbean diaspora. By focusing on a family of middle-class background, the chapter also makes clear that, contrary to common perceptions, immigration to the United States is not just about welcoming "your tired, your poor, your huddled masses," who were celebrated in Emma Lazarus's sonnet on the Statue of Liberty. In this way, the chapter provides a broader perspective on the nature of twentieth-century immigration to the United States.

NEW YORK AS A MIGRANT DESTINATION

A study of migration to New York City is a study of the very creation of the place itself. Since the mid nineteenth century, New York has served as a primary destination for immigrants to the United States (Reimers 1987: 35).[1] Thus, between 1821 and 1975 "over 31 million immigrants . . . entered [the United States] through the Port of New York, equaling about 62 percent of the total immigration into the United States" during that period (Bryce-Laporte 1987: 58). Many settled permanently in New York City. A great deal of this immigration to New York, especially in the past few decades, has involved people from the Caribbean.[2] A study of New York today is hardly complete without considering the large Caribbean presence in the city.

A study of migration to New York is also about the very making of the United States. Indeed, research on migration to New York has traditionally taken place within the wider theoretical framework of American migration studies. In this framework, migration to the United States is seen to set in motion a process of incorporation that only concludes when the immigrants, or their children, become fully integrated into American society and identify with American values. This framework thus emphasizes how foreigners are transformed into Americans, rather than the migration process as such. A special collection of articles in the winter 1997 issue of *International Migration Review*, for example, was devoted specifically to reexamining the contemporary relevance of the incorporation paradigm in North American migration studies. In their concluding discussion of these articles, DeWind and Kasinitz (1997) note that the contributors are not primarily concerned with the phenomenon of migration. Instead they address such questions as "how immigrants and their children are being incorporated into the fabric of American life. What sort of Americans will they be, and what sort of America is being created in the interaction of immigrants and natives?" (1096). Within this conceptualization of migration research, New York is of interest mainly as the place where many migrants have their first encounter with American culture and society.

The significance of New York as a point of transition into American society has also been an important item on the agenda of recent work on Caribbean migration to the city. As stated by Bryce-Laporte, New York is "the arena in which [migrants from the Caribbean] are 'seasoned' and are 'struggling' with the American way-of-life" (1987: 55). In recent years the very nature of this "seasoning" and "struggling" among Caribbean migrants has been the subject of considerable discussion. Two major critical perspectives can be discerned in this debate. One perspective has taken up the question of whether a sort of segmented assimilation occurs, so that certain migrants become integrated into separate subcultures rather than into mainstream American society. In an article on second-generation West Indian and Haitian Americans in New York City, Mary Waters asks whether "processes of immigration and assimilation for nonwhite immigrants resemble the processes for earlier white immigrants? Or do these immigrants and their children face very different choices and constraints because they are defined racially by other Americans" (1994a: 795). She uncovers three different identity strategies (based on American, immigrant, and ethnic identification) among second-generation West Indian migrants whom she interviewed in two New York schools. She is uncertain, however, whether the more separatist "immigrant" and "ethnic" forms of identity will survive in the long run.

The other critical approach to the incorporation paradigm criticizes the notion that migration involves a one-way movement from point of origin to point of destination. This approach argues for a reconceptualization of migration as movement that occurs between places and is embedded in wider systems of relations that crosscut several nation-states. In her introductory article to *Caribbean Life in New York City*, Sutton (1987: 20) thus points to the existence of a "continuous and intense bidirectional flow of peoples, ideas, practices, and ideologies between the Caribbean region and New York City." The result is that the present-day Caribbean population of New York is integrated into a transnational sociocultural system that is only partially grounded in American soil. This integration into a transnational sociocultural system, according to Sutton, means that "the model of immigrant/ethnic incorporation into a 'culturally pluralistic' American society is not the destiny of migrant Caribbeans." The impact of transnationalism on the incorporation of migrants within American society is also a major issue in *Nations Unbound* (Basch, Glick Schiller, and Szanton Blanc 1994), a comparative study of migration to New York from several Caribbean countries and the Philippines. The authors argue that transnationalism constitutes a form of resistance to being subordinated within a specific nation-state such as the United States, with its particular form of "political and economic domination" and "racial and cultural differentiation" (46). An important item on the research agenda pertaining to Caribbean migration to New York therefore has been the nature of the processes of incorporation and exclusion that occur in connection with migration to the United States, and the ways in which these processes influence the continued development of American culture and society.

Processes of incorporation and exclusion in American society are valid concerns of great importance to those who wish to research the history and continued development of American society. They are not, however, the only, or necessarily the best, vantage points from which to study migration as such—or the particular significance of New York in the migratory movements of Caribbean people. We may wish to look for analytic frameworks that are less narrowly focused and ideologically loaded than the incorporation paradigm, which is so closely tied to the cultural and societal interests of the migrant destination.

The basic dictionary definition of migration is simply "to move from one country, place, or locality to another" (Merriam-Webster 1996: 738). In the pages that follow I explore the importance of New York to a Caribbean family network that has engaged in a series of movements since the 1940s. From the point of view of this family, New York attained significance as a destination of movement, as a locus of family life, and as a site to leave behind when new movements were undertaken. New York City figured in the lives of these Caribbean migrants as a future, present, and past place of residence, which was identified with certain phases in the development of the family and the life trajectories of its members. The New York experience, in other words, figured in this family not so much as part of a process of becoming American (or not becoming American), but rather was associated with a place in time where family members had particular experiences and formed certain bonds within an international family network.

Since 1996 I have conducted life-story interviews within three family networks of Caribbean origin.[3] Each of the three family networks can be traced back to a pair of common ancestors in the Caribbean—specifically Jamaica, Dominica, and Nevis—in the early part of the twentieth century. In the course of a few generations, the members of all the family networks have become scattered. At the time of the interviews, members lived in such disparate places as Barbados and the Virgin Islands; Florida, Texas, California, Oregon, New York, and New Jersey; Nova Scotia and Ontario; England, Scotland, and Wales; and in the Caribbean islands of origin. In all three cases, family networks played an important role in knitting members together across a global space. Because New York had a particularly central role in the movements of members of the family network of Jamaican background, this network is the focus here. I explore how New York was constructed as a place in the life stories related by individuals in the Jamaican family whose movements had brought them to the city.[4]

The life-story perspective, a subjective approach, allows us to see how individuals speak about and conceptualize their experiences of moving and settling and thus provides insights into the meaning of these experiences to the migrants themselves. It is important to bear in mind that a subjective perspective, while focusing on individual experiences, views them as taking place within, and therefore reflecting, the social, economic, and cultural context in which the individuals operate. The life stories in this chapter thus reflect the complex interrelationship among individuals, family relations, and the wider social, economic, and cultural environment in which individual lives unfold.[5]

A JAMAICAN FAMILY

The fifty-four members of the Jamaican family I interviewed often spoke of the family's roots in Jamaica. All knew that they had descended from William and Marie, who married and reared eight children in their home in a small Jamaican seaport.[6] William was born in this seaport before the turn of the century; Marie was born on the first day of the twentieth century in a smaller, nearby village. Even though the family members are clear about their Jamaican ancestry, the roots are rather shallow as far as the paternal ancestors are concerned. William's paternal grandfather had moved to Jamaica from Scotland in the mid 1800s; Marie's paternal grandfather from Portugal. Both William and Marie were the issue of unions with local women. Jamaica therefore figures as the meeting place of paternal forebears of European descent and maternal forebears of African Jamaican descent, rather than as a place where the family members' roots reach back to time immemorial.

The family's origins in William and Marie's home in Jamaica is situated not just in a specific geographical location but also in a particular socioeconomic place within the colonial order of the island society. Members of the family made their living by fishing and stevedoring, the stevedoring business having been started by William's father. The family's economic basis in local business and its mixed racial background placed it squarely within the middle strata of Jamaican society. This position was reflected in the cultural values that predominated in the family home. From interviews with Marie and the older generation of siblings, it became clear that the childhood home was oriented toward European middle-class values such as proper manners, mastery of correct English, and educational achievement. Indeed, Marie's family disassociated itself from the local lower classes unless they were of the right "caliber."[7] When I interviewed her in England, Marie, then ninety-seven years old, explained:

> Some locals you would not want your children to marry. We all have our prejudices. It depended on how you were brought up. If you were brought up the same way, you were on equal grounds. If you had manners. Proper manners are important.

Marie never expected her children to remain in the small town where she and her husband lived. She regarded education as providing the best foundation for her children and the family and sent her children to the best possible schools— some even to the finest private secondary schools on the island. When the family fell on hard times as the local harbor, and with it the stevedoring business, underwent a period of decline, Marie started her own store in the town in order to help pay for the children's education. The family members' migration from Jamaica was basically part of this drive for education to consolidate the social and economic status of the family in Jamaican society.

NEW YORK AS A CENTER OF ATTRACTION

Since Marie and her husband did not have the financial means to support their children's education abroad, the children traveled as migrants sponsored by relatives. One son, Henry, explained:

> We had three uncles in America, and my brother and I had decided to further our studies in America. These uncles would send for us, help us get the papers so that we could study there.

Henry gave up on waiting for a visa to enter the United States and instead joined the RAF, leaving for Great Britain in 1943. His brother Bill, however, traveled to New York in 1944:

> I asked one [of my uncles] to sponsor me for the U.S. I got a residency in 1944 and I left Jamaica for New York, where I resided with my uncle and his wife. I traveled around the U.S. seeing several universities, trying to identify the university where I would be the most at ease. Finally, I decided on [a university], which was located in New York City. I enrolled in 1945. I did a pre-med course with a concentration in sciences.

The family had long had high expectations for Bill. Bill's second wife explained:

> When he left [Jamaica] as a boy they all knew he was going off to the U.S. to become a doctor. So they called him doctor. Mom's earnings went to him becoming a doctor. It was difficult for her to support him. I didn't know him then. I was a child in Jamaica.
>
> *Why was it so important for him to become a doctor?*
> Doctor, lawyer, Indian chief. It is a high point in any family. Jamaicans aren't business oriented [i.e., status tends to be identified with the professions rather than with commerce]. Being wealthy is not seen as so great as being a doctor or a lawyer. Most families aspired to have a doctor.

Bill never did become a doctor. Due to economic exigencies—he married and started a family of his own—he took up a career in a large American firm, ending up in a managerial position. Even though he did obtain a B.A. and had a successful business career, Bill could not describe his move to New York without expressing deep regret at not having lived up to his family's expectations:

> I remember in New York I was in the apartment building, back from college, and I was checking the mailbox. There was a large table with chairs and a couch. I found a local paper from Jamaica there, and when I opened it I found inside the paper U.S. dollar bills folded into the paper. My mother had sent them. She also baked plum pudding with money in it.
>
> *She was ambitious for you?*
> Yes, for all. I felt I had let them down, because I didn't achieve what I had set out to achieve by becoming a medical doctor. Quite often in later years I have had the urge to go back to medical school, but the pressure of everyday living made it too difficult.

A few years after Bill came to New York, his younger brother Charles followed. Through Bill's help, Charles obtained a job in the large corporation where Bill worked. Charles told me:

> After the war was over they were placing ex-servicemen in jobs [in Jamaica]. I told you that I was in the home guard [in Jamaica]. I told them that I didn't want a job when I returned there from my three-month vacation. But when my uncle asked whether I wanted to stay, telling me that I could get a job and go to school here [in America], I decided to stay. And this is what I did. I worked for [the corporation], and they sent me to school, taught me drafting, and I worked at that; I made signs, forms, and so on.
>
> *Would this not have been possible in Jamaica?*
> No, Jamaica didn't offer any opportunities. I would depend on my parents, and there were no really good jobs. Here you could get a job, get married, and have children.

Bill and Charles were joined in America by their older sister, Celia, a trained nurse, who entered the United States via Canada. In the late 1950s, after the father had died in Jamaica, the siblings sent for their mother, Marie. During the 1950s another sister, Doreen, began to visit the family in New York for extended periods of time. In the middle of the 1960s, she finally moved there permanently and began working for the same corporation where Bill and Charles were employed. By then, half of the family had, in effect, relocated to New York. The other half had either moved to Great Britain (Henry and Jessica) or stayed in the Caribbean (Amanda went to Dominica and Hubert remained in Jamaica). Three daughters were trained as nurses, but otherwise none of the children became professionals. By 1970 all the children held good jobs; those who had moved to the United States were, generally speaking, doing well and appeared to be firmly settled in the country.

Whereas New York, initially, was a destination to which family members traveled for better educational and economic opportunities, the city became more of a "family place" within the wider network of relatives as the first migrants to New York settled down and started their own families. Thus, when Doreen, who had been living in London for a number of years, arrived in New York with her son and daughter, they found themselves surrounded by family. Doreen's daughter explained:

> There was so much family, it was amazing. They all came along to see [my brother and me].

After the 1950s most of the family members who moved to New York came in order to live with the family, not for educational or economic reasons. Marie, as noted, moved to New York to join her children when she became a widow; Doreen stayed on and off with family in New York before moving there permanently in the mid 1960s and beginning work for Bill's firm; Charles's daughter Barbara, who had been left behind in Jamaica, came to join her family in New

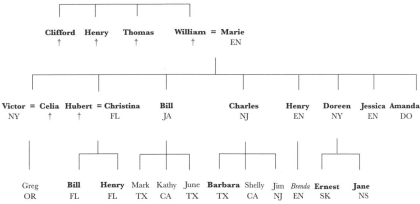

NOTE: This figure includes only those family members who are mentioned in the chapter. In 1996 Marie reckoned that she had twenty-five grandchildren, forty-six great-grandchildren, and two great-great-grandchildren. Names written in **boldface,** a medium font, or *italics* correspond to family members born in Jamaica, New York, or England, respectively. The following abbreviations indicate the place of residence of relatives in 1996: CA = California, DO = Dominica, EN = England, FL = Florida, JA = Jamaica, NJ = New Jersey, NS = Nova Scotia, NY = New York, OR = Oregon, SK = Saskatchewan, TX = Texas. Names marked with a † indicate deceased individuals.

Figure 5.1. The Jamaican Family, 1996

York in 1960 after she had become one of the few family members still living in Jamaica. She expressed the importance of New York as a family place when she described her regret at having had to move to Houston with her husband:

> It was very sad leaving New York, where I had Aunt Celia, Doreen, Grandmother, Bill. . . . I left everybody there.

When Barbara left New York for Houston in 1976, New York had become the place where "everybody" lived. This was also how family members living elsewhere regarded New York. The city had, in fact, become the nexus of the global family network, where family members who lived elsewhere could meet and get to know the family. One of Henry's daughters, Brenda, had been born and raised in southern England. She described her two-year sojourn in New York—when her husband was assigned there by his firm—as a time when she got to know the family:

> We had a fabulous time there. There I met all my other relatives. I knew Grandmother, but I met Aunt Celia and Uncle Victor, Auntie Doreen, Uncle Chuck. It was brilliant. I really met [family members]. . . . It was a nice big happy family.

Her positive impression of New York had actually been formed earlier, while she was a child growing up in Great Britain. She remembered how New York family members had sent boxes of American clothes for their poorer relatives in postwar Great Britain. She recalled with special fondness the pants that she and her sisters had received, which made them the only kids in the area with real American blue jeans. The five children who grew up in England were well aware of the presence of affluent family in New York.

New York had, in fact, been important as a family place since the early decades of the twentieth century. Indeed, if Bill and Charles had not had uncles in the city with whom they could stay and who could help them get visas, they probably would not have been able to undertake the trip at all. At first, New York was an option as a destination; later it became a major center of attraction in family members' travels because of the kin relations associated with it.

Most members of the family had moved to New York in the 1940s, 1950s, and early 1960s, a time when few West Indians migrated to the United States. According to Philip Kasinitz (1992: 23–26), West Indian migration to New York can be divided into three phases: an early phase, in the first decades of the twentieth century until the immigration regulations of 1924, when a large group of West Indians entered the United States; a middle phase, from the mid 1920s until the mid 1960s, when West Indian immigration was severely restricted and mostly involved migrants of middle-class background entering on student visas or joining family who had migrated during the first phase; the latest phase, since 1965, when liberalized U.S. immigration regulations made large-scale West Indian immigration to the United States possible again. With its middle-class background in Jamaica, its members' ambition to migrate for further education, and its dependence on relatives in New York for entry into the United States, the family fits the "stage two migrants" described by Kasinitz. The Jamaican family's middle-class background had an important bearing on the kind of life that family members carved out in the United States. They remained very much oriented toward the social and cultural values of mainstream middle-class society and displayed limited interest in the vast influx of West Indians of lower-class background who began pouring into the city after the mid 1960s.

NEW YORK AS A PLACE TO LIVE

The first family members to arrive in New York in the 1940s initially stayed with uncles who had migrated to the United States in the early part of the twentieth century. This meant living in a racially mixed Harlem. As soon as the new migrants had the economic means, around 1950, they moved to a more upscale area in Brooklyn. Bill described the area in glorious terms:

What was Brooklyn like?
Pristine and beautiful. We lived in a brownstone building owned by my wife's mother. The area was immaculately maintained. When I walked home I met the policeman who patrolled the area. The block was inhabited mostly by professionals, doctors, lawyers, dentists.

The entire family eventually settled in the same part of Brooklyn. Kathy, Bill's daughter, remembered her Brooklyn childhood as a time of growing up surrounded by family:

> We lived on New York Avenue. A close family friend . . . lived two doors down with her husband. Across the street lived a couple of West Indians, and at St. John's Place my aunt and uncle lived with their son. Down the block lived my other aunt and her two children, and half a mile away were my uncle and his wife and their three children. It was very much a family atmosphere. We used to gather together and play. And we used to gather together for family dinners and celebrations, lots of picnics and outings together. Cousins became close friends as well as family members. There is a saying that we can choose our friends but not our family. But clearly there was overlap here.

It seems that much social life took place within the circle of family and family friends. Bill recalled:

> We lived in an apartment in my Jamaican mother-in-law's house. She had married an American who was also of Jamaican descent. Her husband worked with a manufacturing company, and she was a real estate broker.
>
> *Did your wife's background in Jamaica bring you into Jamaican circles?*
> Not really. I was still in college then. I had a brother and two sisters who had migrated. They lived not far away, and my first wife's mother had two sisters who lived not far. The circle was larger, but it was mostly family.
>
> *How much did you see each other?*
> At least three times per week. Just visiting, sometimes we were invited for dinner. Or if there was a function, we might go as a group.
>
> *What kinds of functions would that be?*
> A house party, the theater, movies, primarily. Or a barbecue at family members' homes.

The immediate neighborhood, with its tight circle of relatives and close friends, offered a secure and friendly environment. The wider community, dominated by middle-class white Americans, was not so welcoming, viewing family members in racial terms as "Negro." Indeed, the children experienced direct racism in their virtually all-white private denominational schools. Bill's daughter, Kathy, for example, who is somewhat darker than her father, recollected that in the 1950s her kindergarten teacher, a Catholic nun, did not let her sit with the other children in the classroom, but made her listen to lessons from steps outside the classroom door. Kathy was only permitted into the classroom after her mother informed the principal of what was happening. The parents of the other children in the class did not allow their children to sit next to Kathy during lunch period, and the only girl who had been friendly declined an invitation to come to Kathy's birthday party. The girl's mother would not let her go because, the mother said, "all niggers live in garages."

This explanation was an enormous blow to the family's self-image and pride in having a proper and respectable home. Kathy's mother went to the girl's mother and asked her to have a look at the home for herself:

> When she saw our home, she said: "My God, you live in a nicer home than we do!" And she allowed her daughter to come to my birthday party. But the friendship was never the same.

Most of the time, however, the family ignored racial slights and insults. Kathy told me:

> I wonder why they kept me in that insane school. They may not have realized how bad it was, and they were intent on paying for my good education. They took the stiff upper lip approach that good schooling is most important. It was the ticket to life.

Education was not just the "ticket to life" but also the ticket to (finally) having the doctor in the family that the first generation had failed to produce. When Kathy considered pursuing a career in dancing, it was made clear that this was not a proper choice:

> [My mother] asked me how many black dancers I had seen on stage in ballet productions. None at that time; they were all-white dance companies. So what did I expect to get out of going to the performing arts high school—becoming a ballerina? She reminded me that I wanted to be a pediatrician, so I had to go to the . . . Academy. They were hoping to have a doctor in the family. Eventually I married a pediatrician!

For many years the family and its friends seem to have constituted a very small West Indian enclave in a neighborhood that was otherwise white, initially mainly Jewish and later Italian-Irish. The neighborhood's racial composition changed during the late 1960s, however, as more black people began to enter the area. Mark, one of Bill's sons, elaborated on this change, which he experienced during his childhood and which radically transformed the neighborhood:

> The schools were just being integrated. [I had attended] a mainly Irish-Italian school. My best friend was German American from third to sixth grade. But overnight most of the white families moved out. It all happened within a year.
>
> *Why?*
> Block busting. People panicked, they feared that their property values would deteriorate, and this caused a white flight to the suburbs. The neighborhood went downhill. As kids we were innocent of race, but as we became older it changed. Then my family moved, when I was twelve to thirteen years old, to another Italian-Irish neighborhood. And within two years the same thing happened. We did not move. It was a very nice house, and we were in high school. About 80 percent left, and there were about one to two white families left on the block. Before, the neighborhood had been about 95 percent white.

With white flight and the concomitant influx of blacks, the section of Flat-bush where the family lived changed character entirely. It was no longer an established, middle-class neighborhood of professionals but turned into an immigrant community consisting largely of blacks of Caribbean origin. As Philip Kasinitz (1992: 55) has written, the core of the New York West Indian community shifted during the 1970s to Crown Heights, East Flatbush, and Flatbush in central Brooklyn. Crown Heights, in particular, became an important Caribbean cultural center in the United States, largely because of the Carnival held on Eastern Parkway every Labor Day (43). None of the members of the Jamaican family described the West Indian transformation of the neighborhood in positive terms or mentioned having taken part in West Indian cultural activities in Brooklyn. On the contrary, most of the family members were keen to distance themselves from the present-day neighborhood, which they did not like. Thus, when I asked Charles to describe the Brooklyn neighborhood where he had once lived, he merely stated that it was "much nicer than it is now." He later elaborated:

> Now it has gone drug crazy. I see places in Brooklyn where people line up for drugs. And in the dark you must look over your shoulder all the time.

This distancing does not mean that the family did not identify with West Indian culture or move in New York's West Indian circles. Their ethnic identification, however, was grounded in a rather close and intimate circle of friends and family. Family members maintained close contact with relatives in Jamaica, and while Marie lived there the New York children often spent summers with her. Some of the older children even remembered having spent longer periods of time in Jamaica; Kathy, for example, estimated that she spent about half of her early childhood—before she began school—in Jamaica with her grandmother. After she started school in New York and until she left for college, she spent most of her summers at her grandmother's home in Jamaica, where several cousins also lived. These prolonged stays helped forge a strong Jamaican family identity. Kathy explained:

> A lot of the close feelings we still have for each other stemmed from the time we all spent together in the summers. I think it also served to help our generation feel those close ties to Jamaica. It was not a place where we went to visit Grandma for a week. We "lived" there for eight to ten weeks each year and very much participated in the everyday goings-on in the house and the community as well.

In New York the family, as noted, moved primarily within a small Jamaican circle of family and family friends, who belonged to the same social strata and who knew, or knew of, each other in Jamaica. Indeed, Bill and Charles found their spouses within this circle in New York. Marie told me:

Those who went to the States all married Jamaicans. In the States people are
more clannish, so you tend go with the crowd and you get close to them.
They all met their Jamaican spouses in the States.

Most West Indians who arrived after the late 1960s belonged to a different
"class of people." They represented a rather different sort of West Indianness, with which the family members did not identify. As the neighborhood
turned increasingly lower-class black, many family members felt more and
more out of place.

NEW YORK AS A PLACE TO LEAVE

By the late 1970s members of the younger generation who had been born in
New York City started to move elsewhere. To a certain extent this was a sign
of the family's integration into American middle-class life, in which young people commonly leave home after high school to attend college elsewhere. Kathy,
for example, declined a full scholarship at a local university and opted for a
partial scholarship at a women's college in Massachusetts. Her brother Mark
went to a black college in Virginia; Greg, their cousin, went to a university in
Washington, DC; and Shelly, another cousin, moved to San Francisco, where
she stayed with a maternal aunt and took night classes in business administration. These movements also reflected intergenerational conflict, also quite
common in middle-class American families, which develops as the younger
generation seeks autonomy and "to make it on its own."

Another dynamic was involved in the case of this Jamaican family. Some of
the movements from New York were related to family problems caused by the
death of Bill's and Charles's wives. After these deaths the circle of relatives and
family friends attempted to cushion the effects of the losses. Charles's in-laws
took care of his youngest child, Jim; Bill's youngest sister, Amanda, who had
moved to Dominica, took his younger daughter, June, into her home for several
years until June finished secondary school; and a young West Indian couple,
who had rented an apartment from Bill, moved into his household, maintaining a home for the older children until they were able to manage on their own.
When Bill and Charles remarried, the children were not keen to remain in the
households, and college away from New York therefore became a convenient
way of leaving. Within a few years all of Bill's and Charles's children had moved
out of New York; most never returned to live there again. Whatever the reason
for their initial departure from the city, as they grew older they moved to different parts of the country in accordance with their careers and marital situations.

Movement away from New York City was not confined to the younger generation. In the early 1970s—after having lived in the United States for more
than twenty-five years, rising to the position of district manager in his firm, and
acquiring several residential properties in New York—Bill decided to move
back to Jamaica with his second wife and his new family. He purchased a small

hotel and started a new career there. When I interviewed him in Jamaica, he explained that he had always felt somewhat alienated in the United States:

> I was of mixed origin. I had black, Negro blood within me, but to white Americans I was treated totally different from black students. And that, I think, still permeates American society.
>
> *You continued to be different?*
> Yes, a foreigner. The U.S. has room for foreigners. It amazes me to see a black Spanish-speaking person be more accepted than a well-educated black American. The latter is not accorded the same treatment. There is some respect, but the person is not socially accepted.
>
> *How were you foreign?*
> My way of speaking, and the culture.
>
> *It was an advantage?*
> Yes, in terms of social acceptance. But I didn't yearn for that. You know Marion Anderson? Josephine Baker? Josephine Baker lived in France where she was accepted.
>
> *You didn't feel accepted?*
> I was not genuinely accepted.
>
> *Did you have other places of belonging?*
> I traveled a great deal and I enjoyed it. I got an experience of people living in other parts of the world and how they react to people regardless of color of skin. There was more courtesy and amity than I had experienced in the U.S.—especially in my travels to Spain, where I visited five or six times. Not Germany, I never had the desire to go there.
>
> *Were you disappointed with the U.S.?*
> It made me feel I could leave America and go to other parts of the world and be quite comfortable.

While Bill never developed a strong American identity, he did not identify strongly with Jamaica either. Thus, at the end of the interviews in Jamaica, he concluded that he still identified most with Great Britain, the mother country during colonial times, and that he had always felt at home when he visited there.

Other senior family members also left New York City. At about the same time that Bill returned to Jamaica, Marie, his mother, began to travel a great deal among her children's places of residence, staying for extensive periods of time with her daughter in Dominica, where Bill's daughter was also living. Celia moved out of Brooklyn, at least on a part-time basis, when she and her husband purchased a second home in a Long Island suburb. Only Doreen, who had moved to New York on a permanent basis in the middle of the 1960s, and Charles remained in Brooklyn. In 1995, Celia died. After a heart attack, Charles decided to move to New Jersey to be near his son. Doreen began to spend more time with family elsewhere. When I interviewed her in her Brooklyn home in December 1997, she was planning to move to Nova

Scotia, where she had purchased a house near her daughter, who had lived there for several years.

By 1998 only Doreen—who still kept an apartment and spent considerable time in New York City—remained associated with the former center of the family network. Whereas Barbara had regretted moving away during the 1970s because she was leaving so many family members behind, those who left in the 1980s had no such regrets. Indeed, when Hubert—the only one of Marie's sons never to leave Jamaica—sent a son, Henry, to New York to live with the family and go to school there, the son could not wait to move away from New York. As the son later told me, "there was nobody there" and he felt very alone. His discomfort in New York was exacerbated by the fact that the Brooklyn neighborhood had become racially divided and he did not feel that he fit in. One day he narrowly escaped a severe beating when he chose a shortcut back from high school that took him through an area controlled by an Italian gang. By the late 1970s the racial composition of the old family neighborhood in Brooklyn actually led some relatives to give up entirely on visiting family there. Jane, who looks "white" and had married a Canadian of Scottish origin from a small Nova Scotian village, related that her husband had been so shocked when he visited the family in Brooklyn that he asked never to go there again. Jane herself was quite upset when, later on, her son and his stepbrother insisted on visiting their grandmother there. She explained: "It simply is not a place for whites!" The neighborhood's transformation into an all-black area therefore essentially meant that only the phenotypically "black" members of the family felt comfortable there. The neighborhood, in sum, had changed from being a place that brought the family together to being a place that divided the family along racial lines.

The dispersal of the family, however, did not cause family members to lose contact with each other. Many have kept up close contact over the phone, as is apparent from my interview with Doreen:

> *Whom did you call within the last week?*
> Jane and Ernest [in Canada], my mother and sister in London, my grandson in Canada, Charles [in New Jersey] before he left for Florida. When I am on the phone, I may talk for an hour. This past month I made long distance calls for sixty-eight dollars, but I was told that I had saved two-hundred-forty dollars on the calls at special rates.

> *Who called you during the week?*
> Amanda [in Dominica] and my son [in Canada].

Or listen to Shelly, who lives in California:

> We keep contact by phone, and I have a very expensive phone bill. It is hard for me to write because my fingers go numb.[8]

> *Whom did you talk to last week?*
> Last week I talked to Aunt Doreen (two days ago), Aunt Christina (Hubert's wife), who lives in Miami (also two days ago), and Dad [in New Jersey]. The week before, I talked to Bill in Miami, my cousin [Hubert's son].

Surprisingly, the kinds of movements I have described in the case of this one Jamaican family have received little attention in the scholarly literature. Whereas much has been written on West Indian migration to New York, there has been little study of subsequent movements. One reason for this is that American migration research has tended to focus on movement into the United States. Whatever the reason, subsequent movements, whether inside or outside of the United States, are an important part of the migration experience. They are essential to study if we want to understand migration as a process taking place over time and involving a variety of adjustments, rather than as a movement from one place to another entailing a specific course of incorporation into a new society.

In the Jamaican family I studied, post–border crossing movements among the first generation involved moving away from immigrant black neighborhoods to white, middle-class areas in Brooklyn, suburban Long Island, and New Jersey—or leaving the United States entirely. The second and third generations traveled for further education and career opportunities, in accordance with parental expectations, and they moved to establish personal independence from the parental home. In these movements the second and third generations acted, to a great extent, like middle-class Americans, concerned with establishing independent life trajectories and nuclear families of their own. These life trajectories, however, were informed by social relations and cultural values associated with the wider kin network. The present-day global extension of the family has meant that members of the second and third generation feel at home in many parts of the world. Moreover, they all identify strongly with the family's Jamaican origins, thus reinforcing links outside the United States. The family's racial complexity has also fostered a continued identification with Jamaica among individuals of the second and third generations and a sense that they do not fit easily into rigid North American racial categories.

CONCLUSION

This microstudy of one Jamaican family's migration to New York forms a small part of a much larger study of three Caribbean family networks that demonstrates how extensive movements, over time, both disperse family members and bring them together. By conducting life-story interviews with individuals in migrating family networks rather than doing localized field research in one migrant destination, I have been able to show the role that New York has played in the life trajectories of individual family members and the significance these relatives have attached to New York through time.

Over the course of some fifty years, New York, as I detailed, changed from being an important center of attraction that offered family members social and economic opportunities not available in Jamaica to being a center of family life, a locus of divisive family and racial issues, and, finally, a place remembered for formative childhood experiences. Each life story, of course, is unique, and New York's role for the narrator depended to a great extent on his or her particular life experiences and position in the family network and in society at large. Charles, for example, migrated as a young man to New York, where he received on-the-job training and established a successful career; he has continued to view the city as a place of opportunities unheard of in Jamaica. Bill did not, as his family had hoped, become a doctor, and he ended up investing money earned in the United States in a hotel in Jamaica and moving into the upper echelons of Jamaican society. He described New York as a place of respectable, middle-class life, a place that had to be abandoned as the city declined. Kathy, who lived in California without close family nearby, depicted New York as the place where she grew up in a village-like neighborhood surrounded by close-knit family, and as the place where she first became racially aware. Jane, who married into an all-white community in Nova Scotia, viewed New York as a place of racial divisiveness and tension.

A focus on the ways that New York was constructed as a place in individual life stories provides a multifaceted view of the city as experienced by West Indian migrants rather than a one-dimensional perspective on New York as a point of entry for migrants who are destined, in the long run, to become incorporated into American society. Indeed, the life stories of the Jamaican family make clear that migrants to the United States are not necessarily preoccupied with becoming incorporated into American society and being turned into good American citizens. The first generation of Jamaican migrants whom I interviewed were concerned with obtaining an education and establishing respectable homes in middle-class, white neighborhoods populated by well-mannered and well-educated inhabitants. Those who were disappointed ended up leaving the United States in search of opportunities elsewhere.

In the family as a whole, those who had lived for some time in New York were widely scattered. They lived in such varied places as a wooded mountainside in northern California, an exclusive suburban Texas neighborhood, a housing development in New Jersey, a rural area in Nova Scotia, a village in England, and a major city in Florida. Only one small branch of the family was still living in Jamaica. It may be that this extraordinary variety of settlement was a result, at least in part, of the family's racial complexity. Accorded a respectable position in colonial Jamaica's sociocultural hierarchy, those who left Jamaica had difficulty finding a social and cultural niche in a highly ethnicized and racially divided America.

The dominance of the incorporation paradigm within American migration research is connected with the view of the United States as a country that has received a steady stream of new arrivals who needed to become seasoned as good Americans and fellow citizens. As a result, immigration is seen as initiating a process of incorporation that will, in the long run, lead to full integration into American society unless it is stopped short by societal barriers such as racial discrimination or ethnic politics. There is a danger, however, that this perspective will ignore migratory movements that do not fit the pattern of incorporation. These include movements out of the United States, such as Bill's return to Jamaica, or temporary migration of the kind that Jane's life story reflected. For the study of the long-range historical process of constructing the United States out of new American citizens, these persons may not be of much interest. For understanding West Indian migration to New York and the families that have sustained this migration, however, such persons are central. Bill's case is particularly illuminating. Because of his successful career in the United States, Bill was able to sponsor or offer temporary help to various migrants from Jamaica, most of whom are still in the United States. While Bill played a central role in enabling many family members to move to the United States, he felt that he was not fully accepted there. His marginal social acceptance combined with his economic success led him to return to Jamaica. Ironically, when he returned to Jamaica he was offered a prestigious honorary position by an American institution, in large part because he was an American citizen. Bill's "career" as an American reached a high point after he had, essentially, rejected life in the United States. Jane, in contrast, never stayed in New York for extensive periods of time and did not even have a permanent visa to live in the United States. She probably would not be included in most studies of West Indian migration to New York. Nonetheless, the fact that Jane was part of the family's experiences in New York contributed to her cousins' sense of New York as a family place, and Jane was usually mentioned when they described the family there.

A wider family perspective, as reflected in these life stories, thus brings to the fore aspects of West Indian migration to New York that tend to be ignored or unexamined when the city is seen as a point in a process of incorporation into American society. At a more general level, this family perspective suggests that American migration studies may benefit if they cease to be treated as a sub discipline of the history and sociology of the United States and instead become inscribed within a wider framework of study concerned with the social, economic, cultural, and personal significance of movements between places.

NOTES

1. David Reimers (1987: 35) has noted that, while "Philadelphia, and to a lesser extent Boston, competed successfully in the colonial era for immigrants, by the mid-19th century between two-thirds to three-quarters entered through New York City."

2. In the mid 1980s, Sutton (1987: 19) estimated that New York had a population of two million Caribbean people, if Puerto Ricans were included. Kasinitz's study of Caribbean New York (1992: 4) states that half a million African Caribbean migrants lived in New York in the early 1990s but that this figure might have been twice as large if second-generation migrants and illegal immigrants were included. Waters notes that foreign-born blacks, the vast majority of them African Caribbean, composed 25 percent of the total black population in

New York City in the 1990 Census, and this does not take into account the large and increasing population of second-generation black immigrants, most of whom are from the Caribbean (Waters 1994a: 796–797).

3. This research was sponsored by the Danish Research Council of Development Research and was part of the larger research program "Livelihood, Identity and Organization in Situations of Instability." The Council's support is gratefully appreciated. I also wish to thank the members of the three family networks for helping me with the research. By *family network* I mean a field of social relations linked through kin ties. In a bilateral kinship system, such as exists in the Caribbean, kin networks are not limited in and of themselves. For this reason I have confined my research to the bilateral descendants of three Caribbean couples. The three family networks that I have studied therefore do not constitute the only, or necessarily the most important, set of relatives for all the individuals involved. This is especially the case among members of the younger generations, who also descend from other grandparents or great-grandparents.

4. A preliminary version of this chapter was presented at a seminar at the Institute of Anthropology, Copenhagen. I wish to thank the participants in the seminar for their helpful critiques and comments. I would also like to thank the participants in the conference on "West Indian Migration to New York" for their constructive criticism, in particular Nancy Foner, Don Robotham, and Connie Sutton. Finally, I would like to thank Kay Garth Lee for her perceptive and helpful comments on the revised manuscript.

5. The life (hi)story method has been used in several migration studies in recent years. See Chamberlain (1997), Gmelch (1992), Olwig (1997, 1998a, 1998b), and Sørensen (1995, 1998).

6. "William" and "Marie," like all personal names in this chapter, are pseudonyms.

7. For discussions of the importance of race and culture in Jamaican society, see Alexander (1977), Austin (1983), Austin-Broos (1994), and Robotham (1998).

8. Doreen had neurological problems due to a back injury.

PART THREE

Race, Ethnicity,
and the Second Generation

SIX

"Black Like Who?"

Afro-Caribbean Immigrants, African Americans, and the Politics of Group Identity

Reuel Rogers

Walking along Brooklyn's Flatbush Avenue, one immediately notices that the Caribbean has come to New York. All along the avenue, signals of a vibrant Caribbean immigrant presence shout at even the most casual observer. Storefronts advertise Caribbean symbolism—the bright colors of a flag, a palm tree, a stack of island newspapers in the window. Small, garrulous groups of men and women congregate in front of Caribbean bakeries and restaurants to discuss the news from "back home." Their animated conversations are thick with the distinctive inflections of Caribbean dialect. Jitney vans and dollar cabs perilously jockey for position as they compete for fares along the busy thoroughfare. And above the din, the sounds of calypso and reggae music ring out. This is black New York.

Only a short train ride away is Bedford-Stuyvesant, one of the city's older African American neighborhoods. Mixed in with the brownstones are a few venerable African American churches, where a mostly older segment of the population faithfully worship. Young African American men stand on street corners or sit on stoops, playing spirited rounds of "the dozens." They exchange clever barbs in an endlessly inventive form of American English vernacular. Cars speed by with the aggressive beats of rap and hip-hop music pouring out down-turned windows. This, too, is black New York.

Together these two vignettes provide a snapshot of an increasingly diverse group of black New Yorkers. Within the past three decades the cleavages within the city's black population have multiplied almost exponentially, a pattern reflected among blacks throughout the country. The divisions among blacks nationwide are many: economic, regional, generational, and so on. The most pronounced sign of diversification among black New Yorkers, however, is the division between the native- and the foreign-born. Native-born African Americans predominate, but their numbers are in relative decline. The number of black immigrants from the Caribbean, in contrast, has increased rapidly over the last few decades. Recent estimates put their numbers at roughly six hundred thousand, which constitutes almost one-third of New York's black population.[1] If the current immigration and demographic trends persist, first- and second-generation Afro-Caribbean immigrants will soon outnumber African Americans in the population.[2] To speak of the city's black constituency, then, is to refer to a heavily foreign-born population. To make a more general point, black New Yorkers are a diverse population in flux.

In light of this growing diversity, monolithic categorizations of the city's black population have become increasingly untenable. In much of the influential scholarship on racial and ethnic politics in the United States, there has been a longstanding tendency to treat the black population as if it were a homogeneous lot. Many studies routinely ignore or elide *intragroup* differences, tensions, and conflicts within black politics. Such treatments simplistically assume or imply an undifferentiated black community bound by common experiences and wedded to some unitary vision of a political agenda. In short, these studies often leave us with lamentably superficial, one-dimensional analyses of black politics and the uncomplicated notion of an essential racial community. To posit an undifferentiated black collectivity, however, is to ignore how class, gender, and *ethnic* divisions within race may shape reality differently for members of the group. As Michael Omi and Howard Winant (1994: 23) have noted, "Blacks in ethnic terms are as diverse as whites." Sophisticated analyses of black politics, then, are obliged to take note of this diversity.

In recent years, social scientists have begun to consider the political implications of these emerging patterns of differentiation within the black population.[3] Their inquiries typically focus on three key analytical questions. First, do American blacks in the post–civil rights era share a common set of racial group interests? Second, is there a unified black political agenda? Finally, do blacks in general subscribe to a shared racial group identity that tends to inform their political attitudes and behavior? The growing differentiation among blacks has made these questions the subject of intense scholarly and public debate. To quote one observer, "the meaning of being Black, who is 'allowed' to be Black, and the content of a Black agenda(s), is now more fiercely contested . . . than before" (Dawson 1994a: 195).

The deepening economic division between middle- and lower-class blacks has been the topic of much of this research and debate. In keeping with the predictions of pluralist theory, many scholars expect economic differences between middle-class and poor blacks to lead inevitably to political differentiation. More precisely, conventional wisdom suggests that the divergent material interests of middle- and lower-class blacks will necessarily fragment the black political agenda, dissolve shared racial group interests, and weaken individual attachments to racial group identity. In short, class interests should overwhelm racial group unity in the political sphere.

Counter to these predictions, several researchers have found that many poor and middle-class blacks continue to show strong attachment to their racial identity in their political opinions and behavior (Dawson 1994b; Tate 1993; Gurin, Hatchett, and Jackson 1989; Pinderhughes 1987). The scholarship indicates that many blacks subscribe to a common set of racial group interests, as well as a shared racial group identity. These findings are especially pronounced among middle-class blacks: they show even greater attachment to racial group identity than their lower-class counterparts and routinely elevate their racial interests above their objective class interests. Accordingly, several scholars have concluded that shared racial identity among blacks overwhelms intragroup class differences. To put the point more bluntly, they believe that race trumps class in the political lives of American blacks, leading to a high degree of political unity within the group.[4]

While most of the recent scholarship has focused on economic cleavages among blacks, comparatively little attention has been directed to other divisions within the population, leaving a noticeable lacuna in the literature. The rapidly growing number of Caribbean-born black immigrants in New York invites us to shift the analytical lens to another source of cleavage within the black population: the division between the native- and the foreign-born. Afro-Caribbean immigrants are an especially instructive case for exploring some of the major conundrums in American racial politics, including this latest inquiry into the effects of differentiation within the black population. Although these black immigrants share a racial group classification with African Americans, they also have claim to a distinctive *ethnic* identity separate from the *racial* status they share with native-born blacks. While they share racial minority status with African Americans, they have the option of identifying as voluntary immigrants with a distinct ethnic identity. They are thus black ethnics, with access to both *racial* and *ethnic* markers of group identification.

The intersection of these two identities in this subgroup of the black population prompts several intriguing questions. Do Afro-Caribbean immigrants subscribe to the same strong sense of racial group identity as African Americans? Indeed, does a common racial identity overwhelm the differences between these two groups of blacks, unifying them around some set of collective interests? Alternatively, does ethnic identity override racial group identification among Afro-Caribbean immigrants, giving rise to a distinct set of interests or attitudes that divide them from African Americans? Ostensibly, these questions follow the current fashion of probing into the effects of group differentiation on black politics. While most of the recent studies have explored whether race or class dominates the self-identities and political choices of blacks, the issue in this case is not between race and class but between race and ethnicity.

In the small but rapidly expanding literature on Afro-Caribbeans in the United States, the question of how the immigrants conceive of their group identity—that is, whether they tend to identify ethnically or racially—has already become a fertile site of scholarly inquiry. Some researchers have argued that Afro-Caribbeans tend to emphasize their ethnic identities as voluntary immigrants, often with the aim of distancing themselves from African Americans and avoiding racial stigmatization as blacks in the United States (Reid 1969 [1939]; Bryce-Laporte 1972; Waters 1999a, 1996a). In its least blunt and perhaps most common formulation, this view suggests that ethnic group identification among Afro-Caribbeans might occasionally militate against any strong sense of shared racial identity with their native-born counterparts.

Other researchers, however, maintain that prevailing racial inequalities in American life ultimately compel Afro-Caribbeans to unite with African Americans around a shared racial group identity (Kasinitz 1992; Foner 1987; Sutton and Makiesky-Barrow 1987; Vickerman 1998). While most acknowledge the salience of ethnic group loyalties among Afro-Caribbean immigrants, they nonetheless conclude that racial identification holds more sway in many instances. As long as blacks are subject to categoric racial treatment and discrimination, the argument goes, Afro-Caribbeans will be inclined to identify racially with African Americans. This view is consistent with recent scholarly findings about African Americans' strong attachment to their racial identity, regardless of socioeconomic background. In both cases, scholars argue that persisting racism heightens racial group identification among blacks.

Whether Afro-Caribbeans identify ethnically or racially, the practical implications of both views are clear. If they tend to identify racially, then they may also share many of the political attitudes of African Americans; moreover, they can be expected to join African Americans in coalitions defined by shared racial group interests. On the other hand, if Afro-Caribbeans are more inclined to emphasize their ethnic identities and distance themselves from their native-born counterparts, the prospects for such coalitions will be less certain.

This chapter explores the issue of Afro-Caribbean group identification and the underlying political implications. I avoid framing the question as a matter of Afro-Caribbeans choosing between racial and ethnic identities. That formulation mistakenly implies that the choice is dichotomous, that choosing to emphasize one identity is automatically a negation of the other. Worse, it encourages the misconception that racial and ethnic identities are fixed, or essential, in greater or lesser degrees.[5] Racial and ethnic identities are complex, fluid categories. Individuals may have multiple identities that they hold simultaneously and manage differently within the varying contexts of their social and political lives. Accordingly, Afro-Caribbean immigrants may embrace both their ethnic and racial identities without contradiction. Even more important, they may understand and experience their racial identification differently than African Americans do. As Dawson (1994b: 207) observes, "A black woman working in a textile mill, a black male judge, and a young inner-city gang member all experience race differently." Likewise, black immigrants and their native-born counterparts may attach different meanings to their racial identities.

Drawing from a series of interviews with first-generation Afro-Caribbean immigrants, I argue that most of these foreign-born blacks choose their ethnic or home country identity as their primary or core group identification. That identity frequently informs their political thinking and behavior. Further, the immigrants' ethnic identity and transnational attachments to their home countries make for subtle, but nonetheless important, differences in how they and African Americans make sense of the political world. Nevertheless, the immigrants also identify readily as blacks and see no contradiction between their ethnicity and their racial group identity. Racial self-identification among Afro-Caribbeans is not at all surprising in light of continuing patterns of racial stratification in the United States. Indeed, I argue that persisting racial divisions in this country make racial identification among blacks, both immigrant and native-born, a virtual inevitability.[6] Yet I also suggest that racial identification among Afro-Caribbeans does not occur simply in default of America's grim racial realities; nor is this identity purely a matter of oppositional or adversarial consciousness, as some researchers have insisted. Racial identification has important affirmative meaning for immigrants, a fact that these scholars have tended to overlook.

Moreover, I argue that individual blacks may experience their racial identity differently and embrace it with varying degrees of intensity. Not surprisingly, then, I find that the immigrants' conception of their racial identity and its political entailments does not necessarily comport with African American understandings of that identity. I show that variations in how the two groups understand their racial identity are due to differences in their cognitive frames of reference and the institutional contexts within which their political socialization occurs. First, by virtue of their immigrant status, Afro-Caribbeans define themselves from a different frame of reference than their native-born counterparts. Second, African Americans' sense of their racial identity derives from their socialization within a set of institutions to which Afro-Caribbeans may have little or no connection. Taken together, these two factors give the immigrants a sense of their racial identity that may differ from that of their native-born counterparts.

For the sake of analytical comparison and symmetry, the chapter begins with a brief consideration of the dynamics of racial group identification among African Americans. The discussion then turns to an analysis of Afro-Caribbean group identity and its political implications. I conclude with some tentative predictions about how patterns of group identification among Afro-Caribbean immigrants might evolve over time, particularly into the second generation. These predictions and my analytical inferences about Afro-Caribbean group identity are extrapolated from the response patterns of my interview subjects. I interviewed fifty-nine first-generation Afro-Caribbean immigrants in New York City: thirty-five women and twenty-four men. The respondents were predominantly middle and working class, and more politically active than the average immigrant. I used an open-ended, structured questionnaire and employed snowball sampling techniques to recruit respondents from community board and political club meetings.

The interviews included a series of questions about self-identification, group attachments, and racial identity. For purposes of comparison, many of the questions about racial identity were replicated from the National Black Politics Study, the data source for many recent works on the politics of African American racial group identification. The interview format allowed me to expand on these questions and to prod respondents to elaborate on the more deeply subjective dimensions of group identification. Nevertheless, due to the small size of the interview sample, I take care to make only the most cautious inferences from respondents' answers. More generally, the chapter focuses on patterns in the responses rather than on absolute sizes. Before I delve into those findings, however, let us briefly consider patterns of racial group identification among African Americans and the accompanying political implications.

THE POLITICS OF AFRICAN AMERICAN RACIAL GROUP IDENTITY

Racial group identity has played a pivotal part in the political lives of African Americans. Indeed, racial group attachments have assumed far greater political significance and cognitive utility among black Americans than comparable ethnic group ties among whites. According to pluralist scholars, ethnic group attachments among whites have provided cues for partisan allegiance and functioned as symbolic markers for choosing candidates in elections, especially among the immigrant generation. Even the most casual historian of New York City politics, for example, can point to instances of politicians using ethnic cues to mobilize Italian Catholics, Jews, and so on. Yet these ethnic attachments never crystallized into sustained political identities with identifiable ideological implications.[7] More to the point, while ethnic identities have had important symbolic significance for white voters, they have not had far-reaching instrumental influence on their political attitudes and policy choices. Indeed, whatever limited political influence ethnicity has for whites, it loses much of its salience once they attain middle-class status. Most scholars agree that ethnic identification is often a matter of cultural symbolism or nostalgic fancy—and hence of little practical political significance—for most middle-class whites (see, for instance, Waters 1990; Alba 1990).

Among black Americans, however, racial identity has had much deeper political significance. It has served as a rallying point for group mobilization, as a device for resisting racial discrimination, and as an interpretive lens for making sense of the political world. In short, shared racial identity has had a deep and persisting influence on African American political attitudes and behavior. Most researchers agree that racial identity took on heightened political significance for black Americans during the civil rights era, when it became a flashpoint for group solidarity and collective mobilization of almost epic proportions (McAdam 1982; Morris, Hatchett, and Brown 1989). But the politicization of racial group identity among African Americans can be traced as far back as the emancipationist struggles of the antebellum era.

Researchers have suggested that the salience of racial identity among African Americans is largely a consequence of the sharp racial divisions in American life and the long-standing patterns of racial subordination to which blacks in this country have been subject. This conclusion is practically a matter of scholarly consensus. At least until the 1960s, African Americans' life chances were overwhelmingly determined by their shared ascriptive racial status. Further, those life chances were almost uniformly bleak in the face of persistent racial exclusion and discrimination. African Americans, to quote one writer, were subject to the "perverse equality" of uniform poverty in which even the best-off blacks could seldom pass on their status to their children (Hochschild 1998: 44). Whether judged individually or collectively, African Americans' economic, political, and social opportunities were delimited by the group's racial status.[8] Simply put, "being black did much to determine one's place in the world" (Dawson 1994b: 57). It is no wonder, then, that racial identity has been highly salient among African Americans. Race has cast such an inescapable shadow on African Americans' life prospects that racial identity has in turn taken on heightened significance for group members. Quoting another writer, racial identity matters among African Americans because "race matters" in American life (West 1993).

Linked Racial Fate and Racial Group Consciousness

Still, that explanation alone does not account fully for why and how racial identity matters *politically* for this group—that is, why and how racial group identity has assumed heightened *political* significance among African Americans. Group identity itself is a complex social category that begs for analytical specificity. By the standard definition, group identity is a multidimensional social construct consisting of two integral components: group identification and group consciousness.[9] Group identification is a self-awareness of one's membership in a group and a psychological sense of attachment to that group. Group consciousness is a politicized awareness or ideology about the group's relative position in society and a commitment to collective action aimed at realizing the group's interests. Taken together, these two dimensions of group identity give race its political import among African Americans and transform this social category into a meaningful political identity for group members.

Group identification among African Americans—that is, their sense of racial group attachment and awareness—has had more political significance and utility than comparable ethnic group ties among whites or panethnic identities among Latinos and Asians.[10] Indeed, the sense of racial group attachment is so pronounced among African Americans that many routinely subscribe to a *linked racial fate* outlook. That is, their group identification is not simply a matter of racial self-awareness or group affinity. Rather, many African Americans perceive a determinative link between their own individual fates and the fate of African Americans as a whole. They "believe that their lives are to a large degree determined by what happens to the group" (Dawson 1994b: 57).

This linked racial fate outlook has deep instrumental significance for political decision making among African Americans. It essentially makes the racial group a central analytical category for political and policy choices. In Dawson's formulation, as long as "African-Americans' life chances are powerfully shaped by race, it is efficient [and rational] for individual African-Americans to use their perceptions of [African Americans' group interests] as a proxy for their own interests" (Dawson 1994b: 61). Hence the political thinking of many African Americans is governed, not strictly by their own individual interests, but by their perceptions of racial group concerns. What is more, they see their individual interests as inextricably bound to their racial group interests. Accordingly, their perceptions of what is good for the racial group are central to their evaluations of policy issues, parties, and political candidates. While group identification has been salient for white ethnics, especially in the early stages of their political incorporation, it has never assumed such a high level of instrumental significance and cognitive importance in their political choices and evaluations. Nor do whites perceive the same link between their individual life chances and the status of their ethnic group. In sum, group identification serves as a key cognitive frame of reference for political decision making among African Americans in a way that it has not among whites, or other nonwhite groups for that matter.[11]

Similarly, while radical group consciousness has been largely nonexistent or negligible among whites, it has been highly developed among African Americans. Group consciousness is the component of group identity that gives distinctive ideological thrust to African Americans' political attitudes and behavior. It bears repeating that group consciousness is a politicized sensitivity to the group's relative position in society and a commitment to collective action aimed at realizing the group's interests. African Americans with high levels of racial group consciousness are often dissatisfied with their group's share of social and economic resources and political power. They tend to take stock of the group's relative position in society by drawing comparisons between themselves and whites. They then reject the persisting group disparities as the unjust result of racism and other structural barriers beyond the control of individual African Americans. Accordingly, they seek redress for these inequalities through collective strategies and mobilization.

If strong group identification disposes African Americans to elevate racial group interests in their political thinking, racial group consciousness supplies the interpretive framework for making political decisions. Indeed, scholars like Dawson have argued that group consciousness among African Americans, coupled with a linked racial fate outlook, gives rise to a distinctive "political worldview" with ideological and strategic implications. Group consciousness, then, is the dimension of group identity that shapes political evaluations and behavior. It provides cues for comprehending and acting in the political world.

Racial Group Consciousness and African American Political Behavior

Survey findings suggest that much of what is distinctive about African American political opinion and behavior is driven by this heightened racial group consciousness and the accompanying worldview. In the 1960s and 1970s, when researchers found that African Americans tended to have higher rates of political participation than their white counterparts, many attributed this unexpected disparity to the acute sense of racial group consciousness among African Americans (Shingles 1981; Guterbock and London 1983). Racial group consciousness, the argument went, encouraged norms of community involvement and mobilization among blacks, which in turn led to greater civic and political activity. Now that black and white participation rates have evened out, researchers still point to racial group consciousness to explain why African Americans are more involved than whites in extrasystemic activities—protests, demonstrations, and informal community organizing—while whites show greater participation in system-oriented activities—voting, contributing to political campaigns, and affiliating with political organizations (Bobo and Gilliam 1990; Verba, Schlozman, and Brady 1996). Finally, survey after survey confirms that African Americans are more liberal in their political opinions and policy preferences than any other group in the American electorate. Scholars who study black political life have long contended that racial group consciousness is what gives African American political opinion this particular ideological hue (Dawson 1994b; Tate 1993).

According to Dawson, these patterns of political thinking and behavior grow out of a distinctive "political worldview" that accompanies African Americans' heightened sense of racial group consciousness. He writes, "African

American [racial] group consciousness helps form a political worldview at odds with the 'American ethos' on a number of key points, ranging from evaluations of the local police force to the advisability of expanded government intervention in the economy" (1994b: 58). It is not so much that this worldview is at odds with the American ethos, as Dawson puts it; rather, it is that African Americans often subscribe to a liberal, sometimes even radical, conception of this ethos, which sets their political opinions apart from those of whites and other groups on a number of policy issues and questions. Many African Americans no doubt would insist that their conception of the American ethos is more in keeping with the nation's egalitarian and democratic ideals. Accordingly, they are more supportive than other groups of government intervention in the economy and other arenas, particularly action to redress group inequalities and right racial grievances. Recall that the common thinking among African Americans is that these disparities are the result of systemic racism, the extent of which logically necessitates a governmental response. Although African Americans readily endorse many forms of government intervention, surveys also show that they are, nonetheless, more cynical about government institutions and authority than are other groups in the electorate (Shingles 1981).[12] This cynicism is understandable in light of the innumerable historical instances in which government power has been used to legitimize or support racial discrimination against blacks. Here too, then, ideological concerns about racial group inequality and exclusion underlie African American political attitudes. In sum, racial group consciousness and the attendant worldview furnish African Americans with a distinctive ideological lens for making sense of politics.

African American Institutional Networks and Racial Group Consciousness

As I noted earlier, researchers generally concur that high racial group consciousness and the accompanying political worldview noted among African Americans stem from the group's experiences with racial discrimination. Yet the absence of sustained radical group consciousness among white ethnics or more recent Latino or Asian newcomers—who have encountered significant though less severe discriminatory barriers—suggests that African American racial group consciousness is not the result of discrimination alone. Indeed, as I have argued elsewhere, if politicized group consciousness were an inevitable product of discrimination, we might have seen it among white ethnics earlier this century and certainly should expect it among Afro-Caribbean and other recent nonwhite immigrants (Rogers 1999). African American racial group consciousness is not simply the result of discrimination. Rather it is also an outcome of their political socialization in a network of all-black institutions—churches, colleges, social clubs, community organizations, and so on—that first developed during the era of Jim Crow segregation and continues today, albeit in attenuated form.

Dawson has labeled this network a "black counterpublic," Fred Harris refers to it when he writes of an "oppositional civic culture" among African Americans, and Melissa Harris-Lacewell has deemed it a "black dialogic space" (Dawson 1994a; Harris 1998; Harris-Lacewell 1999). What these writers have in mind is the network of black institutions in which African Americans historically have undergone much of their political socialization. The role of these institutions in African Americans' civil rights struggles is well known. In addition to serving as a staging ground for mobilization and activism, however, these indigenous institutions have also functioned more generally as socializing agents that instill in African Americans a heightened sense of racial group consciousness and a distinctive view of the political world. These institutional sites reinforce African American group identity, sustain a collective memory of the group's racial suffering, and convey values and lessons for how to make sense of the political world, respond to discrimination, and improve group conditions.

As Dawson (1994b: 58) explains, "[These sites] transmit the lessons of how to respond to shifts in race relations, economic climate, and political environment across generations." Evaluations of African American group conditions are typically made with reference to how whites are doing. The values and lessons transmitted through these associational spaces encourage African Americans to question or challenge mainstream values and the political status quo in light of continuing racial inequalities (Harris 1998: 11–15; Dawson 1994b: 56–61). Taken together, then, these institutions serve as a reservoir for "collective experiences, survival tales, and grievances [that] form the basis of a historical consciousness, [the] group's recognition of what it has witnessed, and what it can anticipate in the near future" (Marable 1994: 31). In short, these networks are sites of political learning—the crucible in which African American racial group consciousness and oppositional identity take shape.

Of course, this identity is not static, nor is it uniformly embraced by all African Americans. Although racial group consciousness is transmitted from generation to generation, some African Americans subscribe to a politicized racial identity only tenuously or not at all. The salience of racial group consciousness varies with an individual's political socialization and experiences with discrimination. For example, researchers such as Tate and Dawson have found that middle-class African Americans tend to express a greater sense of racial group consciousness than poor and working-class blacks (Tate 1993; Dawson 1994b; Gurin, Hatchett, and Jackson 1989; Dillingham 1981; Hochschild 1995). Though this finding may run counter to the predictions of pluralist theory, it is not surprising. For one thing, middle-class African Americans are more likely than their poor and working-class counterparts to encounter whites, especially in situations in which they expect to be treated as equals but instead encounter discrimination. Their experiences with racial discrimination in these predominantly white settings tend to heighten their distinctive sense of racial identity.

But this is hardly the definitive reason. In fact, as I have argued and other researchers have concluded, racial group consciousness is not produced simply by
discriminatory treatment (Herring, Jankowski, and Brown 1999).[13]

A second and perhaps more compelling reason is that middle-class African
Americans are more likely than their poorer counterparts to participate in black
institutional networks, which foster a deeper and more assertive racial group consciousness. Black institutional sites historically have brought together African
Americans of divergent economic backgrounds and thus reinforced a sense of
shared racial group consciousness across class lines. In recent decades, however,
participation by the poor in black associational and civic life has declined considerably (Harris 1998; Cohen and Dawson 1993). As Dawson (1994a) notes, the
"black counterpublic" has lost its "multiclass" character. More generally, black
institutional sites have been on the wane. Not surprisingly, then, shared racial
group consciousness among African Americans has diminished—a trend further
encouraged by the end of legalized racial discrimination. Nevertheless, racial
group identity remains salient among poor and middle-class African Americans,
albeit in varying degrees. Even in the face of growing class divisions, then, this
shared group identity continues to play a significant role in black political life.

GROUP IDENTITY AMONG AFRO-CARIBBEAN IMMIGRANTS

Divisions of nationality, however, are another matter. The history of tensions and
conflict between New York's foreign-born Afro-Caribbean population and the
city's African Americans is well known. Despite these documented and sometimes
exaggerated differences, however, there is good reason to expect Afro-Caribbeans
to unite with African Americans around a pronounced sense of shared racial
group identity. As blacks, the immigrants share a racial group classification with
their native-born counterparts. Under the peculiar American system of racial ascription, the two groups are practically indistinguishable by phenotype. As one
writer puts it, Afro-Caribbeans and African Americans wear "the stigmata of
subordination" in their shared physical features (Mills 1998). Ostensibly, Afro-
Caribbeans are thus also vulnerable to the same forms of racial discrimination as
African Americans. Finally, these foreign-born blacks have some obvious history
in common with their native-born counterparts: the deplorable legacy of slavery
and racial domination by whites. The question, then, is whether Afro-Caribbean
immigrants show the same patterns of group identification as African Americans.

Ethnic and Racial Identification

My interviews suggest that there are notable differences. There is some truth
in the two standard views on how these immigrants conceive of their group
attachments and identities. Afro-Caribbeans identify both racially and ethnically. They see no need to make a dichotomous choice, but instead embrace

both their racial and ethnic identities without contradiction. None of my respondents rejected their shared racial identity with African Americans; most of them, however, did choose their ethnic or home country identity as their primary group identification. Of the fifty-nine respondents, forty-eight claimed their ethnic or home country label as their core group attachment. One respondent proudly avowed, "I have been in the United States for many years, but I am a natural Jamaican and a naturalized American."[14] Speaking with the same unequivocal pride, another put it this way: "I'm Jamaican. There is a mixture because I know that my racial ancestry is that of Africa . . . but most immediate is that of the Caribbean. I'm from Jamaica. Jamaica is my home. Not Ethiopia, not South Africa. Those are the homes of my fore-parents. I respect that, but Jamaica is from whence I came." The respondents' strong attachment to their home country identity emerged regardless of how the question was posed. Consider this series of replies:

Some people describe themselves differently according to whom they are speaking. How do you describe yourself when speaking to other Caribbean Americans?
I'm Trinidadian.

African Americans?
Trinidadian.

Whites?
Same thing, Trinidadian.

Do you usually let others know that you're from Trinidad or the Caribbean?
Well, the minute I open my mouth it is sort of self-evident. So, I make it known voluntarily and involuntarily.

A sixty-three-year-old Jamaican man was similarly emphatic about his attachment to his Caribbean identity.

How do you describe yourself when someone asks about your social background?
I'm very proud to be Jamaican. I'm proud to be an American, by citizenship, by virtue of having worked and paid a lot of dues, taxes, rendered service to the community. I have no constraints in saying that I have earned the right to be an American. But I am Jamaican first.

Some people describe themselves differently according to whom they are speaking. How do you describe yourself when you are speaking to others from the Caribbean?
Jamaican. Yes, I have the same pride in speaking to any Caribbean from any country, and hope they have the same pride in their country.

What about when you're talking to African Americans?
I have no problems with that either.

So you don't modify how you identify yourself?
I don't modify. However, I am cognizant of the fact that there is some animosity [between African Americans and Caribbean Americans], and I'm careful how I express that.

What about when you're talking to whites?
I have no problem with that either.

Do you usually let others know you're from the Caribbean?
Yes. Absolutely.

What is most important to you? Being Jamaican, Caribbean, black, American, none?
Jamaican, Caribbean, American, in that order.

Note that the interviewee is a naturalized American citizen who has lived in the United States since 1962, yet he continues to view Jamaica as his home country and define himself primarily as a Jamaican ethnic. Most of the respondents echoed similar sentiments of an abiding attachment to and identification with the Caribbean and their home countries in particular.

Yet even with this strong attachment to their ethnic identity, most of my respondents nonetheless expressed a shared racial group identification, in terms of a sense of awareness and attachment to a racial group, with African Americans. Fifty-two of them reported that they "felt close" to African Americans, and almost as many said that they are personally affected by "what happens to African Americans" in this country. One middle-aged Afro-Caribbean man gave what proved to be a common response: "I feel close to African Americans because we have the same racial background. Our histories are similar." Most of the respondents were quite mindful of the similarities that Afro-Caribbeans share with African Americans and, accordingly, articulated some sense of affinity with or attachment to their native-born counterparts. Indeed, many of the same respondents expressed a somewhat circumscribed notion of linked group fate with African Americans, on which I will elaborate later. Yet it would be a mistake to conclude that Afro-Caribbeans subscribe to the same sense of shared racial identity as African Americans.

Racial Group Consciousness

While my respondents readily acknowledged their shared racial group identification with African Americans, they did not express the same highly cultivated sense of racial group consciousness that researchers have found among many African Americans. That is, they did not attach the same set of ideological and political meanings to their racial identity as do African Americans. The distinction between group identification and group consciousness has often been overlooked or neglected in the debate over the dynamics of group identity among Afro-Caribbean immigrants; however, it is critical to understanding the differences in how Afro-Caribbeans and African Americans conceive of their racial identity. In answering questions designed to tap levels of racial group consciousness, the respondents expressed considerable ambivalence. Take, for instance, this fairly typical set of responses:

Some people think it's harder for blacks to do well in this country. What do you think?
Um. . . . It probably is.

If blacks don't do well in life, is it because they are kept back because of their race, or is it because they don't work hard enough?
Probably half and half.

Although less terse in her response, a middle-aged Afro-Caribbean woman registered similar ambivalence:

Some people think it's harder for blacks to do well in this country. What do you think?
It depends on where they are. I don't know if I would make that blanket statement. Maybe within some systems it is. Where they are—the part of the country, what skills they come with, it could be, but I wouldn't say across the board, nationwide, that is how it is.

If blacks don't do well in life, is it because they are kept back because of their race, or is it because they don't work hard enough?
It depends on the situation. I would really have to look at it more.

Is success in the United States mostly a matter of hard work, or is it more a matter of one's racial or socioeconomic background?
I think it's a combination. I really think it's a combination.

Of the fifty-nine respondents, thirty-eight claimed that success in the United States turned on a combination of individual hard work and environmental factors. Another thirteen believed that success stems from hard work alone. And eight saw race and social background as determinative.

The ambivalence expressed by these first-generation immigrants contrasts with African Americans' attitudes about racial group conditions. African Americans, especially those with high levels of racial group consciousness, often attribute poor black group outcomes to racism and other structural factors (Sigelman and Welch 1991). That particular interpretive view of black group conditions—emphasizing systemic racism and other environmental variables—is informed by the distinctive ideological lens associated with high racial group consciousness. The Afro-Caribbean respondents, in contrast, pointed to a mix of structural and individual factors to account for how blacks fare in American society. Note that these are not diametrically opposed opinions driven by radically different worldviews. Rather, the ambivalence evinced by the Afro-Caribbean respondents suggests that their sense of racial group consciousness may not be as well developed or pronounced as it is among African Americans. More generally, they do not immediately attach the same political and ideological meanings to their racial identity as do African Americans.

Furthermore, although almost all of the respondents declared that they had encountered racial discrimination and that racism was still pervasive in American life, most also claimed that they were not as preoccupied with racism as their African American counterparts. One respondent observed, "We are concerned about racism. But basically we don't walk around with a chip on our shoulders like African Americans, although, like you said, we experience a lot of racial prejudice. America owes African Americans something . . . more opportunity. We feel less owed." A Guyanese man offered a similar theory.

> *You say that Caribbean Americans don't react to racism in the same way as African Americans? What's the difference?*
> You see, they believe that the white man took something from them, which he did, and they're always thinking about how to beat the system to get it back.
>
> *And Caribbean Americans don't have the same attitude?*
> No. We're immigrants. So we come here to uplift ourselves and go back home. So we keep the focus on that.

Such attitudes were prevalent among the interview subjects. Indeed, the respondent's claim that Afro-Caribbeans are less preoccupied with racism than native-born blacks is consistent with the findings of several researchers who have explored Afro-Caribbean attitudes about race, most notably Mary Waters (1994b) and Philip Kasinitz (1992). Yet it would be a mistake to read such responses as an indication of indifference to racial discrimination, a point to which I will return later. Rather, this observation suggests that Afro-Caribbeans recognize that African Americans may have a deeper sense of racial grievance than most other nonwhite groups in America, a sense of grievance tied to their highly cultivated feelings of racial group consciousness.

Differences in Collective Memory and History

Lower levels of racial group consciousness among Afro-Caribbean immigrants can be explained by two key factors. First, while African Americans have direct claim to a collective memory of long-standing racial subordination in this country, Afro-Caribbeans, as recent voluntary immigrants, have no such claim. Many of my respondents were mindful of this historical difference. One man put it this way:

> I was somewhere the other day, and I heard a leading legislator talking about what slavery and segregation had done to the psyche of blacks—but of course, he was talking about American blacks. . . . And I realize that our slavery in the Caribbean passed so many years back before it did in this country . . . and we didn't have segregation. I mean we didn't have much white people to speak of. Well, in Jamaica . . . when I was growing up I never heard anything about slavery and segregation. Whereas for African Americans, those things seem more immediate . . . more recent. And they are still living with the aftereffects.

Here again the respondent recognizes that African Americans have a historically rooted sense of racial grievance that first-generation Afro-Caribbean immigrants, though they might relate to it, do not necessarily share. What is more, that deep sense of racial grievance is a part of the collective memory constitutive of African American racial group consciousness and the accompanying political worldview. With no direct claim to the same memory, first-generation Afro-Caribbean immigrants have correspondingly lower levels of racial group consciousness. The immigrants come from small island nations where the history of systematic racial domination by whites is somewhat more remote and not nearly as extensive as it has been in the United States (Waters 1999a; Vickerman 1999; Kasinitz 1992). There was, for example, no long experience with Jim Crow segregation in the Caribbean. That distinction means that Afro-Caribbeans do not come to the United States with the same long-standing sense of racial grievance that their native-born counterparts have.

Social and Institutional Networks

Second, and perhaps more important, most recent Afro-Caribbean immigrants are not connected to the black institutional networks that have served as sites of political socialization and consciousness raising for African Americans. Recall that these networks foster racial group consciousness among African Americans by sustaining a collective memory of racial suffering and transmitting lessons about how to respond to continuing discrimination and how to make sense of the political world. With fewer ties to these institutions, many recent Afro-Caribbean immigrants do not have the same highly cultivated sense of racial group consciousness as African Americans and, accordingly, do not necessarily attach the same political meanings to their racial identity as their native-born counterparts. Indeed, more than a few of the Afro-Caribbean respondents acknowledged that they did not have the same historically informed interpretive sensibilities about race relations in this country as African Americans, especially during the early years of their adjustment. This is not to say that these immigrants are oblivious to continuing racism or the dynamics of America's race problem; rather, they do not necessarily have the same ready interpretive framework that accompanies racial group consciousness among African Americans.[15]

Those interview respondents who did report frequent or regular participation in black organizations dominated by African Americans—what remains of New York's black counterpublic—expressed the highest levels of racial group consciousness. For example, one respondent, who was an active member of a mostly African American political club, proved to be most emphatic about the linked racial fate of Afro-Caribbeans and their native-born counterparts and the need for collective political action to combat systemic racism.[16]

Do you feel that your fate as an Afro-Caribbean is at all linked to that of African Americans?
Yes. Definitely, in this country.

Why?
Because we're all considered the same—the same, meaning minority or black.
So, we're not separated or separable, in terms of discrimination. And we have
to join together to fight against it.

He also expressed a much stronger sense of racial group consciousness than
many of the other respondents.

Why do some people make it in the United States and others don't? Is it because of their
race, hard work, or a little bit of both?
I think it's race that prevents many of us from not having the same
opportunities, and we have to make it up with hard work. It's not fair, but
that's the reality. So when opportunities do become available, you have
to take advantage of them.

So do you think it's harder for blacks to make it in this country?
Yes, absolutely.

If blacks don't do well in life, is it because of their race or is it because they don't work hard
enough?
It has to be a case-by-case assessment. But one might not have the opportunity
to work hard, because of race. Often black people don't even get the
opportunity in this country.

It is clear that the respondent's contact with African American institutional
networks heightened his sense of a linked racial fate with his native-born
counterparts. This finding confirms the speculation by Herring, Jankowski,
and Brown that racial group consciousness is the result of "socializing experiences that occur within formal and informal [African American] networks"
(1999: 363). In sum, those immigrants who had the most exposure to African
American institutional networks had the most highly developed sense of racial
group consciousness.

The Politics of Transnational Identity

Most of New York's Afro-Caribbeans, however, are not initially socialized in
these traditional black institutional networks. They undergo much of their
political socialization and adjustment to the United States in transnational
immigrant networks, which bring them into contact with coethnics and sustain their ties with their home countries. These networks have developed in
boroughs like Brooklyn and Queens, where Afro-Caribbean immigrants
have carved out distinct residential enclaves with larger black neighborhoods (Crowder and Tedrow, this volume). While the immigrants live in the
same residential zones as African Americans, they have nonetheless established their own residential niches and attendant social networks. In the
context of these social networks, Afro-Caribbeans develop a sense of their
ethnic identity. They come to the United States with their particular island-

based identities, then develop a panethnic Caribbean identity as a result of interacting through these networks with other immigrants from the Caribbean. With their sustained attention to the immigrants' home countries, the networks inevitably give Afro-Caribbean ethnic identity a transnational focus. This transnational identity orients the immigrants toward their home countries. More to the point, it divides their cognitive and emotional attachments, as one writer puts it, "between two nations"—the United States and the countries they left behind. As it turns out, this transnational emphasis makes for a critical difference between how African Americans and first-generation Afro-Caribbean immigrants make sense of the political world and evaluate political options.

Transnational identities are not unique to Afro-Caribbean immigrants. Indeed, they have been attributed to immigrants in general, especially the most recent wave of newcomers to the United States (Basch, Glick Schiller, and Szanton Blanc 1994; Massey 1986; Portes and Grosfoguel 1994; Olwig 1993; Jones-Correa 1998; Bodnar 1985).[17] As one researcher explained, "however settled immigrants actually become, they continue to see themselves in a certain sense as belonging to some other place and retain an idea, albeit increasingly vague and ill-defined, of returning home" (Piore 1979: 65). In short, transnational identities encourage a "sojourner mentality" and fuel the "myth of return." Transnational attachments are quite pronounced among Afro-Caribbean immigrants. Most of the respondents reported strong ties to their home countries, reflected in frequent return trips, remittances to family and friends, and property holdings and other assets on the islands. Of my fifty-nine respondents, forty-eight claimed that they make regular trips to their home countries. A majority also indicated that they read Caribbean newspapers to stay abreast of developments back home and throughout the region. Most Caribbean immigrant associations and organizations in New York have a transnational emphasis. Moreover, almost all Caribbean countries allow dual citizenship, an institutional mechanism that encourages the immigrants to maintain their transnational ties.

Transnational attachments factor heavily in the immigrants' political thinking and help explain why their pattern of group identification does not mirror that of African Americans. Although the two groups share a common racial identity and the experience of discrimination, Afro-Caribbeans and African Americans map their identities on different, albeit overlapping, cognitive fields. African Americans anchor their identities—specifically their oppositional racial group consciousness—in the United States. In contrast, Afro-Caribbeans, as voluntary immigrants with transnational attachments, conceive of their identities on a somewhat wider cognitive map, which divides between the United States and their home countries. They straddle that divide, alternating between transnational attachments. Among these black ethnics, a transnational identity, which they hold in conjunction with their racial group identity, affords them cognitive and strategic options that are not available to African Americans.

Alternate Frame of Reference

First of all, a transnational identity provides the immigrants with an alternate cognitive frame of reference for making political evaluations. Recall from earlier in the chapter that many African Americans—especially those with a highly developed sense of group consciousness—measure their status in American society by comparing themselves to whites. Many of their political judgments, then, are informed by a black/white dialectic. What is more, their sense of oppositional racial group consciousness is often fueled or reinforced when they note the continuing disparities between themselves and whites. Afro-Caribbean immigrants, in contrast, compare themselves not only to groups in the United States but also to compatriots "back home." Or, as Milton Vickerman (1994: 123) has observed, "they . . . measure success by comparing their present condition with their lives in the [Caribbean]." Nor are the comparisons strictly retrospective. With frequent trips to their home countries and continued contact with family and friends, Afro-Caribbean immigrants can readily evaluate their status relative to that of groups "back home."

Simply by migrating, immigrants secure a somewhat higher status in their home countries, where they are often viewed as a highly motivated and select group. Although migration to the United States is hardly uncommon among Caribbean populations, those who immigrate still acquire a measure of prestige—or at least generate curiosity and the burden of expectations— as "locals" determined to "make good" in America.[18] Frequent trips and remittances to the home country allow Afro-Caribbean immigrants to signal mobility and status. Many immigrants, especially men, initially suffer a decline in occupational status after immigration; nevertheless, there is still social prestige associated with migration. Even if immigrants experience only modest, incremental mobility, they can compare themselves favorably to those back home. Whether the comparisons ultimately prove favorable or not, many Afro-Caribbeans make evaluations about their status from this transnational frame of reference.

Often with little or no prompting, respondents, both men and women, made comparisons between "their present condition and their lives in the Caribbean." Consider this representative pair of responses to questions about life in the United States.

> *How would you describe your standard of living?*
> Fairly good. I mean, probably better than on the island. But I'm not sure.

> *Are you saying that you're better off now than you were on the island?*
> Well, not really. You have to consider the age difference.

Sure. But even looking at your family as a whole then and now, what would you say?
I'd say better off. It's hard to determine what's better off. One might say we
have more amenities and material things. But I'm not sure about other areas.
Better off is really subjective.

A Jamaican woman used a similar transnational lens to assess the quality of
her children's schooling.

What local political issues do you most care about?
Education for sure, and quality-of-life issues.

Are you satisfied with the quality of education at your children's schools?
Not really. My children are doing okay. But the teachers don't seem to care
about the kids' learning like they did back in Jamaica. If I could afford it, I
would send them to private school.

As these exchanges indicate, the transnational frame of reference surfaced
particularly in respondents' answers to questions involving assessments of
some qualitative dimension of their lives. The immigrants' political decisions, then, may often be based on assessments made from a transnational
frame of reference and not necessarily on the basis of the black/white dialectic that frequently informs African American political thinking and behavior. While Afro-Caribbean immigrants are saddled with the same racial
minority label as African Americans, they also derive their own sense of status, self-definition, and perspective from their transnational attachments to
their home countries. Thus we should not expect them to respond to racial
frustrations in exactly the same manner as African Americans, nor should we
be surprised that they understand their racial identity differently from their
native-born counterparts.

Exit Option

A transnational identity also furnishes Afro-Caribbean immigrants with a
strategic option for responding to racial discrimination, an option not available to African Americans. Some scholars have argued that the transnational
frame of reference disposes immigrants to dismiss or minimize racial barriers
as temporary inconveniences. John Ogbu, for instance, contends that "voluntary immigrants tend to interpret the economic, political, and social barriers
against them as more or less temporary problems, as problems they will overcome or can overcome with the passage of time and with hard work" (Ogbu
1990: 526). He contrasts this immigrant outlook with that of African Americans, who often view racial barriers as systematic or entrenched and thus have
a more radical response to them. While Ogbu and others are correct in their
emphasis on the immigrants' alternate frame of reference, he reaches the
wrong interpretive conclusion, at least in the case of Afro-Caribbean immigrants. It is not that Afro-Caribbean immigrants view racial discrimination as

temporary or insignificant. In fact, they are quite cognizant of the stubbornly persistent patterns of antiblack racism that often limit their incorporative possibilities and frustrate their adjustment to life in America. Yet they recognize that, as immigrants with transnational attachments, they have a distinct strategic option for alleviating racial frustrations.

Afro-Caribbean immigrants have an *exit* option for responding to American racism. If the immigrants find their mobility blocked by insuperable racial barriers, they will likely maintain their transnational attachments and keep the "myth of return" alive. In such instances the myth of return becomes an option for escape or exit, which coincidentally may dampen the immigrants' interest in political participation in general, or radical political action or systemic reform more specifically. Rather than make costly political demands for reform, the immigrants can simply exit the political system.

When asked how they cope with American racism, many of the interview respondents spoke of this exit option. They repeatedly declared that if racial barriers proved too daunting they would return to their home countries. One Jamaican woman explained, "If things get impossible, I can always go home to Jamaica." A middle-aged Trinidadian man reported that he increasingly has begun to view his home country as a place of refuge from the rigors of American racism.

> *Do you feel affected by the recent cases of police brutality?*
> Of course, yeah man. It's so bad now even in my neighborhood. My teenage sons are always complaining that the police harass them. It's getting so bad that I feel like I should just take my family and move back home to Trinidad. I think about it seriously more and more these days. You know, we don't have this nonsense in Trinidad. Here you can't even feel safe with the police.

A Guyanese woman expressed a similar outlook with no prompting.

> *Have you ever experienced racial discrimination?*
> Are you kidding?! Many times. Americans are some racist people. They look at you funny on the street. They turn up their nose at you in stores when you ask a question. It's terrible, man. Make[s] me feel like just packing my bags, selling everything, and going back to Guyana. I just thank God nothing really serious never happen, like what's going on with the police in this city. I tell you if something like what happened to Louima ever happened to me or one of my children, I'd be on the next plane out of New York back home.

An elite respondent elaborated on the cognitive and instrumental utility of the exit option among her coethnic constituents.

> I go back to the psychological and emotional ties to the Caribbean. People feel that, "I have an option, I have an option. If things don't work here for me, I'll work, make some money, and go back home. If I don't get respect, or I meet prejudice, I can always pack my bags and go back home, where at least people will respect me."

Vickerman found this same pattern of invoking the exit option in his interviews with Caribbean immigrants. Reflecting on a past encounter with racism, one of his respondents explained his determination to return home: "This redneck guy looked around and told us that . . . he used to . . . kill people like us, meaning he used to kill black people. That only crystallized my resolve to leave here [the United States] and go home" (Vickerman 1994: 102).

Even if Afro-Caribbean immigrants never resort to this exit option—and few actually ever do—it nonetheless informs their political thinking and their identity or view of themselves. Although it remains only a contemplated choice for most immigrants, it continues to factor in their outlook. The exit option was invoked even by those immigrants who had lived in the United States for two decades or more. The choice to return to Jamaica remained a viable option for my respondent, although she had been in the United States since the 1960s. Similarly, Vickerman reports that the immigrants he interviewed "were 'birds of passage' in the sense that, though they evinced little desire to actually return to Jamaica, they wanted to feel that the option was always there for them. As they expressed it to the writer, they could always return to Jamaica if conditions became intolerable in the United States" (90). In appealing to the exit option, Afro-Caribbean immigrants stand in contrast with African Americans, especially those with a highly cultivated sense of racial group consciousness, who look to collective mobilization and government intervention to eliminate racial barriers. Bear in mind that earlier European immigrants maintained transnational ties as well—many resorted to the exit option in the face of the harsh realities of immigrant life in America. Yet for those who remained, transnational identity never took on the kind of instrumental significance that it has among today's Afro-Caribbean immigrants.

First, with improvements in travel and technology, maintaining transnational ties is far easier for newcomers from the Caribbean and Latin America than it was for European immigrants in the early twentieth century. For one or two European groups, like the Jews from Russia, grim conditions in their home countries made the possibility of return less practicable. Even more significantly, transnationalism among earlier European immigrants diminished under the pressure of the Americanization movement and the patriotic fervor of World War II (Gerstle 1996, 1993). Afro-Caribbean immigrants and other recent nonwhite immigrants have not had to face comparable pressures. Indeed, since the 1960s there has been far greater acceptance and tolerance of immigrants' ties to their home countries.

Finally and perhaps most important, transnational ethnic identity among European immigrants gradually declined as they gained entry to almost all arenas of American life after World War II, in keeping with the predictions of the pluralist model. It is not clear, however, that the discriminatory barriers facing blacks—both immigrant and native-born—will disappear anytime soon. Hence Afro-Caribbean immigrants may continue to hold on to the exit option that their transnational identities provide.

The continuing utility of the exit option among Afro-Caribbeans also sets them apart from contemporary immigrants from Asia and Latin America. While the latter groups also encounter racial obstacles, the ones they meet are not nearly as imposing or pervasive as those faced by blacks. Asian and Latino immigrants may thus have less reason than Afro-Caribbeans to hold on to the exit option afforded by their own transnational ties. Consider for example Jones-Correa's thoughtful work on Latino immigrants in New York (Jones-Correa 1998). Much like this study, his research emphasizes the importance of transnational attachments in the political lives of Latinos. But there is little in his account to suggest that these attachments function for Latino immigrants as they do for Afro-Caribbeans—that is, as a device for responding to racial discrimination.

The persisting cognitive and instrumental utility of transnational attachments among Afro-Caribbeans is a clear contravention of pluralism's assimilationist logic. In the pluralist version of American history, immigrants have always profited from assimilation; relinquishing ties to their home countries and adopting the customs of this one have sped their entry into the mainstream. Afro-Caribbeans, however, may be the first group of immigrants for whom this is not the case. In fact, the racial barriers that block their path into the mainstream make it necessary for these black immigrants to hold on to their transnational ties and the accompanying exit option. Their transnational attachments give them an out for responding to the racial obstacles—a device that their native-born counterparts do not have.

The Question of Group Belonging

A number of researchers have argued that Afro-Caribbeans emphasize their transnational attachments and ethnic identity in an effort to distance themselves from African Americans and avoid racial stigmatization (Reid 1969 [1939]; Bryce-Laporte 1972; Waters 1996b). That argument is, in fact, the emerging consensus. Even scholars who argue that Afro-Caribbeans also evince strong racial identification often imply that the immigrants do so only by sheer default (Kasinitz 1992). That is, they identify racially because they are forced to do so in the face of persisting racial discrimination and limited "ethnic options." In one view, then, ethnic identification among Afro-Caribbean immigrants is a means for avoiding discrimination and stigmatization. In the other, racial identification among Afro-Caribbean immigrants develops only because it is necessitated by the terrible racial constraints of American life. The first argument is not entirely supported by the findings from my interviews. The second, though not wholly inaccurate, misses the affirmative dimensions of the immigrants' racial identification with their native-born counterparts.

The Afro-Caribbeans in this study were hardly convinced that their ethnicity would spare them from discrimination. While many of the respondents noted that whites sometimes compared them favorably to African Americans, they had no illusions about their own vulnerability to racism. In fact, respondents tended to identify most strongly with African Americans as targets of discrimination. As I noted earlier, many expressed a somewhat circumscribed sense of linked racial fate with African Americans, particularly in their shared vulnerability to racism. One respondent's sentiments typified those of many in the sample:

> *Do you feel close to African Americans?*
> Oh, yes. . . . Our histories are similar. It just so happens that some got
> dropped off here, and some in the West Indies. Yes, and how we are viewed
> in this country today. It's a matter of color. We basically face the same kinds
> of stigmas.

This sense of linked racial fate expressed by the respondents was, however, somewhat qualified. That is, the immigrants acknowledged the differences between their own history and that of African Americans and also made note of cultural differences between the two groups. Nevertheless, virtually all of the respondents expressed some sense of shared racial group identification with African Americans.

Many also spoke admiringly of African Americans' long history of resistance to racism and their struggles for civil rights. It is here that the affirmative dimensions of their shared racial identification with African Americans surfaced most clearly. One woman remarked, "You have to respect black Americans. They knocked down doors to make it better for the immigrants who come today." When asked whether he felt close to African Americans, another respondent offered, "Yes, of course. Mostly I empathize, and sometimes I'm sorry that I wasn't here longer to help them fight the fight that they fought for all the things they have now." Neither response suggests that the immigrants' racial identification with African Americans is strictly a matter of unlucky default, as some scholars have implied. Nor do these responses lend much credence to the argument that identification with African Americans leads to oppositional or adversarial consciousness (Portes and Zhou 1993; Waters 1996a). Rather, they indicate that some Afro-Caribbean immigrants feel a measure of proud racial group solidarity with African Americans, notwithstanding the differences in their histories and cultures. The immigrants recognize that African Americans have a long, impressive history of inverting what has been a stigmatized racial identity into a site of empowerment, mobilization, and solidarity. Scholars who have written about the adversarial or oppositional nature of racial group consciousness and its potentially negative consequences among Afro-Caribbean immigrants often overlook this point.[19] Not surprisingly, the most emphatic declarations of respect for African

Americans and identification with their antidiscrimination struggles came from those Afro-Caribbean immigrants who had ties to traditional black institutional networks and those who had resided in the country for the longest periods.[20]

One final point about Afro-Caribbean ethnic identity deserves mention. Respondents were quick to stress cultural values as part of their ethnic identity. They viewed themselves as hardworking, disciplined, and inclined to put a strong emphasis on education and professional achievement. Very few were willing to say that African Americans were lacking in the same values, although they tended to make these attitudinal attributions only to middle-class African Americans. While that itself is an interesting finding, there is an even more intriguing irony here. The cultural values that Afro-Caribbean immigrants attribute to themselves are precisely the ones that American society, as they understand it, is ideally supposed to reward. This process of striving and reward is the lure of the American Dream that brings many immigrants to this country. If Afro-Caribbean immigrants display the correct values, play by the rules, follow societal norms, yet find their mobility hampered by racism and prejudice, there is a distinct possibility that they may develop the same kind of racial group consciousness that researchers have noted among middle-class African Americans.

The same applies to second-generation Afro-Caribbeans. It may be that they will have little or no connection to their parents' transnational ethnic identity and, hence, no cognitive or practical recourse to an exit option. If they continue to encounter racial hurdles that impede their mobility and diminish their prospects for improving on the socioeconomic outcomes of their parents, they may develop an oppositional racial group consciousness much like that of many African Americans. There is already some evidence that this process has begun among the "new second generation."[21] Of course, a newly ignited sense of racial group consciousness among Afro-Caribbean immigrants or their children may not necessarily assume the same forms and content that it has taken among African Americans, especially with the weakening of traditional black institutional networks. Hence the question of what it means to be black in America is still an open and highly contingent one for Afro-Caribbeans and African Americans alike.

CONCLUSION

The contingency of black identity suggests that scholars should exercise due caution in making predictions and generalizations about the future of black politics in this country. The divisions between African Americans and Afro-Caribbean immigrants are a signal of the increasing demographic diversity and political complexity within the black population. Despite their ostensible commonalities with African Americans, New

York's first-generation Afro-Caribbean immigrants do not necessarily conceive of their racial identity or its political entailments in the same manner as their native-born counterparts. While Afro-Caribbeans and African Americans both experience racial discrimination and concur on many relevant policy issues, it would be unreasonable to expect the two groups to have the same views of the political world. Indeed, the findings from these interviews suggest that the immigrants and their native-born counterparts may have very different frames of reference for making sense of the political world.

What is more, the political responses of blacks to continuing racism can be expected to vary. Both Afro-Caribbean immigrants and African Americans agree that racism is still a looming impediment to their mobility; however, the two groups do not share a uniform response to the challenges that racism poses. When asked about their reactions to American racism, my Afro-Caribbean respondents spoke of the exit option furnished by their continuing transnational attachments. African Americans, in contrast, often look to their long history of collective mobilization and demands for government redress for lessons on how to respond to persisting racial discrimination. Even among African Americans there are significant differences. Middle-class blacks, for example, have higher levels of racial group consciousness than their lower-strata counterparts. Accordingly, these two groups might also be expected to have different political responses to racial discrimination. In short, there is no essential black political community that holds forth over all issue domains and political contexts. Perhaps with the smashing of Jim Crow the notion of a politically unified black community has become more difficult to sustain.[22] Like some of the recent work on class differentiation among African Americans, this chapter illustrates that there are various layers of diversity and political complexity within the black population that remain to be explored.

More practically, African American political leaders cannot take for granted the support of Afro-Caribbeans, or that of other nonwhite immigrants for that matter. Many minority politicians and some social scientists have predicted that the prejudices of American society will force new nonwhite immigrants into common cause with African Americans. This chapter and recent research on Latinos and Asians, however, suggest that a grand rainbow coalition of African Americans and nonwhite immigrants is not an inevitability. Perhaps African Americans could revitalize deteriorating black institutions by reaching out more aggressively to nonwhite immigrants, thereby enhancing the prospects for coalition building with these groups. Afro-Caribbean immigrants, at least, would arguably stand to gain a great deal from such a coalition. My respondents' ready identification with African Americans as targets of antiblack discrimination suggests that there is considerable basis for coalition building between the two groups. With their continuing transnational ties, however, the immigrants' support cannot be readily assumed; rather, it must be cultivated.

More generally, there are still troubling commonalities in the political experiences of African Americans and Afro-Caribbean immigrants that bear consideration. While race may matter differently for these two groups, it is clear that racism complicates the political incorporation process for both African Americans and Afro-Caribbean immigrants. With their high levels of racial group consciousness, African Americans have developed a fairly politicized awareness of the persisting racial inequalities in American life that disadvantage blacks. Afro-Caribbeans seem to have somewhat lower levels of racial group consciousness, but they nevertheless see racism as an obstacle to their full integration into American society. What is more, race may assume even greater political salience for these immigrants and their children as they continue to encounter racial obstacles, thereby contravening the "melting pot" logic of the pluralist model of political incorporation.

Like African Americans, Afro-Caribbean immigrants worry about being relegated to a kind of marginal citizenship in this country. Although the immigrants respond to this marginalization somewhat differently than African Americans, it leaves them no less conflicted about American citizenship and their prospects for full inclusion. Indeed, pessimism about their chances for incorporation ultimately may depress political participation among Afro-Caribbeans. Already there is evidence that black immigrants naturalize at lower rates than immigrants from Europe (Mollenkopf, Olson, and Ross 1999). Whites continue to achieve incorporation with relatively more ease and security than blacks and perhaps other nonwhites as well. In light of that continuing dilemma, Dahl's (1961) predictions for the full incorporation of all groups into American political life still seem all-too-giddily sanguine. Edmund Morgan's much more sobering view of an American liberal democracy predicated on the exclusion of a racially marked group has the ring of reasonable prediction (Morgan 1975). So long as racial stratification and discrimination persist in America, there is a distinct possibility that the promises of pluralist democracy will prove uneven, or altogether hollow, for yet another group of blacks.

NOTES

My sincere thanks to Jennifer Hochschild, Tali Mendelberg, Michael Danielson, Nancy Foner, Philip Kasinitz, Michael Hanchard, Dennis Chong, John Mollenkopf, Hawley Fogg-Davis, and Janelle Wong for their helpful comments on this chapter and project. Special thanks must go to Mary Waters for the title and her scholarly example. Research for the chapter was supported in part by grants from the Social Science Research Council and the Ford Foundation.

1. 1998 *Current Population Survey.*

2. I use *Afro-Caribbean* to refer to black immigrants from the Anglophone Caribbean region and to distinguish them from their counterparts in the French- and Spanish-speaking Caribbean.

3. While many of these cleavages have become more pronounced in recent decades, some of them are long-standing divisions that have simply gone unexamined.

4. Despite the high levels of political consensus among African American voters, Dawson and a few other scholars have found that middle-class and poor African Americans express divergent views and preferences on several key policy questions, such as the advisability of economic redistribution. Not surprisingly, poor blacks are more supportive of redistributive policies than their middle-class counterparts. See Dawson (1994b) and Cohen and Dawson (1993).

5. More than a few of the recent studies on the effects of increasing class stratification on African American group identity are vulnerable to this same criticism. For a trenchant critique of some of the more notable works in this vein, see Reed (1999).

6. Whites, in contrast, have much greater latitude in choosing whether or not to signify ethnic group attachments. As Waters (1990) has convincingly argued, expressions of ethnicity among whites are voluntary and symbolic—they are fundamentally a matter of choice.

7. Jews may represent the notable exception, although ethnicity no longer seems to have the same strong ideological meanings for group members that it had earlier in this century (Mollenkopf 1992).

8. Space does not permit a recital of the historical details here. Other writers have recounted this history with meticulous care and far more skill than I could manage in this short chapter.

9. Social psychologists and sociologists have developed most of the literature on group identity. For some important works on group identity that also devote attention to political behavior, see Tajfel (1981), Brown (1986), Conover (1984), Shingles (1981), and Miller, Gurin, Gurin, and Malanchuk (1981).

10. The political significance of panethnic identities among Latinos and Asians is still an open research question. However, extant research has turned up almost no consistent evidence that panethnicity has the same deep political meaning among Latinos or Asians as racial identity has among African Americans.

11. One study found that African Americans are twice as likely as whites to conceptualize politics in terms of *group* benefits (Hagner and Pierce 1984).

12. Recently, African Americans' cynicism and mistrust of government institutions has surfaced dramatically in their attitudes toward police and courts.

13. Herring, Jankowski, and Brown speculate that black racial group identity has less to do with status inconsistency and discriminatory treatment by whites than with the socializing experiences that occur within formal and informal black networks. For a useful discussion of status inconsistency among middle-class African Americans, see Hochschild (1995).

14. The interviews quoted in this chapter were conducted between 1996 and 1997 in New York.

15. For a related line of argument, with an intriguing case to illustrate it, see Waters (1996a).

16. In his detailed study of Afro-Caribbean New Yorkers, Kasinitz profiles Guyanese activist lawyer Colin Moore. This prominent immigrant furnishes another example of how exposure to African American institutional networks can produce a pronounced sense of racial group consciousness. As Kasinitz writes, Moore is "a black power advocate . . . who has led demonstrations against the harassment of blacks by Hasidic security patrols" and the like. By Kasinitz's description, then, Moore appears to have a keen sense of group consciousness. Hence it is not surprising to learn that Moore was involved in African American institutional networks just after he immigrated to New York. As he recalls, "I became involved in the United Democratic Club [and] was a member of the . . . NAACP" (Kasinitz 1992: 204–205).

17. For a discussion of incipient transnationalism among earlier European immigrants, see Bodnar (1985).

18. On the long-standing prevalence of migration in Caribbean countries, see Thomas-Hope (1978), Toney (1986), and Kasinitz (1992), especially Chapter 1.

19. To be fair, most of these studies focus on second-generation immigrants, but the caveat applies no less to this group.

20. Similarly, recent research indicates that Latino immigrants who have lived in the United States longer tend to express views on racial discrimination that conform more closely to the liberal attitudes of African Americans than to the attitudes of more recent arrivals (Uhlaner 1991; Garcia, Falcon, and de la Garza 1996).

21. Recent studies have discovered downward mobility, as well as burgeoning racial group consciousness, among second-generation immigrants from Latin America and the Caribbean (Portes 1996). Socioeconomic backsliding by the second generation contravenes the predictions of the pluralist model and the pattern established by the children of earlier European immigrants.

22. Kasinitz develops a similar argument to explain why ethnic politics did not emerge among Afro-Caribbean immigrants until the 1970s. As he convincingly shows, racial constraints in the earlier part of the century precluded the development of Afro-Caribbean ethnic politics. In the face of these constraints, he contends, Afro-Caribbean political elites identified with their African American counterparts as representatives of New York's black population at large rather than emphasizing their ethnic distinctiveness. In short, the pervasive racial discrimination faced by both African Americans and Afro-Caribbean immigrants made their ethnic differences less politically significant (Kasinitz 1992).

SEVEN

Growing Up West Indian and African American

Gender and Class Differences in the Second Generation

Mary C. Waters

In the early 1990s I began a study of West Indian immigrants and their teenage children in New York City. I was interested in exploring how they developed a racial and ethnic identity, given the overwhelming attention to race in American society. I was also interested in whether the first and second generations would follow the same patterns of assimilation as did immigrants of European origin at the beginning of the twentieth century. I conducted in-depth interviews and participant observation in order to examine the ways in which first- and second-generation West Indian immigrants balance their identities as West Indian and American. I found that, for both the first and the second generations, part of coming to terms with being an American is coming to terms with American race relations and specifically with American discrimination against black people.[1] In this chapter I briefly review the main findings of my study of West Indians, highlighting the ways in which class and gender shape the understandings of race and the ways in which the second generation identifies itself. I then examine the implications of the identity choices of the first and second generations for the future of West Indians in American society, and for race relations in American society more generally.

THE STUDY

The overall study was designed to explore the processes of immigrant adaptation and accommodation to the United States, to trace generational changes in adaptation and ethnic and racial identification, and to explore the reactions of immigrants and their children to American race relations. Interviews with black and white Americans who interacted with the first and second generations were included in order to understand the dynamic and interactive processes of self- and other-identification and the development of ethnic attitudes and stereotypes.

The 212 in-depth interviews conducted included seventy-two first-generation immigrants from the English-speaking islands of the Caribbean, twenty-seven native-born whites, and thirty native-born blacks, as well as eighty-three adolescents who were the children of black immigrants from Haiti and the English-speaking islands of the Caribbean. The first-generation respondents were drawn from two populations: unskilled workers at a food service company in downtown Manhattan (given the pseudonym American Food), and middle-class school teachers in the New York City school system. At American Food a sample of black American coworkers and white American employers (all of the whites who worked at American Food were in management) were interviewed. Samples of black American and white American teachers were also interviewed. The in-depth life-history interviews lasted between one and two hours and were conducted by myself, a white female, and a team of three research assistants, two of whom are second-generation Caribbean Americans and one of whom is a black American.

The second-generation sample included eighty-three adolescents drawn from four sources selected to tap a range of class backgrounds and class trajectories:

1. A public school sample, consisting of teenagers attending two public inner-city high schools in Brooklyn, New York, where I did extensive interviewing and participant observation (forty-five interviews).
2. A church and church school sample, consisting of teenagers attending Catholic parochial schools or a Catholic after-school program in the same inner-city neighborhood as the public schools (although most of these students were not themselves Catholic) (fourteen interviews).
3. A street-based snowball sample, consisting of teenagers living in this same inner-city neighborhood who could not be reached through the schools—either because they had dropped out or because they would not have responded to interviews conducted in a formal setting (fifteen interviews).
4. A middle-class snowball sample, consisting of teenagers who had ties to this same neighborhood, who were now living there and attending magnet schools or colleges outside of the district, or whose families had since moved to other areas of the city or to the suburbs (nine interviews).

RACIAL AND ETHNIC IDENTITIES

First-generation immigrants from the West Indies identify themselves according to their national origins, going to great lengths to differentiate themselves from black Americans. These immigrants have a particular culture that reflects their status as immigrants and serves as an aid in the assimilation process and to the immigrants' relative success in the economy. First-generation West Indian parents face many hurdles in trying to raise a family in New York. The materialist American culture, oppressive racial environment, and segregated city schools and neighborhoods pose serious obstacles to the children of West Indian immigrants.

The dilemma facing immigrant children is that they grow up exposed to the negative opinions voiced by their parents about American blacks and to the belief that whites respond more favorably to foreign-born blacks. But they also realize that, because they lack their parents' accent and other identifying characteristics, other people, including their peers, are likely to identify them as American blacks.

I found some clear divisions in the ways in which the second generation balances their racial and ethnic identity. This variation was related to attitudes toward school and work and to the socioeconomic backgrounds and trajectories of these young people. Some of the adolescents we interviewed agree with their parents that the United States holds many opportunities for them. Others disagree with their parents because they believe that racial discrimination and hostility from whites will limit their ability to achieve their goals. By contrasting the ideas these young people have about their own identities and the role of race in American society, I found a great deal of variation within the West Indian group. Some Jamaican Americans, for example, are experiencing downward social mobility, while others are maintaining strong ethnic ties and achieving socioeconomic success.

The key factors for these youth are race, class, and gender. The daily discrimination that the young people experience, the type of racial socialization they receive at home, and the understandings of race they develop in their peer groups and at school strongly affect how they react to American society. The ways in which these young people experience and react to racial discrimination influences the type of racial and ethnic identity they develop. The most important influences on how these young people experience race are the social class background of their parents, the type of neighborhood they grow up in and the schools they attend, and their gender. Youth who grow up in poor households in inner-city neighborhoods are most likely to adopt an "oppositional identity." Middle-class teens from integrated neighborhoods and schools are more likely to adopt an "ethnic identity." Girls and boys differ in the meanings they attach to these identities, and in the extent to which they see these identities as mutually exclusive.

THREE PATHS OF IDENTITY DEVELOPMENT

The interviews with the teenagers suggest that, while the individuals in this study vary a great deal in their identities, perceptions, and opinions, they can be sorted into three general types: identifying as an American; identifying as an ethnic American, with some distancing from black Americans; and identifying as an immigrant in a way that does not reckon with American racial and ethnic categories.

A black American identity characterized the responses of approximately thirty-five (42%) of the eighty-three second-generation respondents we interviewed. These young people identified with other black Americans. They did not see their "ethnic" identities as important to their self image. When their parents or friends criticized American blacks or described perceived fundamental differences between Caribbeans and American blacks, these young people disagreed. They tended to downplay Jamaican or Trinidadian identities, instead describing themselves as American.

There were definite elements of an "oppositional identity" among the American-identified teens. They were more likely than the ethnic and the immigrant teens to describe racial prejudice as pervasive and as limiting their chances in life. They talked of school as representing white culture and white requirements much more often than the other teens. They also were more likely to report that they sometimes describe a person as not "acting black" or as "acting white." The ethnic and immigrant teens were aware of these terms but were much less likely to see them as unproblematic and were less likely to use the term to describe other people.

Another twenty-six (31%) of the respondents adopted a strong ethnic identity that involved a considerable amount of distancing from American blacks. It was important for these respondents to stress their ethnic identities and for other people to recognize that they were not American blacks. These respondents tended to agree with parental statements that there were strong differences between Americans and West Indians. This often involved a belief that West Indians were superior to American blacks in their behaviors and attitudes.

Twenty-two (27%) respondents had more of an immigrant attitude toward their identities than either the American-identified or the ethnic-identified youth. Most, but not all, of these respondents were more recent immigrants themselves. Of crucial importance for these young people was that their accents and styles of clothing and behavior clearly signaled to others that they were foreign born. In a sense, their identities as immigrants precluded having to make a "choice" about what kind of American they were. These respondents had strong identities as Jamaican or Trinidadian but did not evidence much distancing from American blacks. Rather, their identities were strongly linked to their experiences on the islands, and they did not worry much about how they were seen by other Americans, white or black.

These categories capture the general identifying tendencies of each of the individuals we interviewed. Yet it is best to understand these categories as ideal types that simplify a much more complicated reality. Identity was situational and fluid for all of the teens we studied, and if any individual generally identifies as African American, for instance, this does not mean that there are no situations in which he or she might identify as Jamaican.

While the identity choices did not differ by gender, there tended to be a strong relationship between types of identity and outlook on American race and ethnic relations and social class backgrounds and/or trajectories. The ethnic-identified young people were most likely to come from a middle-class background. Of the second-generation teens and young adults interviewed, 57 percent of the middle-class[2] teens identified ethnically, compared with only 17 percent of the working-class and poor teens. The poorest students were most likely to be immigrant or American-identified. Only one out of the thirteen teens whose parents were on public assistance identified ethnically. The American-identified, perhaps not surprisingly, were also more likely to be born in the United States. Sixty-six percent of the American-identified were native born, as opposed to only 14 percent of the immigrant-identified and 38 percent of the ethnic-identified.

Parents with more education and income were better able to provide good schools for their offspring. Some of the middle-class families had moved from the inner-city neighborhoods to middle-class neighborhoods in the borough of Queens or to suburban areas where the schools were of higher academic quality and more likely to be racially integrated. Other middle-class parents sent their children to Catholic parochial schools or to citywide magnet schools like Brooklyn Tech or Stuyvesant. The children were thus far more likely than poorer children to attend schools with other immigrant children and with other middle-class whites and blacks (although some of the Catholic high schools the students attended were all-black).

Middle-class children who did attend the local high schools were likely to be recent immigrants who identified as immigrants. Because of their superior education in the West Indies, these students were the best in the local high schools, attended honor classes, and were bound for college. Middle-class children who were American-identified, pessimistic about their own future opportunities, and prone to antischool attitudes were likely to have arrived in New York early in their lives and to have attended inner-city public schools from an early age.

The social networks of parents also influenced the type of identity the children developed. Regardless of social class, parents who were involved in ethnic voluntary organizations or heavily involved in a church seemed to instill a strong sense of ethnic identity in their children. Parents whose social networks transcended neighborhood boundaries seemed to have more ability to provide guidance and social contacts for their children.

The parents of these teens grew up in a situation where blacks were the majority. The parents do not want their children to be "racial," that is, overly concerned with race, using it as an excuse or explanation for lack of success at school or on the job. The first generation tends to believe that, while racism exists in the United States, it can be overcome or circumvented through hard work, perseverance, and the right values and attitudes. The second generation constantly experiences racism and discrimination and develops perceptions of the overwhelming influence of race on their lives and life chances, perceptions that differ from their parents' views. These teens experience being hassled by police and store owners, being denied jobs, and even being attacked if they venture into white neighborhoods. The boys adopt black American culture in their schools, wearing flattops, baggy pants, and certain types of jewelry, thus contributing to the image of the "cool pose," which in turn causes whites to be afraid of them. This fear, in turn, makes the teens angry and resentful. Moreover, the media also tells these young people that blacks are disvalued by American society. While parents tell their children to strive for upward mobility and to face discrimination by working harder, the American-identified teens think their chances of succeeding with that strategy are very slim.

Thus a wide gulf arises between the parents and their children. The parents are absolutely terrified of their children becoming Americans. For the children to be American is for them to have freedom from parental controls. This is an old story in the immigrant saga, which one sees, for example, in novels and movies about conflicts between Jewish and Italian immigrants and their children. But the added dimension in the situation of Caribbean immigrants is that these parents are afraid of the downward social mobility that becoming an American black represents to them, an idea reinforced constantly in the claim made to them by whites that Caribbean blacks are better than their American counterparts.

One question—about how things had changed since the civil rights movement—elicited responses that demonstrate the teens' different perceptions of the role of race in American society. The ethnic-identified gave answers that I suspect most white Americans would give, saying that things are much better for blacks and pointing out that they now can ride at the front of the bus and go to school with whites.

> Things are much better now. Cause I mean, during the sixties, you couldn't
> get into white high schools. And you couldn't drink from the same water
> fountain as whites. You had to go to the back of the bus. Now it's a lot of
> things have changed (eighteen-year-old Guyanese female, born in the United
> States, American-identified).

The irony is that we were sitting in an all-black school when this young woman made her statement. American-identified teens saw things differently. The vast majority told us that things were not better since the civil rights movement. They think that the only change is that discrimination is now "on the down low," that is, covered up, more crafty.

> It's the same discrimination, but they are more careful of the way they let it
> out. It's always there. You have to be very keen on how to pick it up. But it's

always there. But it's just on a lower level now (seventeen-year-old Grenadian male, three years in the United States, American-identified).

Some of the American-identified teens pointed out that we were in an all-black school, and they concluded that the fight against segregation had been lost. The result of these different worldviews is that parents' faith in opportunity and a structure open to hard work is systematically undermined by their children's peer culture and, more importantly, by the actual experiences of these teens.

> It's worse now because back then at least you know who didn't like you and who like you. But now you don't know who's after you. I mean we don't have anyone to blame for anything. I mean, we know what we feeling. We know when we got there to get a job, we can't get a job. We know it is our color. . . . If you know who your enemy is, you can fight him. But if you don't know who your enemy is you can't fight him. And they're tearing you down more and more and you don't know what is going on. And there's a lot of undercover racist people out there, institutions and firms and corporations, that's directly keeping people out (twenty-two-year-old Jamaican male, six years in the United States, immigrant-identified).

The following response, given by a fifteen-year-old American-born Trinidadian female, points to the difference between de facto and de jure rights for blacks. She is taught in school about the accomplishments of the civil rights movement and her mother tells her all the time not to be "racial," yet her peer group and her own "mental map" of her surroundings gives her a very different picture.

> *Do you think things are better for black people now than they were before the civil rights movement?*
> In some ways I would say yes and in some ways no. Because, it's like they don't say that you can't go in this neighborhood anymore. But you know you really can't, because there will be trouble if you do. I mean you could go there, but you know you will get those looks and stares and everything like that.
>
> *What neighborhoods can't you go to?*
> My friends say Sheepshead Bay is bad. They say Coney Island too, but I have to deal with that. They say by South Shore, around there. And near Kings Plaza. They say over there. And by Canarsie. They say that's really bad (fifteen-year-old Trinidadian female, born in the United States, American-identified).

On the other hand, ethnic-identified teens, whose parents are more likely to be middle class and doing well or who attend parochial or magnet schools, see clearer opportunities and rewards ahead, despite the existence of racism and discrimination. Their parents' message that hard work and perseverance can circumvent racial barriers does not fall on unreceptive ears. Ethnic-identified youngsters embrace an ethnic identity in direct line with their parents' immigrant identity. Such an identity is formed partially in opposition to peer identities and partially in solidarity with parental identities. Ethnic-identified youngsters stress that they are Jamaican Americans, and, while they may be proud of their black racial identity, they see strong differences between themselves and black Americans. Specifically, they see their ethnic identities as keys to upward social mobility, stressing, for instance, that their parents' immigrant values of hard work and strictness will provide the opportunity to succeed in the United States. The teens' ethnic identity is very much an American-based identity—it is in the context of American social life that these youngsters base their assumptions of what it means to be Jamaican or Trinidadian. In fact, often a panethnic identity—Caribbean or West Indian—is the most salient label for these youngsters. They see little difference between the various West Indian groups, and the more important thing for them is differentiating themselves as second-generation nonblack Americans.

The teens' ethnic and racial identifications were also correlated with what they thought of being American. While all three groups contained individuals who spoke in somewhat patriotic terms of the privileges of being American, there was a difference in the overall interpretation of American identity. Ironically, the American-identified teens had more negative things to say about being American in the abstract:

What does it mean to you to be an American?
To be an American? The question's kinda hard for me cause I don't believe in the American dream. My parents believe in it because that's what they came here for. But I don't know, for me, the American dream. I would have to see equality among everybody. You know there's a lot of corruption and prejudice in this country and racism. People always brush it under the rug. But I'm very, you know, vivid about that. So, I'm like, the American dream, does it exist? Or is it a myth of something? I think it's something they portray to attract people to come here and to work for what they call the American dream is. And they actually getting a bum rap. The American dream does not exist, unless you have money (eighteen-year-old Haitian female, born in the United States, American-identified).

What does it mean to you to be an American?
American? Well, I live in America, so I call myself American. But America is just like—we were brought here to do work for Americans. So like, we work for Americans really (seventeen-year-old Jamaican male, born in the United States, American-identified).

The ethnic-identified respondents, who were also more likely to be middle class, often gave more positive appraisals:

What does it mean to you to be an American?
To be an American is to, one, be free. I think that's the main thing we have in our Constitution and the Declaration of Independence. Free to vote. Free to express our ideas. Free to go out and do what we want to do. That may be to go out and start our own business. I think that being an American gives the

individual the opportunity to make the choice to succeed, to be better. . . . I felt proud to be an American when I went overseas . . . or when America as a whole has done something great. Most of the time though I think of myself as a West Indian (twenty-two-year-old Montserrat male, born in the United States, ethnic-identified).

GENDER AND IDENTITY

Although there was no overall gender difference in the teens' choice of identities, there were significant gender differences in the meanings attached to being American. The two main differences were that girls experienced greater restrictions and control by parents and that racism appeared to have a different impact between genders. Boys discussed being black American in terms of racial solidarity in the face of societal exclusion and disapproval. Girls also faced exclusion based on race, but they discussed being American in terms of the freedom they desired from strict parental control, which was a much more salient issue in their lives.

Although parents monitored girls' activities more than they did boys' activities, the boys face a more violent environment because of the differential effects of American racism. Boys reported far more racial harassment from whites and from the police than did girls, and they felt less at ease when they left their all-black neighborhoods than did the girls. The types of incidents reported by the boys included instances of gangs of whites threatening or starting fights with them when they ventured into white neighborhoods.

In the two high schools where we interviewed, it was far more likely for girls to graduate from high school than for boys. The girls also perceived themselves as having more job opportunities than did the boys. The message that boys get from the behavior of whites, the police, and from negative educational outcomes is that they are unwelcome in mainstream society. This message appears to create a rigidity in their attitudes toward racial solidarity that is not present so much among the girls. Two pieces of evidence in our data suggest that boys pay acute attention to racial boundaries: first, boys are more likely to suffer social stigma if they speak standard English among their friends, and second, boys were more likely to report that they accuse others of "acting white" than were the girls.

In effect, girls experience less overt hostility and exclusion by mainstream society, while boys experienced a greater number of attacks on their rights to be full-fledged members of society. In terms of identity, this discrepancy created more of a direct choice for the boys. The African American identity many of them adopted has an adversarial or oppositional character to it— inverting many of the values of mainstream society and highly prizing racial solidarity. The girls also experienced exclusion and denigration by the wider society, but because it was not as virulent, direct, and all-encompassing, the black identity adopted by the girls is not as sharply differentiated from the mainstream as is the boys' identity.

IMMIGRANT AND AMERICAN IDENTITIES

What does this study of West Indians tell us about American society in general and, more specifically, about the present and future of American race relations? Early models of the relationship between immigration, identity, and assimilation tied together identity, political loyalty, and economic integration. Becoming American meant learning the language, voting, adopting the culture, and achieving economic security for oneself and social mobility for one's children. A number of studies of European immigrants who arrived in the nineteenth and early twentieth centuries and their children were conducted based on these theoretical expectations. The simple conclusion of these studies was that by the second generation most people had become hyphenated Americans. By the third generation the descendants of the original immigrants were thoroughly American, with a continuing emotional and cultural, yet rarely behavioral, tie to their ethnic ancestries. In these "straight line assimilation studies," successful incorporation into society was automatically associated with the loss of ethnic, social, and cultural attachments.

Recent decades have produced many critiques of this model of identity and assimilation. Ethnic and racial identities and American identity have been shown to be very complex, even in the case of European immigrants. However, one facet of these early models of identity and assimilation has always been central—that it raised an immigrant's social status to become American (Warner and Srole 1945). Becoming American was coupled with economic success. Yet the experiences of post-1965 immigrants and their children challenge this central assumption. In fact, especially for nonwhites, remaining immigrant or ethnic-identified can lead to greater success in the labor market and beyond. The theories of segmented assimilation and second-generation decline suggest that there are major benefits to being firmly ensconced in an ethnic or immigrant community, including access to social networks with ties to jobs, social networks and institutions that support parental authority, and protection from the stigmatized identity and discrimination directed towards native racial minorities (Portes and Zhou 1993; Rumbaut 1994, 1997a; Zhou 1997; Zhou and Bankston 1994).

West Indians are perhaps the quintessential postmodern peoples. The influence of the capitalist system, the interpenetration of cultures in the created societies of the Caribbean, and the long-standing role of migration in the everyday lives and life cycles of the region's population all point to the kinds of situational, multilayered, and socially constructed identities that are said to characterize the postmodern world.

The identities of these immigrants and their children must be understood in context. The identity chosen by any one individual is always chosen in relation to others, and it can change in response to different situations.[3] Yet current power relations in the United States mean that West Indians face a particular situation that narrowly shapes their identity choices. Assimilation involves becoming American blacks, who have traditionally been the most stigmatized and abused people in American history (along with American Indians). If anyone has an incentive to maintain either loyalty to another country or a transnational identity, West Indians in the United States do.

The story of how West Indians become Americans reflects many complexities and changes and demands a more complex model of what it means to become American. I have paid particular attention to the ways in which class, gender, and generation have shaped the individual identities adopted by Caribbean immigrants, the ways in which race and ethnicity interact and intersect for these immigrants, and the ways in which these characteristics shape how white Americans categorize and react to the immigrants.

Middle-class families, their institutions, and the environments in which they live provide substantial support for the maintenance of a distinct West Indian identity and for sharp cultural boundaries around the group. Working-class and poor families live in environments in which the children come to see little difference between themselves and African Americans. (In part this occurs because the high concentration and strong presence of West Indian immigrants in New York have "Caribbeanized" native black New Yorkers.) Class shapes how race and culture are used in the development of identity. Middle-class second-generation West Indians use their cultural identities to claim an American identity as a member of a "model minority." While not denying their black racial identity, these youth distance themselves from the underclass image of American blacks. Working-class second-generation youth, in contrast, simply become African Americans.

These patterns may surprise readers who hold popular conceptions of how immigrants become Americans. The people most likely to resist Americanization, for instance, were the middle-class teachers, not the working-class food service workers. Recall, in contrast, Warner and Srole's (1945) study of European immigrants, in which they suggest that ethnicity is a sort of "consolation prize" for people who do not achieve social mobility.

Yet even among the teachers we interviewed only a minority showed active resistance to becoming American. Most people very much wanted to become American, even though they thought that America was in many ways still a "white world." Among the second generation about a third of the sample was classified as immigrant-identified. The few teens who were born in the United States and yet maintained an immigrant identity came the closest to representing any evidence of sustained transnational identities. They were very likely to have traveled back to visit relatives in the islands or were even sent back for schooling, for child care, or on summer vacations. Besides these teens, most of the people with an immigrant identity were more recent immigrants. The immigrant identity seemed the most difficult identity to maintain under the constant pressure to come to terms with how others identified you—as American black.

Teens who traveled back and forth between New York and the islands were the exception. Most immigrants could not afford to send their children back, nor to travel to the islands much themselves. Among the food service workers, only six out of thirty-four immigrants had ever been back to visit their homeland. Most of the workers could not afford visits or even frequent phone calls back home. They were struggling to get by in America, and, as much as they liked to entertain thoughts of retiring to the islands, most were firmly planted in the United States. Even among the more economically secure teachers, travel back to the islands was seen as a big expense. Only nine of the twenty-five teachers we interviewed had traveled home within the last ten years.

Most of the immigrants we spoke to, like earlier immigrants, came to the United States for selfish, individual reasons. They wanted to make a better life for themselves and realized they could make more money in the United States than back home. There were also greater opportunities for employment in the United States and, for many, greater educational opportunities.

The debate over immigration has misplaced its emphasis in asking whether these new immigrants truly want to become American. No political or ideological considerations or policies of multiculturalism will keep them from assimilating. For these immigrants, choosing to become American is an economic decision. They come here to attain a better standard of living for themselves and their children, and becoming American is part of the journey.

The highest economic payoff, however, seems to go to the least Americanized among the post-1965 immigrants. One reason is that American culture seems to negatively affect the children of immigrants. The less Americanized they are, the better they do in school, the more time they spend on homework, the less materialistic they are, and the less they challenge their parents' and teachers' discipline and authority (Rumbaut 1994; Suarez-Orozco and Suarez-Orozco 1995; Suarez-Orozco 1987). Discrimination is the other key to this puzzle. The more foreign or ethnic the immigrants are, the more likely they are to have access to jobs and information from social networks, and the more likely employers are to prefer them to native minority individuals.

If there is a problem in the Americanization of immigrants, it lies not with the immigrant but with American society and most especially with the urban areas in which many poor immigrants find themselves. Public policy analysts concerned over whether current immigrants demonstrate loyalty to America should be less concerned with questions of civic incorporation and transnational ties and more concerned with the paradox of modern American society. The best Americanization program for earlier waves of immigrants con-

sisted not of civics lessons in public high schools but in the enormous economic payoff that the descendants of European immigrants enjoyed. Today's
working-class immigrants, who come for many of the same reasons as earlier
immigrants, are rewarded for maintaining strong ethnic ties and punished for
assimilating into American minority communities. A concrete example of this
process is the belief on the part of some second-generation youth that culti-
vating a West Indian accent opens doors to housing and employment that are
shut to American blacks. The study described in this chapter suggests that the
kinds of discrimination members of America's native minority groups encounter is an important part of the process of assimilation and should be central to the immigration debate. We should not only be asking, "How can we
structure our immigration policy and our institutions to facilitate immigrants
adopting our civic culture and becoming American?" We should also be asking, "What can we do about the pervasive inequalities in American life that
sustain the perception that becoming American rather than remaining an immigrant leads to a less bright future?"

WEST INDIANS AS A MODEL MINORITY

For decades, liberals and conservatives have squared off over the question of
whether structure or culture is responsible for the problems of black Americans. Conservatives tend to blame the culture of black Americans for their
failures, arguing that they have a "victim mentality" that keeps them from taking advantage of the opportunities that exist in American society. Sowell
(1978), for instance, points to the success of West Indians in American society
to show that racial discrimination cannot triumph over "correct" cultural values. Liberals, on the other hand, point to the immense structural problems of
poverty and racial discrimination as an explanation for why black Americans
are not doing well in American society. They tend to argue that any attention
to the culture of black Americans is "blaming the victim" and takes away
from the real task of changing the structure of society to alleviate the problems of black Americans.

The story conservatives tell is that West Indians represent a "model
minority"—a group which, despite black skin and sometimes humble beginnings, triumphs over adversity with a strong work ethic and commitment to
education (Sowell 1978). Immigrants prefer this image and use it to differentiate themselves from black Americans. Empirical evidence lends some small
support to this stereotype—West Indians do have very high labor force participation rates (Kasinitz 1988; Model 1991; Waldinger 1996). Yet many careful analysts have concluded that other claims of West Indian success have
been overstated (Butcher 1994; Model 1991; Model 1995). By 1990 they did not
earn any more than comparable African Americans and their educational advantage had evaporated because of rising African American education levels

and declining education levels among more recent West Indian immigrants (Model 1995; Model 1997a).

I believe that white hiring preferences, along with a different metric for evaluating jobs and dense social networks that connect individuals to jobs, explain much of the difference between native blacks and West Indians in labor force participation. I have also argued that these are structural reasons for West Indian success—any group that found itself in the same position would behave in the same ways.

I do give more credence to cultural explanations for West Indian attitudes and behaviors with regard to race relations. I would also argue that the West Indian approach to black/white race relations can lead to acceptance and socioeconomic mobility in the service economy.

The immigrants' preparation for and militance about structural racism, together with their lack of anticipation of interpersonal racism, leads to more comfortable on-the-job relations with whites, as well as ambitious and vigilant monitoring of progress in job hierarchies. In an age of affirmative action, West Indians have the potential for success—they push for promotions and perks yet have easygoing relations with whites. One teacher told us that her principal actually came to her one summer, said he was under pressure to hire more blacks, and asked "where could he find some Jamaican teachers like her to fill his quota?" The food service company we studied has an extensive internal labor market, and, aside from one black American supervisor, all of the internal promotions of blacks went to West Indians. The food service managers were not at all reticent in expressing their strong preferences for foreign-born over American-born blacks.

In arguing that there are cultural expectations about race that explain some of the dynamics of West Indian success in the service economy, I am not in agreement with the classic cultural explanations for West Indian success put forth by other analysts (Forsythe 1976; Glazer and Moynihan 1970; Sowell 1978). The beliefs and practices I am describing do not stem from differences that arose generations ago, but from recent experiences in the Caribbean and from the immigration process itself. Indeed, the structural realities of American race relations quickly begin to change the beliefs and behaviors of the immigrants, and most especially of their children.

All too often, cultural explanations of West Indian success appeal to whites because of a wish to believe that something in African Americans' behavior and beliefs is responsible for their low status in American society, an explanation especially preferred by whites who do not believe that there is continuing prejudice and discrimination in American society. Whites who want blacks to "forget about race and past injustice" profess that blacks need only shed their "victim mentality" to do well. The experiences of the immigrants described in this chapter indicate that there is a small kernel of truth to this argument. The immigrants' lack of expectation of interpersonal racism makes whites feel comfortable with West Indians, thus providing a small advantage in the workplace. But the weight of the evidence leads to a different overall conclusion. It is the continuing discrimination and prejudice of whites, along with ongoing structural and interpersonal racism, that creates an inability among American, and ultimately West Indian, blacks to ever "forget about race." The behavior and beliefs about race among whites create the very expectations of discomfort that whites complain about in dealings with their African American neighbors, coworkers, and friends. Those expectations are not some inexplicable holdover from the days of slavery but rather a constantly recreated expectation of trouble, nourished by every taxi that does not stop and every casual or calculated white use of the word "nigger." If the West Indian experience teaches us anything about American race relations, it should refocus our attention on the destructive, everyday prejudice and discrimination for which whites are still responsible.

THE FUTURE OF THE SECOND GENERATION

Analysis of the experience of West Indians in the United States shows how rapidly structure affects culture. Within one generation the combination of structural racism—substandard schools, racially segregated and disinvested neighborhoods, and the discrimination of employers who fear urban black men in their workplaces—and interpersonal racism—blacks being killed by modern lynch mobs, followed in stores, stopped by police, called "nigger" on the street, being "looked at as if we have germs on our skin"—has its effects on people. Rightful anger, correct diagnoses of blocked mobility, and prudent protection of one's inner core from these assaults give rise to cultural and psychological responses best described as disinvestment and oppositional identity. To protect themselves from indignities, some blacks disinvest, especially from school, redefining social norms and behaviors such as success in school, speaking standard English, and so forth as oppositional to their core identities.

The story I have told here is, on balance, a sad one. Declining city services, a materialistic American culture, failing inner-city schools, an economy that offers little hope to the least educated, and a society where black skin still closes doors and awakens hatred can destroy the chances of people who have sacrificed a great deal for a better life. Many West Indian immigrants face the prospect of stagnant standards of living or intergenerational downward mobility. While a significant minority of immigrants and their children are rewarded with significant social mobility, many others, indeed a majority, face bitter disappointments.

Our study, because of the limitations of the non-random and relatively small sample, cannot ascertain what percentage of second-generation West Indian Americans will do better or worse than their parents. Because the U.S.

Census does not include a "birthplace of parents" item, it will be difficult for any study to address the question of how well second-generation West Indians are doing in the economy. One finding of this study should inform future studies that use the census ancestry question, a subjective measure, to identify West Indian Americans. If the less successful children of West Indians identify as African American and the more successful identify as West Indian, and if we continue to gather data in a subjective fashion on West Indians and their descendants, the image of West Indians as a model minority will continue to garner statistical support. Such support will reflect the situational identities of second-generation youth and not some statistically valid reality.

The key fact brought to light by West Indian immigrant experiences is that continuing racial inequality—the institutional failures of our inner cities to provide jobs, education, and public safety—sustains a cultural response of disinvestment in the face of discrimination, rather than increased striving. A lifetime of interpersonal racial attacks can lead to bitterness and anger on the part of an individual. A community of people coping with economic marginality and a lack of institutional support for individual mobility often adopts a culture of opposition. That culture might serve an individual at times, as a protection against the sting of racism and discrimination, but as a long-term political response it only prevents people from taking advantage of the opportunities that do arise. Those opportunities are reserved by whites for immigrants who make them feel less uncomfortable about race relations and who do not mind taking orders from white supervisors or customers.

One African American teacher eloquently described how just one act of cruelty or disdain by a white person can have long-lasting effects on a young black person, as well as on the whole cycle of black/white relations:

> I have had this happen to me so let me relate this incident. I have been going or coming from a building and held the door for some old white person and had them walk right past me, as if I am supposed to hold the door for them. Not one word, a thank you, or an acknowledgment of your presence was made. A seventeen-year-old, when he has something like that happen to him, the next time he is going to slam that door in the old lady's face, because I had that tendency myself. I had the hostility build up in me. The next time it happens I won't do that because I am older, but when I was seventeen it might not have made any difference to me that this was a different old lady. I would have flashed back to that previous incident and said, "I am not holding that door for you." Now that old lady who may have been a perfectly fine individual, who got this door slammed in her face by this young black person, her attitude is, "Boy, all those people are really vicious people." Her not understanding how it all came to pass. That on a large scale is what is happening in our country today. That's why our young people are very aggressive and very, very hostile when they are put in a situation of black/white confrontation. They say to themselves, "I am not going to let you treat me the way you treated my grandparents, or the way I have read or

seen in books or movies that they were treated." I would rather for you to
hate me than to disrespect me, is the attitude I think is coming out from our
black youth today (black American male teacher, age forty-one).

The policy implications of this study emerge from an understanding of the
ways in which economic and cultural disinvestment in American cities erodes
the social capital of immigrant families. The families need recognition of
their inherent strengths and the structure necessary to support their ambitions. The erosion of the first generation's optimism and ambition that occurs
in the second generation could be stopped if job opportunities were more
plentiful, inner-city schools were nurturing and safe environments that provided good educations, and neighborhoods were safer. Decent jobs, effective
schools, and safe streets are not immigrant-oriented or race-based policies.
They are universal policies that would benefit all urban residents. Indeed, the
strengths of immigrant families may be, in part, due to their immigrant status, but the problems they face are more likely due to their class status and
urban residence. Policies that benefit immigrants would be policies that benefit all Americans.

But the experience of West Indian immigrants also urges us to recognize
the continuing role of interpersonal racism in creating psychological tensions
and cultural adaptations in the black community. The cycle of attack and disrespect from whites, anger and withdrawal by blacks, and disengagement and
blame by whites must be broken by changing whites' behaviors, a process that
must involve policies that specifically address racial discrimination. Immigrants' tales of blatant housing and job discrimination point to the need for
vigilance in protecting all blacks in the United States from unequal treatment
in the private sector. The more difficult problem is dealing with the subtle,
everyday forms of prejudice and discrimination that plague foreign- and
American-born blacks. We cannot pass laws forbidding white women from
clutching their hand bags when black teenagers walk past them. We cannot
require old white women to thank young black men who show them courtesy.
Behaviors will only change when whites no longer automatically fear blacks
and begin to perceive the humanity and diversity of the black people they encounter.

The genuine correlations that exist among race, poverty, and criminality
explain some of the fears of whites that encourage them to behave poorly
(Franklin 1991). Policies that improve the positions of blacks in the overall class
structure of society could remove whatever correlations there are between
poverty, race, and criminal behavior. But what is really needed is for whites no
longer to see blacks as the "other," but rather as the "self." Why was it so easy
for the white managers we interviewed to describe immigrants as "like you
and me" and their American black coworkers as "those people"? If whites
recognized the basic humanity and individuality of the black people they encountered, they might consider how they would feel if, while walking down

the street, strangers clutched their handbags or quickened their pace. Sadly, the color line and the ingrained stereotypes and segregation we have constructed all too often prevent or undermine human connections between whites and blacks in American society.

THE FUTURE OF THE COLOR LINE IN AMERICAN SOCIETY

West Indian immigrants are part of the large wave of immigrants who have arrived in the United States since 1965. This wave has been predominantly nonwhite, mostly from the Caribbean, Latin America, and Asia. The immigrant influx has forever changed the demography of the United States. Before 1965, race relations in America revolved largely around a black/white dichotomy and excluded the nation's small nonblack, nonwhite populations of Asians, American Indians, and Hispanics. Perlmann (1997) notes that, in 1970, blacks represented 66 percent of all nonwhites in the United States. By 1990 the figure had fallen to 48 percent, and the Census Bureau forecasts that it will fall to 30 percent by 2050.[4]

How will the recent wave of immigration affect American race relations? Where will the color line be drawn in the twenty-first century? Do these demographic changes mean that color and race will take on new meanings in American society? Aside from the common question of whether immigrants take jobs from black Americans, how will the growing presence of nonwhite immigrants affect relations between blacks and whites?

One model of the impact of immigration on American race relations rests on the simplistic assumption that American society will continue to be divided between those people historically identified as white and those historically identified as nonwhite. This model is often used in discussions of population projections for racial and ethnic groups. In 1990, *Time* ran a cover story that posed the question, "What Will the United States Be Like When Whites Are No Longer a Majority?" The "rainbow coalition" that Jesse Jackson tried to enlist in his 1984 presidential campaign spoke to this idea, claiming that nonwhite groups in the United States have common cause in challenging the white majority's privileges and should come together politically. The popular phrase *people of color* also implies a model based on a division between white and nonwhite. Supporters of this model would suggest that immigration and the increasing diversity of American society will empower nonwhite peoples, and that new immigrants will ally with black Americans to challenge white hegemony.

Recent scholarship on the historical absorption of immigrants in the nineteenth and early twentieth centuries provides reason to be skeptical of such a simple model. Groups such as Southern and Central Europeans and the Irish were originally seen as racially different than established white Americans. In the nineteenth century, Irish immigrants were referred to as "niggers turned inside out," and Negroes were referred to as "smoked Irish." Yet over time the category "white" absorbed these European groups, identifying them as "not black." By assiduously distancing themselves from black Americans, these groups "became white" (Ignatiev 1995).

Even groups still thought of as racially distinct from whites have used some of the same tactics. James Loewen (1988) argues that, between 1870 and 1960, Chinese immigrants and their descendants in the Mississippi delta succeeded in changing their racial position. Loewen found that the Chinese, who were legally and socially considered nonwhite in the mid nineteenth century, slowly changed their status so that by the 1960s they were accepted as equivalent to whites. (Loewen's book opens with the following quote from a white Baptist minister in the delta: "You're either a white man or a nigger here. Now, that's the whole story. When I first came to the Delta, the Chinese were classed as nigras. [And now they are called whites?] That's right.") The price they paid for this social movement included the ostracism of Chinese who had married blacks, and continued social distance between blacks and Chinese on every level. In effect, the Chinese accepted the color line in Mississippi in order to step over it.

Speculating about post-1965 non-European immigrants, historian Gary Gerstle (1996: 54) proposes that they might also put themselves on the white side of the color line:

> Whiteness is a cultural category, not a biological one; its boundaries were stretched once before to admit immigrants from southern and eastern Europe and they can be stretched again to accommodate a wide range of people who today are considered nonwhite. It may be too that Hispanics and Asians will want to pursue whiteness much as the Irish, Italians and Poles did before them, as a way of securing their place in American society.

One can see evidence of this occurring now, especially among Hispanics and Asians. Many Asian groups such as the Koreans, Chinese, and Japanese have achieved far more economic success and structural assimilation with whites than have black Americans. In the nation's black ghettos, Koreans have taken over many of the middleman minority positions that were once filled by Jewish Americans. There is some evidence that whites are more accepting of Asians and Hispanics than they are of blacks. Intermarriage rates between whites and Asians are quite high. Among native-born Asians ages twenty-five to thirty-four, over 50 percent have out-married (Farley 1996). Residential segregation is also very low for Asians—even first-generation Asians. The tensions between blacks and Koreans in the Los Angeles riots, as well as those between Hispanics and blacks in many neighborhoods, point to a lack of any solidarity based solely on nonwhite status.

West Indians, however, provide an extreme test case for the social construction of race. It is relatively easy to imagine Chinese or Koreans becoming socially defined as nonblack or even white, but is this a possibility for people from societies where they have long identified as black? Despite their black skin, can West Indians distance themselves from black Americans and become nonblack?

Historians who stress that race is a cultural, not biological, category would believe this to be possible. Indeed, a few scholars such as Gilroy (1990) and Appiah and Gutmann (1996) argue that present-day racism is rooted in cultural definitions and explanations, not biological ones. Arguing that there has been a decline in outright racist thinking since World War II, especially in biologically based racial essentialism, Gilroy notes that racism now "frequently operates without any overt reference to either race itself or the biological notions of difference that still give the term its common-sense meaning. Before the rise of modern scientific racism in the nineteenth century the term race did duty for the term culture. No surprise then that in its postwar retreat from racism the term has once again acquired an explicitly cultural rather than biological inflection" (265–266).

Gilroy defines this change as a shift from vulgar to cultural racism. Moreover, Rogers (1996) notes that American cultural pluralism allows cultural racism to flourish. According to this line of thinking, American blacks in the 1990s are not left behind in the economy or overrepresented in the prison system because of biological inferiority (as old time vulgar racists would argue) but because black culture is lacking.[5]

Indeed, one finds cultural distancing from black Americans among the immigrants we interviewed. They argued that West Indians merited inclusion in American society because of their strong work ethic, the value they placed on education, and their lack of pathological behaviors. By asserting a cultural identity as immigrants and as members of a model minority, West Indians make a case for cultural inclusion in American society based on being different from black Americans. This is a strategy that many new immigrants adopt. However, when Koreans "become American" by distancing themselves from the underclass black image, the status of the group itself improves. This is how the process worked for the Irish, the Poles, and even the Mississippi Chinese. In contrast, when West Indians and middle-class black Americans attempt the same distancing, a boomerang effect occurs. Cultural distance may help individual black Americans and West Indians, but it leaves intact and reinforces stereotypes of blacks as inferior, thus harming other group members.

Middle-class black Americans often face this dilemma of self-definition. Because of ingrained images of African Americans as unworthy and as failures, middle-class blacks have not been able to develop a "symbolic ethnicity" to accompany their socioeconomic status. As I have argued elsewhere, middle-class white ethnics are able to selectively identify with their ethnic origins, picking and choosing between the various aspects of their backgrounds

(Waters 1990). Moreover, as they succeed in society the image of their group changes. Jews are no longer seen as uniquely athletically talented, and Irish are no longer seen as stupid. With European groups, two things happen over time. First, middle-class individuals attain leeway in deciding how or whether to identify ethnically. Second, if they do ethnically identify they do so with a group that maintains its positive characteristics and loses its negative ones as it is increasingly associated with its middle-class members rather than its poor immigrant members. For example, most Irish Americans no longer even recognize "paddy wagons" as an ethnic slur against their supposed proclivity for criminal behavior. Instead, politicians of every ethnic background flock to Saint Patrick's Day celebrations to become "Irish for a day."

For middle-class blacks both these aspects of a symbolic ethnicity are missing. Because being black involves a racial identity, people with certain somatic features—dark skin, kinky hair, and so on—are defined as blacks by others regardless of their own preferences for identification. Racial identification does not allow "passing" except for a very few light-skinned people. Furthermore, the group itself is not seen as changing. For most nonblack Americans the image of blacks as poor, unworthy, and dangerous is still very potent, despite the success of many black Americans and the growth of a sizeable black middle class. The existence of an urban underclass of very poor blacks who exhibit "ghetto-specific behaviors"—no matter how small in comparison with America's total black population—reinforces the same cultural stereotypes that whites developed long ago to justify and shore up slavery.

Middle-class black Americans often encounter whites who are so convinced that all American blacks are poor, criminal, hostile, or nasty that they will not even admit that a nice, successful person might be black. A thirty-four-year-old black American teacher described one such experience:

> I had a white person I work with say, "That Mary, she is not white, she is not black." Or people say I'm better or I'm different. To me that's ignorance. They probably feel that I would feel better if they said that. When you don't know you say a lot of stupid things.

The white coworker who wanted to compliment Mary was forced to say that she was raceless—neither phenotypically white nor culturally and behaviorally black. For whites who adopt the image of West Indians as a model minority, identifying a person as West Indian provides a useful alternative. A West Indian is a successful black, a person who may have black skin but who is not "the other," defined as "not like us." This thirty-two-year-old white female teacher described the positive image many white Americans have of West Indians:

> *What is your impression of West Indians?*
> They are educated. They have high values for education. A lot of times their accent is more British than American. It's sort of somehow people with a

British accent; you always think that they are really intelligent no matter what they say.

Images of race and ethnicity that "fit" with the immigrants were more acceptable to the whites we interviewed than the images they held of African Americans. West Indians are seen often, though not all the time, as immigrants. Whites see themselves as the descendants of immigrants, thus recognizing a shared history and, in some ways, allowing for a shared future—a future that whites have trouble visualizing with regard to their relationship with black Americans.

Yet to erase the color line we must move beyond both cultural and vulgar racism, preventing new Americans from accepting the color line in order to cross over to its advantageous side. By taking seriously the experiences of West Indian immigrants and their children, I hope that I have shown how much race still shapes everyday life for those our society defines as black. If the color line is redrawn to sharply distinguish between black and nonblack, the results could be disastrous for black Americans. Four hundred years after coming to this country and one hundred years after the end of slavery, a new generation of black Americans would watch as immigrants from around the globe leapfrog over them and achieve greater success and inclusion in American society. For immigrants, the outcome of such a scenario would be bifurcated, with those socially defined as white or nonblack doing well and those defined as black doing poorly. West Indians and African Americans would suffer greatly from the resulting continuation of inequality. Indeed, all Americans would suffer greatly if we had once again missed an opportunity to overcome the inequality that has been present at the core of our society since its founding.

NOTES

This chapter is a revised version of a paper presented at the Conference on West Indian Migration to New York: Historical, Contemporary and Transnational Perspectives, sponsored by the Research Institute for the Study of Man, New York, 17 April 1999. The research was supported by the Russell Sage Foundation and by the John Simon Guggenheim Foundation. I am grateful to Nancy Foner for comments on an earlier version. This chapter draws from the full-length work *Black Identities: West Indian Immigrant Dreams and American Realities* by Mary C. Waters, published by Harvard University Press, Cambridge, Mass., Copyright © 1999 by the Russell Sage Foundation.

1. The complete study is described in Waters (1999a).

2. Middle-class status was defined as having at least one parent with a college degree or professional or business employment. Working-class status was defined as having parents (or one parent, the other unemployed) with low-skill jobs. Poor students were those whose parents were both unemployed.

3. In my larger study I deal with the intriguing issue of the variety of identities open to these immigrants, contrasting times when immigrants identify with a particular coun-

try or island with times when they choose a panethnic West Indian identity (Waters 1999a, Chapter 3).

4. A major weakness of these Census Bureau projections is that they do not take into account intermarriage and assimilation. They are premised on the idea that ethnic and racial groups do not intermarry. With rising intermarriage among some groups, the potential for a particular group to either increase (if children of intermarried couples identify with the minority group) or decrease (if they identify as white non-Hispanics) becomes a reality—a reality ignored by the Census Bureau in making these projections. The very meaning of these ethnic and racial groups could change significantly over time, causing ethnic and racial boundaries to appear very different. I have explored these issues in other writing (Alonso and Waters 1993; Waters 2000).

5. Gilroy notes that, when culture is used to explain the place of groups in the social structure, the concept of culture is used in a specific way, "not as something intrinsically fluid, changing, unstable and dynamic, but as a fixed property of a social group" (Gilroy 1990: 266).

EIGHT

Experiencing Success
Structuring the Perception of Opportunities
for West Indians

Vilna F. Bashi Bobb
and
Averil Y. Clarke

The question of social mobility is a critical one for West Indian migrants in the United States and for the lives of their children. Much of the literature on this question focuses on the success or lack of success of black immigrants relative to native-born blacks. In this chapter we explore the way first- and second-generation West Indian immigrants perceive the possibilities and opportunities for social mobility, and we analyze these perceptions as a function of immigrants' social experience in global and local stratification systems. We use the words of our sample group and the resulting ethnographic insights to understand the social bases for ethnic identification among West Indians. By diagraming the social experiences that lead to particular types of ethnic identification for black West Indian immigrants and those born in the United States of black West Indian immigrant parents, we hope to shed light on the way social experiences and ethnic identification produce particular kinds of perceptions about the possibilities for achieving higher socioeconomic outcomes.

It has often been argued that "success" among West Indian blacks is due to their West Indian culture (Kalmijn 1996; Sowell 1978) and that "failure," "hopelessness," or "lack of optimism" (particularly in the second generation) may be a result of their downward assimilation into the "inner-city" culture of black Americans (Waters 1996a; Portes 1995a; Kao and Tienda 1995). Our conclusion is that racial adaptation to American society (not socialization to an "inner-city," underclass, or otherwise aberrant black culture) is the key ingredient for explaining how the second generation comes to lose "hope" and "optimism" when assessing the possibilities for its economic future.

RESEARCH ON THE WEST INDIAN GENERATIONS

Using data from the 1970 U.S. Census, Thomas Sowell (1978) argued that second-generation West Indians exceeded the socioeconomic status of the immigrant generation and that the immigrant generation showed higher status attainment relative to African Americans. Sowell suggested that West Indian immigrant socioeconomic success relative to that of African Americans "undermines the explanatory power of current white discrimination as a cause of current black poverty" (Sowell 1978: 49). Since the 1978 publication of Sowell's writings, much debate has centered on disproving or verifying and then explaining differential success among West Indians of the first (immigrant), second, and third generations, as compared to African Americans (American-born blacks).

Not surprisingly, given this emphasis, much of the research on first-generation West Indians has been structured to assess their success relative to American-born blacks, who are seen as a "natural" comparison group because of their shared racial ascription. These works have documented West Indian placement in labor and housing markets (Crowder 1999; Butcher 1994; Model 1991; Farley and Allen 1987; Sowell 1978), their economic success or lack thereof relative to people of African descent born in the United States (Kalmijn 1996; Waldinger 1996; Butcher 1994; Model 1991; Farley and Allen 1987; Sowell 1978), and aspects of the reception West Indians encounter in the United States and the immigrants' adaptive responses (Vickerman 1999; Kasinitz 1992; Basch 1987a; Foner 1978; Bryce-Laporte 1972). Research on the second generation of West Indians in the United States has investigated whether they represent a model of the continued success of West Indian immigrants or if theirs is an assimilation of a different kind (Kalmijn 1996; Waters 1996a; Kao and Tienda 1995; Portes 1995a).[1]

Various explanations have been advanced by researchers employing both qualitative and quantitative methods, but cultural explanations for the success of West Indian ethnics are by far the most popular. West Indian success in mobility has been attributed to a seemingly superior culture, oriented toward optimism (Waters 1996a; Kao and Tienda 1995), "hard work and achievement" (Kalmijn 1996), and a commitment to socioeconomic independence from the social welfare structure (Sowell 1978). Failure (of the second generation) to thrive in schooling or in the economic arena has been attributed to "downward leveling," or assimilation to the "inner-city culture" of blacks (Waters 1996a; Kao and Tienda 1995; Portes 1995a). We do not wish to dismiss the role of cultural values in immigrant achievement. Nor do we deny that assimilation for black immigrants often involves assimilation to a negative social niche. Yet academic analysts too often equate this negative social niche with culture—that is, the culture of American black "ethnics" (i.e., African Americans).[2] We argue instead that the ethnicity and assimilation issue has been misconstrued. Rather than assimilating to a pathological culture, blacks of the first and second generation—whether socioeconomically successful or not—must assimilate into a social system with a racial hierarchy that structurally relegates black people of all classes to the bottom of the racial ladder (Bashi 1998a).

The extent to which West Indians and their American-born offspring have achieved high social status and economic success or have "assimilated" is not our concern. Rather, we want to look at what first- and second-generation West Indians believe about the possibilities and opportunities for "getting ahead" in American society. Research to date has focused on "objective" indicators of socioeconomic status attainment, but none has assessed what members of the different generations believe about this success or lack thereof in their own social experience.[3] Although writings on West Indians have shown that social experience is important in explaining first- and second-generation perceptions of the social structure of economic opportunity, few works have emphasized social experience directly, and even fewer have compared the social experience of the first generation with that of the second. Here we use respondents' own words to report what the immigrant and second generations understand success to be. The actuality of mobility is less important to this study than the extent to which our respondents believe mobility can be achieved and the factors they perceive as influencing their chances for socioeconomic success. In our analysis we make the important distinction between race—in which categories are hierarchical and ascribed to individuals— and ethnicity—in which categories are self-imposed and generally nonhierarchical (Bashi 1998a; Cornell and Hartmann 1998; Omi and Winant 1994).

This study is based on two sets of interviews with West Indian immigrants and U.S.-born children of immigrants from the West Indies. The data on the immigrant generation's perspectives on social mobility come from Vilna Bashi's 1996 interviews with forty-four black immigrants from St. Vincent and the Grenadines and Trinidad and Tobago who migrated to New York City between 1930 and 1980. These immigrants were connected to one another by virtue of their social networks, through which they helped each other migrate to and resettle in New York (Bashi 1997). From 1998 to 1999, Averil Clarke (2001) interviewed fifty-five college-educated women of African American and West Indian ancestry to study how fertility and nuptiality decisions affected the ability to earn a college degree. For the present chapter, Clarke used data only for those women whose parents emigrated from the West Indies to New York, and supplemented their stories with fifteen additional interviews of native-born persons, all between the ages of fifteen and forty-five, whose parents migrated from these same islands to New York City.[4]

The rest of the chapter is organized as follows. First, we explain West Indians' understandings of the role of education in facilitating success. Second, we explain their understandings of the role of race in limiting success. Using a structural rather than culturally deterministic mode of analysis, we then argue that it is the two generations' separate social experiences that bring them to different conclusions about the opportunities for success and advancement in the economic arena. To conclude, we explain what variables account for their different social experiences and summarize what our findings imply for understanding racializing assimilation for West Indians in the United States.

EDUCATION AND SOCIAL MOBILITY FOR WEST INDIANS

The first-generation immigrants interviewed for this study strongly believed that education would generate returns in the labor market; they were also committed to the idea of getting an education themselves. Many came to the United States expressly to gain an education, some exclusively for education and others in order to work and obtain schooling simultaneously.[5] A well-known and common scheme—for women at least—was to enter the country under a visa that allowed them to start work as babysitters or housekeepers (employers in these niches typically filed the necessary papers under exceptions to the usual immigration laws), and then to go to school to learn the skills that would permit a career change (Bashi 1998b). Several respondents told stories of working and attending school simultaneously in order to get specialized job training and certification, college-level training, associate's, bachelor's, and master's degrees, or, in one case, a doctorate. Only one man reported being chastised by his coethnic coworkers for working and going to school—but this was because they saw his job (in New York City Water Tunnel construction) as a well-paying career track. As word of immigrant advancement through education was passed around in social networks, successful mobility experiences served to reinforce the idea among the immigrant generation that education leads to social mobility.

The second generation was just as committed to the belief in education as a tool necessary for advancement. Almost every second-generation respondent directly or indirectly mentioned education as a key factor in what they had achieved (or failed to achieve) to date. Roy[6] told us that his professional success was due to "the ability to learn and understand what I do." Others spoke about education's influence more indirectly, including Kareen, who emphasized her parents' and her peers' role in her success so far. When discussing peer influence, she said, "[With] my friends like all through elementary in and high school . . . it was always like friendly competition to get good grades and stuff like that. It was kinda keeping up with them that kept me going." Thus, she explained that her performance in school was an important factor in her success and that a competitive relationship with peers helped to facilitate success. Jonathan maintained that "some of the values" that he possessed were "due to [his parents] being immigrants." He continued, "My mom and my dad always explained to me that you had to work to get whatever you wanted. Education was one of the ways of getting something in this country. So they came here and worked hard and I believe they instilled those things into me."

Although second-generation West Indians agreed with their parents that education was the key to success or failure in the economic sector, some perceived limitations in the value of an education and felt that a singular focus on education was not likely to suffice for economic advancement. For example, although Nordrick did not attribute his career success to his record of educational achievement, he added that, when he discovered the fact that his educational credentials surpassed those of his white coworkers, he realized he was being discriminated against in terms of salary and promotions. Kyle explained that the major obstacles to his success were the structure of society and racial barriers. Consider his comments on how a degree from a black institution did not carry the same weight as one from a majority white institution when applying to graduate school.

> Like going to my university. The way this world in America views that is that I can have the same grades as a person in a University of Penn, and just because he or she went to Penn and I went to Virginia State, I would get overlooked with a quickness. I feel like to be coerced to go to a predominantly white school or some other school because of a reputation—you know, I feel the person should speak for himself not the reputation of the school. There's a few black schools that do get recognition. I mean you hear about the Howards, the Morehouses, but maybe you won't hear so much about the Morgan States, the Norfolk States, or the Virginia States. . . . I mean, I'm sorry if we can't have the high Ph.D. people that fly in from France to teach a class, to teach one class a week, you know. My school gave me the opportunity and I made use of my opportunity. I love my school. I think it's the society.

When we asked second-generation respondents to tell us what advice they would give a twelve-year-old who wanted to achieve what they had achieved, at least one-third of the respondents made no response that directly stressed education. Roy explained that his ability to learn his work accounted for his success; he did not even mention education. "Get as much background about the industry right now as possible, and also to begin meeting and getting to know as many people as possible who are already in the industry." Linda insisted that one has to "know the work" and "know what you're doing" to succeed in her field, but maintained that the "old boy network" had certainly held her back.

Much like their parents, second-generation West Indians continue to hail the value of an education for gaining economic success, and they often attribute failure to inadequate, misdirected, or inappropriate education. Yet the second-generation and long-resident immigrants[7] also perceive that there are limits to the returns to education, and more than a few of them would be suspicious of claims that education is the only or even the main ingredient to success in their field. In this chapter we argue that these perceptions emerge from the U.S.-born generation's understanding of how the racial structure in the United States negatively affects black people who seek to achieve higher social or economic status.

SOCIAL EXPERIENCE AS A FACTOR IN UNDERSTANDING THE ROLE OF EDUCATION

What are the social experiences that underpin the attitudes we have described? First-generation immigrants bring with them extensive experience in the economic and education systems of "Third World" immigrant-sending countries. This includes but is not limited to the idea that "education was a privilege, not a right, in the West Indies," as Randall, a first-generation immigrant, put it. During colonialism the West Indian education system was modeled after the British education system, which, albeit in neocolonial fashion, still exists today. In the West Indies it is not the case that all students can advance as far as they like. At various points one must take examinations in order to move to the next level, and there are only a very limited number of slots available for advancement. Thus, not only must you take qualifying examinations, but it is your placement among all exam-takers that determines whether you will win a coveted slot that allows you to further your education.

Sufficient experience in this context generates investment in the idea that lack of educational opportunity limits one's economic mobility (since it literally does so). Such experience also encourages investment in education once the opportunity presents itself, as it does with migration to a country where access to education is more open. In many cases, then, the decision to migrate from the Caribbean is bound up in the desire to take advantage of educational opportunity. As James explained,

> Everybody knows that when you come here, you've got to survive on your own. The key is to get here, and when you get here the second step is not to forget why you came. In the event that you have to return, then you will return with what you came for, which is basically an education. Life in the Caribbean is beautiful; furthering your education is a problem.

Jonita, another first-generation respondent, spoke of the complexity of messages about the relationship between economic mobility and education in the United States relative to the Caribbean. She described her poor rural upbringing and how she and her childhood friends shared books: "We didn't have Xerox machines! So we wrote out the chapters for each other by hand." Here in the United States, she quipped, "books are free, yet people can't read." While immigrants may attempt to pass their intense emphasis on education to their children, most of those children have no experience of being denied access to education. Immigrant West Indians encourage their second-generation children to adopt the West Indian immigrant worldview in an environment where, despite severe inequities, education appears to be free and available to all. However, in the United States, education does not always translate into attractive social positions. In this context, black immigrant parents' attempt to pass on their intense attachment to education is a "harder sell" to black children who know the "raw deal" of the black experience in this different racial structure. Education is the culturally accepted means for achieving social mobility, and our second-generation respondents (only two-thirds of whom held college degrees) generally agreed with this but saw race as a mediating factor. Moving our lens from the first to the second generation, we move from a generation that wholly believes in education as a means for mobility to one that does not. What needs to be explained is not why some young black people believe in the power of education, but why it is that many young blacks do not. We emphasize that this difference between the generations is due to structural limitations that restrict blacks in the United States and the fact that these limitations differ from those that affect blacks who live in other nations.

In addition to social experience in an environment where educational opportunities are both limited and overtly linked to movement up the class hierarchy, first-generation West Indians share other kinds of social experience that, in turn, structure their perceptions of opportunities in the United States. The first generation's experience with interisland migration, for instance, is an important factor in producing immigrants' particular understanding of success in their receiving country. Here we discuss this factor, beginning with a summary of the specific history of interisland migration and then turning to the way in which this interisland migration experience colors first-generation perceptions of mobility opportunities.

It is evident that West Indians have used geographic mobility to take advantage of opportunities for socioeconomic mobility for more than a century. "Strategic flexibility" is the term Carnegie (1987) has coined to describe the West Indian philosophy of organizing one's life in order to be ready to take advantage of whatever opportunities for work and migration may arise. This philosophy is evident in the islanders' social practices; for example, a person may take a series of unrelated jobs in order to diversify and collect skills in order to prepare for subsequent jobs and eventual emigration. Since opportunities for advancement in one's own village or island are few and far between, preparedness and flexibility go hand in hand with migration. Emigration has long been a primary means of economic advancement, from the emancipation in 1834 of black slaves in the islands until today. For a time, emigration was the only means for securing work and averting starvation for the bulk of the population (D. Marshall 1987). For fifty years (1835–1885), interisland migration moved people out of their homelands, mainly to Trinidad and Tobago and British Guiana, countries from which planters recruited labor on the smaller islands. An "ebb and flow" of migration to "foreign" territories marked the period from 1885 to 1920, in which out-migration was primarily to Cuba and the Dominican Republic (to work sugar plantations), Central America (for railroads and banana plantations), Bermuda (dry-dock labor), and Panama (1850–1855 for railroad construction, 1880–1914 to work on the Panama Canal, 1906–1914 for railroad relocation)—with a small proportion going as far as the United States. Crisis marked the period from 1920 to 1940, when migration flows nearly ceased as the First World War and the Great Depression shrank opportunities for mobility. Since 1940, however, Caribbean emigration has increased, dominated by movement to the United Kingdom, the United States, and Canada. In this period, geographic mobility and wider access to education have gone hand in hand.

Our first-generation informants corroborated the existence of and adherence to the "strategic flexibility" philosophy, particularly as it relates to seeking education for job advancement. For example, one informant explained that when he first came to New York, he "did a little of everything," starting with jobs in carpentry and then moving on to spraypainting. "You've gotta have more than one skill," he said. Joycelyn, after rejoining her immigrant mother in New York, was told by her mother that she should become a dietitian. Following the suggestion, she went to school for training, worked as a dietitian for six months, and hated it. Her brother suggested that she might like to work in banking, and she agreed, immediately switching to a job he found for her as a secretary in a bank. She worked her way to the top and made a career of banking. Randall told a similar story when asked if his work history consistently used one of the skills he had honed. "No, I did a couple of other jobs, I work other little places. Listen, let me tell you, any place that was offering me five or ten dollars more than what I was doing, I'm gone. Oh yes, that's the way." To take advantage of opportunities for advancement, some people moved, not only from one job to another, but across state borders. Consider Charmaine's case. In the late 1970s, she and her future husband were enrolled in New York schools—she in nursing school and he in medical school. Neither had green cards. When she found herself pregnant, as Charmaine put it, "We had two choices—well, one choice, really. We had to find someone to sponsor us so that we could get our green card. In order for that to be done, I had to go and do domestic work and have someone sponsor me." Thus, after the child's birth, Charmaine left nursing school and applied for legal residence through an employer for whom she began working as a maid. For nearly three years she lived in her employer's New Jersey home during the week and in New York on the weekends. Finally she received her green card. In that time she had earned a two-year-college degree and a nursing certificate. In the end, she was able to sponsor her husband's application for a green card and secure a job as a nurse's aide in a New York City hospital.

Among other things, strategic flexibility depends upon an understanding of the world in which personal accommodation to economic and social systems is part and parcel of economic mobility. Struggling to gain an education becomes just one kind of adjustment or accommodation that one must make. Furthermore, education is bound up with the migration act itself. Many immigrants now living in New York began migrating at very young ages, as they had to move to other islands for schooling once they had passed the primary-school level. Immigrants from Union Island (in St. Vincent and the Grenadines), for example, were only able to continue schooling past primary school by migrating to mainland St. Vincent or to Trinidad, since at the time they were growing up there was no upper-level school on their island. These young migrants stayed with family or friends of their parents while attending school, coming home only for holidays and summers.

With regard to socialization in the educational system of the United States, second-generation immigrants experience a system in which all education is not equal (e.g., "black" schools are valued less than "white" schools), and this inequality affects their belief in the value of an education. Recall Kyle's comments, in which he explains that "society" has rendered his education at a "black" school less valuable than educations at other schools. In the end, he was forced to accept a judgement that, although his education followed appropriate guidelines, it was insufficient preparation for his chosen field, and Kyle was forced to change careers. It is well known that primary education systems in the United States differ in quality by regional status within and across counties. The children of West Indian immigrants living in urban areas (as most do) are likely to attend a school with a predominantly black student body and inadequate funding and resources (Massey and Denton 1993; Wilson 1980). McLeod (1995) finds that some combination of tracking and lackluster performance levels the aspirations of minority youth. The American school system is not always helpful in educating young blacks, despite their high aspirations and hard work.

In sum, although both generations see education as the primary factor in social advancement, their differing social experiences lead them to interpret the importance of education somewhat differently. For the second generation, a lack of experience in the postcolonial Third World education system and economy has a dampening influence on their perceptions about the rewards associated with education. The investment in strategic flexibility driven by Third World–style limits to social and economic opportunity is another quality possessed by the first generation but lacking in the second.[8]

While these experiences are enough to cause differences in the generations' perspectives on the rewards to education, we also believe that racial socialization has its own independent effect. The way in which black West Indian immigrants as a group are able to distance themselves economically and psychologically from racism in the United States leaves intact their beliefs about the rewards of education. In contrast, the second generation, as well as those who immigrated at young ages or have remained in the United States for long periods of time, becomes immersed in the American racial hierarchy and has no such distance. These West Indians have a less optimistic understanding of the meaning of blackness for their chances for advancement opportunities in the economic arena.

RACISM AND SOCIAL ADVANCEMENT FOR WEST INDIANS

West Indian immigrants arrive in the United States with one understanding of race and racism and come to learn quite another after living here for some time (Bashi 1996). James explained,

> Oh man, you know, you may realize my personality is a jovial one, so maybe they used to give me a racist remark and maybe I used to just overlook it and say it's stupid. But when you just come to the United States and because you're not accustomed to racism, you're not sensitive to it. Yet after [some time] you become sensitive to racism. I mean, I start knowing what is a racist remark, but when I just came, I didn't know. I thought they were just making a joke or something.

West Indians in the immigrant generation are shocked or surprised by racism in the United States. "We don't have that back home," as one person explained and many others expressed in similar words. West Indian migrants come to the United States with an idea of race developed in their Caribbean homelands. Immigrants described the West Indian racial structure as akin to a class system, where access to sources of human capital—particularly education—makes a significant difference in one's ability to achieve social mobility (Gopaul-McNichol 1993; Foner 1985; Dominguez 1975). As Jonita explained,

> Racism is not really a priority there, you know. You don't look at a black and white situation. You more look at an economic situation, you know. It doesn't matter really whether you're black or white or whatever it is. If you don't have the money you don't have the position in society that I'm talking about. If you have the money you have the position. But when I came here I realized that not only is there economics you have to deal with, you have to deal with the color of your skin, so that was kind of a shock to me.

Evidence suggests that there is an ideal typical trajectory for the adaptation of West Indian immigrants to racism in the United States (Bashi 1996). When they arrive, West Indians believe that, because they are committed to hard work and social advancement, and because they are foreigners, racist behavior will not be directed toward them. They soon learn that racism is directed toward all black people (i.e., racism is not a set of social behaviors applied by white Americans just toward black Americans, as many immigrants initially believe). Once they learn that racism indeed applies to them, West Indians develop coping strategies to ignore, avoid, or overlook it. Then they learn a second lesson—that living with racism is a demoralizing process, and that racism cannot be wholly ignored or avoided.

Immigrant responses to racism in the United States indicate an understanding of how racism has demoralized African Americans, though only one immigrant reported being demoralized herself. Although they saw themselves as targets of racism, West Indians still reported that they did not let racism bother them or get in the way of achieving their dreams.

> I lived in St. Vincent, where there is a good enclave of so-called white people, and we worked together but we didn't see black and white, we saw people. We worked together, socialized together. . . . So when coming to America, and they were calling you "black" . . . You work in the hospital and they would spit on you and tell you don't touch them and tell you to take your black so-and-so away from them. . . . That was dramatic to me because I never had experience of people spit on me. I mean, my first [response] was to hit back. Someone spit on me and call me black! And then my cousin say, "If you want a job you can't do it." You got to swallow your teeth and take it. . . . After a while you learn to rise above it, like water off the duck's back.

Of course, racism did bother some immigrants enough that it became one reason for deciding to leave New York City and return home. Still, they did not seem to think that racism was a problem that hindered mobility. One man, who has several brothers in New York, said that he never took the opportunity to live there because he found American society so distasteful.

> You know, you have blacks on one side and whites on one side and unless you're a foreign black they look at you like you're diseased or something, you know. Where black folks are afraid to walk on the same side of the streets as the white folks. It was just gross. A country so advanced to be so stupid, you know. I could never see the reason for it and I really never accepted it.

Responses such as this one are quite different from those of the U.S.-born ethnic West Indians we interviewed, as well as the West Indian–born individuals who immigrated as children, all of whom believed that racism—rather than something to be ignored or overlooked—is a huge problem for blacks in American society. Consider fourteen-year-old Ellie's summary of the state of racial affairs in New York:

> When I came here I had to start learning what racism was. Because when you go to the stores and stuff like that, people follow you around; you go on the bus and people hold their pocketbooks. So I want to know why, you know, why when I come to America people do this? What is so different? They don't discriminate because you're West Indian. They are discriminating against you because you're black. Period.

Second-generation respondents unanimously stated that racism should be an issue of great concern in our society. They readily recited incidents and sit-

uations that they believed were indicative of racism and its deleterious consequences for blacks. As Nordrick said in a matter-of-fact tone, "Racism is still
a big problem. It's still nowhere near equal." He explained that affirmative action should be kept in place: "It's needed to even out some of the past wrong-
doings." Other respondents also focused their discussions of racism on specific arenas of society, particularly the social control systems. Christopher
mentioned race as one of the social markers that officers in the military use
to keep the gates of their status group closed and to hinder the mobility of
others. Shana argued, "Police in general, they treat black people and Hispanics different than the way they treat white people." Kyle was vehement in his
comments about the New York City police force:

> It's terrible! It's terrible! These cops and Giuliani, I mean, they focus in these
> black neighborhoods, and it's like they're trying to personally kill us and do it
> underhandedly by feeling it's our fault. . . . You got people fightin', walking on
> Washington, DC, you know, unity, anything, 'cause it's still there! It's still
> there. It might not be as prominent, and that is straight up. You know it's
> there in the workplace, I mean—and if you're not, you know, an educated
> black person, you won't see it.

Nordrick stated that he was affected by racism early in his professional life.

> During my eight years of working construction management, just seeing
> numerous white bosses bring their children, nieces, sons, and daughters in,
> bring them into a position above me, making more money than me, and they
> had no formal education and I had been working there for years. There was
> basically no question for me to ask. So eventually I caught on and knew that I
> had to move on.

Jonathan, also in the second generation, said that racism is American society's
"number one problem" and argued that it affects the decision making of
black and white people "all the time." Like Jonathan, Kyle felt very strongly
about racism, repeatedly saying that he thought it was "terrible." Kyle also felt
personally affected by racism. In the course of his interview, he related the following incident. After just one week on a new job, Kyle was asked to take what
was supposed to be a random drug test. Four days later his supervisor asked
him to pick up a handwritten paycheck because his name had not yet been
entered into the computer. So Kyle asked the supervisor how he had been
randomly picked for a drug test from a computer list that had not included his
name. The day before the drug test Kyle had shown up at the job site in a
brand new car, and he was sure that the new car and his race together had
falsely signaled drug trade involvement to his employer.

While the U.S.-born and U.S.-raised respondents were unanimous in their
perceptions of the problem of racism, there was more variance in the degrees
to which they felt that racism affected them personally. At the other end of the
spectrum from Jonathan and Kyle were a few second-generation women who

did not feel personally affected by racism. Carla declared that minorities face racism as they attempt to climb the rungs of the job ladder. However, when she spoke about racism's effect on her own life, Carla said that she herself had not been its victim. Although Shana talked about how the police were against blacks and Hispanics, she did not believe that she herself had been affected by racism. Kareen expressed a similar set of opinions, stating that she thinks racism is a "big problem" but at the same time maintaining that "it's hard for me to say because I haven't really encountered anything like that that I know of." Furthermore, some respondents who considered racism to be a major problem said that, even when treated in racist ways, they were able to evade its effects or somehow keep it from affecting them. Nadine said, "I am sure that I have been discriminated against. I know that I have been mistreated and ignored." Yet she followed these assertions by saying, "I counteract it pretty well." She described one response to salespersons who followed her around stores asking whether she needed help in order to keep an eye on her:

> You usually just politely take whatever service they want to give you. You can either work 'em to death or say, "No, that's okay, I'm just browsing." Or you can say, "Is Julie here today?" Julie's their boss; they don't know you know their boss. "How does this black woman know my boss?"

In the same vein, Christopher, who mentioned racism in the military, said, "Me, no, I haven't been personally affected by racism. I rise above the top when it comes to that. I know how to deal with it, I guess. I don't let it really get to me."

Thus, second-generation West Indians seemed to be well aware of racism's existence and unanimously declared it to be a big problem for blacks, detailing the way it negatively affects the level and shape of blacks' participation in economic and social life. However, they varied as to whether they felt it had affected them personally. While some felt that they had been treated unfairly by the system in general or by particular white persons, others felt that they had not encountered unfair treatment. Still others thought that, although they had encountered racism, they were able to ignore, circumvent, or counteract the expected negative consequences.

SOCIAL EXPERIENCE AS A FACTOR IN UNDERSTANDING RACE AND RACISM

As with attitudes regarding education, perceptions about racism are linked to social experience. This includes experience in the West Indian racial system, immersion in the immigrant social network, and one's possession or lack of markers of West Indian ethnicity that are immediately observable to others.

First-generation immigrants, having experienced life in another racial hierarchy, take a different perspective on the American racial system than their children born and raised in the United States (Bashi 1996; Foner 1978). The foreign reference point orients the immigrants to an outsider perspective that encourages them to avoid personalizing the American culture of racism that their native-born children are hard-pressed to ignore. Moreover, in the sociopolitical arena the foreign reference point brings to the migrant a transnational perspective, which shapes identity construction and the international flows of cultural ideas and material goods, thereby allowing migrants to resist subordination to a globally racialized capitalist system (Glick Schiller, Basch, and Blanc-Szanton 1992). Although their understanding of American society may change over time, immigrants consistently interpret their new social circumstances in relation to the circumstances under which they lived in their country of origin. Note, for example, what Heddy says about her first experiences with racism in the United States.

> I took anything racial, especially then [when I first arrived], at face value. The older woman I was tutoring in math was pleasant. But my friend was telling me, "Oh, you're so stupid. She's racist! What in the hell make you think these white people are your friends? She's just using you!" Well, that was my first time [experiencing racism] and I just couldn't understand. I said, "You don't even know her. How could you just look at a person and hate them?" She said, "Oh, I don't hate them, they hate me." Ha, ha, ha. . . . And now, in retrospect, I see exactly what she was saying.

Without the foreign reference point, second-generation West Indians can draw upon only their experience of American racial and class hierarchies. They experience life embedded in a class and status hierarchy of roles and social positions filled with distinct sets of people in both the bottom and the top rungs of the economic ladder. Piore (1979) described the socially embedded nature of the capitalist labor hierarchy as one in which jobs are not described simply by wages and specific vocational functions and activities, but are value-laden occupations. Jobs fit into a status as well as a wage hierarchy and are thus associated with attendant amounts of scorn or esteem. Second-generation West Indians conceptualize economic mobility and understand labor force participation as occurring through and existing within such job ladders. They also know that race is one factor that limits their ability to move up the job ladder, even though they believe that they deserve to climb just like any other person.

> If you aspire only to those things that have been deemed traditionally either work that minorities or the poor or the disenfranchised perform, then you won't have too many problems with that. If you step out of the natural bounds that have been set, and start to look at things that have not been traditionally done by minorities or females, then I think that race is just as prevalent as it ever has been.

Unlike immigrants, who are prepared to take low-status jobs that pay higher wages than those in the West Indies, second-generation adults eschew association with such low-status positions and reject minimal wages. They do so, not because they believe they deserve more than or are better than their parents, but because their worldview locates these jobs at the bottom of a ladder the second generation is trying to climb. Their immigrant parents see the bottom in the United States as a step up in a climb that began on a rung in the Third World.

Max Weber's model of class in industrial society offers another way to look at the socioeconomic context in which second-generation West Indians are reared. Randall Collins (1986) uses Weber's model to argue that labor ladders such as Piore (1979) describes are maintained by the monopolization of privileged labor market positions by status groups. These groups are most obviously marked by the educational credentials and lifestyles of their members, although other behaviors and ascribed characteristics can be used to establish membership boundaries. For example, status groups may have more stringent standards of behavior for persons who belong to ethnic, religious, or racial minorities, or for women. Christopher, a second-generation West Indian, explained how success in the military is dependent upon similarity to or compatibility with persons who hold power:

> We have a problem in the United States military about race today. It's a fear that, just 'cause you can do your job just as good as the other person, because of your race or the other person doesn't like you they will hinder you from moving up. There's a lot of people, some of 'em it's not their fault, it's just the way they were brought up. I mean, we can get along, but due to the fact that some people feel that the way they were raised—that "black people this, black people feel that." It's in their mind that's causing so much havoc.

Thus second-generation West Indians compete with other persons for entry into racialized, educationally credentialed status groups. Because they recognize that members of these groups control secure, prestigious, and lucrative positions, second-generation West Indians seek to mimic the behaviors, practices, and life trajectories of persons in these privileged positions. On the one hand, they face the same requirements for status group attainment as other active participants in American society. On the other hand, they may be barred from participation by the stigma of race. Racial minorities, particularly blacks, not only must struggle to mimic the lifestyles and credentials of the members of higher status groups, but they must also distance themselves from negative racialized stereotypes. Patricia Hill Collins (1991) has argued that African American women must deal in their everyday interactions with the stereotypes of Hot Momma, Mammy, Welfare Queen, and Matriarch. Given the negative connotations of these stereotypes, distancing seems to be a necessary step toward elite status group entry (Collins 1991; Feagin and Vera 1995).

In addition to the foreign reference point, the first generation's perceptions about its ability to negotiate the American racial hierarchy are influenced by membership in the social networks that supported immigrants' arrivals and resettlements in New York. Through the immigrant social network, veteran immigrants assist newcomers in getting into the country, provide coresidence for extended periods of time, and assist in finding employment and secure housing (Bashi 1997).

Data on the life trajectories of first-generation immigrants demonstrate that the social network shields its members in two ways from the racism present in society. First, even if a group only participates in the primary and secondary labor markets and not in ethnic enclaves, immigrants work and live alongside other immigrants because their social space is within ethnic job and housing niches. If a group operates within an enclave economy (which is not the case among West Indians), the ethnic isolation or insulation effect in the labor and housing markets is even greater. Living, working, and having needs met through the network creates something of a "micro-society," which, though not totally self-sufficient, reduces contact with nonimmigrant persons and institutions (Bashi 1997, 1996; Portes 1995a).

Second, ethnically isolated economic niches and enclave economies reduce the chances that immigrants will interact with persons who are not predisposed to hire or rent to them because of their race. Working with and living among West Indians in economic niches brings to the immigrant population a degree of socioeconomic success higher than that of their native-born black counterparts, and thus a measure of socioeconomic separation from them. The labor market success that members achieve belies racist stereotypes about the inability of black people to succeed in America. Thus life in an immigrant network is constituted by a series of socially supported experiences in the American housing and labor markets. Network and niche memberships both structure goals (i.e., influence living preferences and the direction of job searches) and support the attainment of those goals. The support that first-generation West Indians experience, as well as their concentration in workplaces and communities of residence, translates into an easier experience securing jobs and housing. This experience reinforces an insulation—both psychological and physical—from racist enmity and an ability to disregard racist stereotypes. For West Indians, movement to the United States introduces the unique problem of being rendered invisible (Bryce-Laporte 1972), because to most Americans they are indistinguishable from African Americans. It is the foreign reference point—an orientation to home societies demographically, socially, and politically structured to inhibit "thinking like a minority"—coupled with the socioeconomic isolation that network membership provides, that allows West Indian immigrants to discount the effect of racism on their lives—at least for a time.

There is also the role of what we call "the foreign marker," that is, an accent that may lead whites—especially those employers and providers of goods with whom the network has negotiated special status for its members—to treat West Indians better than American blacks. To the degree that West Indians

separate themselves ethnically (and an accent helps greatly here) or socioeconomically (aided by the immigrant social network, particularly in terms of
labor and housing niches), they may come to believe that they can disregard
racist animosity.

Second-generation respondents confirmed that an ability to invoke West
Indian ethnic status changed the way they were treated by others. Roy said
that his West Indian status gave him "drive," while Carla maintained that it
gave her a "work ethic." Adele asserted that she inherited from her parents
the sense that she was "capable of much more" than other Americans. Nadine, however, described being West Indian as involving rigid and impersonal
parental expectations. Still, she was quick to recognize that this same ethnicity, which she had come to reject, distinguished her in the eyes of others.

> People treat you different when you say that you're Trinidadian. We were
> discussing something in class, and I said to one of the other black students in
> class—and he's from Florida—"Well, my folks just didn't play that. My folks were
> born in the islands. I am a child of West Indian parents." And the professor heard
> me and he goes, "Oh, that makes you very different." But he never elaborated, and
> I never asked. But he did recognize a difference. I wasn't imagining it. It does exist.

Thus, even if sometimes experienced negatively, West Indian ethnicity generally buffers the second generation from some of the negative characterizations
associated with their racial status.

To summarize, we have identified three variables that explain differences in
the perception of racism between first- and second-generation immigrants. The
first is the foreign reference point that the experience of growing up in a black-
majority society provides the first generation. This perspective enables immigrants to hold the American racial system at a distance and bolsters their ability
to resist internalizing minority status. The second variable is social experience in
an immigrant social network, which shields first-generation immigrants from
racism and structures their lives so that they are able to avoid or withstand racism
when they face it. Finally, the foreign marker and the ability to invoke West Indian ethnic status leads to better treatment from others, which in turn builds motivation to duplicate or demonstrate ethnic distinctiveness.

CONCLUSION

Both first- and second-generation West Indians believe that education is key to
achieving social mobility. In a racialized society, however, race and ethnicity
mediate the impact of education. Both generations experience racism, but they
perceive its personal and societal impact differently. Our second-generation
respondents unanimously felt that racism in America is a huge problem, and
many believed that there are limits to the returns to education because of
racism. They varied, however, in their perceptions of the extent to which

racism affects their own attempts at mobility. Some felt that racism had limited their opportunities, others felt that they had been able to circumvent those limitations, while still others said that racism had not in any way limited their opportunities. The first generation, however, did not see racism as a huge problem. Despite having experienced racism in the United States, immigrants believed that racism need not be an obstacle to mobility, but that it is something readily ignored or avoided. We believe that these differences can be explained largely by one's ability to invoke West Indian ethnic status, which is related to the degree that the social experience common to a foreign-born, foreign-raised West Indian is incorporated into one's socialization.

The first generation has the maximum opportunity to invoke West Indian ethnic identity—they have the social experiences of a foreign reference point, a network of coethnics with which to live and work, and a foreign accent—all of which translate into social distance from a racially hierarchical social system. The second generation is less strategically flexible, particularly in those areas most influenced by the racial system. Social experience variables, rather than immigrant status or cultural ethnicity, best explain differences between the generations. What characterizes the first generation is not just their foreign birth but that they have moved from a black-majority society to the white-majority United States and successfully remained, reaching employment and educational goals that most of those who stayed behind can only dream of. What characterizes the second generation is not just their American birth but that they have difficulty marshaling their West Indianness in a society that racializes black people with little regard to ethnicity. As Linda, a second-generation respondent, told us,

> We are affected by race 'cause a lot of people just see us as black Americans. We're treated, as far as I know, the same ways black Americans are treated because we're clumped in that category. But I think our own perception is different than that of a black American because our parents had such a drive and a strive that other Americans did not have. We come from a totally different perspective of work ethic and a different perspective of, you know, their education. With, you know, my father's education is probably so much better probably than mine when I reached the level that he reached because of, you know, that British influence. You know, they far exceed us in math and other areas. So I think we're affected because we are clumped in those categories, but I think that our perception is different.

Since subsequent American-born generations will have less and less ability to invoke West Indian ethnicity, they may end up exposed to the oppressive aspects of American racial structure. In contrast, ethnic West Indians may be relieved of racism's worst effects if West Indian ethnicity continues to be recognized as a marker of difference. Thus, West Indians of both the first and the second generations may gain from investing in the cultural difference stereotype.

Invoking cultural arguments to explain socioeconomic difference reifies existing racial structures by reinforcing the dichotomy of ethnic West Indian success and black American failure. On the flip side of the coin is the persistent stereotype that blacks (including people not readily identifiable as ethnically West Indian) have a poor work ethic and other cultural failings that lead to socioeconomic failure (Feagin and Vera 1995). This stereotype persists despite the many examples of black socioeconomic success represented by blacks in the working and middle classes. The socioeconomic success of an ethnically undifferentiated black person is thus seen as an anomaly (Feagin and Sikes 1994).

Black success is more readily accepted when cloaked in West Indian ethnicity, and American society equates that ethnicity with "positive" cultural values. A lack of hope, optimism, or even socioeconomic success among second-generation West Indians is in turn associated with assimilation to the "negative" cultural values of African Americans. That we ignore social structure in favor of cultural arguments to explain West Indian failure and success serves as yet another example of how racialized societies use ethnic myths (Steinberg 1989) to maintain and reinforce the mechanisms that justify and perpetuate racism and hierarchical racial structures.

NOTES

1. Of course, many factors influence one's chances for social mobility. Some work has been done to understand the factors that affect success differently between the generations, but so far no studies have examined both the first and second generations' own ideas about socioeconomic success or failure and the likelihood of either. Most published work has either studied the first generation while speculating on second-generation sentiment (Foner 1978), studied the second generation without studying notions of success held by the first (Portes 1995a; Waters 1996a), or studied both while using preconceived but "objective" ideas (GPA, income, etc.) of what success means (Kalmijn 1996; Portes 1995a; Kao and Tienda 1995). One of the more intergenerationally comparative of these works, Foner's (1978) ambitious study of Jamaicans in London, tackled a myriad of factors relating to the status attainment afforded by international migration. In one chapter she explained the differing obstacles to success faced by first- and second-generation West Indians in London. But while her data on the first generation came from interviews with respondents, Foner did not directly interview second-generation respondents to gather data on the second generation.

2. Some studies of the second generation emphasize culture and others ethnicity, but most tend to downplay the effect of race (i.e., racism, residential segregation, white prejudice) and instead emphasize intragroup attributes of American blacks as primary explanatory factors.

Kalmijn (1996) uses the language of culture to explain observed differential socioeconomic success among second-generation West Indians as compared to native-born blacks in his quantitative analysis of 1990 U.S. Census data. Kalmijn does not define what this "culture" is, but rather implies that the first and second generations share cultural attributes that bring about success. Sowell (1978) is the most well-known proponent of cultural determinism as it applies to explaining differential outcomes between black West Indians and African Americans.

Kao and Tienda (1995), who studied educational outcomes for native-born and first- and second-generation immigrants, conclude that, since first-generation blacks are high achievers, there is support for the "immigrant optimism hypothesis," the theory that differences between African American and West Indian *parents* explain the difference in educational achievement between African American and West Indian youth. They also suggest that immigrant parents' policing of children's after-school behavior differs from that of native parents, although they do not explain how this translates into the "optimism" that subsequent generations supposedly "benefit from" (15). Still, they note that for blacks "the presence of an immigrant parent may be insufficient to prevent regression of educational achievement toward that of U.S.-born blacks with native parents" (12). Their study suffers from methodological problems as well. While the authors compare Asian and Hispanic groups on the basis of educational outcomes, they do not compare blacks of different generations because the groups, they argue, do not share ethnicities. However, it is unclear whether all the Asians and Hispanics in the study share the same ancestry or country of origin. Thus one suspects that their analysis of pancthnic groups labeled "Asian" or "Hispanic" has similar comparison problems (are all the Asians or Hispanics from the same country of origin?)—yet they complete these comparisons anyway.

Portes (1995a) studied four second-generation groups to understand what he calls "downward leveling," the tendency for some second-generation groups to assimilate (or to resist assimilation) to values that differ from the immigrant parent generation's aspirations for their children. He notes that the density of social networks may make the difference between whether or not second-generation youth avoid such downward assimilation, but he states that his findings are not conclusive on this point. Portes uses social network density and differential leveling pressures to explain why some second-generation youth face pressures to be less than academically successful, but he gives only passing mention to the importance of a hierarchy of racial categories. For example, although he notes that some second-generation students in his study (Cubans) attended private schools while others (Haitians) lived in racially segregated poor neighborhoods, Portes's main explanation for differential exposure to "inner city values" is the varying densities of immigrant social networks; his silence on other, racial issues suggests that he believes neither the extent of racial residential segregation nor the accompanying poverty rates are factors that make a difference.

In any event, we argue that, whether because of limitations on the data or problematic construction of theoretical arguments, prior work has been unable to sufficiently explain intergenerational variation in West Indian aspirations and achievement.

3. By *social experience*, we mean immersion in a social context of sufficient duration to socialize a person or group so that they are fully familiar with the way that social context operates.

4. Although the immigrants interviewed for this study all migrated to and lived in New York, second-generation respondents did not all live in the New York City area. We justify inclusion of these non–New Yorkers by noting that, for native-born persons, social mobility often requires geographic mobility, just as it did for their parents. The first generation's mobility strategy required geographic movement *into* the New York area, in many cases with the help of social networks that then constrained immigrants to remain in New York City (Bashi 1997). However, second-generation mobility strategies are more likely to require

moves *away from* the New York area. In any event, we argue that immigrant social networks are not likely to geographically restrict the second generation.

5. Over 95 percent of the first-generation respondents arrived in New York City well before 1980. They were here, then, before the 1986 crackdown on employers who hired foreigners without proper working papers. They were also here before New York City's near bankruptcy and fiscal crisis in 1975–76, which brought about restrictions in City University of New York admission policies for bachelor's degree programs. Thus, it was relatively easy for these immigrants to combine both work and schooling under the immigration, employment, and college admissions climates they faced in New York City between 1965 and 1976.

6. We invented pseudonyms to refer to our respondents. None of their real names are used in this chapter.

7. Like other researchers, we separated the first generation from subsequent ones for the purpose of our sociological analysis, but in many ways this separation was merely a heuristic device to organize our ethnographic and interview material. "First" and "second" generations are ideal types used to characterize people with different "values" across a variable best labeled as "ethnicity." We develop these generational categories not because birth on different soil produces different human beings; instead, generational status is used as a dummy variable to reflect the effect of nativity on ethnic status. A better analytic tool would break ethnicity and the effects of nativity down into discrete and observable social experiences. Although we do not abandon the simplifying language of "first" and "second" generations, we refer to the differences between the two groups by the immigrant status variables that correspond with the differential social experiences each group faces in their respective social contexts.

8. People from islands that were more economically self-sufficient (e.g., Jamaica) or linguistically distinct (e.g., former Dutch or French colonies) may have participated less fully in the interisland migration that marked the former British colonies of the Lesser Antilles in the Eastern Caribbean (D. Marshall 1987).

NINE

Tweaking a Monolith
The West Indian Immigrant Encounter with "Blackness"

Milton Vickerman

Although "blackness" has long been an issue in American society, this fact has not always been self-evident. American racism has created and thrived on a uniform—almost monolithic—view of people of African ancestry.[1] Until recent times this view has effectively disguised the complex variations that are inherent in conceptions of race. However, as racism has become less monolithic, the contested nature of "blackness" has slowly become more apparent. Though racism is still crucially important in the lives of individuals of African ancestry, its relative decline in the decades following the civil rights revolution has led to a multiplicity of viewpoints as to what it means to be "black." A number of social trends both contribute to and serve as indicators of these changes. One such trend is the growing ideological diversity among individuals of African ancestry. Another trend is the well-known bifurcation, in the African American community, between the so-called underclass and the upwardly mobile. A third trend is the rise in the number of individuals of mixed race.[2]

There is, however, a fourth important trend that is contributing to the contestation of ideas of blackness, and this is the one on which I wish to focus. It is the large-scale influx of African ancestry immigrants—mostly West Indians—into the United States. In core areas of settlement such as New York City and Miami, these immigrants are diversifying the African American population and introducing African-ancestry individuals with a different culture and history. A significant aspect of this difference is that West Indians hold conceptions of blackness that are at odds with those held by many Americans. In this essay, I advance the thesis that the meeting of contending West Indian and American conceptions of race is helping to *slowly* erode the traditional monolithic conception of blackness. However, this erosion must be seen in proper context since systematic racism remains a powerful force and rigid views of what it means to be black remain entrenched. Hence, assessments as to how much conceptions of blackness are changing need to be phrased very cautiously. I proceed by presenting brief historical summaries of how notions of blackness developed in the United States and the West Indies. I then show how, through immigration, West Indian perspectives on the issue are influencing monolithic American conceptions of blackness. This discussion includes an examination of the views and experiences not only of the immigrants but also of their children who were born in the United States.

FRAMING "BLACKNESS": THE "ONE-DROP RULE"

Although by now a truism, it bears repeating that race is a social construction. In America, the "one-drop rule" defining "blacks" is perhaps the single best example of this fact. As many writers have noted, being "black" in America has meant having only the slightest trace of African ancestry. Historically, such inheritance has damned individuals designated "black" to subjugation, brutalization, and the state of being indelibly stamped with a mark of inferiority. Blackness, in this traditional view, has strongly resembled the biblical "mark of Cain."[3]

But the engraining of this view has occurred only after a great deal of struggle. This struggle originated in the early decades of the country's colonization and revolved around the legal status of Africans and mulattoes. Scholars of colonial America disagree over the exact status of Africans in the earliest decades of the American colonies (see, for example, Handlin 1957; Degler 1984; Quarles 1987). What is certain is that the early English settlers in Virginia and the surrounding colonies harbored deep prejudices against Africans—prejudices, according to historian Winthrop Jordan (1969), that stemmed from white settlers' fixation on Africans' skin color and religious status as nonbelievers in the Christian faith. These prejudices meant that, one way or another, the lot of Africans in early America was a hard one. In fact, according to historian Joel Williamson (1980), by 1630, Africans had already been reduced by the courts to slavery. In the following decades, the Virginia legislature progressively systematized and reinforced this status. By the end of the seventeenth century, it had become accepted that to be African— "black"—meant being a slave. The one-drop rule reified this association between African ancestry, skin color, and inferiority by holding that all individuals of even remote African ancestry were to be defined as "black."

Although the equation of blackness with slavery became widespread throughout the thirteen original colonies, this consensus did not completely resolve the issue of what it meant to be black. The status of mulattoes remained a significant problem for almost two more centuries. As writers such as Williamson (1980) and F. James Davis (1991) have shown, the one-drop rule, though profoundly influential, was not universally embraced. For a significant portion of American history it faced a rival viewpoint, which predominated mostly in the Lower South, especially in Charleston and New Orleans. This alternate vision of blackness moderated the one-drop rule by separating mulattoes into an intermediate category between the dominant whites and their slaves. In Charleston and New Orleans this buffer group, existing by the leave of whites, flourished for a time. Some mulattoes became quite wealthy, even to the point of owning slaves. In general they insisted on a status apart from their enslaved cousins and emphasized their physical characteristics—such as skin shade and hair type—as symbols of superiority to darker-skinned individuals. A humorous but apparently effective device described by Davis (1992) was the brown paper bag test, whereby only mixed-race individuals whose skin shade was lighter than a brown paper bag were allowed into certain clubs.

Despite their advantages, mulattoes had an ambivalent sense of self. As Williamson has noted, "The ultimate absurdity in America's attempt to draw a race line with the one-drop rule was the fact that many mulattoes themselves simply did not know whether they were white or black. Their African origins were lost to certain memory, and they were left only with lingering doubts" (1980: 98). These lingering doubts also affected white southerners, who were anxious to preserve the principle of white purity and constantly worried about "invisible blackness." Such fears gradually intensified as slavery came under increasing attack. The upshot was that, by the middle of the nineteenth century, whites had redefined mulattoes as being distinctly "black." If the one-drop rule had had a competitor in the seventeenth and eighteenth centuries, by the end of the nineteenth century it stood absolutely unopposed as the law and custom of the land. Significantly, those persons defined as black also came to embrace this rule. One indicator of the extent to which this is still true was the response of some African Americans to attempts to include a separate mixed-race category in the 2000 Census. For instance, the NAACP opposed the proposal on the grounds that it would dilute the political power of African Americans (Frisby 1996). Implicit in this opposition was the idea that mixed-race individuals are "black" and that attempting to claim a different identity is illegitimate.

"BLACKNESS" IN THE WEST INDIES

Historically, West Indian ideas regarding race have resembled their American counterparts in fundamental ways. But they have also differed significantly, and it is these differences that underpin the enormous difficulties that West Indian immigrants experience in adjusting to life in America. If American race relations have traditionally been organized around a black-white dichotomy buttressed by the one-drop rule, West Indian race relations have been organized around a trichotomy. This trichotomy would have been recognizable to eighteenth- and nineteenth-century residents of Charleston and New Orleans, whose system shared a similar pyramidal structure: a small white elite at the top, a large mass of blacks in the base, and an intermediate mixed-race group. However, while the tripartite model of race relations gained only a toehold in the United States and eventually lost out to the one-drop rule, in the West Indies it became the standard model. Thus, significantly, in the West Indies blackness has traditionally been conceptualized within a more complex framework than has been the case in the United States.

Most important in terms of the similarities between West Indian and American views of race, slavery flourished for centuries in both regions and led to entrenched pejorative views of individuals possessing African ancestry. This is such a truism in the United States that it hardly requires comment. In the West Indies an oft-cited example is that of beauty contests. In Jamaica, for instance, beauty contestants have traditionally possessed features that are noticeably Caucasian—although in recent years the winners have been darker-skinned. That women with Caucasian features consistently win even though Jamaica's population is over 90 percent of African origin suggests that notions of feminine beauty are biased in favor of a Caucasian ideal. To put it another way, African features traditionally have not been highly esteemed (Nettleford 1972: 25–26; Brodber 1989: 66). However, it should also be noted that the pro-black ideologies embodied in Garveyism and Rastafarianism, the self-confidence engendered by independence from Britain, and economic growth since World War II have mitigated antiblack biases.[4]

Despite similarities, notions of race in the West Indies differ markedly from those in the United States: a tripartite model of race relations promotes a complex view of race, whereas America's dichotomous model promotes a more simplistic view. Historically, individuals were ranked within the tripartite model according to shade of skin and access to wealth, income, honor, and power. During the slavery period, society was more than just whites on top, free persons of color (largely light-skinned) in the middle, and slaves (largely dark-skinned) on the bottom. Among slaves the lighter-skinned were often house servants as opposed to fieldhands, and, among intermediate mulattoes, the lighter-skinned had certain advantages—some were even accepted by Caucasians as "white." After emancipation and throughout the colonial era, it came to be expected, though never entirely realized, that "white persons should belong to the upper class, colored to the middle, and black to the lowest class" (Philip Mason, quoted in Foner 1978: 27).

The focus on skin shade encouraged West Indians to conceive of race as a continuum. The introduction of East Indian and Chinese indentured workers in the nineteenth century magnified this tendency since it led to even more miscegenation. Unlike in the United States, the criteria for defining race in the West Indies were diffuse rather than sharp. Moreover, after the end of slavery and as the nineteenth century wore on, West Indians, unlike Americans, lowered the barriers to full black participation in society. Although slow, the trend was toward greater freedom, whereas the United States increasingly restricted its black population, particularly through Jim Crow segregation. Throughout the twentieth century, West Indians increasingly tended to downplay race. Typically, West Indians stigmatized black skin but argued that it could be "compensated" for through such factors as higher education and the attainment of prestigious professional careers (Norris 1962).

As far back as the nineteenth century, West Indian societies were relatively tolerant compared to American society. For instance, in *The English in the West Indies* (1888), the nineteenth-century English writer and traveler A. J. Froude barely hid his incredulity at the fact that a black man had become attorney general of Barbados. Some West Indian opinion makers highlighted such successes as a way of de-emphasizing race. For instance, in *Two Jamaicas,* Philip Curtin (1970: 172–173) noted the eagerness of some mid-nineteenth-century European Jamaicans to present a raceless face in appealing to potential immigrants:

> The question of race was beneath the surface of every Jamaican problem, intermingling with other issues and making all solutions more difficult. . . . The threefold racial division helped to ease tensions somewhat—racial, as opposed to class, lines were never as tightly drawn in Jamaica as in the southern United States. In Jamaica, the race question was often hidden behind other issues, while in the American South other issues tended to hide behind racial conflict. Many Jamaicans took a certain pride in their lack of overt racial distinctions, and the racial equality of Jamaica was frequently stressed in immigration appeals.

Of course, as Curtin notes, racism was deeply embedded within Jamaican society. Nevertheless, white foreigners, used to the more rigid conditions prevailing in other countries (especially the United States), found West Indian race relations to be disconcertingly liberal. Speaking of nineteenth-century Jamaica, John Bigelow, editor of the *New York Evening Post,* noted that, "One unacquainted with the extent to which the amalgamation of races has gone here, is constantly liable to drop remarks in the presence of white persons, which, in consequence of the mixture of blood that may take place in some branch of their families, are likely to be very offensive" (quoted in Broom 1954: 119).

Historically, the key factor behind West Indians' relative looseness in matters of race has been the predominance of persons of African ancestry. Among the more important effects of this demographic reality is that "blackness" is normal in the West Indies in the way that "whiteness" is normal in the United States. In the West Indies, possessing black skin is taken for granted and excites no special comment. In their daily lives, West Indians are much more interested in the problem of how to make ends meet in countries that are poor and in which the costs of living are high. To the extent that they take note of race, West Indians see that levels of wealth often—though by no means exclusively—correlate with shades of skin. But they also see that most people—the impoverished as well as prominent opinion makers—look much like them. Moreover, and very significantly, their entire socialization teaches them that race is unimportant. This is true of political socialization, which deliberately and effectively removes race from the public agenda and substitutes an "all are equal in a diverse society" ideology.[5] It is even more true of socialization in the home and in the educational system, where West Indians learn to place extreme stress on the cultural ideal for achieving upward mobility: education.[6] All this effectively minimizes the role of race in West Indian societies. By contrast, in the United States most people do not look like the average West Indian, and West Indians' skin color often excites not only comment but fear and contempt as well. West Indian immigrants gradually realize the large social costs of possessing black skin. Their assertion that they discover what it means to be black only after immigrating is a recognition that African ancestry carries far more serious consequences in American society than it does in their home societies (Vickerman 1999; Foner 1987).

"BLACKNESS" IN AMERICA'S FUTURE: THE ROLE OF WEST INDIANS

Were it not for the fact of their large-scale, sustained immigration to the United States, West Indians' tendency to minimize race as a life-shaping factor would be irrelevant to American society. As it stands, however, it is highly relevant—especially in places, such as New York City, where there is a large West Indian presence. In the current social climate, where received ideas about what it means to be black are more unsettled than they once were, any factor that raises questions about racist ideas[7] regarding blackness has the potential to further unsettle the issue. This is the context in which West Indian immigration must be seen—as raising one more question regarding standard American assumptions about blackness. To frame the analysis in these terms is to argue for the existence of marginal changes that could, in the future, have larger societal effects. To phrase the argument another way, such an analytical framework allows us to recognize the entrenched nature of traditional ideas regarding blackness while cautiously suggesting that these ideas now face many more overt challenges than they did in previous times. The suggestion is not that racist ideas regarding blackness will disappear any time soon. Rather, because of factors such as upward mobility in the black community and large-scale immigration, the *potential* exists that racist ideas will be progressively undermined. Thus one speaks of the "tweaking" of notions of blackness rather than, say, their crumbling.

To understand why cautious optimism is warranted, one need only look at data on intermarriage. The rate of black/white intermarriage is much higher today than it was decades ago. For instance, Table 9.1 shows that, between 1970 and 1980, marriages between all couples increased by 11.5 percent; but interracial marriages increased by 110 percent in the same period and those between blacks and whites by 157 percent. For the years 1990 through 1994, black/white marriages increased by 40 percent. Since intermarriage is a good indicator of assimilation, on the surface it looks as if racial distinctions between blacks and whites are blurring at a rapid rate. However, other data show that these initial appearances are deceiving. For one, only about 5 percent of all marriages in the United States are interracial; secondly, when intermarriage rates are broken down by group, the black/white intermarriage rate looks anemic. Reynolds Farley's (1996) analysis of 1990 census data shows that, among those aged twenty-five to thirty-four, 70 percent of Asian wives and 39 percent of Hispanic wives had white husbands. In contrast, only 2 percent of black wives married white husbands.[8]

These data suggest that the traditional black/white dichotomy is still well entrenched but is beginning to incorporate more nonblacks. Thus, the black/white dichotomy might metamorphose into a black/nonblack one. When we also consider other data showing continuing systematic discrimination against blacks,[9] the argument that racism is crumbling looks even weaker.

This is not to say, however, that what it means to be black will remain static. Indeed, the assumptions associated with blackness are likely to undergo some measure of change. Consider the stereotype that blackness entails being poor, of any number of hues, and politically liberal. First, while the poverty rate among African Americans continues to hover around 27 percent, it is also true that a growing number of African Americans are affluent. Second, despite the one-drop rule, which compressed individuals of a wide range of skin shades into a single "African American" community, the existence of groups such as PROJECT RACE and the recent push to include a mixed-race category on the 2000 Census show that the monolithic conception of blackness is being openly contested by more and more Americans. Finally, as is well known, conservative blacks, while not necessarily flourishing, are more outspoken today than they have been in the past.

Changes that affect what it means to be black will likely impact the African American community first and most strongly and then, perhaps, the entire society. The immigration of West Indians could also play a role in altering the meaning of blackness in society at large. As shown, their entire socialization pushes them away from conceiving of the world in racial terms. If they are reluctant to embrace a racial consciousness with their ethnic kin, they are even more unlikely to see automatic connections between themselves and African Americans. While strong bonds are found between many West Indians and African Americans, they take time to develop—West Indians must undergo a period of learning through experience to understand truths about social injustice in America that African Americans have long known. As writers such as Foner (1987) have shown, West Indians learn to "become black" through immersion in American racism, and the process is most definitely a painful one.

TABLE 9.1 Married Couples of Same or Mixed Race, 1970–1994
(in thousands)

	1970	1980	1990	1994	Percentage increase 1970–1980	Percentage increase 1980–1990	Percentage increase 1990–1994
All married couples	44,598	49,714	53,256	54,251	11.5	7.1	2.0
Interracial couples	310	651	964	1,283	110.0	48.1	33.0
Black/white	65	167	211	296	156.9	26.3	40.2
White/other race[a]	233	450	720	909	93.1	60.0	26.3
Black/other race[a]	12	34	33	78	183.3	-2.9	136.0
All other couples[b]	366	799	1,401	1,764	118.3	75.3	26.0

SOURCE: Adapted from Table 61, *Statistical Abstracts of the United States* (Washington, D.C.: Government Printing Office, 1995)
[a]Excluding white and black
[b]Excluding same-race couples

One of the most salient features to emerge from my previous research among West Indian immigrants in the New York City area is the sense of astonishment they feel at being discriminated against because of their skin color.[10] For most this is a brand-new experience, one that they would rather not get used to. A financial consultant put the problem this way:

> I still can't fathom why, because of the color of your skin, certain privileges are not available to you. I still can't understand it; I just can't understand it. . . . When you come here it's almost like after a while you learn to accept your fate. . . . So, for instance, if you know you are not going to be welcome in certain places, you just don't go there . . . because you alone cannot fight this war. . . . And this situation has been here long before we came here and it will be here . . . for as long as I can see into the future. So it's just a matter of working within the system to extract the benefits that you will need for yourself. That's how I see it.

Another person stated:

> I go to the track once day a year—the Belmont stakes. . . . There are . . . benches around the place that you can sit on; not reserved, not paid for. Everybody pays five dollars and you go into the clubhouse. . . . We were feeling a little tired and we went . . . to sit down. . . . And we sat and these people started to tell us that these seats were reserved. So we said, "Look, these seats are not reserved. If you want to reserve a seat you have to pay extra because I have one of the tags." . . . And this redneck guy looked around and told us that . . . he used to . . . kill people like us, meaning he used to kill black people!

In a third example, a thirty-seven-year-old computer programmer stated:

> Race was important [in Jamaica] but not on a day-to-day basis. The difference I find is that when you get to America, you have to start thinking about race when you walk into the store. . . . In Manhattan you walk into a store, you'll find that people will be following you around. Things like that you have never been accustomed to. To me, what has been a shocker here is to walk on the train and for women to clutch their handbags. That has never happened to me before. So you realize that you have to develop a . . . thick skin . . . because if you have never been taken as a thief before and all of a sudden you have to deal with this! That has been, to me, my worst problem to overcome since I have been here.

Experiences such as these, which manifest the ever-present reality of racism, move West Indians toward a strong sense of affinity with African Americans. This affinity is evident, for instance, in their criticism of the police for targeting blacks and of the media's negative portrayal of blacks, as well as in West Indians' pro-black voting patterns. Nonetheless, their whole history and culture acts as a counterpressure against conceptualizing the world in racial terms, and, just as important, so does their achievement orientation in the United States. Generally speaking, West Indian immigrants are highly pragmatic, focusing primary attention on material and educational advancement and paying only secondary attention to social issues such as racism. They are, on the whole, socially conservative; moreover, to the extent that they consider race, they view African ancestry positively. The result of these cross-pressures is that West Indians live in a state of dynamic tension between what they would like to focus their attention on and what they have to deal with because of skin color.

West Indians who migrated to the United States before the 1960s generally resolved this tension by casting their lot with African Americans. Whether or not they wished to do so, they had little choice in the matter: Jim Crow segregation was monolithic.[11] Increasingly, however, West Indians of the "new" immigration cohort have the option of resolving the tension by becoming more "West Indian." One reason for this is the decline of blatant racism, which has enabled West Indians to manifest their unique culture distinct from an overarching "black" culture. At the same time, their increasing numbers in cities such as New York have enabled West Indians to achieve a critical mass that has allowed them to expand the borders of the ethnic community such that they can spend large amounts of time surrounded by West Indian culture. Although this culture is often Americanized, it is authentic enough to bolster a strong "West Indian" sense of self.

Immersion in a West Indian community has implications for notions of blackness in that it reinforces a less overt interest in race than is found among African Americans and Americans in general. Although exposure to American society causes West Indians to become more conscious of race, the influence of their socialization in the West Indies is thorough enough to keep racial consciousness at fairly low levels. While exposure to American racism is jarring, West Indians still tend to subordinate racial considerations to their overriding goal of achieving material success in the United States. This orientation probably mutes feelings of racial solidarity with African Americans that derive from shared experiences of discrimination. Thus the social circumstances in which present-day West Indian immigrants find themselves and their achievement orientation counter the long-standing idea that all individuals of African ancestry feel automatic kinship. This contrast is likely to become more evident as the West Indian share of New York City's black population increases. According to census data, by 1990 West Indians already constituted 25 percent of the black population (32 percent in Brooklyn). And, as Philip Kasinitz (1992) has shown, some New York City politicians have already sought to appeal to West Indians, not as "blacks" but as a distinct ethnic voting block.

THE SECOND GENERATION AND "BLACKNESS"

The growth of the West Indian population in the United States—especially in New York City—raises a question as to whether the American-born children of West Indian immigrants will influence ideas about blackness in this country. The question is more problematic for the second generation than it is for their immigrant parents. First, because more research has been conducted on West Indian immigrants than on the second generation, more is known about the immigrant generation. Second, since the children of these immigrants were born in America, they face more identity options than do their parents. Research on West Indian immigrants has shown that they strongly identify with their countries of birth or, more generally, as "West Indians." Indeed, historically, West Indian immigrants' tendency to cling to these identities has been central to the friction between themselves and African Americans. However, it is more difficult to say how the children of these immigrants view themselves since, like their parents, they may identify with a particular West Indian country or, generally, as "West Indian." Alternatively, they may choose a racial designation such as "black" or "East Indian," view themselves simply as "American," or opt for some combination of these identities.[12]

Concerning American ideas of blackness, the self-identification of second-generation West Indians is important mainly because these self-identifications give some indication of whether the children of West Indian immigrants support the prevailing societal views of what it means to be black or, like their parents, raise further questions about these views. In reality the choice is not that stark since second-generation West Indians assimilate into the African American community. This implies an acceptance of, for instance, the expressive aspects of African American culture—music, dress, slang phrases, and so on. More important, it suggests an embracing of the idea that individuals of African ancestry experience discrimination because of that ancestry. In this context, blacks' history of struggle against racism is a powerful unifying force between second-generation West Indians and their African American peers. However, the second generation's assimilation into the African American community does not imply an automatic and rapid acceptance of all customary beliefs regarding what it means to be black. Most problematic is the common equation of blackness with socially disruptive behavior and with inferiority in such areas as academics and occupational status. In their vocal rejection of such stereotypes some second-generation West Indians raise yet another question regarding negative perceptions of blackness, thus contributing in a small way to larger social forces that represent dissatisfaction with antiblack views.[13]

Research by sociologist Mary Waters (1996a) has shown that social class, the experience of discrimination, and perceptions of discrimination significantly affect the terms on which second-generation West Indians assimilate into the African American community. Specifically, she argues that second-generation West Indians in New York City fall into three categories: the American-identified, the ethnic-identified, and the immigrant-identified. American-identified second-generation West Indians mostly come from poor families in which parental involvement in social networks is limited. These youth attend all-black inner-city schools and view themselves as black Americans. As Waters notes, "They most definitely assimilate to black America;

they speak black English with their peers, they listen to rap music, and they accept the peer culture of their black American friends" (183–184). One crucial aspect of this assimilation is that American-identified second-generation West Indians develop pessimistic attitudes about racial discrimination and view racism as an insurmountable barrier. Consequently, concludes Waters, they are likely to experience downward mobility.

In contrast, ethnic-identified second-generation West Indians mostly come from middle-class families, which possess the resources to send children to challenging, racially mixed schools. Moreover, parents of ethnic-identified individuals are part of extensive social networks that help to boost the children's achievements. Although the ethnic-identified are aware of racial discrimination against blacks, they are also achievement-oriented and do not view racism as an insurmountable barrier. Most importantly, ethnic-identified second-generation West Indians tend to distance themselves from poorer African Americans in an attempt to claim higher status. They argue that whites view West Indians more favorably than African Americans, and, as Waters notes, they try to stress that "being black is not synonymous with being black American" (1996a: 181). Although the ethnic-identified may eventually assimilate into the African American community, Waters's work implies that they will do so more slowly than do the American-identified.

Immigrant-identified West Indian youth are characterized by a strong orientation toward the West Indies. They signal this through their dress, speech, and behavior, and, according to Waters, are so West Indian–oriented that the question of whether to choose a black American identity or an ethnic identity does not exist for them. Because they adopt this stance, immigrant-identified West Indian youth are able, to some extent, to opt out of the identity conflicts that affect both American- and ethnic-identified second-generation West Indians.

Waters's research is relevant to my main theme, that is, whether second-generation West Indians contribute to the larger social forces raising questions about the meaning of blackness. In this regard, Waters makes the important point that West Indian immigrants consciously try to inculcate in their children the notion that West Indians are distinct from certain African Americans. This means that the parents, who reject what Waters refers to as "the generalized negative view of blacks," encourage their children to make this same rejection. The parents want their children to instead associate being black with positive traits, especially achievement and success.

Based on research I have conducted among West Indian immigrants and second-generation West Indians, I would argue that the desire to establish this positive association in the consciousness of the larger society is deeply held by many West Indian immigrants. If realized, such a view would represent a significant departure in the way blackness is perceived in America. However, a large gap separates desire from reality. Indeed, even some members of the second generation do not accept their parents' notions of blackness. Waters's research shows that, though parents of both the American- and the ethnic-identified send pro–black achievement signals to their children, such messages only find a receptive audience where parents possess enough material and social resources to actualize their optimistic beliefs. Thus ethnic-identified second-generation West Indians respond positively to their parents' pro–black achievement signals while the American-identified do not. Moreover, given American society's tendency to view all individuals of African ancestry as the same, Waters is even skeptical about the ethnic-identified's ability, over the long run, to continue responding positively to parents' pro–black achievement signals. Similarly, she wonders whether the immigrant-identified can, over time, maintain their intermediate status between the American- and the ethnic-identified. Ultimately, Waters suggests, they may be forced by the intensity of American racism to choose between identifying as "black" or as ethnics.

My own research tends to support Waters's findings. The West Indian immigrants whom I interviewed in New York City generally agreed that West Indians prize achievement over all else and are willing to sacrifice to attain success. Moreover, the respondents desired to pass on the same orientation to their children. One ethnic-identified young man whom I interviewed stated, "For the most part, foreign blacks are the ones that set a more positive example for blacks here because the American blacks, as far as the foreign blacks are concerned, let themselves down and let us down. . . . [If] you choose not to take advantage of . . . opportunity, then whose fault is that?"[14] More recent research that I have conducted among second-generation West Indians echoes these sentiments.[15] Most of the thirty-seven individuals whom I interviewed were, by Waters's definition, "ethnic-identified," but in important respects these individuals were also Americans.[16] Asked to choose from a list of identity options—"American," "hyphenated American," "national origin" (e.g., Barbadian), "racial," or "other"—60 percent chose "hyphenated American," saying that, because they were born in this country, they were Americans. They viewed their immigrant parents as more enmeshed in West Indian culture than themselves and more likely to maintain contact with relatives in the West Indies.

In general my second-generation respondents reported being more conscious than their immigrant parents of race as a life-shaping issue. They were acutely aware that American society views them as "black" and reacts to them according to negative stereotypes. For instance, one young female graduate student recounted how she had been harassed, for racial reasons, in a supermarket near the university she attended. A manager who worked for a large multinational corporation told of being stopped by the police and of having white women shy away from him as he walked on the street. A third respondent—an analyst at a Wall Street bank—reported that, while he was searching for an apartment in an affluent neighborhood, the receptionist in one building threatened to call the police if he did not leave the premises. In our conversation, the analyst underlined the seriousness of racial discrimination in America by arguing that the mere fact of being "black" in America can even result in murder.

Despite such experiences and a heightened sense of shared bonds with African Americans, most second-generation young people I interviewed still viewed themselves as being partially West Indian—more specifically, West Indian blacks. Indeed, this aspect of their identity was important to them—they viewed it as setting them apart from generalized negative perceptions of blacks. Although the respondents numbered African Americans among their close friends, they also argued that being West Indian gives them an edge in American society because of a perception that West Indians are achievement-oriented. They wanted those around them to perceive that they did not conform to American society's negative perceptions of blackness—that they were succeeding in school and obtaining high-status jobs, and that they respected authority figures such as elders and teachers. Many of the second-generation respondents believed that blackness should encompass elements from the African American, white, and West Indian communities rather than from only the African American community.

In our discussions, second-generation West Indians attributed their outlook mostly to the influence of their immigrant parents, who had stressed certain core values, notably, the importance of attaining education and finding high-status jobs, respect for elders, and religiosity. Only occasionally did respondents mention the role of West Indian parents' social class in actualizing these cherished values. Instead, they gave primarily cultural explanations as to why they differed from their African American peers. Sue, a high school student, stated: "School is the most important—well, other than, for my family, other than God—school is the most important. Work hard. Never do a job half done but to the best of your abilities and things like that. My parents never accepted mediocre. And I think that . . . a lot of West Indians and West Indian parents [are] teaching . . . things of that nature."

At the same time as ethnic-identified second-generation West Indians assimilate into the African American community, they also seek to retain their West Indian culture. West Indians' tendency to de-emphasize race becomes relevant here. Some second-generation respondents reported conflict with African American friends over how much stress to place on race and how to define blackness. Some respondents complained that their African American friends too narrowly defined being "black." Being "black," these respondents argued, is not incompatible with embracing other aspects of the wider American—especially "white"—culture.

Sue discussed differences between her views of blackness and those held by her African American friends:

Is racial discrimination an issue with you in your everyday life?
No. . . . It is with friends of mine, and I think that's another comparison; because my parents have raised me to . . . accept every part of people. You

know, you have white people, you have black people, you have Asians. . . . For instance . . . I accept different types of music, whereas my . . . black friends are into plain old rap, and they don't want to hear anything else because it is not "black people music." . . . That I don't like. They have a problem with white people and what they did to their African descendants. Me . . . I really don't have that problem.

How do your friends respond to that attitude?
They get upset. They get all flustered and sometimes fight over . . . my views. They argue with me over it, and they tell me how I should be angry, but I don't see why. Even if white people . . . did that to West Indians, it didn't happen to me, and that was then, this is now. The people now did not do it. . . . I don't think I've ever dealt with either a white teacher or any other nationality sort of being racist against me. I've never had this problem. I've actually been more appreciated in the white communities than in the black ones.

In what ways?
Because the black people think I am too, let's see, stoosh.[17] . . . I am considered white, and they think of me this way simply because I have respect for teachers. I know my place. I try . . . to speak properly. If . . . they mess up I correct them, and if they are cursing, I don't—I don't like that. They think of that as something bad. I listen to alternative music, as well as a whole lot of other music . . . usually listened by the white people. I do not prefer rap. I . . . can't stand harsh rap. It annoys me. It has no beat. It's nothing to me and that gets them upset.

Judith, a young professional woman, expressed similar sentiments. Shortly after migrating to the United States, her parents moved from New York City to an all-white suburb in another state and educated their children in a school system that had very few blacks. During her upbringing, her parents pointedly emphasized their West Indian origins and the need for achievement. Despite the racism of white neighbors and the children's classmates, the parents downplayed the racial problems experienced by blacks. Because of this upbringing, Judith was ambivalent about her identity, shifting back and forth between "African American," "black," and "West Indian." Also, she did not perceive being black in narrow terms—for instance, as having only African American friends. To Judith, blackness can entail mixing elements of West Indian, "white," and African American cultures:

I perceive myself as . . . black American or African. It's funny, I go back and forth. Sometimes it's African American—I guess that's the proper term. Sometimes I just say "black," because I'm black . . . I say "black" . . . and I know that means I'm supposed to include West Indians as well, but sometimes it kinda doesn't. . . . Sometimes I feel like I really don't fit in anywhere because . . . even though I do have close friends who are African American . . . I have a diverse group of friends. . . . In general I find that the people that I have met whose parents are from the Caribbean tend to have friends from different backgrounds—especially if they were raised in the suburbs. . . . They don't seem to have as much angst or issues with . . . having friends of different backgrounds, listening to different types of music, eating different types of food—because they grew up in a multicultural household . . . and things are not just black and white. . . . Like I said, I am generalizing, and most of the people [friends] I happen to have come from similar socioeconomic background as well; so that can have something to do with it too. I'm sure if they grew up in a very impoverished situation maybe they wouldn't be so open-minded.

According to Waters's typology of second-generation West Indians, individuals such as Sue and Judith, like most of the people I interviewed, are, essentially, ethnic-identified. As for the five second-generation respondents who identified as "American" and/or "black," they were more deeply assimilated into the African American community than the ethnic-identified. They were less ambivalent about identifying themselves as African American and less critical of their African American peers. They also felt less attachment to West Indian culture. Still, in terms of the issue of what it means to be "black," they, too, somewhat downplayed race. Thus, although James (whose wife is Latino) self-identified as African American, the thought of interacting only with people of African ancestry was anathema to him: "I go places where it's all Spanish people. I go to . . . Chinatown where it's all Chinese people, and I [go] places with white people."

Becky emphasized her identification, as a "black" person, with African Americans, especially in her struggle against racism. She told me that she disliked reggae music, preferring to listen to rap. Still, her parents' emphasis on the importance of hard work and excellence had influenced her view of herself as a black person. She noted: "I find that a lot of West Indians are very dedicated to their work. . . . It's like that adage . . . if you gonna do something, do it well. They tried to instill that in us." Becky believed that these values added a distinctive element to her identity as an African American, values that she hoped to pass on to her children: "I definitely want them to know that they have [a] Caribbean background . . . but, you know, obviously they are going to know that they are African American."

The most distinctive aspect of second-generation West Indians' view of blackness is an intuitive understanding of the deepest concerns of African Americans combined with a tendency to resist restrictive worldviews based on racial considerations. Because they were born in America, members of the second generation grasp more quickly than do their parents the pressures that individuals defined as black experience in America. Although many West Indian immigrants identify with African Americans, this identity usually arises only after an extended period of struggling to reconcile the differing West Indian and American views of what it means to be black. Immigrant children experience less conflict between West Indian and American racial views because they are already assimilated into the African American community and have only a secondhand understanding of West Indian culture.

Still, conflicts between West Indian and American views have not disappeared, especially for second-generation youth who identify with their West Indian heritage. This fact directly relates to the idea that West Indians are "tweaking a monolith." Some members of the second generation, like their parents, are
openly resisting widespread, deeply held expectations concerning the attitudes
that black people should have, the way they should behave, and what they can
achieve. By behaving contrary to these expectations, the second generation helps
to unsettle received ideas about what it means to be black. In this they resemble
African Americans who attain high-status jobs that society does not typically associate with African Americans, and mixed-race individuals who lay claim to a
"black" identity but also insist that other racial and ethnic components of their
identity be recognized. By playing against societal expectations, these individuals
force observers to re-evaluate—even if only momentarily—their assumptions
about blackness. As the number of second-generation West Indians, mixed-race
persons, and successful African Americans grows, there also grows the possibility
that they will cause society to question its standard assumptions about blackness.

CONCLUSION

In the United States, ideas of what it means to be "black" have tended to be
rigid—even monolithic—because of the social and historical circumstances
under which individuals of African ancestry were originally incorporated into
American society. The "one-drop rule" represents the clearest expression of
this rigidity since, under the rule, all individuals of even remote African ancestry have been considered "black." This definition of blackness has been accompanied by unflattering assumptions about how black individuals think
and behave, as well as about their abilities. Importantly, being "black" has involved the experience of racial discrimination. From the perspective of individuals of African ancestry in the United States, however, being "black" has
held more positive connotations—for instance, an association with distinctive
and cherished cultural attributes. Historically, the balance of power between
external definitions of blackness and group self-definitions has rested on the
side of society at large. In general, the wider American society's claims about
people of African ancestry have tended to overshadow the claims that these
individuals have made about themselves.

Over the past several decades a number of social trends have emerged which
have raised the possibility that, in the future, individuals of African ancestry in
the United States may gain somewhat greater leeway in defining their own
identities than they have had in the past. Trends that are unsettling received notions of what it means to be black include the growth of the black middle class,
ideological diversity among people of African ancestry, the rising numbers of
mixed-race individuals, and immigration. These social trends challenge the validity of negative stereotypes of individuals of African ancestry. Because these

stereotypes are deeply entrenched, it is unlikely that they will be eradicated any time soon. Yet, in raising questions about the stereotypes, social changes over the past few decades serve notice that long-standing assumptions about people of African ancestry will increasingly be met with skepticism. Although mono-lithic notions of what it means to be "black" are still evident in American soci-ety, emerging social trends, in small degrees, push negative stereotypes regard-ing people of African ancestry toward change. It could be said that these social trends "tweak," rather than fully dispel, monolithic conceptions of blackness.

In this essay I have focused on immigration, arguing that the largest group of African-ancestry immigrants—West Indians—conceive of race differently than do Americans. Generally speaking, West Indians view race as a complex phenomenon, whereas Americans have tended to condense racial issues into a simplified black/white dichotomy. More importantly, West Indians are so-cialized not to see race as important in their daily lives or to their aspirations. Although on some levels race remains important in the West Indies, antiracial socialization has proven effective. Consequently, West Indian immigrants ex-perience difficulty coping with blatant racism in the United States.

However, the relative decline of blatant racism and the growing size of West Indian communities—especially in New York City—have given West In-dian immigrants increased scope for laying claim to a "West Indian" identity instead of undergoing submersion into a larger "black" identity. The attempt to claim such an identity is not a rejection of African ancestry but an attempt to substitute a West Indian conception of what it means to be "black" for an American one. The most important aspect of this substitution is the linking of African ancestry with achievement and with "good" (i.e., socially acceptable) behavior. The attempt at self-definition, however, must still contend with American society's powerful tendency to homogenize blacks. Consequently, the success of West Indian self-definitions is not assured. Still, with the grow-ing size of the West Indian community, efforts by ethnic politicians and ordi-nary West Indians to spur recognition in the larger society of a distinctive West Indian identity have made some progress. Perhaps the best measure of this progress lies in the overtures that nonethnic politicians have made to West Indians as "West Indians."

In looking to the future, the attitudes and experiences of the second genera-tion are crucial. West Indian immigrant parents attempt to inculcate their chil-dren with the notion that African ancestry, high aspirations, and "good" behav-ior go together. How successful they are in transmitting these values depends largely on the family's financial and social resources. Parents who cannot com-mand many resources and whose children grow up in poor inner-city neighbor-hoods—and who thus represent a significant number of West Indian immi-grants—are unable to effectively pass on their "West Indian" values to the second generation.[18] These children tend to experience downward mobility as they become overwhelmed by the racial discrimination and poverty that surround them. Relatively affluent West Indian parents are more successful in transmitting their values to their children. The measure of such success is children who typically identify as "West Indian" and who, though they assimilate into the African American community, often have a heightened desire to defy stereotypes about people of African ancestry. Like their parents, ethnic-identified second-generation West Indians consciously attempt to link blackness with material and educational success. At the same time, unlike some of their parents, they identify closely with other aspects of being "black" in America—chiefly the expressive aspects of African American culture and the reality of facing racial discrimination. The end result of the assimilation of second-generation West Indians into the African American community may be a greater awareness within that community and, possibly, in the larger society as well of the diversity of origins and attitudes within the "black" population.

Many West Indians are thus helping to undermine the notion that blackness is incompatible with attaining socioeconomic success in the United States. Moreover, the example of West Indians makes clear that people of African ancestry can identify as African American at the same time as they embrace cultural elements from other heritages. In the long run, then, the enormous influx of West Indian immigrants into the United States in recent years is likely to broaden Americans' understanding of race and to help transform long-held racial conceptions. West Indian immigrants may well contribute to modifying, if only slightly, monolithic views of blackness.

NOTES

1. I use this term as an alternative to *black*. As such, it broadly refers to African Americans, West Indians, African immigrants, and other immigrants who can trace their heritage back to Africa.

2. Of course, *mixed race* is problematic in that it usually refers to individuals whose parents are of different "races." However, this designation is arbitrary since most individuals possess a mixed heritage—one that becomes more uncertain the further back in time the lineage is traced. On this point see Lieberson (1991).

3. On this point see, for example, Jordan (1969). For discussion of the one-drop rule (or "rule of hypodescent"), see Davis (1991), Harris (1964), Root (1996), and Williamson (1980).

4. The change in racial attitudes is evident in a 1980 study in which a sample of middle-class Jamaican university students accorded the highest prestige scores to blacks (M. Richardson 1983).

5. This perspective is best exemplified in the national mottoes of several West Indian territories. For instance, Jamaica's is "Out of Many, One People"; Guyana's, "One People, One Nation"; and Trinidad's, "Together we aspire, together we achieve." See Lowenthal (1972: 18).

6. For discussions of West Indians' focus on education, see Austin (1987), Foner (1973), Kuper (1976), and Smith (1965).

7. By *racist ideas* I mean the traditional equation of African ancestry and dark skin with inferiority.

8. The same trend is evident for men. While 33 percent of Hispanic husbands and 40 percent of Asian husbands had white wives, this was true of only 5 percent of black husbands (Farley 1996: 264–265).

9. See, for instance, Feagin and Sikes (1994) and Vickerman (1999).

10. This research consisted of 106 interviews that I conducted with Jamaican immigrants between 1988 and 1990 using a "snowball" sample. The average age of the men was forty-one and they had resided in the United States for an average of 11.5 years. See Vickerman (1999).

11. As much of the literature has noted, early West Indian immigrants (i.e., those migrating before the 1960s) had a strong sense of ethnicity. Indeed, the intensity of their ethnic identity was the source of the reputed conflict between West Indian immigrants and African Americans. To many whites, however, West Indians' racial identity as "blacks" was more important than their ethnicity as "West Indians." Consequently, West Indians were confined, like African Americans, to living in certain areas of the city, and those who took on public roles often did so as African Americans (see, for example, Kasinitz 1992).

12. Of course, an individual's racial and/or ethnic identity is only partially voluntary. An equally—and in some cases more—important aspect of identity construction is the process whereby societies impose labels on individuals.

13. Of course, African Americans also reject these stereotypes. At this juncture, however, I wish to draw attention to the fact that the desire to reject antiblack stereotypes is particularly acute among some second-generation West Indians—especially those who identify as West Indians. This desire stems from the immigrant parents' wish to see their American-born children achieve.

14. Most of the people whom I interviewed in New York City were fairly recent immigrants. However, a few had migrated at a very early age. This young man had immigrated to the United States at the age of one.

15. This research consists of a snowball sample of thirty-seven second-generation West Indians who lived in New York City, New Jersey, Washington, DC, and Los Angeles. New Yorkers (twenty-seven respondents) predominated in the sample. The sample is best characterized as upwardly mobile, since 62 percent were college educated. However, most of the respondents' parents (46 percent of fathers and approximately the same percentage of mothers) had achieved only a high school education. Jamaicans dominated the sample, with 62 percent of the respondents having parents from Jamaica. Other respondents' parents originated in Barbados, Grenada, Guyana, Haiti, Panama, St. Martin, and Trinidad and Tobago. Cross-national marriages were fairly common among parents of different nationalities. On average, mothers had lived in America for twenty-eight years and fathers for thirty-one. The telephone interviews (only one interview was face-to-face) were tape-recorded (with permission) and were an average of thirty-eight minutes long. However, fifteen of the interviews were between forty and sixty minutes long (with one running 110 minutes).

16. None were immigrant-identified in the sense of being recent immigrants. However, three of the respondents self-identified in terms of an island nationality. Their responses were similar to those of the ethnic-identified.

17. Jamaican slang for being standoffish.

18. In her study of second-generation West Indians in New York City, Waters states that 42 percent of her sample could be classified as American-identified, 30 percent as ethnic-identified, and 28 percent as immigrant-identified (1996a: 178–79).

Invisible No More?

West Indian Americans
in the Social Scientific Imagination

Philip Kasinitz

In his 1972 landmark essay on West Indian Americans, Roy Bryce-Laporte described the group as the "invisible" immigrants. It's a telling image. The essays collected in this volume and the larger body of research on which they draw show clearly that West Indian Americans have become a good deal more visible in the last quarter century—both in the social scientific literature and in the popular imagination. Yet the confluence of race and ethnicity that may have rendered West Indians invisible at earlier times is still very much with us, as the essays by Waters, Vickerman, Rogers, and Bashi Bobb and Clarke all show. Today West Indians are the largest immigrant group in the nation's largest city.[1] They constitute about 8 percent of New York's population—more if their U.S.-born children are included. They are a major contributor to the huge wave of international migration that has altered the nature of several of America's largest cities since the mid 1960s, yet they are still most often written about in terms of what their experience does (or does not) imply about African Americans. They are almost always seen relative to other blacks—and only rarely relative to other immigrants. Given the central place the question of race plays in U.S. history, it could hardly be otherwise. Indeed, many of us who have written about West Indian migration were initially drawn to the topic precisely for this reason. Yet this focus, if no longer rendering West Indians as invisible as they were twenty-five years ago, still ignores parts of their experience.

Drawing on Ralph Ellison, Bryce-Laporte's notion of invisibility was both apt and ironic. On one level West Indian Americans, at that time overwhelmingly the second- and third-generation descendants of people who came to the United States between 1900 and 1930, were obviously members of what the Canadians call a "visible" minority. To the extent that the group was primarily marked by its "racial" (in this case meaning phenotypical) identity as people of African descent,[2] West Indian immigrants had come to share Ellison's African American paradox of stigmatized physical visibility and social invisibility. For West Indians, Bryce-Laporte argued, incorporation into the larger African American community carried with it an additional layer of invisibility: invisibility as immigrants or as "ethnics." Although most West Indian Americans were, or were descendants of, early-twentieth-century immigrants to New York City—that is to say, immigrants in the quintessential immigrant town—their racial identity obscured their ethnic distinctiveness.

A quick look back at the literature confirms Bryce-Laporte's point. In 1920, West Indian immigrants constituted about a quarter of New York's black population. Over the next five decades their numbers would fall relative to those of native-born African Americans. They would, however, continue to play a disproportionately prominent role in the political and social leadership of New York's African American community (Kasinitz 1992). Yet, in both the social scientific and journalistic accounts of New York's pre-1965 immigrant groups, West Indians are rarely seen.[3] On the rare occasions when the mainstream press noticed West Indians prior to the 1970s it was usually in the context of mildly humorous human interest stories, underlining the fact that, for most white readers, the very fact that black people might play cricket or celebrate the birthday of the British monarch was amusing.[4]

It should be noted that West Indians do appear prominently in both fiction and nonfiction about pre–World War II New York written by African Americans. Both during the Harlem Renaissance and in the later memoirs of Harlem Renaissance figures, West Indians play a noteworthy role.[5] Yet the general thrust of this literature is that West Indians should and inevitably would become part of an African American melting pot, in parallel to the mainstream melting pot bubbling away downtown. While they might add a bit of Caribbean seasoning to the African American cultural melange, West Indians were, these writers noted, rapidly becoming indistinguishable from the rest of the black community. Attempts to assert otherwise were often derided as dangerously divisive and ethnocentric (see, for example, DuBois 1920).

West Indian immigrants and their children probably also contributed to their own invisibility. However much early-twentieth-century West Indian New Yorkers and their children may have sought to distance themselves from native African Americans, the overwhelming role of race in shaping their life chances inevitably made them part of this group. In many cases this inclusion entailed taking up the struggle of African Americans, often with enthusiasm and perhaps with an even greater sense of injustice. Thus it was not unusual for West Indians themselves to downplay their cultural distinctiveness for the sake of black unity (Kasinitz 1992) and at times to emphasize the African heritage that united the two groups (James 1998). Those writers who did not downplay ethnicity often found it hard to maintain an audience. Claude

McKay's prose work (in contrast to his poetry, which continued to have a broad readership) was briefly popular in the 1920s but would then wait decades to be rediscovered. Paule Marshall's now nearly canonical coming-of-age novel, *Brown Girl, Brownstones,* had only a modest reception when first published by Random House in 1959. Too much a "second-generation immigrant" story to be easily pigeonholed as a "black novel," it was also too much about race to be comfortably shelved next to Kazin, Roth, Malamud, and all of the other New York writers who told stories of a neighborhood kid finding his or herself (usually *his* self) as an intellectual while struggling with neighborhood parochialism and immigrant parents' lack of understanding. Marshall's book would achieve its current status only after being rediscovered following a Feminist Press reprint in 1981.

The pre-1970s social scientific literature on West Indian immigrants largely begins and ends with one important study, Ira De A. Reid's 1939 *The Negro Immigrant.* When West Indians appear in the secondary literature, it is almost always to serve one purpose: comparison to African Americans. Moreover, data was almost always drawn solely from Reid's work. As late as the 1970s, Reid's book, then more than thirty years old, was being cited as if it were a contemporary work (see, for example, Light 1972). In what is probably the most widely read study of New York's ethnic groups, Glazer and Moynihan astutely devote several pages to West Indians. Yet their main point is to emphasize the "striking difference" between West Indians and "Southern Negroes," particularly in terms of the former's supposed entrepreneurial orientation: "The ethos of the West Indian, in contrast to that of the Southern Negro, emphasized savings, hard work, investment and education" (Glazer and Moynihan 1970: 35). The evidence for this business orientation is entirely anecdotal and comes from a handful of sources: two West Indian writers (McKay and Marshall), the memoirs of the Harlem Renaissance writer James W. Johnson, and some fairly casual remarks in Reid (Glazer and Moynihan 1970: 34–38). Recently, more systematic research has found that, compared to other immigrants or even to white natives, West Indians actually have low rates of self-employment today and probably did during earlier periods as well (see, for a summary of this work, Kasinitz 1988). What self-employment did exist was largely in the professions, not in the types of small business that we usually associate with immigrant entrepreneurial activity.[6] Indeed, the level of West Indian entrepreneurial activity, even in its alleged heyday of the 1920s, was notable only in comparison with its almost complete absence among native African Americans. The wonder with which contemporary observers greeted the small amount of West Indian self-employment in the 1920s probably reflects both the celebration of "business" in the West Indian community and, more significantly, the low expectations that observers, black as well as white, had for black entrepreneurs.

I do not mean to blame Glazer and Moynihan for this error. Indeed, they deserve credit for even noticing ethnic diversity among New York's African

American population—few other social scientific observers of the time did. The sources they used were the best available, and their interpretation was consistent with what was then received wisdom among black writers as well as white. Their conclusion that "West Indians have by now pretty much merged into the American Negro group and their children do not feel themselves to be particularly different" (Glazer and Moynihan 1970: 36) was probably accurate in 1963—the changes in immigration law of the next few years would completely transform the situation by producing an entirely new wave of West Indian immigrants. Still, by passing on Reid's and Johnson's observations, Glazer and Moynihan helped enshrine a small myth—that of the West Indian small businessman—within the social scientific canon.

Thomas Sowell took this myth and ran with it in his 1981 book, *Ethnic America.* Sowell focused on one key piece of data, the fact that in the 1970 Census second-generation West Indian men had incomes roughly the same as those of native whites and far higher than those of African Americans of native parentage. This fact, Sowell argued, indicated that the negative effects of racial discrimination on African Americans were less pernicious than was widely assumed. If second-generation West Indians, presumably indistinguishable from African Americans in the eyes of most whites, had higher incomes than African Americans, it must have been because their behaviors and their "culture" were more conducive to economic upward mobility.[7] While Sowell's data did not clearly show where the relatively high second-generation West Indian incomes came from (the number of men reported in the 1970 public use microsample was in fact quite small), he was quick to fall back on Reid, Johnson, and others in invoking the idea of a West Indian "ethos" for business. Presumably a pro-business mentality in the first generation produced higher incomes in the second. There is an interesting neoconservative assumption here: that the economic success of a group must be due to private-sector and presumably entrepreneurial activity. (This rests on a deeper neoconservative assumption, namely, that entrepreneurial activity is wealth-producing and thus inherently virtuous, whereas public-sector activity is expropriative, at best redistributive and at worst morally suspect.) Sowell went on to assert that West Indian private-sector success provides a better model of the route to prosperity than do civil rights–based activities, but that, ironically, the disproportionate prominence of West Indians in civil rights organizations has given the group something akin to a class interest in denying this fact.

The debate that Sowell helped to inspire over the existence of West Indian economic success and its implications for African Americans is now a thoroughly familiar one, and there is little reason to rehash it here.[8] My point is simply that, even granting Sowell's interpretation, West Indians can only be seen as an economic success story relative to African Americans. Indeed, as Sowell's data showed, second-generation West Indian incomes were about the same as those of native whites and were far below those of other ethnic groups we usually think of as exhibiting a business "ethos" (particularly Jews and Japanese Americans). West Indian incomes, quite modest when compared to those of other second-generation immigrants, become noteworthy only relative to those of native blacks. The characterization of West Indians as an entrepreneurial minority and indeed as something of a model minority rests on the assumption that this is the meaningful comparison.[9]

In light of Sowell's assumptions it is also worth noting—as Reid noted for the earlier period and Model (this volume) makes clear for the present—that West Indians have extremely high rates of public-sector employment *for immigrants*. This is particularly noteworthy since most areas of public-sector employment are off-limits for undocumented immigrants as are some for legal noncitizens, a fact that partially explains the low rates of public-sector employment among almost every other immigrant group (Waldinger 1996). It is also important in light of the fact that New York has a larger public sector than most places in the United States, and it may in part explain the devotion of so many West Indians (both today and in the past) to electoral politics. Yet the fact is often missed, because the rate of West Indian public-sector employment does not dramatically differ from that for native African Americans. Once again, the focus on race, while important, renders an important ethnic distinction invisible. Other observers point to a Caribbean cultural emphasis on education in attempting to explain the relative economic success of West Indians (Lowenthal 1972). It should be noted, however, that among many other immigrant groups high rates of education actually decrease entrepreneurial activity, while opening the door to the professions and civil service.

In part because of the many attempts to refute Sowell, and in part because a new generation of scholars (many of whom are represented in this volume) are reacting to a new generation of immigrants, the notion of West Indians as a model minority has more or less disappeared from the academic literature. With the increased visibility of West Indian populations, the notion is also less common in the popular media, at least in New York, where stereotypes of joyous Carnival revelers and "hardworking" West Indian immigrants are now balanced with those of Uzi-tooting posse men and ganja-smoking Rastas (for an account of the changing image of West Indians in popular films, see Vickerman 1998). The reader may judge whether this change constitutes any improvement. At the national level, however, the popular image of West Indians as a model minority remains with us, and, as in all model minority arguments, it carries with it strong implications about the "other" minorities for whom the group is supposed to be a model. Just a few years ago I was contacted by the producers of one of network television's pseudo–news magazines, who told me that they were doing a feature on West Indians in Brooklyn. I gave them what information I could until after several conversations it became clear what kind of story they wanted to run. The thrust of the program was how America had turned into a nation of "whiners" complaining about the unfairness of life.

The segment on West Indians emphasized how this admirable group did not "whine" about racial discrimination but rather got on with their productive lives, in marked contrast to (as the reader will have guessed) African Americans. What was shocking, though perhaps not completely surprising, was how remarkably data-proof the television executives were in sticking to this foolish conclusion. They listened to me politely, but, when it became obvious that I was telling them a more complex story than what they wanted to hear, they stopped calling and moved on to a series of other academic sources. When none of the scholars gave support to the story line, the producers simply ran it anyway, without expert endorsement. Once again New York's West Indians were seen as worthy of popular interest to the extent that they could be juxtaposed with African Americans or used to make a point about the nature of race in America. West Indians as immigrants in their own right remain, apparently, of little interest (for another example, see Traub 1981).

The West Indian "model" minority image is invoked highly selectively. The most recent conspicuous case is that of U.S. Secretary of State Colin Powell, whose background as the son of "hardworking" lower-middle-class West Indian immigrant parents and strong early attraction to the Anglican Church are key points in his oft-repeated autobiographical narrative. The almost identical description that could be made of the early years of Nation of Islam leader Louis Farrakhan is less well known, probably because it is less consistent with the popular stereotype of upwardly mobile West Indians. It is also noteworthy, given the importance accorded to business in the West Indian model minority mythology and among West Indians themselves, that Secretary Powell's life and career have been entirely dependent on the public sector. The son of a postman, he was educated in a free public university and, immediately upon graduation, joined the nation's largest public-sector bureaucracy, where he spent his entire career until retiring to become wealthy writing about it. Farrakhan, by contrast, is a well-known advocate for, though not exactly a practitioner of, black small-business activity.

NEW IMMIGRANTS, A NEW LITERATURE

A lot has changed since the early 1970s. If the image of West Indians as simply the "other" blacks remains with us, it is clearly no longer the only image available. As the present volume shows, a new body of scholarship on West Indian migration, much of it focused on New York City, has emerged in the past three decades. With it has emerged a new body of historical work that reassesses what we thought we knew about the earlier period in light of new evidence and new theory. The main reason for this resurgence of scholarship is the renewal of massive immigration from the Anglophone Caribbean following the passage of the Hart-Celler immigration reforms in 1965. The new immigrants have come from a different Caribbean than that of their predecessors, and they immigrate to a far different New York—thus they raise new issues for scholars. However, race continues to be a central theme, in both this work and others.

Starting in the mid 1970s, several edited collections and monographs on Caribbean migration appeared, most of which dealt with both Afro-Caribbean and Latino-Caribbean migration (Safa and du Toit 1975; Bryce-Laporte and Mortimer 1976; Mortimer and Bryce-Laporte 1981). In 1979 Elsa Chaney and Constance Sutton edited a special issue of the *International Migration Review* that dealt specifically with Caribbean migration to New York City. Revised versions of the articles from this issue, along with a number of new pieces (full disclosure: including one of my own), were published as a book edited by Sutton and Chaney, *Caribbean Life in New York City*, which appeared in 1987. In addition to mainstream social science venues, important work on West Indian migration also began to appear in the then emerging fields of black studies and ethnic studies (in addition to the Bryce-Laporte essay, important examples include Henry 1977 and Holder 1980).

From the beginning this literature was strikingly interdisciplinary; at times it seemed institutionally homeless (this is one reason why edited volumes have played a more important role in its development than discipline-based journals). I remember complaints about "falling through the cracks" between Latin American studies and African American studies, as well as between immigration history and the sociology of race. The 1977 panel that gave birth to the Chaney and Sutton collection actually occurred at a conference cosponsored by the Latin American Studies Association and the *African* Studies Association. In retrospect this marginality had decided benefits, bringing a variety of fresh perspectives to the field. Few of the early contributors to this literature started out as immigration or U.S. ethnicity specialists. Many were anthropologists (like Sutton) or area studies specialists (like Chaney) who had previously worked in the Caribbean. Some, most notably Nancy Foner, had also studied other parts of the Caribbean diaspora (London in Foner's case), and most were well versed in the postcolonial "empire strikes back" literature on race and immigration that had emerged in Britain in the previous decade. Whereas traditional American immigration studies have sometimes been faulted for ignoring migrants' backgrounds and connections to their countries of origin, this new wave of Caribbean immigration scholarship was, from its beginnings, "transnational" in focus, concerned with the continuous, multidirectional flows of people across numerous nation-state boundaries that often characterize Caribbean migration. It was also particularly sensitive to the importance of migration for the sending societies (early examples include Philpott 1973 and B. Richardson 1983). Thus when *transnationalism* emerged as a fully formed perspective at the end of the 1980s it was not surprising that many of the key theorists would be scholars who had studied Caribbean migration, most notably Nina Glick Schiller and Linda Basch. This new scholarship also paid attention to the international power relations of the colonial and postcolonial worlds. The international processes of importing labor and exporting capital for the benefit of metropolitan societies were often seen as inextricably connected (Sassen 1981). While race continued to be a central issue in this literature, many of the writers were more versed in the anthropological tradition of viewing the Caribbean as a lab for the study of racially plural societies (in line with the work of M. G. Smith, Sidney Mintz, and others) than in the U.S. literature on race relations and immigrant incorporation.

Finally, while this new group of scholars was at first largely, though not entirely, made up of ethnic "outsiders,"[10] that is, non–West Indians—we were fairly quickly joined by a number of scholars who were themselves West Indian immigrants or the children of West Indian immigrants (in this volume, for example, Bashi Bobb, Vickerman, and Rogers), as well as a few native African Americans (Watkins-Owens and Clarke). Indeed, whereas in the earlier literature a clear distinction can be made between mainstream academic accounts and those produced by intellectuals based within the ethnic community, such a distinction can no longer be as clearly drawn. Today many young West Indian American scholars, who in earlier times might well have spoken and wrote mainly for West Indian or black community audiences, find themselves based within the academy. At the same time, academic writers sometimes publish in community venues, and some institutions, such as the Medgar Evers Center for Caribbean Studies and its new journal *Wadabagei,* straddle the border between West Indian communities and the academy.

More grounded in the Caribbean than previous studies, the new scholarship was able to see West Indians as a people in their own right, rather than simply as the "other" blacks. Yet still often missing from the literature (at least until recently) has been a willingness to place the experience of West Indian migrants in the context of other post–Hart-Celler immigrants. Today most immigration specialists still pay little attention to black immigrants; scholars often compare Latino and Asian groups among contemporary immigrants as if these were the only two possible reference populations. In general, U.S. policymakers and journalists continue to display an appalling ignorance about Caribbean immigrants and the Caribbean region in general. In a particularly stunning recent example, in 1999 the U.S. Department of Housing and Urban Development prepared what was supposed to be a pamphlet for clients versed in Haitian Creole. Somehow the HUD officials decided to compose the pamphlet in "Jamaican Creole," consisting in this case of phonetic renderings of an absurdly stereotypical version of a Jamaican accent. The section entitled "Yuh Rispansabilities" included "Payin de carrek amount a rent pan a timely basis everi muhnt" and "Conduktin yuhself in a mannah dat wuhduhn distrub yuh neighbahs." The pamphlet was withdrawn only after HUD received complaints (*Harper's* 2000).

Caribbeanists, however, have their own weaknesses. Often focused on the historical uniqueness of the people they study, Caribbeanists have been slow to make connections to the larger issue of how West Indians, as immigrants in a period of high immigration, are reshaping their receiving society and particularly, in this case, New York City. If I may be excused some special pleading, I think that sociologists, who have a tradition of studying immigration, may have a special role to play in addressing this issue. In recent years they have become far more prominent in the literature; I would point, in particular, to the work of Milton Vickerman and Mary Waters.

What does it mean to think of West Indians as immigrants as well as blacks? When compared to other contemporary immigrants, West Indians and their children stand out in two crucial respects: ease of acculturation and race. On the one hand, "becoming American" is a shorter journey for them than for most other immigrants. They arrive as native speakers of English. They come from homelands thoroughly penetrated by American mass media and in which the tourist industry has created considerable personal exposure to Americans. They also come from tiny nations where a large portion of the population emigrates to the United States and where emigration has been a normal and expected part of the adult life experience for a long time (Olwig, this volume). Thus many West Indian immigrants have obtained considerable knowledge of the United States from friends and family members, and many have ready-made social networks upon arrival. These advantages have particular importance for economic incorporation.

As Model (this volume) shows, West Indians have done relatively well economically in New York in recent years (see also Kasinitz and Vickerman, forthcoming). In New York their median household incomes are higher and the percentage of households in poverty is lower than for most other immigrant groups, as well as for African Americans. West Indians' labor force participation rates are strikingly high, particularly for women, and their high household incomes are partially explained by the fact that nearly a quarter of West Indian–headed households report three or more wage earners.

Like most immigrant workers in New York, West Indians tend to concentrate in certain occupations and sectors. These occupational niches have grown up over time and reflect a combination of the skills, cultural preferences, and human capital within the group, the structures of opportunities available to the group within the regional economy, and actions taken by the group to create "ethnic networks" through which employment information and referrals may flow (Waldinger 1996; Waters 1999a).

West Indian immigrants' particular circumstances, however, have shaped their experience in several unusual ways. First, West Indian ethnic niches are notably gendered. West Indian women are almost as likely as West Indian men to work outside the home and are more likely to be in the labor force than either American native women, black or white, or women of most other immigrant groups. This situation may partially, though not entirely, reflect premigration backgrounds. The percentage of women in the labor force in most Anglophone Caribbean nations is higher than in most other sending societies; however, the percentage of West Indian women in New York's labor force is higher still. West Indian women, who actually outnumber West Indian men in the labor force, are also far more heavily niched—that is, they are far more likely to work in occupations and industries where West Indians are heavily concentrated. Niching is most evident in nursing and among nurse's aides and domestic child-care workers. Yet West Indian women are also heavily represented in teaching and in the finance, insurance, and real estate (FIRE) sector, a major employer in New York that has grown rapidly in recent years (Kasinitz and Vickerman, forthcoming). None of these jobs are particularly high paying—the FIRE positions are largely clerical and data entry jobs—but they are all in sectors that have grown in the years since substantial West Indian immigration resumed in the late 1960s and in which jobs have been plentiful more often than not. Indeed, if one was to summarize the story of West Indian female employment in New York over the past three decades in a single phrase, it might be: "bad jobs in good sectors."

The story for West Indian men is harder to characterize. They have a more diverse employment profile and are less heavily niched than women and thus far less likely to work in a largely coethnic world. Yet they too are concentrated in services and in the public sector. Compared to other immigrants, West Indian men are much less likely to work in manufacturing.

What most of the jobs held by West Indians have in common is a fair amount of face-to-face interaction and the requirement of language skills. West Indian immigrants' English-language abilities and high rate of literacy have allowed them access to growing sectors of the mainstream economy to a degree unknown to most other immigrants or, for that matter, many native minority graduates (and particularly nongraduates) of New York's public school system. Thus West Indians were able to take advantage of the growing number of personal service, clerical, and retailing jobs in the New York urban region during the late 1970s and the 1980s, and, by largely avoiding manufacturing (the sector in which non-English-speaking immigrant groups tended to concentrate), West Indians avoided the worst impacts of economic restructuring.

At the same time, precisely because they have had access to primary sector jobs, West Indians have not had the need to create an autonomous ethnic enclave of the sort that Portes, Zhou, and others have depicted as central in the upward mobility of other immigrant groups. An "ethnic enclave," in the sense that Portes and his colleagues have used the term, is more than just a niche.

It implies a multilevel structural linking of coethnic workers, bosses, service providers, and customers (Portes and Manning 1986). For example, in New York's Chinatown, Chinese factory owners often attain credit from Chinese financial institutions, rent space from Chinese landlords, buy equipment and materials from Chinese vendors, and employ primarily Chinese workers, who in turn consume products from local Chinese merchants (Zhou 1992). There is considerable debate over how widely distributed the benefits of such an arrangement are (Sanders and Nee 1987; Kwong 1998; Kwong 1987). Wages within such an enclave are often lower than in the mainstream economy, and there is little doubt that many workers would escape the enclave if they only had the necessary language skills, legal status, and knowledge of the wider world. Yet enclaves do allow immigrant communities to build capital, promote self-employment, and transform social bonds into economic ones; to some degree they also serve as a buffer between communities and the ups and downs of the larger economy, as well as a haven for groups who suffer discrimination outside the enclave. A potential springboard for the upward mobility of the most successful members (and their children), enclaves can also serve as a safety net for the less fortunate, providing employment for those who might be unemployable in the mainstream economy.

West Indian niches do not generally serve such functions. Of course, personal networks are used to pass on information about jobs, and West Indian supervisors may discriminate in favor of West Indian workers. Further, non–West Indian employers may come to rely on ethnic networks in the form of referrals from current employees. Yet workers within the resulting niches usually have only informal and limited means of restricting employment access to coethnics (what Waldinger [1996] terms "closure"). Further, in white-collar and particularly in public-sector employment, educational credentialing and bureaucratic requirements limit the scope of network hiring and thus the effectiveness of any safety net function that an enclave more oriented toward employment in other sectors might perform. Finally, West Indian ethnic niches rarely create the opportunity for capital formation or establishment of credit that is created by entrepreneurial activity. The five or six most skilled and knowledgeable workers in a Chinese-owned garment factory can (and frequently do) pool their resources, borrow a small amount of capital from a community credit institution, and become a subcontracting firm, sometimes stealing the best workers and clients from their former employers. Chefs and cooks frequently open their own restaurants, and among many immigrant groups it is common for the managers of small retail outlets to eventually open their own shops, often with the blessing and assistance of their former employers (Kim 1999; Zhou 1992). But a half dozen nurses, no matter how skilled or well networked, cannot open their own hospital!

Unfortunately, many researchers have been so intent on explaining why West Indians are marginally more entrepreneurial than African Americans (and debating what that does or does not imply about African Americans) that by and large we have missed the significance of the lack of a West Indian economic enclave and of the very low rates of West Indian entrepreneurialism compared to those of other immigrant groups. The main reason many West Indians have avoided starting small businesses is probably because they have not needed to do so. For all the celebration of small business both within and outside the West Indian community, the fact remains that running a small business is a terribly difficult way to make a living, often paying less and incurring far more risk than skilled labor or mid-level white-collar employment. For many immigrant-entrepreneurs, self-employment is simply the sole alternative to unemployment (and sometimes is thinly disguised unemployment, as it often is in the Caribbean).

The easy assimilation of most West Indian immigrants into the mainstream economy (albeit within certain niches) and the lack of a need for an ethnic enclave might be viewed as wholly benign, were it not for the other major factors shaping West Indian trajectories: racial identity and the continuing reality of racial discrimination. To the extent that assimilation means assimilation into black America, the lack of an enclave can be a major disadvantage, at least for the less educated parts of the population and certainly, as Waters notes, for the less educated children of West Indian immigrants.

The process of "becoming black American" (Woldemikael 1989) is perhaps the most frequently described aspect of the experience of contemporary West Indian immigrants and their children. Comparing different cohorts of first-generation immigrants, I have argued that the racial structure of the United States discouraged the formation of a distinct ethnic identity for most of the twentieth century, at least in the public arena. For post-1965 immigrants, by contrast, America's social environment has provided considerably more social space for ethnic differentiation within the African American population (Kasinitz 1992). Foner's comparative study of Jamaicans in New York and London also points to the importance of context, showing how the presence of the African American community in the United States has shaped Jamaican attempts to maintain ethnic distinctiveness, in a manner unshared by their cousins in Britain (Foner 1985). Vickerman's study of first-generation immigrant men further expands on this theme by describing the circumstances under which West Indian immigrants to the United States feel compelled to "distance" themselves from African Americans and the circumstances (often, ironically, exposure to racism through encounters with whites) under which they "identify" with African Americans in a form of reactive solidarity (Vickerman 1999).

Finally, Waters, in her study of the children of immigrants, points to three possible paths for the West Indian second generation. Some choose an "ethnic" response, asserting a Caribbean American identity and distancing themselves from African Americans. This attempt may prove futile if whites do not recognize ethnic difference or if parents lack the material resources to effectively shield second-generation youth from the influence of the street. Other young people assert an immigrant identity, stressing their national origins and emphasizing their own or their parents' early experiences in the "home" country (Waters 1999a). Yet in the long run, Waters argues, many, probably most, will express an American—that is, *African* American—identity, assimilating into African American culture while also transforming it, at least on the margins. Not surprisingly, this last scenario is often accompanied by considerable conflict between children and parents.

With respect to the issue of assimilation, the two most extensive and important studies of West Indian racial identity, those of Vickerman (an "insider") and Waters (an "outsider") are more or less in agreement: the historical fact of race in America may not be as monolithic as it once was, but it is still likely to overwhelm notions of ethnic difference, at least in the second generation. The monolith may be "tweaked," as Vickerman puts it, and the overall situation is more complex and bidirectional than in times past. Still, both scholars see race in the long run as the central force shaping the life chances of West Indian Americans.

There is another mode of resisting incorporation into black America: staying tied to one's nation of origin. Here again one of the great benefits of the prominence of anthropologists and area studies specialists among students of the post-1965 West Indian migration has been a sensitivity to transnational connections and a more global frame of reference than that traditionally adopted by immigration scholars. It makes sense that people, when forced to choose between a home society in which they face severely limited economic possibilities and metropolitan societies in which they are socially devalued as members of a historically oppressed minority, might try to live socially in the former society and materially in the latter. While such efforts might have been futile in earlier times, the speed of travel and communication today may make possible such a transnational strategy. Many nations, particularly those of the Anglophone Caribbean, are now coming to grips with this new, deterritorialized reality by extending citizenship rights and broadening the participation in homeland affairs of their nationals abroad and the nationals' children (Basch, this volume).

Still, it remains to be seen how long West Indian migrants will remain transnational and which segments of West Indian American society will do so. As the continuing deterioration of the economies of most Anglophone Caribbean nations makes return less and less likely for most migrants, many observers are skeptical of the durability of transnationalism (Waters, Kasinitz, and Mollenkopf, forthcoming; Vickerman, forthcoming). For some middle-class West Indian Americans, regular trips "back home" are now taken for granted and seen as a vital part of socializing children. Yet for the poor and for undocumented migrants, steady back-and-forth migration is no easy matter.

On the other hand, low-cost telephone service and the spread of telephones to even remote parts of the Anglophone Caribbean have put one form of frequent communication within the grasp of almost everyone.

It should be noted that assimilation into "black America" need not be negative in terms of economic outcomes. The black middle class is far larger than it was during earlier periods of West Indian migration. As Neckerman and her colleagues have argued, there are instances in which incorporation into African American life may facilitate upward mobility (Neckerman, Carter, and Lee 1999). There is a considerable African American middle class, and when it embraces new immigrants (as, for example, the fraternal organizations of black professionals and the alumni groups of historically black colleges have often done) it can be a considerable resource for upward mobility. Black professional networks can help to incorporate immigrant professionals, and African American communities can provide markets for goods and services, while programs promoting African American educational advancement (originating both from within and outside the African American community) have clearly been used to good effect by black immigrants and their children. Further, the conditions which hinder incorporation and upward mobility in one arena may prove beneficial in another. Residential segregation, for example, while disadvantageous in many respects, can be an advantage in attaining political representation since it often creates electoral districts in which even relatively small groups constitute a plurality. This is particularly true when an immigrant group such as West Indians is routinely categorized as simply "black" for purposes of the Voting Rights Act. In New York, West Indian immigrants now hold several seats in the New York City Council and the State Assembly.

It is also true that incorporation into "black America" is no longer a one-way process. As popular culture clearly demonstrates, African American New Yorkers are being influenced by their immigrant peers. Listen to dance hall music and watch the dance steps that accompany it—or, for that matter, check out the attempts of central Brooklyn African American teenagers to imitate Jamaican patois. You can clearly see signs of assimilation in reverse. Indeed, at least in New York, "blackness" no longer simply means African American. In many New York neighborhoods the population is overwhelmingly "black" and sees itself as such, despite the fact that native African Americans are a decided minority. What this means for African Americans and for black identity in general is among the least researched, but potentially most important, aspects of contemporary black immigration to New York.

RACE, IDENTITY, AND THE NEXT
GENERATION (OF MIGRANTS—AND OF SCHOLARS)

How will the children of these now visible, still ambivalent West Indian immigrants find their way in U.S. society? And how will the next generation of scholars and intellectuals characterize them? In some ways this volume, published a quarter century after Bryce-Laporte's essay, is a good place to start that discussion.

Until recently most academic work on the possible trajectories of the children of the post-1965 West Indian immigrants (and for that matter, of all post-1965 immigrants) has been, of necessity, speculative. Nevertheless, since the early 1990s several highly influential models have been proposed. While not specifically concerned with West Indians, Herbert Gans's "Second Generation Decline" (Gans 1992) provides an important starting point. In Gans's scenario, second-generation immigrants who are restricted by racial discrimination and a lack of economic opportunities to poor inner-city schools, bad jobs, and shrinking economic niches will experience *downward* mobility relative to their immigrant parents. In this case, Gans argues, substantial acculturation may take place without much structural assimilation. This is particularly likely for those children of post-1965 immigrants for whom becoming American means, in effect, "becoming black American." Clearly, if assimilation means joining the street culture of the urban ghetto, a child's "becoming American" is every immigrant parent's worst nightmare. Gans hypothesizes that the children of immigrants will refuse to accept many of the jobs that their parents hold and will thus experience downward mobility. The other possibility he cites is that the children of immigrants will refuse to "become American" and will stay tied to their parents' ethnic community. Thus Gans turns traditional, "straight line" assimilation theory on its head: "The people who have secured an economically viable ethnic niche are acculturating less than did the European second and third generations and those without such a niche are escaping condemnation to dead-end immigrant and other jobs mainly by becoming very poor and persistently jobless Americans" (188).

Portes and Zhou make a similar argument in their article on "segmented assimilation," perhaps the most influential theoretical formulation concerning the contemporary second generation. The segmented assimilation model describes the various outcomes of different groups of second-generation youth and suggests that the mode of incorporation for the first generation provides the second generation with access to different types of opportunities and social networks as well as differing amounts of cultural and social capital. Those who, like West Indians, are socially closest to American native minorities, may adopt an oppositional, reactive ethnicity. Groups that arrive with strong ethnic networks, access to capital, and fewer ties to American minorities experience a "linear" ethnicity that creates networks of social ties, may provide access to job opportunities, and reinforces parental authority and values. Thus, Portes and Zhou argue that those groups which most effectively *resist* acculturation may end up with better opportunities for second-generation upward mobility (Portes and Zhou 1993).

This theme has been further elaborated and amplified in the recent work of Rubén Rumbaut. Acculturation, Rumbaut notes, may in many ways prove a hindrance to upward mobility and in some cases negatively influences the quality of life and even the physical well-being of immigrants and their children (Rumbaut 1995, 1997b). Similarly, Zhou and Bankston's work on Vietnamese youth in New Orleans makes a case for preserving ethnic social capital, at times even at the expense of acquiring connections with the host society (Zhou and Bankston 1998). But this begs the question of what will happen to those immigrants, such as West Indians, who do not or cannot maintain an economic ethnic enclave, but whose racial identity may prevent assimilation into the mainstream middle class. It is important to avoid applying the segmented assimilation model mechanistically. West Indian migrants have never been a monolith: among the "model minority" of immigrant "strivers" are plenty of "rude boys" and "sufferers" from the slums of Kingston and Port of Spain. The English-speaking Caribbean has produced a considerable oppositional culture of its own, one that has been a major influence on African American popular culture.

Ultimately, the future life chances of the children of West Indian immigrants will probably be shaped by race. The fact that many West Indian youth have a keen sense of themselves as victims of discrimination, combined with the lack of a distinctly West Indian economic enclave, points to a growing, if probably highly ambivalent, identification with African Americans. This identification need not lead to "downward" assimilation. In terms of household income, the children of West Indian immigrants are among the better-off children in New York's immigrant groups. As the black middle class has grown, many West Indians have taken advantage of new opportunities for economic upward mobility and residential suburbanization. Yet apart from a few distinct ethnic niches, most notably in health care, West Indian middle-class opportunities lie, by and large, where African American middle-class opportunities lie, in white-collar and upper-level service-sector employment. Thus, more than for most other immigrant children, schooling will play a crucial role in the future of the West Indian second generation. The success of English-speaking West Indians in acquiring jobs in the mainstream service sector has put them in positions where the usefulness of ethnic connections and networks is highly contingent on educational credentials. Knowing many nurses, physical therapists, or mid-level white-collar financial service workers will be of little use to second-generation youth if they do not have the college degrees that such positions require.

Residential segregation is a particularly important obstacle for West Indians, if only because it keeps their children in dangerous neighborhoods and inferior schools. Given the connection between educational success and two-parent families, the large number of West Indian immigrant children now growing up in single-parent households is also cause for concern. The struggle against the pernicious effects of "the street" is one that few single parents can win. It is also probable that children in poorer families will be reluctant to take the kinds of jobs their parents now hold: home attendants, domestic workers, drivers, security guards, and the like. Many will no doubt conform to high parental expectations, benefit from parents' ethnic characteristics and networks, and thus not have to take such jobs. Yet without a viable ethnic enclave to serve either as a springboard or a safety net, the future of a West Indian middle class is ultimately linked to that of the African American middle class.

Incorporation into African America, however, will be different for today's West Indian immigrants than it was for their earlier counterparts. Barring drastic changes in immigration law, high levels of immigration from the Anglophone Caribbean are likely to continue for the foreseeable future. Thus today's second and third generations will grow up alongside recent immigrants of the same age, something that generally did not occur from the 1930s to the 1960s. Transnational connections are easier to maintain, and even if most West Indian immigrants do not maintain such connections, a minority surely will, thus creating connections that others will utilize when it is in their interests to do so. The growth of the black middle class and continuing black migration will create a more diverse African American community, particularly in New York. Culturally, this trend may well lead to an emphasis on things African as a source of common ground. Finally, the number of West Indians and people of West Indian descent is much larger today than ever before, a fact that, by itself, makes the group "visible" in a way it was not when Bryce-Laporte wrote his essay a quarter century ago.

Ethnicity and race will no doubt continue to shape the experience of West Indian Americans. The key for the next generation of scholars, however, may be to move beyond seeing race and ethnicity as an either/or proposition or even seeking to understand the circumstances that make one more crucial than the other. Instead, scholars might hope to understand how race and ethnicity interpenetrate in people's daily lives. Viewing West Indians only in comparison to other blacks rendered their ethnic distinctiveness invisible, except insofar as it could be used to say something about African Americans. Viewing them only in comparison to other contemporary immigrants, while it draws our attention to some important and often neglected aspects of people's lives, no doubt obscures other central issues. The challenge now is to fully capture the dynamic interplay of race, ethnicity, and generation as it shapes the lives of West Indian New Yorkers, a group that now includes fourth-generation Americans—and their cousins, who may have arrived just this morning.

NOTES

1. This fact often goes unnoticed because demographers are accustomed to classifying immigrants by political nation of origin. While the Dominican Republic is now the largest single nation of origin of foreign-born New Yorkers, the thirteen tiny nations of the former British Caribbean—that is, the nations that prior to 1962 were all part of the "British West Indies"—constitute a far larger total when statistically reunited. While each of these new nations is distinct, it makes sense to combine them in this context, not only because of their common history, but also because in New York immigrants from these nations tend to live in common neighborhoods (Crowder and Tedrow, this volume; Kasinitz 1992), work in similar occupations (Model, this volume), and intermarry. Thus for most purposes they constitute a common ethnic group.

2. Throughout this essay I refer only to West Indians of at least partially African descent. Some of these people are considered, or consider themselves, African or "black" in their home societies, yet that racial designation generally comes to play a central role in their social status only in the United States (Olwig, this volume). The even more complicated status of the growing population of East Indian–descended West Indian New Yorkers, a minority within a minority within a minority, is beyond the scope of this work.

3. The one major social scientific account of Caribbean immigration published in the prewar period, Ira De A. Reid's *The Negro Immigrant*, deals with a variety of groups throughout the country but devotes several chapters to New York's West Indian community (Reid 1969 [1939]). For more recent historical accounts of West Indians and their activities in early-twentieth-century New York, see Watkins-Owens (1996) and James (1998).

4. See, for example, the following bemused stories from the pages of *The New Yorker:* "Coronation Ball," 27 May 1937; "Houdini's Palace," 6 May 1939; "Well Caught Mr. Holder," 25 September 1954.

5. See in particular the 1925 special issue of *Survey Graphic* magazine on "The New Negro" (vol. 6, no. 6). See also Ottley and Weatherby (1967).

6. The benefits of high rates of entrepreneurialism for immigrant communities, one of the key assumptions behind the notion of the "ethnic enclave" developed by Portes and his collaborators, are laid out quite lucidly by Glazer and Moynihan (1970: 36–38). They note that, while immigrant small businessmen often have lower incomes than professionals and skilled workers in immigrant communities, small business owners are important for the community as a whole because they have the opportunity to accumulate capital, have access to credit, and can serve as employers and clients of coethnics. This is far less true for professionals and is even less true for public-sector employees.

7. Sowell's use of *culture* has caused a great deal of angst. In fairness it should be noted that, while he occasionally evokes the term in an essentialist, almost mystical way that could be interpreted as an assertion of "superior" versus "inferior" cultures, for the most part Sowell uses the notion of culture in a fairly narrow, limited, and economic sense to denote the sum of a group's human capital characteristics. It should also be noted that Sowell is highly critical of genetic explanations of differences between human groups.

8. For summaries of the various arguments, see Foner (1979), Model (1995), and Kasinitz and Vickerman (forthcoming).

9. Indeed, one could argue that Sowell's data actually point to the profound effects of racial discrimination. The children of white immigrants earn more than the children of white natives, and the children of black immigrants earn more than the children of black

natives. Second-generation black immigrants earn less than second-generation white immigrants. Thus the effect of discrimination may be seen across the board—it is simply not enough to nullify the "immigrant advantage."

10. For more on the significance of "insider" versus "outsider" scholars of ethnicity, see Gans (1999).

REFERENCES

Alba, Richard. 1990. *Ethnic Identity: The Transformation of White America*. New Haven: Yale University Press.

Alba, Richard, and John Logan. 1991. "Variation on Two Themes: Racial and Ethnic Patterns in the Attainment of Suburban Residence." *Demography* 28: 431–453.

———. 1993. "Minority Proximity to Whites in Suburbs: An Individual-Level Analysis of Segregation." *American Journal of Sociology* 98: 1388–1427.

Alba, Richard, John Logan, and Kyle Crowder. 1997. "White Ethnic Neighborhoods and Assimilation: The Greater New York Region." *Social Forces* 75: 883–909.

Alexander, Jack. 1977. "The Culture of Race in Middle-Class Kingston, Jamaica." *American Ethnologist* 4: 413–435.

Alexander, M. Jacqui, and Chandra Talpade Mohanty. 1997. "Introduction: Genealogies, Legacies, Movements." In M. Jacqui Alexander and Chandra Talpade Mohanty (eds.), *Feminist Genealogies, Colonial Legacies, Democratic Futures*. New York: Routledge.

Alonso, William, and Mary C. Waters. 1993. "The Future Composition of the American Population: An Illustrative Projection." Paper presented at the winter meetings of the American Statistical Association. Fort Lauderdale, Florida, January.

Anderson, Benedict. 1991. *Imagined Communities: Reflections on the Origins and Spread of Nationalism*. Rev. ed. London: Verso.

Appadurai, Arjun. 1990. "Disjuncture and Difference in the Global Culture Economy." *Theory, Culture and Society* 7: 295–310.

———. 1993. "Patriotism and Its Futures." *Public Culture* 5: 411–429.

———. 1996. *Modernity at Large: Cultural Dimensions of Globalization*. Minneapolis: University of Minnesota Press.

Appiah, Anthony, and Amy Gutmann. 1996. *Color Conscious: The Political Morality of Race*. Princeton: Princeton University Press.

Arnold, Faye W. 1996. "Los Angeles West Indian Immigrant Women: Claimin' De Not Black, De Jus' Tillin' De Bitter Harvest." Paper presented at the annual meeting of the American Sociological Association, New York, August.

Association for Improving the Conditions of the Poor. 1924. "Health Work for Mothers and Children in a Colored Community." Report of the Association for Improving the Conditions of the Poor, New York.

Austin, Diane J. 1983. "Culture and Ideology in the English-Speaking Caribbean: A View from Jamaica." *American Ethnologist* 10: 223–240.

———. 1987. *Urban Life in Kingston, Jamaica: The Culture and Class Ideology of Two Neighborhoods.* New York: Gordon and Breach.

Austin-Broos, Diane J. 1994. "Race/Class: Jamaica's Discourse of Heritable Identity." *Nieuwe West-Indische Gids* 68 (3&4): 213–233.

Bair, Barbara. 1992. "True Women, Real Men: Gender, Ideology, and Social Roles in the Garvey Movement." In Dorothy Helly and Susan M. Reverby (eds.), *Gendered Domains: Rethinking Public and Private in Women's History.* Ithaca, N.Y.: Cornell University Press.

Baker, Ella, and Marvel Cooke. 1935. "The Bronx Slave Market." *Crisis* 42: 330–332.

Ballard, Roger. 1987. "The Political Economy of Migration: Pakistan, Britain, and the Middle East." In J. Eades (ed.), *Migrants, Workers, and the Social Order.* New York: Tavistock Publications.

Basch, Linda. 1987a. "The Vincentians and Grenadians: The Role of Voluntary Associations in Immigrant Adaptation to New York City." In Nancy Foner (ed.), *New Immigrants in New York.* New York: Columbia University Press.

———. 1987b. "Ethnicity, Race and Migration: Changing Dimensions of West Indian Identity in New York and Trinidad." Paper presented at the annual meeting of the American Anthropological Association, Chicago, November.

———. 1992. "The Politics of Caribbeanization: Vincentians and Grenadians in New York." In Constance R. Sutton and Elsa M. Chaney (eds.), *Caribbean Life in New York City: Sociocultural Dimensions.* Rev. ed. New York: Center for Migration Studies.

Basch, Linda, Rosina Wiltshire, Winston Wiltshire, and Joyce Toney. 1990. *Caribbean Regional and International Migration: Transnational Dimensions.* Ottawa, Canada: International Development Research Centre.

Basch, Linda, Nina Glick Schiller, and Cristina Szanton Blanc. 1994. *Nations Unbound: Transnational Projects and the Deterritorialized Nation-State.* Langhorne, Pa.: Gordon and Breach.

Bashi, Vilna. 1996. "'We Don't Have That Back Home': West Indian Immigrant Perspectives on American Racism." Paper presented at the annual meeting of the American Sociological Association, New York, August.

———. 1997. "Survival of the Knitted: The Social Networks of West Indian Immigrants." Ph.D. diss., University of Wisconsin, Madison.

———. 1998a. "Racial Categories Matter Because Racial Hierarchies Matter: A Commentary." *Ethnic and Racial Studies* 21: 959–968.

———. 1998b. "Racist Ideology in Immigration Policy and its 'Effect' on Black Immigrant Social Networks." Paper presented at the annual meeting of the Social Science History Association, Chicago, November.

Benta, Helena M. 1933. "Address to a Group of Benevolent Associations." In Evangeline Pollard, *Harlem As Is: The Negro Business and Economic Community.* Master's thesis, City College of New York.

Beshkin, Abigail. 1999. "Immigrants Build a Bridge of Barrels." *New York Times* (City section), 10 October.

Best, Tony. 1998. " U.S. 'Greed' Peels Away at Caribbean's Banana." *Carib News,* 21 July.

———. 1999. "Corporate Greed Can Topple Caribbean Economy." *Carib News,* 20 April.

Bhabha, Homi K. 1990. "DissemiNation: Time, Narrative and the Margins of the Modern Nation." In Homi K. Bhabha (ed.), *Nation and Narration.* New York: Routledge.

Bigelow, Poultney. 1906. "Our Mismanagement at Panama." *The Independent* 45: 9–21.

Bobo, Lawrence, and Frank Gilliam, Jr. 1990. "Race, Socio-political Participation, and Black Empowerment." *American Political Science Review* 84: 377–393.

Bolles, A. Lynn. 1996. *We Paid Our Dues: Women Trade Union Leaders of the Caribbean.* Washington, D.C.: Howard University Press.

Bodnar, John. 1985. *The Transplanted: A History of Immigrants in Urban America.* Bloomington: Indiana University Press.

Bodnar, John, Roger Simon, and Michael Weber. 1982. *Lives of Their Own.* Urbana: University of Illinois Press.

Bonner, Raymond. 2000. "Donating to the First Lady, Hoping the President Notices." *New York Times,* 14 March.

Bonnett, Aubrey W. 1981. *Institutional Adaptation of West Indian Immigrants to America: An Analysis of Rotating Credit Associations.* Washington, D.C.: University Press of America.

Bouvier, Leon. 1999. *Embracing America: A Look at Which Immigrants Become Citizens.* Center Paper 11. Washington, D.C.: Center for Immigration Studies.

Brodber, Erna. 1989. "Socio-cultural Change in Jamaica." In Rex Nettleford (ed.), *Jamaica in Independence.* Kingston, Jamaica: Heinemann Caribbean.

Broom, Leonard. 1954. "The Social Differentiation of Jamaica." *American Sociological Review* 19: 115–125.

Brown, Roger. 1986. *Social Psychology.* 2d ed. New York: Free Press.

Bryce-Laporte, Roy S. 1972. "Black Immigrants: The Experience of Invisibility and Inequality." *Journal of Black Studies* 3: 29–56.

———. 1987. "New York City and the New Caribbean Migration: A Contextual Statement." In Constance Sutton and Elsa Chaney (eds.), *Caribbean Life in New York City.* New York: Center for Migration Studies.

Bryce-Laporte, Roy S., and Delores S. Mortimer (eds.). 1976. *Caribbean Immigration to the United States.* Washington, D.C.: The Smithsonian Institution.

Butcher, Kristin F. 1994. "Black Immigrants in the United States: A Comparison with Native Blacks and Other Immigrants." *Industrial and Labor Relations Review* 47: 265–284.

Calley, Malcolm. 1965. *God's People: West Indian Pentecostal Sects in England.* London: Oxford University Press.

Carnegie, Charles V. 1987. "A Social Psychology of Caribbean Migration: Strategic Flexibility in the West Indies." In Barry Levine (ed.), *The Caribbean Exodus.* New York: Praeger.

Chamberlain, Mary. 1997. *Narratives of Exile and Return.* London: Macmillan.

Chaney, Elsa M., and Constance L. Sutton (eds.) 1979. "Caribbean Migration to New York." *International Migration Review* 13: 213–332.

Chatterjee, Partha.1986. *Nationalist Thought and the Colonial World: A Derivative Discourse.* London: Zed Books.

Chisholm, Shirley. 1970. *Unbought and Unbossed.* Boston: Houghton Mifflin.

Chiswick, Barry R. 1979. "The Economic Progress of Immigrants: Some Apparently Universal Patterns." In William Fellner (ed.), *Contemporary Economic Problems*. Washington, D.C.: American Enterprise Institute.

—. 1988. *Illegal Aliens: Their Employment and Employers*. Kalamazoo, Mich.: W. E. Upjohn Institute.

Clarke, Averil. 2001. "Black Women, Silver Spoons: How African American Women Manage Social Mobility, Fertility, and Nuptiality Decisions." Ph.D. diss., University of Pennsylvania.

Cohen, Cathy J., and Michael J. Dawson. 1993. "Neighborhood Poverty and African-American Politics." *American Political Science Review* 87: 286–302.

Colen, Shellee. 1986. "'With Respect and Feelings': Voices of West Indian Child Care and Domestic Workers in New York City." In Johnnetta Cole (ed.), *All American Women: Lines That Divide, Ties That Bind*. New York: Free Press.

Collins, Patricia Hill. 1991. *Black Feminist Thought: Knowledge, Consciousness, and the Politics of Empowerment*. New York: Routledge.

Collins, Randall. 1986. *Weberian Sociological Theory*. New York: Cambridge University Press.

Collins, Sharon. 1983. "The Making of the Black Middle Class." *Social Problems* 30: 369–382.

Conover, Pamela Johnston. 1984. "The Influence of Group Identification on Political Perceptions and Evaluations." *American Journal of Political Science* 46: 760–785.

Conway, Dennis, and Ualthan Bigby. 1987. "Residential Differentiation among an Overlooked Black Minority: New Immigrant West Indians in New York." In Constance R. Sutton and Elsa M. Chaney (eds.), *Caribbean Life in New York City*. New York: Center for Migration Studies.

Cordasco, Francesco. 1985. *The Immigrant Woman in North America: An Annotated Bibliography*. Metuchen, N.J.: The Scarecrow Press.

Cornell, Stephen, and Douglas Hartmann. 1998. *Ethnicity and Race: Making Identities in a Changing World*. Thousand Oaks, Calif.: Pine Forge Press.

Crowder, Kyle. 1999. "Residential Segregation of West Indians in the New York/New Jersey Metropolitan Area: The Roles of Race and Ethnicity." *International Migration Review* 33: 79–113.

Curtin, Philip. 1970. *Two Jamaicas: The Role of Ideas in a Tropical Colony, 1830–1865*. New York: Atheneum.

Dahl, Robert. 1961. *Who Governs? Power and Democracy in an American City*. New Haven: Yale University Press.

Davis, Carole Boyce. 1994. *Black Women, Writing and Identity: Migrations of the Subject*. New York: Routledge.

Davis, F. James 1991. *Who is Black? One Nation's Definition*. Philadelphia: University of Pennsylvania Press.

Dawson, Michael C. 1994a. "A Black Counterpublic? Economic Earthquakes, Racial Agenda(s), and Black Politics." *Public Culture* 7: 195–223.

—. 1994b. *Behind The Mule: Race and Class in African-American Politics*. Princeton: Princeton University Press.

Deere, Carmen et al. 1990. *In the Shadows of the Sun*. Boulder, Colo.: Westview Press.

Degler, Carl. 1984. *Out of Our Past*. New York: Harper and Row.

Denton, Nancy A., and Douglas S. Massey. 1988. "Residential Segregation of Blacks, Hispanics, and Asians by Socioeconomic Status and Generation." *Social Science Quarterly* 69: 797–817.

————. 1989. "Racial Identity among Caribbean Hispanics: The Effect of Double Minority Status on Residential Segregation." *American Sociological Review* 54: 790–808.

Department of City Planning. 1999. *The Newest New Yorkers 1995–1996*. New York: Department of City Planning.

DeWind, Josh, and Philip Kasinitz. 1997. "Everything Old is New Again? Processes and Theories of Immigrant Incorporation." *International Migration Review* 31: 1096–1111.

Dillingham, Gerald. 1981. "The Emerging Black Middle Class: Class Conscious or Race Conscious?" *Ethnic and Racial Studies* 4: 432–451.

Domingo, W. A. 1925. "The Tropics in New York." *The Survey* 53: 648–650.

Dominguez, Virginia. 1975. *From Neighbor to Stranger: The Dilemma of Caribbean Peoples in the United States*. Occasional Papers #5. New Haven: Yale University, Antilles Research Program.

Dodoo, F. Nii-Amoo. 1991. "Earning Differences among Blacks in America." *Social Science Research* 20: 93–108.

DuBois, W. E. B. 1920. "The Rise of the West Indian." *Crisis* 20: 214–215.

Durr, Marlese, and John R. Logan. 1997. "Racial Submarkets in Government Employment: African American Managers in New York State." *Sociological Forum* 12: 353–370.

Eisner, Gisela. 1961. *Jamaica, 1830–1930*. Manchester: Manchester University Press.

Epstein, A. L. 1958. *Politics in an Urban African Community*. Manchester: Manchester University Press.

Erickson, Alana J. 1996. "'I Don't Want Her in My Home': Bias Against African American Domestic Servants, 1810–1980." *Race & Reason* 3: 26–31.

Fairclough, Alice Brown. 1929. "A Study of Occupational Opportunities for Negro Women in New York City." Master's thesis, New York University.

Farley, Reynolds. 1996. *The New American Reality: Who We Are, How We Got There, Where We Are Going*. New York: Russell Sage Foundation.

Farley, Reynolds, and Walter R. Allen. 1987. *The Color Line and the Quality of Life in America*. New York: Russell Sage Foundation.

Feagin, Joe R., and Melvin P. Sikes. 1994. *Living with Racism: The Black Middle Class*. Boston: Beacon Press.

Feagin, Joe R., and Hernan Vera. 1995. *White Racism: The Basics*. New York and London: Routledge.

Feldman-Bianco, Bela. 1994. "The State, Saudade and the Dialectics of Deterritorialization and Reterritorialization." Paper presented at the International Symposium on Transnationalism, Nation-State Building, and Culture. Wenner-Gren Foundation, Mijas, Spain, June.

Fern, David. 1990. "Racial and Ethnic Differences in United States Census Omission Rates." *Demography* 27: 285–302.

Flores, Ronald, and Joseph Salvo. 1997. "Foreign-for-Native Replacement Patterns in the New York Urban Region." Paper prepared for the Regional Plan Association, New York.

Foner, Nancy. 1973. *Status and Power in Rural Jamaica: A Study of Educational and Political Change*. New York: Teachers College Press.

————. 1978. *Jamaica Farewell: Jamaican Migrants in London*. Berkeley: University of California Press.

————. 1979. "West Indians in New York City and London: A Comparative Analysis." *International Migration Review* 13: 284–297.

————. 1983. "Jamaican Migrants: A Comparative Analysis of the New York and London Experience." Occasional Paper No. 36. New York: Center for Latin American and Caribbean Studies, New York University.

————. 1985. "Race and Color: Jamaican Migrants in London and New York City." *International Migration Review* 19: 708–727.

————. 1986. "Sex Roles and Sensibilities: Jamaican Women in New York and London." In Rita Simon and Caroline Brettell (eds.), *International Migration: The Female Experience*. Totowa, N.J.: Rowman and Allenheld.

————. 1987. "The Jamaicans: Race and Ethnicity among Migrants in New York City." In Nancy Foner (ed.), *New Immigrants in New York*. New York: Columbia University Press.

————. 1997. "The Immigrant Family: Cultural Continuities and Cultural Change." *International Migration Review* 31: 961–974.

————. 1998a. "West Indian Identity in the Diaspora." *Latin American Perspectives* 25:173–188.

————. 1998b. "Towards a Comparative Perspective on West Indian Migration." In Mary Chamberlain (ed.), *Caribbean Migration*. London: Routledge.

————. 2000. *From Ellis Island to JFK: New York's Two Great Waves of Immigration*. New Haven and New York: Yale University Press and Russell Sage Foundation.

Ford-Smith, Honor. 1988. "Women and the Garvey Movement in Jamaica." In Rupert Lewis (ed.), *Marcus Garvey: His Work and Impact*. Kingston, Jamaica: Institute of Social and Economic Research, University of the West Indies.

Forsythe, Dennis. 1976. "Black Immigrants and the American Ethos: Theories and Observations." In Roy S. Bryce-Laporte and Delores M. Mortimer (eds.), *Caribbean Immigration to the United States*. Washington, D.C.: Smithsonian Institution.

Foucault, Michel. 1990. "Governmentality." In Graham Burchell, Colin Gordon, and Peter Miller (eds.), *The Foucault Effect*. Chicago: University of Chicago Press.

Franklin, Raymond S. 1991. *Shadows of Race and Class*. Minneapolis: University of Minnesota Press.

Friedman-Kasaba, Kathie. 1996. *Memories of Migration: Gender, Ethnicity, and Work in the Lives of Jewish and Italian Women in New York, 1870–1924*. Albany: State University of New York Press.

Frisby, Michael. 1996. "Black, White or Other." *Emerge* (December 1995/January 1996).

Froude, James A. 1888. *The English in the West Indies*. New York: Charles Scribner.

Gabaccia, Donna. 1989. *Immigrant Women in the United States: A Selectively Annotated Multidisciplinary Bibliography*. Westport, Conn.: Greenwood Press.

Gaines, Kevin. 1996. *Uplifting the Race: Black Leadership, Politics, and Culture in the Twentieth Century*. Chapel Hill: University of North Carolina Press.

Gans, Herbert. 1992. "Second Generation Decline: Scenarios for the Economic and Ethnic Futures of Post-1965 American Immigrants." *Ethnic and Racial Studies* 15: 173–193.

————. 1999. "Towards a Reconciliation of Assimilation and Pluralism: The Interplay of Acculturation and Ethnic Retention." In Charles Hirschman, Philip Kasinitz, and Josh DeWind (eds.), *The Handbook of International Migration*. New York: Russell Sage Foundation.

Garcia, F. Chris, Angelo Falcon, and Rodolfo de la Garza. 1996. "Ethnicity and Politics: Evidence from the Latino National Political Survey." *Hispanic Journal of Behavioral Sciences* 18: 91–103.

Garcia, John A. 1986. "Caribbean Migration to the Mainland: A Review of Adaptive Experiences." *The Annals of the American Academy of Political and Social Sciences* 487: 114–125.

Gellner, Ernest.1983. *Nations and Nationalism*. Ithaca, N.Y.: Cornell University Press.

Gerstle, Gary. 1993. "The Working Class Goes to War." *Mid-America* 75: 303–322.

———. 1996. "European Immigrants, Ethnics, and American Identity, 1880–1950." Paper presented at the Becoming American/America Becoming conference of the Social Science Research Council, Sanibel Island, Florida, January.

Gilroy, Paul. 1990. "One Nation Under a Groove: The Cultural Politics of Race and Racism in Britain." In David Theo Goldberg (ed.), *Anatomy of Racism*. Minneapolis: University of Minnesota Press.

Glazer, Nathan, and Daniel Patrick Moynihan. 1970 [1963]. *Beyond the Melting Pot: The Negroes, Puerto Ricans, Jews, Italians, and Irish of New York City*. Cambridge: MIT Press.

Glick Schiller, Nina, Linda Basch, and Cristina Blanc-Szanton. 1992. "Transnationalism: A New Analytic Framework for Understanding Migration." In Nina Glick Schiller, Linda Basch, and Cristina Blanc-Szanton (eds.), *Towards a Transnational Perspective on Migration*. New York: New York Academy of Sciences.

Glick Schiller, Nina, and Georges Fouron. 1998. "Transnational Lives and National Identities: The Identity Politics of Haitian Immigrants." In Michael Peter Smith and Luis Eduardo Guarnizo (eds.), *Transnationalism from Below*. New Brunswick, N.J.: Transaction Publishers.

Gmelch, George. 1992. *Double Passage: The Lives of Caribbean Migrants Abroad and Back Home*. Ann Arbor: University of Michigan Press.

Gmelch, George, and Sharon Bohn Gmelch. 1997. *The Parish Behind God's Back: The Changing Culture of Rural Barbados*. Ann Arbor: University of Michigan Press.

Goldstein, Ira, and Clark White. 1985. "Residential Segregation and Color Stratification among Hispanics in Philadelphia: Comment on Massey and Mullan." *American Journal of Sociology* 91: 391–396.

Gopaul-McNichol, Sharon-Ann. 1993. *Working with West Indian Families*. New York: The Guilford Press.

Gordon, Linda. 1995. *Pitied But Not Entitled: Single Mothers and the History of Welfare*. New York: The Free Press.

Grasmuck, Sherri, and Ramon Grosfoguel. 1997. "Geopolitics, Economic Niches, and Gendered Social Capital among Recent Caribbean Immigrants in New York City." *Sociological Perspectives* 40: 339–364.

Guarnizo, Luis Eduardo, and Michael Peter Smith. 1998. "The Locations of Transnationalism." In Michael Peter Smith and Luis Eduardo Guarnizo (eds.), *Transnationalism from Below*. New Brunswick, N.J.: Transaction Publishers.

Guest, Avery M., and Barrett A. Lee. 1984. "How Urbanites Define Their Neighborhoods." *Population and Environment* 7: 32–56.

Gupta, Akhil. 1992. "The Song of the Nonaligned World: Transnational Identities and the Reinscription of Space in Late Capitalism." *Cultural Anthropology* 7: 63–77.

Gurin, Patricia, Shirley Hatchett, and James S. Jackson. 1989. *Hope and Independence: Blacks' Response to Electoral and Party Politics*. New York: Russell Sage Foundation.

Guterbock, Thomas, and Bruce London. 1983. "Race, Political Orientation, and Participation: An Empirical Test of Four Competing Theories." *American Sociological Review* 48: 439–453.

Gutman, Herbert G. 1976. *The Black Family in Slavery and Freedom, 1750–1925*. New York: Vintage Books.

Guy, Rosa. 1990. "The Human Spirit." In Selwyn R. Cudjoe (ed.), *Caribbean Women Writers*. Wellesley, Mass.: Calaloux Publishers.

Hagner, Paul, and John Pierce. 1984. "Racial Differences in Political Conceptualization." *Western Political Quarterly* 37: 212–235.

Hall, Stuart. 1990. "Cultural Identity and Diaspora." In J. Rutherford (ed.), *Community, Culture, Difference*. London: Lawrence and Wishart.

Handlin, Oscar. 1957. *Race and Nationality in American Life*. New York: Anchor Books.

Harper's. 2000. "Owne Sweet Owne." *Harper's* (January): 20

Harris, Fred. C. 1998. "Will the Circle Be Unbroken? The Erosion and Transformation of African-American Life." Paper presented at the Center for the Study of Race, Inequality, and Politics, Yale University, New Haven, December.

Harris, Marvin. 1964. *Patterns of Race in the Americas*. New York: Columbia University Press.

Harris-Lacewell, Melissa. 1999. "Barbershops, Bibles, and B.E.T.: A Dialogic Theory of African-American Political Thought." Ph.D. diss., Duke University.

Harrison, Lawrence E. 1992. *Who Prospers?* New York: Basic Books.

Hathaway, Heather. 1999. *Caribbean Waves: Relocating Claude McKay and Paule Marshall*. Bloomington: Indiana University Press.

Haynes, George. 1968 [1912]. *The Negro at Work in New York City*. New York: Arno Press.

Henry, Frances. 1994. *The Caribbean Diaspora in Toronto*. Toronto: University of Toronto Press.

Henry, Keith. 1977. "The Black Political Tradition in New York: A Conjunction of Political Cultures." *Journal of Black Studies* 7: 455–484.

Hepner, Randal. 1998. "The House That Rasta Built: Church-Building and Fundamentalism among New York Rastafarians." In R. Stephen Warner and Judith Wittner (eds.), *Gatherings in Diaspora*. Philadelphia: Temple University Press.

Herring, Mary, Thomas B. Jankowski, and Ronald E. Brown. 1999. "Pro-Black Doesn't Mean Anti-White: The Structure of African-American Group Identity." *The Journal of Politics* 61: 363–386.

Hill, Robert A. 1983. *The Marcus Garvey Papers*. Berkeley: University of California Press.

Hine, Darlene Clark. 1989. *Black Women in White: Racial Conflict and Cooperation in the Nursing Profession, 1890–1950*. Bloomington: Indiana University Press.

Ho, Christine. 1993. "The Internationalization of Kinship and the Feminization of Caribbean Migration: The Case of Afro-Trinidadian Immigrants in Los Angeles." *Human Organization* 52: 32–40.

Hobsbawm, Eric J. 1990. *Nations and Nationalism since 1780: Programme, Myth and Reality*. New York: Cambridge University Press.

Hochschild, Jennifer L. 1995. *Facing Up to the American Dream: Race, Class, and the Soul of the Nation*. Princeton: Princeton University Press.

———. 1998. "American Racial and Ethnic Politics in the 21st Century: A Cautious Look Ahead." *Brookings Review* 16: 43–46.

Holder, Calvin B. 1980. "The Rise of the West Indian Politician in New York." *Afro-Americans in New York Life and History* 4: 45–59.

———. 1987. "The Causes and Consequences of West Indian Immigration to the United States, 1900–1952." *Afro-Americans in New York Life and History* 11: 6–18.

———. 1998. "Making Ends Meet: West Indian Economic Adaptation in New York City, 1900–1952." *Wadabagei* 1: 31–84.

Hondagneu-Sotelo, Pierette. 1994. *Gendered Transitions: Mexican Experiences of Immigration.* Berkeley: University of California Press.

Hunter, Albert. 1974. *Symbolic Communities: The Persistence and Change of Chicago's Local Communities.* Chicago: University of Chicago Press.

Ifill, Vera Clarke. 1986. Interview #402, conducted by Patricia Gloucester-Coates. New York: National Park Service, Statue of Liberty National Monument, 2 May.

Ignatiev, Noel. 1995. *How the Irish Became White.* New York: Routledge.

Insley-Casper, R. 1934. "The Negro Unmarried Mother of New York." *Opportunity* 12: 172–173.

James, Winston. 1998. *Holding Aloft the Banner of Ethiopia: Caribbean Radicalism in Early Twentieth-Century America.* London: Verso.

Johnson, Violet. 1995. "Culture, Economic Stability, and Entrepreneurship: The Case of British West Indians in Boston." In Marilyn Halter (ed.), *New Migrants in the Marketplace: Boston's Entrepreneurs.* Amherst: University of Massachusetts Press.

Jones, Claudia. 1949. "An End to the Neglect of the Problems of Negro Women." *Political Affairs* 43: 29–42.

Jones-Correa, Michael. 1998. *Between Two Nations: The Political Predicament of Latinos in New York.* Ithaca, N.Y.: Cornell University Press.

Jordan, Winthrop. 1969. *White Over Black.* New York: Penguin.

Kalmijn, Matthijs. 1996. "The Socioeconomic Assimilation of Caribbean American Blacks." *Social Forces* 74: 911–930.

Kao, Grace, and Marta Tienda. 1995. "Optimism and Achievement: The Educational Performance of Immigrant Youth." *Social Science Quarterly* 76: 1–19.

Kasinitz, Philip. 1988. "From Ghetto Elite to Service Sector: A Comparison of the Role of Two Waves of West Indian Immigration to New York City." *Ethnic Groups* 7: 173–203.

———. 1992. *Caribbean New York: Black Immigrants and the Politics of Race.* Ithaca, N.Y.: Cornell University Press.

Kasinitz, Philip, Juan Battle, and Ines Miyares. Forthcoming. "Fade to Black? The Children of West Indian Immigrants in South Florida." In Rubén Rumbaut and Alejandro Portes (eds.), *Ethnicities.* Berkeley: University of California Press.

Kasinitz, Philip, and Milton Vickerman. Forthcoming. "Ethnic Niches and Racial Traps: Jamaicans in the New York Regional Economy." In Hector Cordero-Guzman, Ramon Grosfoguel, and Robert Smith (eds.), *Migration, Transnationalism, and the Political Economy of New York.* Philadelphia: Temple University Press.

Kearney, Michael. 1991. "Borders and Boundaries of State and Self at the End of Empire." *Journal of Historical Sociology* 4:52–74.

———. 1995. "The Effects of Transnational Culture, Economy, and Migration on Mixtec Identity in Oaxacalifornia." In Michael Peter Smith and Joe R. Feagin (eds.), *The Bubbling Cauldron: Race, Ethnicity, and the Urban Crisis.* Minneapolis: University of Minnesota Press.

Kim, Dae Young. 1999. "Beyond Co-Ethnicity: Mexican and Ecuadorian Employment in Korean-Owned Businesses in New York City." *Ethnic and Racial Studies* 22: 581–605.

Kine, Edith. 1934. "The Garment Union Comes to the Negro Worker." *Opportunity* 12: 107–110.

Knight, R. 1989. "The Emergent Global Economy." In R. Knight and G. Gappert (eds.), *Cities in a Global Society.* Newbury Park, Calif.: Sage.

Krueger, Alan B., and Lawrence H. Summers. 1988. "Efficiency Wages and the Inter-Industry Wage Structure." *Econometrica* 56: 259–293.

Kuper, Adam. 1976. *Changing Jamaica.* London: Routledge and Kegan Paul.

Kwong, Peter. 1987. *The New Chinatown.* New York: Vintage.

———. 1998. *Forbidden Workers.* New York: New Press.

Ladipo, David. 1998. "West Indians in Britain and North America." Ph.D. diss., Cambridge University.

Laguerre, Michel S. 1984. *American Odyssey: Haitians in New York City.* Ithaca, N.Y.: Cornell University Press.

Lessinger, Johanna. 1992. "Investing or Going Home? A Transnational Strategy among Indian Immigrants in the United States." In Nina Glick Schiller, Linda Basch, and Cristina Blanc-Szanton (eds.), *Toward a Transnational Perspective on Migration.* New York: New York Academy of Sciences.

Levitt, Peggy. 2000. "Migrants Participate Across Borders: Towards an Understanding of Forms and Consequences." In Nancy Foner, Rubén Rumbaut, and Steven Gold (eds.), *Immigration Research for a New Century: Multidisciplinary Perspectives.* New York: Russell Sage Foundation.

Lieberson, Stanley. 1963. *Ethnic Patterns in American Cities.* New York: Free Press.

———. 1980. *A Piece of the Pie: Black and White Immigrants Since 1880.* Berkeley: University of California Press.

———. 1991. "A New Ethnic Group in the United States." In Norman Yetman (ed.), *Majority and Minority: The Dynamics of Race and Ethnicity in American Life.* Boston: Allyn and Bacon.

Lieberson, Stanley, and D. K. Carter. 1982. "Temporal Changes and Urban Differences in Residential Segregation: A Reconsideration." *American Journal of Sociology* 88: 296–310.

Light, Ivan. 1972. *Ethnic Enterprise in America.* Berkeley: University of California Press.

Loewen, James. 1988. *The Mississippi Chinese: Between Black and White.* Prospect Heights, Ill.: Waveland Press.

Logan, John R., and Richard D. Alba. 1993. "Locational Returns to Human Capital: Minority Access to Suburban Community Resources." *Demography* 30: 243–268.

Logan, John R., Richard D. Alba, and Thomas L. McNulty. 1994. "Ethnic Economies in Metropolitan Regions: Miami and Beyond." *Social Forces* 72: 691–724.

Lorde, Audre. 1981. *Zami, A New Spelling of My Name: A Biomythography.* Freedom, Calif.: The Crossing Press.

Lowenthal, David. 1972. *West Indian Societies.* London: Oxford University Press.

Mahler, Sarah J. 1998. "Theoretical and Empirical Contributions Toward a Research Agenda for Transnationalism." In Michael Peter Smith and Luis Eduardo Guarnizo (eds.), *Transnationalism from Below.* New Brunswick, N.J.: Transaction Publishers.

Manners, Robert. 1965. "Remittances and the Unit of Analysis in Anthropological Research." *Southwestern Journal of Anthropology* 21: 179–195.

Marable, Manning. 1994. "Building Coalitions among Communities of Color." In James Jennings (ed.), *Blacks, Latinos, and Asians in Urban America.* New York: Praeger.

Marks, Carole. 1989. *Farewell—We're Good and Gone: The Great Black Migration.* Bloomington: Indiana University Press.

Marshall, Dawn. 1982. "Towards an Understanding of Caribbean Migration." In Mary Kritz (ed.), *U.S. Immigration and Refugee Policy.* Lexington, Mass.: D.C. Heath.

———. 1987. "A History of West Indian Migrations: Overseas Opportunities and 'Safety-Valve' Policies." In Barry Levine (ed.), *The Caribbean Exodus.* New York: Praeger.

Marshall, Paule. 1959. *Brown Girl, Brownstones*. New York: Feminist Press.

———. 1987. "Black Immigrant Women in *Brown Girl, Brownstones*." In Constance Sutton and Elsa Chaney (eds.), *Caribbean Life in New York City: Sociocultural Dimensions*. New York: Center for Migration Studies.

Massey, Douglas S. 1985. "Ethnic Residential Segregation: A Theoretical Synthesis and Empirical Review." *Sociology and Social Research* 89: 874–888.

———. 1986. "The Social Organization of Mexican Migration to the United States." *Annals of the American Academy of Political and Social Science* 487: 102–113.

Massey, Douglas S., and Nancy Denton. 1987. "Trends in the Residential Segregation of Blacks, Hispanics, and Asians: 1970–1980." *American Sociological Review* 52: 802–825.

———. 1988. "The Dimensions of Residential Segregation." *Social Forces* 67: 281–315.

———. 1993. *American Apartheid: Segregation and the Making of the Underclass*. Cambridge: Harvard University Press.

Massey, Douglas S., and Mitchell L. Eggers. 1990. "The Ecology of Inequality: Minorities and the Concentration of Poverty, 1970–1980." *American Journal of Sociology* 95: 1153–1188.

Massey, Douglas S., Andrew B. Gross, and Kumiko Shibuya. 1994. "Migration, Segregation, and the Geographic Concentration of Poverty." *American Sociological Review* 59: 425–445.

Massey, Douglas S., and Brendan Mullan. 1984. "Processes of Hispanic and Black Spatial Assimilation." *American Journal of Sociology* 89: 836–873.

Massiah, Joycelin. 1993. "Living with Dignity: Barbadian Women in the Work Force." In Woodville Marshall (ed.), *Emancipation IV: A Series of Lectures to Commemorate the 150th Anniversary of Emancipation*. Kingston, Jamaica: Canoe Press.

Matthews, Victoria Earle. 1898. "Some of the Dangers Confronting Southern Girls in the North." In *Hampton Negro Conference Annual Proceedings*. Hampton, Va.: Hampton Institute Press.

Mayers, Janice. 1995. "Access to Secondary Education for Girls in Barbados, 1907–1943: A Preliminary Analysis." In V. Sheperd, B. Brereton, and B. Bailey (eds.), *Engendering History: Caribbean Women in Historical Perspective*. Kingston, Jamaica: Ian Randle.

McAdam, Doug. 1982. *Political Process and the Development of Black Insurgency, 1930–1970*. Chicago: University of Chicago Press.

McCullough, David. 1977. *Path Between the Seas: The Creation of the Panama Canal, 1870–1914*. New York: Simon and Schuster.

McLeod, Jay. 1995 [1987]. *Ain't No Making It: Aspirations and Attainment in a Low-Income Neighborhood*. Boulder, Colo.: Westview Press.

Merriam-Webster. 1996. *Collegiate Dictionary, Tenth Edition*. Springfield, Mass.: Merriam-Webster.

Miles, Robert. 1993. *Racism after "Race Relations."* London: Routledge.

Miller, Arthur, Patricia Gurin, Gerald Gurin, and Oksana Malanchuk. 1981. "Group Consciousness and Political Participation." *American Journal of Political Science* 25: 494–511.

Mills, Charles. 1998. "Dark Ontologies: Blacks, Jews, and White Supremacy." In Charles Mills (ed.), *Blackness Visible: Essays on Philosophy and Race*. Ithaca, N.Y.: Cornell University Press.

Mitchell, J. Clyde. 1956. *The Kalela Dance*. Rhodes-Livingston Papers No. 27. Manchester: Manchester University Press.

———. 1969. *Social Networks in Urban Situations*. Manchester: Manchester University Press.

Model, Suzanne. 1988. "Mode of Job Entry and Ethnic Composition of Firms: Early Twentieth Century Migrants to New York City." *Sociological Forum* 3: 110–127.

————. 1991. "Caribbean Immigrants: A Black Success Story?" *International Migration Review* 25: 248–276.

————. 1993. "The Ethnic Niche and the Structure of Opportunity." In Michael Katz (ed.), *The Underclass Debate: Views from History*. Princeton: Princeton University Press.

————. 1995. "West Indian Prosperity: Fact or Fiction?" *Social Problems* 42: 535–553.

————. 1997a. "An Occupational Tale of Two Cities: Minorities in London and New York." *Demography* 34: 539–550.

————. 1997b. "Ethnic Economy and Industry in Mid-Twentieth Century Gotham." *Social Problems* 44: 445–463.

Model, Suzanne, and David Ladipo. 1996. "Context and Opportunity: Minorities in London and New York." *Social Forces* 75: 485–510.

Model, Suzanne, and Gene Fisher. 1999. "Intermarriage among Caribbean Blacks: A Cross-National Analysis." Unpublished paper.

Mollenkopf, John. 1992. *A Phoenix in the Ashes: The Rise and Fall of the Koch Coalition in New York City Politics*. Princeton: Princeton University Press.

Mollenkopf, John, David Olson, and Tim Ross. 1999. "Immigrant Political Participation in New York and Los Angeles." Paper presented at the conference Democracy and Difference, International Center for Migration, Ethnicity, and Citizenship, New School University, New York, April.

Moore, Gary Ward. 1913. "A Study of a Group of West Indian Negroes in New York City." Master's thesis, Columbia University.

Morgan, Edmund W. 1975. *American Slavery, American Freedom: The Ordeal of Colonial Virginia*. New York: W. W. Norton.

Morris, Aldon D., Shirley Hatchett, and Ronald E. Brown. 1989. "The Civil Rights Movement and Black Political Socialization." In Roberta S. Sigel (ed.), *Political Learning in Adulthood: A Sourcebook of Theory and Research*. Chicago: University of Chicago Press.

Mortimer, D. M., and R. S. Bryce-Laporte (eds.). 1981. *Female Immigrants into the United States: Caribbean, Latin American, and African Experiences*. Washington, D.C.: The Smithsonian Institution.

Moss, Philip, and Chris Tilly. 1996. "'Soft' Skills and Race: An Investigation of Black Men's Employment Problems." *Work and Occupations* 23: 252–276.

Neckerman, Kathryn, Prudence Carter, and Jennifer Lee. 1999. "Segmented Assimilation and Minority Cultures of Mobility." *Ethnic and Racial Studies* 22: 945–965.

Nettleford, Rex. 1972. *Identity, Race and Protest in Jamaica*. New York: William Morrow.

Norris, Kathleen. 1962. *Jamaica, the Search for an Identity*. London: Oxford University Press.

Ogbu, John. 1990. "Cultural Model, Identity, and Literacy." In James W. Stigler, Richard Shweder, and Gilbert Herdt (eds.), *Cultural Psychology: Essays on Comparative Human Development*. New York: Cambridge University Press.

Olwig, Karen Fog. 1993. *Global Culture, Island Identity: Continuity and Change in the Afro-Caribbean Community of Nevis*. New York: Harwood Academic Publishers.

————. 1997. "Toward a Reconceptualization of Migration and Transnationalism." In Bodil Folke Frederiksen and Fiona Wilson (eds.), *Livelihood, Identity and Instability*. Copenhagen: Centre for Development Research.

————. 1998a. "Constructing Lives: Migration Narratives and Life Stories among Nevisians." In Mary Chamberlain (ed.), *Caribbean Migration*. London: Routledge.

————. 1998b. "The Mobile Middle Class." *Anthropology Newsletter* (November): 11–12.

Omi, Michael, and Howard Winant. 1994 [1986]. *Racial Formation in the United States: From the 1960s to the 1990s.* 2d ed. New York: Routledge.

Ong, Aihwa. 1993. "On the Edge of Empires: Flexible Citizenship among Chinese in the Diaspora." *Positions* 1: 745–778.

Ottley, Roi, and William Weatherby. 1967. *The Negro in New York.* New York: Oceana.

Palmer, Ransford. 1974. "A Decade of West Indian Migration to the United States, 1962–1972: An Economic Analysis." *Social and Economic Studies* 23: 571–587.

———. 1995. *Pilgrims From the Sun: West Indian Migration to America.* New York: Twayne.

Pareles, Jon. 1999. "The Drum Master Prepares for a Carnival." *New York Times,* 3 September.

Peach, Ceri. 1995. "Profile of the Black Caribbean Population in Great Britain." In Ceri Peach (ed.), *Profile of the Ethnic Minority Populations of Great Britain.* London: Office of the Population Censuses and Surveys.

Perez, Lisandro. 1992. "Cuban Miami." In Guillermo Grenier and Alex Stepick (eds.), *Miami Now!* Gainesville: University of Florida Press.

Perlmann, Joel. 1997. "Reflecting the Changing Face of America: Multiracials, Racial Classification and American Intermarriage." Public Policy Brief 35. Annandale-on-Hudson, N.Y.: The Jerome Levy Economics Institute of Bard College.

Pessar, Patricia R. 1999. "Engendering Migration Studies." *American Behavioral Scientist* 42: 577–600.

Petras, Elizabeth McLean. 1986. "Jamaican Women in the U.S. Health Industry: Caring, Cooking, and Cleaning." *Annals of the American Academy of Political and Social Sciences* 487: 304–321.

Philpott, Stuart. 1968. "Remittances, Obligations, Social Networks and Choice among Montserratian Migrants in Britain." *Man* 3: 465–475.

———. 1973. *West Indian Migration: The Montserrat Case.* London: The Athlone Press.

Philpott, Thomas L. 1979. *The Slum and the Ghetto: Neighborhood Deterioration and Middle-Class Reform, Chicago, 1890–1930.* New York: Oxford University Press.

Pinderhughes, Dianne. 1987. *Race and Ethnicity in Chicago Politics: A Reexamination of Pluralist Theory.* Urbana: University of Illinois Press.

Piore, Michael J. 1979. *Birds of Passage: Migrant Labor in Industrial Societies.* Cambridge: Cambridge University Press.

Portes, Alejandro. 1995a. "Children of Immigrants: Segmented Assimilation and Its Determinants." In Alejandro Portes (ed.), *The Economic Sociology of Immigration: Essays on Networks, Ethnicity, and Entrepreneurship.* New York: Russell Sage Foundation.

———. 1995b. "Transnational Communities: Their Emergence and Significance in the Contemporary World System." Keynote address, Conference on the Political Economy of the World System, University of Miami.

———. 1996. Ed. *The New Second Generation.* New York: Russell Sage Foundation.

Portes, Alejandro, and Ramon Grosfoguel. 1994. "Caribbean Diasporas: Migration and Ethnic Communities." *Annals of the American Academy of Political and Social Science* 536: 48–69.

Portes, Alejandro, Luis Guarnizo, and Patricia Landolt. 1999. "Introduction: Pitfalls and Promises of an Emergent Research Field." *Ethnic and Racial Studies* 22: 217–237.

Portes, Alejandro, and Robert D. Manning. 1986. "The Immigrant Enclave Theory and Empirical Examples." In Susan Olzak and Joanne Nagel (eds.), *Competitive Ethnic Relations.* Orlando, Fla.: Academic Press.

Portes, Alejandro, and Min Zhou. 1993. "The New Second Generation: Segmented Assimilation and Its Variants among Post-1965 Immigrant Youth." *Annals of the American Academy of Political and Social Science* 530: 74–96.

Prescod-Roberts, Margaret, and Norma Steel. 1980. *Black Women: Bringing It All Back Home.* Bristol, England: Falling Wall Press.

Quarles, Benjamin. 1987. *The Negro in the Making of America.* New York: Collier Books.

Reddock, Rhoda. 1993. "Transformation in the Needle Trades: Women in Garment and Textile Production in Early Twentieth Century Trinidad." In Janet H. Momsen (ed.), *Women and Change in the Caribbean.* Bloomington: Indiana University Press.

———. 1994. *Women, Labor and Politics in the Caribbean.* London: Zed Books.

Reed, Aldophe. 1999. *Stirrings in the Jug: Black Politics in the Post-Segregation Era.* Minneapolis: University of Minnesota Press.

Reed, Ruth. 1926. *Negro Illegitimacy in New York City.* New York: Columbia University Press.

Reid, Ira De A. 1969 [1939]. *The Negro Immigrant: His Background, Characteristics, and Social Adjustments, 1899–1937.* New York: Columbia University Press.

Reimers, David. 1987. "New York City and its People: An Historical Perspective up to World War II." In Constance R. Sutton and Elsa M. Chaney (eds.), *Caribbean Life in New York City: Sociocultural Dimensions.* New York: Center for Migration Studies.

Reitz, Jeffrey G. 1990. "Ethnic Concentrations in Labour Markets and Their Implications for Ethnic Inequality." In R. Breton, W. W. Isajiw, W. E. Kalbach, and J. G. Reitz (eds.), *Ethnic Identity and Equality.* Toronto: University of Toronto Press.

Richards, Yvette. 1994. "'My Passionate Feeling about Africa': Maida Springer Kemp and the American Labor Movement." Ph.D. diss., Yale University.

Richardson, Bonham. 1983. *Caribbean Migrants: Environment and Human Survival on St. Kitts and Nevis.* Knoxville: University of Tennessee Press.

———. 1985. *Panama Money in Barbados, 1900–1920.* Knoxville: University of Tennessee Press.

———. 1992. *The Caribbean in the Wider World, 1492–1992.* New York: Cambridge University Press.

Richardson, Mary. 1983. "Out of Many, One People—Aspiration or Reality? An Examination of Attitudes to the Various Racial and Ethnic Groups within Jamaican Society." *Social and Economic Studies* 32: 143–167.

Roberts, George. 1955. "Emigration from the Island of Barbados." *Social and Economic Studies* 4: 244–288.

Robinson, Harry. 1939. "The Negro Immigrant in New York." In *Migration and the Negro Population of New York City.* WPA Research Report, Schomburg Center for Research in Black Culture, New York.

Robotham, Don. 1998. "Transnationalism in the Caribbean: Formal and Informal." *American Ethnologist* 25: 307–321.

Rogers, Reuel. 1996. "Somewhere Between Race and Ethnicity: Afro Caribbean Immigrants, African Americans, and the Politics of Group Identity." Unpublished paper.

———. 1999. "White, Black, and In-Between: Reconsidering Theories of Political Incorporation." Ph.D. diss., Princeton University.

Root, Maria P. P. 1996. "The Multiracial Experience: Racial Borders as a Significant Frontier in Race Relations." In Maria P. P. Root (ed.), *The Multiracial Experience.* Thousand Oaks, Calif.: Sage.

Rouse, Roger. 1992. "Making Sense of Settlement: Class Transformation, Cultural Struggle, and Transnationalism among Mexican Migrants in the United States." In Nina Glick Schiller, Linda Basch, and Cristina Blanc-Szanton (eds.), *Towards a Transnational Perspective on Migration: Race, Class, Ethnicity and Nationalism Reconsidered*. New York: New York Academy of Sciences.

Rubenstein, Hymie. 1987. *Coping with Poverty: Adaptation Strategies in a Caribbean Village*. Boulder, Colo.: Westview Press.

Ruggles, Steven, and Matthew Sobek. 1997. Integrated Public Use Microdata Series: Version 2.0. Minneapolis: Historical Census Projects, University of Minnesota (http://www.ipums.umn.edu).

Rumbaut, Rubén. 1994. "The Crucible Within: Ethnic Identity, Self Esteem, and Segmented Assimilation among Children of Immigrants." *International Migration Review* 28: 748–794.

———. 1995. "The New Californians." In Rubén Rumbaut and Wayne Cornelius (eds.), *California's Immigrant Children*. San Diego: Center for U.S. Mexican Studies.

———. 1997a. "Ties that Bind: Immigration and Immigrant Families in the United States." In Alan Booth, Ann C. Crouter, and Nancy Landale (eds.), *Immigration and the Family: Research and Policy on U.S. Immigrants*. Mahwah, N.J.: Lawrence Erlbaum Publishers.

———. 1997b. "Assimilation and Its Discontents: Between Rhetoric and Reality." *International Migration Review* 31: 923–960.

Safa, Helen, and Brian du Toit (eds.). 1975. *Migration and Development: Implications for Ethnic Identity and Political Conflict*. The Hague: Mouton.

Salvo, Joseph, and Ronald Ortiz. 1992. *The Newest New Yorkers: An Analysis of Immigration Into New York City During the 1980s*. New York: Department of City Planning.

Sanders, Jimy, and Victor Nee. 1987. "The Limits of Ethnic Solidarity in the Ethnic Enclave Economy." *American Sociological Review* 52: 745–767.

Sassen, Saskia. 1981. "Exporting Capital and Importing Labor: The Role of Caribbean Migration to New York City." Occasional Paper 28. New York: Center for Latin American and Caribbean Studies, New York University.

Schneider, Dorothy, and Carol J. Schneider. 1994. *American Women in the Progressive Era, 1900–1920: Change, Challenge and the Struggle for Women's Rights*. New York: Anchor.

Schneider, Mark, and John Logan. 1982. "Suburban Racial Segregation and Black Access to Local Public Resources." *Social Science Quarterly* 63: 762–770.

Sheperd, Verene A. 1995. "Gender, Migration and Settlement: The Indentureship and Post-Indentureship Experience of Indian Females in Jamaica." In V. Sheperd, B. Brereton, and B. Bailey (eds.), *Engendering History: Caribbean Women in Historical Perspective*. Kingston: Ian Randle.

Shingles, Richard D. 1981. "Black Consciousness and Political Participation: The Missing Link." *American Political Science Review* 75: 76–91.

Sigelman, Lee, and Susan Welch. 1991. *Black Americans' Views of Racial Inequality: The Dream Deferred*. Cambridge: Cambridge University Press.

Singham, A. W. 1968. *The Hero and the Crowd in a Colonial Polity*. New Haven: Yale University Press.

Smith, Albert Edgar. 1933. "West Indians on the Campus." *Opportunity* 11: 238–241.

Smith, M. G. 1965. *The Plural Society in the British West Indies*. Berkeley: University of California Press.

Smith, Robert C. 1993. "De-territorialized Nation Building: Transnational Migrants and the Re-imagination of Political Community by Sending States." Paper presented at the Seminar on Migration and the State, Center for Latin American and Caribbean Studies, New York University, New York, May.

———. 1998. "Transnational Localities: Community, Technology, and the Politics of Membership within the Context of Mexico and U.S. Migration." In Michael Peter Smith and Luis Eduardo Guarnizo (eds.), *Transnationalism From Below*. New Brunswick, N.J.: Transaction Publishers.

Sørensen, Ninna Nyberg. 1995. "Telling Migrants Apart: The Experience of Migrancy among Dominican Locals and Transnationals." Ph.D. diss., University of Copenhagen.

———. 1998. "Narrating Identity Across Dominican Worlds." In Michael Peter Smith and Luis Eduardo Guarnizo (eds.), *Transnationalism from Below*. New Brunswick, N.J.: Transaction Publishers.

Soto, Isa Maria. 1987. "West Indian Child Fostering: Its Role in Migrant Exchanges." In Constance R. Sutton and Elsa M. Chaney (eds.), *Caribbean Life in New York City: Sociocultural Dimensions*. New York: Center for Migration Studies.

South, Scott J., and Kyle Crowder. 1997. "Escaping Distressed Neighborhoods: Individual, Community, and Metropolitan Influences." *American Journal of Sociology* 102: 1040–1084.

———. 1998. "Leaving the 'Hood: Residential Mobility between Black, White, and Integrated Neighborhoods." *American Sociological Review* 63: 17–26.

Sowell, Thomas. 1978. "Three Black Histories." In Thomas Sowell (ed.), *Essays and Data on American Ethnic Groups*. Washington, D.C.: The Urban Institute.

———. 1981. *Ethnic America*. New York: Basic Books.

Steber, Joseph A. 1987. "Our Family History." Typescript.

Steinberg, Stephen. 1989 [1981]. *The Ethnic Myth: Race, Ethnicity, and Class in America*. Boston: Beacon Press.

Stinner, William, Klaus de Albuquerque, and Roy Bryce-Laporte. 1982. *Return Migration and Remittances: Developing a Caribbean Perspective*. Washington, D.C.: Research Institute on Immigration and Ethnic Studies, Smithsonian Institution.

Stone, Carl. 1982. *The Political Opinions of the Jamaican People, 1976–1981*. Kingston, Jamaica: Blackett.

Suarez-Orozco, Carola, and Marcelo M. Suarez-Orozco. 1995. *Transformations: Immigration, Family Life, and Achievement Motivation among Latino Adolescents*. Stanford, Calif.: Stanford University Press.

Suarez-Orozco, Marcelo M. 1987. "Becoming Somebody: Central American Immigrants in U.S. Inner City Schools." *Anthropology and Education Quarterly* 18: 287–299.

Sutton, Constance R. 1969. "The Scene of the Action: A Wildcat Strike in Barbados." Ph.D. diss., Columbia University.

———. 1987. "The Caribbeanization of New York City and the Emergence of a Transnational Socio-cultural System." In Constance R. Sutton and Elsa M. Chaney (eds.), *Caribbean Life in New York City*. New York: Center for Migration Studies.

Sutton, Constance R., and Elsa M. Chaney (eds.). 1987. *Caribbean Life in New York City*. New York: Center for Migration Studies.

Sutton, Constance R., and Susan Makiesky-Barrow. 1987. "Migration and West Indian Racial and Ethnic Consciousness." In Constance R. Sutton and Elsa M. Chaney (eds.), *Caribbean Life in New York City*. New York: Center for Migration Studies.

Tajfel, Henri. 1981. *Human Groups and Social Categories*. Cambridge: Cambridge University Press.

Tate, Katherine. 1993. *From Protest to Politics: The New Black Voters in American Elections.* Cambridge: Harvard University Press.

Thomas-Hope, Elizabeth. 1978. "The Establishment of a Migration Tradition: British West Indian Movements in the Hispanic Caribbean after Emancipation." In Colin Clarke (ed.), *Caribbean Social Relations.* Monograph Series No. 8. Liverpool: Centre for Latin American Studies.

———. 1992. *Explanation in Caribbean Migration.* London: Macmillan.

Thompson, Paul, and Elaine Bauer. n.d.. "Jamaican Transnational Families: Points of Pain and Sources of Resilience." Unpublished paper.

Thottam, Jyoti. 2000. "Housing Brings Richmond Hill's Indo-Caribbeans into the New World of Politics." *City Limits* 25: 26–28.

Tienda, Marta. 1991. "Poor People and Poor Places: Deciphering Neighborhood Effects on Poverty Incomes." In Joan Huber (ed.), *Macro-Micro Linkages in Sociology.* Newbury Park, Calif.: Sage.

Tilly, Charles. 1990. "Transplanted Networks." In Virginia Yans-McLaughlin (ed.), *Immigration Reconsidered.* New York: Oxford University Press.

Toney, Joyce Roberta. 1986. "The Development of a Culture of Migration among a Caribbean People: St. Vincent and New York, 1838–1979." Ph.D. diss., Columbia University.

———. 1987. "Emigration from St. Vincent and the Grenadines: Contextual Background." Unpublished manuscript.

Toulis, Nicole Rodriguez. 1997. *Believing Identity: Pentecostalism and the Mediation of Jamaican Ethnicity and Gender in England.* Oxford: Berg.

Traub, James. 1981. "You Can Get It If You Really Want." *Harper's* 264: 27–31.

Turner, W. Burghardt, and Joyce Moore Turner. 1988. *Richard B. Moore: Caribbean Militant in Harlem.* Bloomington: Indiana University Press.

Uhlaner, Carol J. 1991. "Perceived Discrimination and Prejudice and the Coalition Prospects of Blacks, Latinos, and Asian Americans." In Bryan O. Jackson and Michael B. Preston (eds.), *Racial and Ethnic Politics in California.* Berkeley: IGS Press.

U.S. Immigration Commission Reports. 1911. *Immigrants in Cities.* Vols. 1 and 2. Washington, D.C.: Government Printing Office.

U.S. Immigration and Naturalization Service. 1997. *Statistical Yearbook of the Immigration and Naturalization Service, 1996.* Washington, D.C.: Government Printing Office.

Van Slambrouck, Paul. 1999. "Immigrants Shift Status: No Longer Sojourners." *Christian Science Monitor,* 21 September.

Verba, Sidney, Kay Lehman Schlozman, and Henry Brady. 1996. *Civic Voluntarism in American Politics.* Cambridge: Harvard University Press.

Verdery, Katherine. 1998. "Transnationalism, Nationalism, Citizenship, and Property: Eastern Europe Since 1989." *American Ethnologist* 25: 291–306.

Vickerman, Milton. 1994. "The Responses of West Indians to African-Americans: Distancing and Identification." *Research in Race and Ethnic Relations* 7: 83–128.

———. 1998. "Representing West Indians in Film: Ciphers, Coons and Criminals." *The Western Journal of Black Studies* 23: 83–96.

———. 1999. *Crosscurrents: West Indian Immigrants and Race.* New York: Oxford University Press.

———. Forthcoming. "Transnationalism among Upwardly Mobile Second Generation West Indians." In Mary C. Waters and Peggy Levitt (eds.), *Transnationalism and the Second Generation.* New York: Russell Sage Foundation.

Wacquant, Loic, and William J. Wilson. 1989. "The Cost of Racial and Class Exclusion in the Inner City." *Annals of the American Academy of Political and Social Science* 501: 8–25.

Waldinger, Roger. 1987. "Beyond Nostalgia: The Old Neighborhood Revisited." *New York Affairs* 10: 1–12.

————. 1995. "The 'Other Side' of Embeddedness: A Case Study of the Interplay of Economy and Ethnicity." *Ethnic and Racial Studies* 18: 555–580.

————. 1996. *Still the Promised City? African-Americans and New Immigrants in Postindustrial New York.* Cambridge: Harvard University Press.

Waldinger, Roger, and Mehdi Bozorgmehr (eds.). 1996. *Ethnic Los Angeles.* New York: Russell Sage Foundation.

Waldman, Amy. 1998. "Old Places, New Faces: In Southern Brooklyn, Coexistence but Not Quite Community." *New York Times* (City section), 12 April.

Warner, W. Lloyd, and Leo Srole. 1945. *The Social Systems of American Ethnic Groups.* New Haven: Yale University Press.

Warren, Robert, and Jeffrey Passel. 1987. "A Count of the Uncountable: Estimates of the Undocumented Aliens in the 1980 United States Census." *Demography* 24: 375–393.

Waters, Mary C.. 1990. *Ethnic Options: Choosing Identities in America.* Berkeley: University of California Press.

————. 1991. "The Role of Lineage in Identity Formation among Black Americans." *Qualitative Sociology* 14: 57–77.

————. 1994a. "Ethnic and Racial Identities of Second-Generation Black Immigrants in New York City." *International Migration Review* 28: 795–820.

————. 1994b. "West Indian Immigrants, African-Americans and Whites in the Workplace: Different Perspectives on American Race Relations." Paper presented to the American Sociological Association, Los Angeles, August.

————. 1996a. "Ethnic and Racial Identities of Second-Generation Black Immigrants in New York City." In Alejandro Portes (ed.), *The New Second Generation.* New York: Russell Sage Foundation.

————. 1996b. "Ethnic and Racial Groups in the USA: Conflict and Cooperation." In Kumar Rupesinghe and Valery Tishkov (eds.), *Ethnicity and Power in the Contemporary World.* London: U.N. University.

————. 1997. "Immigrant Families at Risk: Factors That Undermine Chances for Success." In Alan Booth, Ann Crouter, and Nancy Landale (eds.), *Immigration and the Family.* Mahwah, N.J.: Lawrence Erlbaum.

————. 1999a. *Black Identities: West Indian Immigrant Dreams and American Realities.* Cambridge and New York: Harvard University Press and Russell Sage Foundation.

————. 1999b. "Explaining the Comfort Factor: West Indian Immigrants Confront American Race Relations." In Michele Lamont (ed.), *The Cultural Territories of Race.* Chicago: University of Chicago Press.

————. 1999c. "West Indians and African Americans at Work: Structural Differences and Cultural Stereotypes." In Frank Bean and Stephanie Bell-Rose (eds.), *Immigration and Opportunity.* New York: Russell Sage Foundation.

————. 2000. "Multiple Ethnicities and Identity Choices: Some Implications for Race and Ethnic Relations in the United States." In Paul R. Spickard and W. Jeffrey Burroughs (eds.), *We Are a People: Narrative in the Construction and Deconstruction of Ethnic Identity.* Philadelphia: Temple University Press.

Waters, Mary C., Philip Kasinitz, and John H. Mollenkopf. Forthcoming. "Second Generation Transnationalism in New York Today." In Mary C. Waters and Peggy Levitt (eds.), *Transnationalism and the Second Generation*. New York: Russell Sage Foundation.

Watkins-Owens, Irma. 1996. *Blood Relations: Caribbean Immigrants and the Harlem Community, 1900–1930*. Bloomington: Indiana University Press.

West, Cornel. 1993. *Race Matters*. Boston: Beacon Press.

White, Deborah Gray. 1999. *Too Heavy a Load: Black Women in Defense of Themselves, 1894–1994*. New York: W. W. Norton.

White, Michael L. 1986. "Segregation and Diversity Measures in Population Distribution." *Population Index* 52: 198–221.

Williamson, Joel. 1980. *New People: Miscegenation and Mulattoes in the United States*. New York: New York University Press.

Wilson, Franklin D. 1998. "Ethnic Concentrations and Labor Market Opportunities." Paper presented to the American Sociological Association, San Francisco, August.

Wilson, William Julius. 1980 [1978]. *The Declining Significance of Race: Blacks and Changing American Institutions*. 2d ed. Chicago: University of Chicago Press.

Wiltshire, Rosina, Linda Basch, Winston Wiltshire, and Joyce Toney. 1990. *Caribbean Transnational Migrant Networks: Implications for Donor Societies*. Ottawa, Canada: International Development Research Centre.

Woldemikael, Tekle M. 1989. *Becoming Black American: Haitians and American Institutions in Evanston, Illinois*. New York: AMS Press.

Woofter, R. J. Jr. 1969 [1928]. *Negro Problems in Cities*. College Park, Md.: McGrath.

Wright, Richard, and Mark Ellis. 1996. "Immigrants and the Changing Ethnic-Racial Division of Labor in New York City, 1970–1990." *Urban Geography* 17: 317–353.

———. 1997. "Nativity, Ethnicity, and the Evolution of Intraurban Division of Labor in Metropolitan Los Angeles, 1970–1990." *Urban Geography* 18: 243–263.

Yinger, John. 1995. *Closed Doors, Opportunities Lost: The Continuing Costs of Housing Discrimination*. Newbury Park, Calif.: Sage.

Zane, Wallace. 1999. "Spiritual Baptists in New York City: A View from the Vincentian Converted." In John W. Pulis (ed.), *Religion, Diaspora, and Cultural Identity: A Reader in the Anglophone Caribbean*. Amsterdam: Gordon and Breach.

Zhou, Min. 1992. *Chinatown: The Socioeconomic Potential of an Urban Enclave*. Philadelphia: Temple University Press.

———. 1997. "Growing Up American: The Challenge Confronting Immigrant Children and the Children of Immigrants." *Annual Review of Sociology* 23: 63–96.

Zhou, Min, and Carl Bankston III. 1994. "Social Capital and the Adaptation of the Second Generation: The Case of Vietnamese Youth in New Orleans." *International Migration Review* 28: 821–845.

———. 1998. *Growing Up American: How Vietnamese Children Adapt to Life in the United States*. New York: Russell Sage Foundation.

NOTES ON CONTRIBUTORS

Linda Basch is Executive Director of the National Council for Research on Women. She previously served as Vice President for Academic Affairs at Wagner College, Dean of Arts and Sciences at Manhattan College, where she was also a faculty member in the Anthropology Department, and Director of Special Academic Programs at New York University. She spent a decade directing programs on social and economic development and gender issues at the United Nations and has conducted fieldwork in the Caribbean, Africa, Iran, and the United States on issues of migration, race, ethnicity, nationalism, and gender. She has written widely on these topics, with works including the coauthored *Nations Unbound: Transnational Projects, Postcolonial Predicaments, and Deterritorialized Nation-States* (Gordon and Breach, 1994) and the coedited *Towards a Transnational Perspective on Migration: Race, Class, Ethnicity and Nationalism Reconsidered* (New York Academy of Sciences, 1998) and *Transforming Academia: Challenges and Opportunities for an Engaged Anthropology* (American Anthropological Association, 1999).

Vilna Bashi Bobb, Assistant Professor of Sociology at Rutgers University, received her Ph.D. from the University of Wisconsin–Madison in 1997. She has taught at Northwestern University, where she was a faculty fellow in the Institute for Policy Research. She was also a Mellon Foundation postdoctoral fellow at the Population Studies Center, University of Pennsylvania. Her dissertation focused on two social networks of West Indian immigrants in New York City. Her current research project, for which she received a Ford Foundation postdoctoral fellowship, compares the West Indian immigrant experiences in New York City, London, Toronto, and Montreal. Her most recent publications include "Neither Ignorance nor Bliss: West Indian Perspectives on American Racism," in the forthcoming *Migration, Transnationalism, and the Political Economy of New York* (Temple University Press, 2001), and "Racial Categories Matter Because Racial Hierarchies Matter," in *Ethnic and Racial Studies.*

Averil Clarke is a Ph.D. candidate in sociology at the University of Pennsylvania. She has a B.A. from Williams College and an M.A. in demography from the University of Pennsylvania. Her dissertation, "Black Women, Silver Spoons: How African American Women Manage Social Mobility, Fertility, and Nuptiality Decisions," focuses on the relationship between economic mobility and family formation among African American women. She has also done research on the transition from welfare to work in Philadelphia and Pensacola, Florida.

Kyle Crowder is Assistant Professor of Sociology at Western Washington University. He received his Ph.D. in 1997 from the State University of New York at Albany, where he also completed a postdoctoral research fellowship at the Center for Social and Demographic Analysis. His research on the residential patterns of West Indian blacks has recently appeared in the *International Migration Review.* He has published articles on urban politics, family demography, residential mobility and segregation, and the consequences of neighborhood context in a number of journals, including *Social Forces,* the *American Sociological Review,* and the *Journal of Marriage and the Family.* He is currently conducting research on the interactive effects of family composition and neighborhood mobility on adolescent well-being.

Nancy Foner, Professor of Anthropology at the State University of New York at Purchase, has conducted research among Jamaicans in rural Jamaica, London, and New York. She is the author or editor of eight books, including *Status and Power in Rural Jamaica: A Study of Educational and Political Change* (Teachers College Press, 1973), *Jamaica Farewell: Jamaican Migrants in London* (University of California Press, 1978), *New Immigrants in New York* (Columbia University Press, 1987), and *The Caregiving Dilemma: Work in an American Nursing Home* (University of California Press, 1994). Her most recent books are *From Ellis Island to JFK: New York's Two Great Waves of Immigration* (Yale University Press, 2000) and *Immigration Research for a New Century: Multidisciplinary Perspectives,* edited with Rubén Rumbaut and Steven Gold (Russell Sage Foundation, 2000). She has been a visiting scholar at the Russell Sage Foundation and is a member of the International Migration Committee of the Social Science Research Council.

Philip Kasinitz holds a joint appointment as Professor of Sociology at Hunter College and the Graduate Center of the City University of New York. He is the author of *Caribbean New York: Black Immigrants and the Politics of Race* (winner of the 1996 Thomas and Znaniecki Award; Cornell University Press, 1992), the editor of *Metropolis: Center and Symbol of Our Times* (New York University Press, 1995), and coeditor of *The Handbook on International Migration: The American Experience* (Russell Sage Foundation, 1999). He is currently working on a long-term ethnographic and historical project on the Red Hook section of Brooklyn and (with Mary Waters and John Mollenkopf) a major multimethod study of the young-adult children of immigrants in New York City. He has been a National Endowment for the Humanities Fellow, a visiting scholar at the Russell Sage Foundation, and chair of the American Sociological Association's Section on International Migration. Prior to coming to CUNY in 1993, he taught at Williams College.

Suzanne Model received her Ph.D. in Social Work and Social Science from the University of Michigan in 1985. She is currently Professor in the Department of Sociology at the University of Massachusetts, Amherst. Her publications on West Indians include "Caribbean Immigrants: A Black Success Story?" in the *International Migration Review,* "West Indian Prosperity: Fact or Fiction?" in *Social Problems,* and "Black Caribbeans in Comparative Perspective," in the *Journal of Ethnic and Migration Studies.* She is currently working on a book that is tentatively titled *The Cost of Being West Indian: Caribbean Immigrants in the U.S. and Beyond.*

Karen Fog Olwig is Associate Professor at the Institute of Anthropology, University of Copenhagen. She has carried out fieldwork on St. John in the U.S. Virgin Islands and the Caribbean Leeward island of Nevis, as well as among Caribbean migrant communities in the United States, England, and within the Caribbean. Her major publications include *Cultural Adaptation and Resistance on St. John: Three Centuries of Afro-Caribbean Life* (University of Florida Press, 1985), *Global Culture, Local Lives: Continuity and Change in the Afro-Caribbean Community of Nevis* (Harwood Academic Publishers, 1993), and *Siting Culture: The Shifting Anthropological Object,* edited with Kirsten Hastrup (Routledge, 1997). Her most recent research is a multilocal ethnography of three global family networks of Caribbean origin.

Reuel Rogers is Assistant Professor of Political Science at Northwestern University. His recently completed dissertation explores the impact of racial difference and inequality on the political incorporation process for Afro-Caribbean New Yorkers and for African Americans more generally. His primary research interests are race, ethnicity, immigration, urban politics, and African American politics. He is the author of "Afro-Caribbean Immigrants, African-Americans, and the Politics of Incorporation," in *Black and Multiracial Politics in America,* edited by Yvette Alex-Assensoh and Lawrence Hanks (New York University Press, 2000), and coauthor with Jennifer Hochschild of "Race Relations in a Diversifying Nation," in *New Directions: African-Americans in a Diversifying Nation,* edited by James Jackson (Russell Sage Foundation, 2000). He has been a dissertation research fellow with the Social Science Research Council and the Ford Foundation. He received his Ph.D. in Political Science from Princeton University.

Lucky M. Tedrow, Director of the Demographic Research Laboratory at Western Washington University, holds a B.S. in sociology and an M.A. in sociology-demography from Western Washington University. His research has focused on the patterns, causes, and consequences of migration as well as fertility and population estimates, and has appeared in *Demography, Population Studies,* and *Family Planning Perspectives.* He is also the recipient of several National Science Foundation grants for the advancement of undergraduate research.

Milton Vickerman, Associate Professor of Sociology at the University of Virginia, has conducted research on immigration and issues pertaining to race. He has carried out extensive fieldwork among West Indian immigrants in New York City and among blacks in Prince William County, Virginia. His publications include *Crosscurrents: West Indian Immigrants and Race* (Oxford University Press, 1999) and various chapters and articles dealing with West Indian immigrants in the United States.

Mary C. Waters is the Harvard College Professor of Sociology at Harvard University. She is the author of *Black Identities: West Indian Immigrant Dreams and American Realities* (Harvard University Press, 1999), *Ethnic Options: Choosing Identities in America* (University of California Press, 1990), *From Many Strands: Ethnic and Racial Groups in Contemporary America* (with Stanley Lieberson) (Russell Sage Foundation, 1988), and numerous articles on racial and ethnic identity and immigrant assimilation. Her current research focuses on patterns of assimilation among the second generation in New York City and patterns of racial intermarriage and identity formation in the United States.

Irma Watkins-Owens is Associate Professor and Chair of the Department of African and African American Studies at Fordham University at Lincoln Center. She teaches undergraduate and graduate courses in African American history and in ethnic and women's studies. The author of *Blood Relations: Caribbean Immigrants and the Harlem Community, 1900–1930* (Indiana University Press, 1996), she is currently working on a book-length study of the migration, work, and community activity of southern and Caribbean women in New York City between 1898 and 1950 and is a member of the Executive Board of the Immigration and Ethnic History Society.

Index

African American New Yorkers: employment of, 69–74; niche earnings of, 75–78; West Indian relations with, 11, 13–15, 54, 176, 186–188

African Americans: and black institutional networks, 172–174, 179–180; class differences of, 173–174, 213; linked racial fate outlook of, 169–171; politics of, 168–174, 188–190; and racial group identity, 168–174, 177; socialization in black institutions, 173; West Indian relations with, 243, 246

Afro-Caribbean immigrants. *See* West Indian New Yorkers

American identity of immigrants, 200–201, 202–205

Asian immigrants, 211–212

Assimilation of immigrants in America, 202–205

Banana crisis, 136

Basch, Linda, 263

Bashi Bobb, Vilna, 264

Bishop, Maurice, 118, 130, 134

Black Americans: class consciousness of, 164–165; differentiation criteria, 164; economic divisions of, 164–165; political differentiation of, 164–165, 188–190; and socioeconomic failure, 234

"Blackness": in America, defined, 238–239; in New York, defined, 12, 13; "one-drop rule"

of, 238-239; redefined in the future, 242 243, 246; in West Indies, defined, 12, 13, 239–242

Black New Yorkers: causes for division among, 163, 164; division between native- and foreign-born, 163–165, 174; population distribution of, 93–95

Blaize, Herbert, 117–119, 130

Briggs, Cyril, 26

Brooklyn: in the 1950s, 150–154; racial division of, 156; transnational immigrant networks in, 180–182

Bryce-Laporte, Roy, 257, 273

Caribbean-born New Yorkers. *See* West Indian New Yorkers

Caribbean migration. *See* West Indian migration

Chaney, Elsa, 263

Child fostering by West Indian New Yorkers, 39–42

Chinese immigrants, 211, 267

Chiquita corporation, 136

Clarke, Una, 135–138

Class, identity development influenced by, 195, 197, 203

Class consciousness of Jamaican New Yorkers, 146, 150, 153–154

Communist party, 47

Copperbelt (northern Rhodesia) studies, 121

Crown Heights riots, 11

Deterritorialized nation-states, 119–120, 123–124, 130–137
Dole corporation, 136
Domingo, W. A., 26
Dual citizenship, 9, 137–138

Education: and racial inequality, 220, 224; as transnational project, 126–127
Ellison, Ralph, 257
Emigration regulation, 28
Employment: in administration work, 71, 72; in apparel, 69; in banking, 69; in communications, 69; data on West Indian New Yorkers, 54–55, 266; in department stores, 70; ethnic niche, defined, 52; in government work, 79; in hospitals, 70, 72; industry employment of West Indian New Yorkers, 58–67; and job changing, 223; niche distributions of West Indian New Yorkers, 67–74; niche earnings of West Indian New Yorkers, 74–78; in postal service, 71; in private households, 70, 72, 78; public-sector, 261; in repair, 69; in schools, 70; in transportation, 68, 69, 78; in trucking, 69; in warehousing, 69; West Indian, post–civil rights era, 6; of West Indian women, 35–38
Enclave locations in New York, 105–108, 152–153
Ethnicity: and economic success, 204; of West Indian New Yorkers, 10–16, 81, 85–86, 111–112, 164–167, 186–188, 194–195, 197, 199–200
European immigrants, 185, 202, 205, 210–211, 213

Family as a West Indian social unit, 126. *See also* West Indian Families
Farrakhan, Louis, 262

Garvey, Marcus, 46–47
Garvey movement, 46–47, 240
Gender identity and race issues, 201–202
Glick Schiller, Nina, 124, 263
Grenadians: Bishop, Maurice, 118, 130; Blaize, Herbert, 117–119, 130; family ties of, 126–127; and migration history, 124–126; political community of, defined, 132; political independence of, 125; and state practices that maintain the nation-state, 133–134; transnational economic activities of, 128; transnational identities of, 130–137; transna-

tional organizational ties of, 128–130; transnational practices of, 117–120, 123–135, 137

Harrison, Hubert, 26
Hart-Celler immigration reforms, 262
Haynes, George, 56
Hispanics, 211
Howard Beach incident, 11

Immigration law (U.S.), 5, 150, 262
Index of dissimilarity as measure of racial segregation, 88–93
Intermarriage between blacks and whites, 242–244

Jamaicans: British immigrants compared to U.S. immigrants, 268; as Brooklyn residents, 150–154; career choice customs of, 147, 152; enclave locations in New York, 105, 107, 108, 152–153; and job opportunities in home society, 148; middle-class educational ambitions of, 146–148; transnational practices of, 10, 157
Johnson, James W., 259

Lorde, Audre, 27, 30, 39

Marshall, Paule, 27, 39, 259
McKay, Claude, 258–259
Migration, defined, 145
Migration traditions in Caribbean island societies, 3, 125
Mintz, Sidney, 264
Mixed-race individuals, 238–240, 243–244
Moore, Richard B., 26
Mulattoes, 238–239

Nation-states: and globalization, 123; importance of, 123–124; and politics and identity, 134–137
New York (New York City): African American neighborhoods in, 82; black population of, 6, 7, 93–95; comparison of early- to late-twentieth-century, 6; as destination for migrants, 142–145; diversity within West Indian enclaves of, 104–109; role in global family network, 145–157; socioeconomic characteristics of West Indian enclaves in, 100–104; statistics on immigrants to, 4, 143; transnational economic activities in, 127–128;